T0217540

HTML5 Game Development Insights

Colt McAnlis, Petter Lubbers, Brandon Jones,
Duncan Tebbs, Andrzej Manzur, Sean Bennett,
Florian d'Erfurth, Bruno Garcia, Shun Lin, Ivan Popelyshev,
Jason Gauci, Jon Howard, Ian Ballantyne, Jesse Freeman,
Takuo Kihira, Tyler Smith, Don Olmstead, John McCutchan,
Chad Austin, and Andres Pagella

apress·

HTML 5 Game Development Insights

ISBN-13 (pbk): 978-1-4302-6697-6

ISBN-13 (electronic): 978-1-4302-6698-3

President and Publisher: Paul Manning
Lead Editor: Ben Renow-Clarke
Technical Reviewer: Phil Sherry, Rob Evans, David Gash and Rita Turkowski
Developmental Editor: Gary Schwartz
Editorial Board: Steve Anglin, Mark Beckner, Ewan Buckingham, Gary Cornell, Louise Corrigan, Jim DeWolf, Jonathan Gennick, Jonathan Hassell, Robert Hutchinson, Michelle Lowman, James Markham, Matthew Moodie, Jeff Olson, Jeffrey Pepper, Douglas Pundick, Ben Renow-Clarke, Dominic Shakeshaft, Gwenan Spearing, Matt Wade, Steve Weiss
Coordinating Editor: Christine Ricketts
Copy Editor: Mary Behr and Lisa Vecchione
Compositor: SPi Global
Indexer: SPi Global
Artist: SPi Global
Cover Designer: Anna Ishchenko

Distributed to the book trade worldwide by Springer Science+Business Media New York, 233 Spring Street, 6th Floor, New York, NY 10013. Phone 1-800-SPRINGER, fax (201) 348-4505, e-mail orders-ny@springer-sbm.com, or visit www.springeronline.com. Apress Media, LLC is a California LLC and the sole member (owner) is Springer Science + Business Media Finance Inc (SSBM Finance Inc). SSBM Finance Inc is a Delaware corporation.

For information on translations, please e-mail rights@apress.com, or visit www.apress.com.

Apress and friends of ED books may be purchased in bulk for academic, corporate, or promotional use. eBook versions and licenses are also available for most titles. For more information, reference our Special Bulk Sales–eBook Licensing web page at www.apress.com/bulk-sales.

Any source code or other supplementary material referenced by the author in this text is available to readers at www.apress.com. For detailed information about how to locate your book's source code, go to www.apress.com/source-code/.

Contents at a Glance

Contents

About the Authors

Colt McAnlis is a Developer Advocate at Google, focusing on games and performance. Before that, he was a systems and graphics programmer in the games industry working at Blizzard, Microsoft (Ensemble), and Petroglyph. He's a UDACITY course professor for HTML5 games, and he also spent four years as an Adjunct Professor at SMU Guildhall's school for game development. When he's not working with developers, Colt spends his time preparing for an invasion of giant ants from outer space.

Peter Lubbers is a Program Manager in the Google Developer Relations team, focused on scalable developer programs. He is the author of *Pro HTML5 Programming* (2nd Ed. Apress, 2011) and the founder of the San Francisco HTML5 User Group (SFHTML5), the largest HTML5 User Group in the world with over 10,000 members. Prior to joining Google, Peter headed up the HTML5 training division at Kaazing. A native of the Netherlands, Peter served as a Special Forces commando in the Royal Dutch Green Berets. Peter lives on the edge of the Tahoe National Forest and in his spare time he loves to run around Lake Tahoe. You can follow him on Twitter at @peterlubbers.

Brandon Jones works on Chrome's WebGL implementation at Google, and he is a big advocate of WebGL in any form. After taking a web development job ten years ago before eagerly moving on to "real programming," he came to his senses and now gleefully spends any time that he's not hacking on Chrome or building 3D things in JavaScript or Dart.

Duncan Tebbs is a Senior Software Engineer at Turbulenz Limited, developing technology to allow developers to bring high quality game content to the Web. He has previously held roles at Electronic Arts, NaturalMotion, and Square-Enix, where he has worked on various games technology and research projects.

Andrzej Manzur is an HTML5 game developer; founder of the Enclave Games indie development studio, which is focused on mobile HTML5 games; creator of the js13kGames competition; and Gamedev.js Meetups organizer. He's a front-end developer and JavaScript programmer, active blogger and conference speaker, HTML5 games evangelist, and a huge fan of the Firefox OS. In his free time, he loves playing Neuroshima Hex, eating sushi, running around with a paintball marker, and driving go-karts, plus everything SciFi/post-apo/cyberpunk related.

Sean Bennett is a Software Engineer at Crowdtilt, and he is passionate about using the Web as a platform for awesome, immersive experiences. Sean's background is in web development and developer education. When he isn't working on building a better Web, Sean likes running, hiking, and preparing for the inevitable zombie apocalypse.

Florian d'Erfurth is a new game developer who's been doing freelance web development for the last five years. In early 2013, he won the Udacity HTML5 Game Development contest, and ever since he's been obsessed with JavaScript and its performance so that he can deliver ubiquitous gaming experiences. Florian is currently working on Foxes and Shotguns, a video game featuring wererabbits.

Bruno Garcia is co-founder at 2DKit, helping developers build cross-platform games. Before that, he engineered browser and mobile games at Three Rings and Zynga. He is a member of the Haxe compiler team, contributes to the Flump open source project, and writes the occasional game on the side. His favorite color is #202020.

Shun Lin is the founder of the Cocos2d-HTML5 open source game engine and a Senior Technical Director at ChuKong, where he focuses on creating a cross-browser and cross-platform game engine. He spends most of his time on improving the performance and compatibility of mobile web games. Shun is also the co-founder of the Cocos2d-x game engine, working alongside the "x-men" to bring JavaScript Binding to Cocos2d-x, which provides developers an easy way to publish their HTML5 games as native apps with very little or no change to their existing code.

Ivan Popelyshev is an MMO game developer and founder of Matroid Games, a company that focuses on real-time and massively multiplayer games. He's passionate about HTML5 cutting edge technologies, building game servers and sports programming. During his career, he won the ACM as well as other contests, and he participated in many well-known competition finals, including TopCoder 2013. Previously, he worked at Wargaming and Yandex, where he supported the Russian sports programming community.

Jason Gauci is a Research Scientist at Apple. Prior to joining Apple, Jason worked in the labs of Google Research and Lockheed Martin Applied Research, focusing on behavior prediction and predictive analytics. Jason is the lead developer for several netplay-enabled emulators, including MAMEHub, NES Together, and SNES Together. He also co-hosts the Programming Throwdown podcast.

Jon Howard is the Executive Product Manager for Future Development at the BBC (CBBC & CBeebies). In this role, he works closely with interactive/TV producers, user experience designers, the BBC Research and Development department, and many of the world's best digital agencies to promote innovation and set strategy for the games portfolio on the UK's most successful children's web sites. Over the years, Jon has designed, developed, and served as tech lead on many hugely successful games for major UK and international childrens' brands, including Tree Fu Tom, Scooby Doo, Rastamouse, Shaun the Sheep, Charlie & Lola, Dick & Dom, Horrible Histories, Sarah Jane Adventures, Scorpion Island, and many more. Jon takes a keen interest in game design developments. He is a creative coder, a prolific game prototyper, and an enthusiastic mathematician/statistician with a great passion for BBC Children, rich media, innovation, and technology.

Ian Ballantyne is a Software Engineer at Turbulenz, developing HTML5 games, tools, and technology. He is responsible for managing the Turbulenz Engine and SDK. He is all too aware of the complex details of delivering high-fidelity 3D games to the web platform. Having worked with indie developers, small studios, and large publishers, he knows a thing or two about helping game developers make the best use of new technologies. When he's not giving talks on high performance HTML5 games, he's involved in their creation, making them run on anything from desktops to mobile devices. By day he is a mild-mannered software engineer; by night he is a rogue coder, hacking away at secret projects and game jams. Prior to Turbulenz, he worked at Philips Electronics on a gaming/lighting technology known as amBX. A graduate of Imperial College London, Ian is still glad to be putting his Masters of Engineering in Computing to practical use.

Jesse Freeman is a Developer Evangelist at Amazon focusing on HTML5 and gaming. He is an active leader in New York's developer community. For more than 13 years, Jesse has been on the cutting edge of interactive development, focused on the web and mobile platforms. As an expert in his field, Jesse has worked for Microsoft, MLB, HBO, the New York Jets, VW, Tommy Hilfiger, Heavy, and many more. In addition to development, Jesse has a background in Art with a Masters in Interactive Computer Art from the School of Visual Arts. He can be found on Twitter at @jessefreeman. Jesse also speaks at conferences and does workshops, which you can learn about on his web site, http://jessefreeman.com.

Takuo Kihira is the HTML5 Manager and Chief Engineer at DeNA, and he specializes in JavaScript and HTML5 development for mobile platforms. Takuo created the HTML5 Flash Player Pex, which is distributed by DeNA free of charge. Takuo is a serial entrepreneur who has started two companies.

Tyler Smith is the HTML5 Game Evangelist at Intel, focusing on helping the HTML5 game developer community grow. He has participated in numerous app and game development hackathons, both as a speaker and facilitator. Tyler was also the project manager and lead developer of Boom Town, an HTML5 game that was deployed on more than seven platforms with single code base. He is also the founder and CTO of LocalGhost Media, a small HTML5 development studio. All opinions expressed in the chapter he wrote for this book are his and his alone. They do not reflect the opinion of his employers.

Jon Olmstead is a Senior Software Engineer at Sony Network Entertainment, working on the underlying web platform for PlayStation hardware. On the native side, he advances the browser, supporting the rendering bits. For the application side, he develops the rendering engine, built using WebGL, which provides the backbone for the Playstation Store, and portions of the UX on the PS4. He is interested in how the Web can be leveraged by game developers as a target platform.

John McCutchan is a Software Engineer at Google working on the Dart Virtual Machine. While an undergraduate, John created inotify, the Linux kernel filesystem event notification system used in every Linux distribution and Android phone. After receiving a M.Sc. in Computer Science from McMaster University, John joined Sony Computer Entertainment of America, where he optimized the Bullet Physics library for the PlayStation 3. In 2013, John created a highly-performant SIMD programming model for dynamically compiled languages, such as Dart and JavaScript.

Chad Austin is a Senior Technical Director at IMVU, where he focuses on client application structure and the web platform. When he's not in meetings or evangelizing technical strategy, he likes to get his hands dirty—demonstrating what is possible and shaving milliseconds off critical execution paths as well. In a previous life, he wrote a 2D RPG game engine still in use today.

Mario Andrés Pagella is the founder of Warsteed Studios, an independent HTML5 game development studio, and he is also a Technical Project Leader at R/GA. He has authored *Making Isometric Social Real-Time Games with HTML5, CSS3, and JavaScript and HTML5 Transition and Animation*, and he advocates the use of HTML5, CSS3, and JavaScript for game development through his web site, Twitter account, and in meetups and events.

About the Technical Reviewers

Phil Sherry hails from Liverpool (a.k.a. the Best City in the WORLD). He is a Professional Scouser and a self-taught Nerd. He somehow became the author of *Foundation Mac OS X Web Development*, and co-author, geek wrangler, and brains behind Blog Design Solutions. He's also been a pedantic, nit-picking, soul-destroying technical reviewer for many friends of ED & Apress books over the last decade. He currently builds the British Airways web site and lives in the frozen wasteland that is Newcastle, where the folk talk funny but the pubs are mostly okay, especially the Brandling Arms. Some rules: lowercase, not camelCase; hyphens, not underscores; spaces, not tabs; Mac, not MAC; cats, not dogs; and... WarGames is still one of the best movies—ever.

Rob Evans is the CEO of Irrelon Software Limited and the developer of the Isogenic Game Engine, a JavaScript 2D and isometric multiplayer engine. He loves programming and writes advanced web applications for a living. You can reach him at `www.irrelon.com`.

Dave Gash is the owner of HyperTrain, a Southern California firm specializing in technology consulting and training for hypertext developers, with an all-new website at `www.davegash.com`. He is a veteran technical publications specialist with extensive experience in software development, technical documentation, and technology training. He holds degrees in both Business and Computer Science. Dave is well known in the technical publications community as a proficient and engaging technical speaker, and is a frequent presenter at User Assistance conferences in the U.S. and around the world.

Rita Turkowski works for AMD as a Senior Embedded Gaming Marketing Manager. Rita came to AMD from Unity Technologies, where she was the Sales Team Channel Manager for 20 months. While there, Unity had more developer adoption in the game industry than any other game development technology company—ever. She was a Graphics and Media Software Product Manager at Intel from 2007 until December 2009, working on graphics and game industry software tools. Before that, Rita was the Executive Director of the Web3D Consortium from 2005–2007, where she worked on projects internationally for the adoption of ISO 3D standards, as well as establishing joint working group cooperation with related industry consortia such as Khronos, the OGC, and W3C.

Introduction

Making games is *hard*.

Even most veteran game developers don't fully grasp the scale of how difficult it is to weave together technology, code, design, sound, and distribution to produce something that resonates with players around the world. As industries go, game development is still fairly young, only really gaining traction in the early 1980s. This makes it an even more difficult process, which, frankly, we're still trying to figure out.

In 30 years of game development, we've seen the boom of console games, computer games, Internet bubbles, shareware, social gaming, and even mobile gaming. It seems that every five to eight years, the entire industry reinvents itself from the core in order to adjust to the next big thing.

As hardware trends shift and user tastes change, modern game developers scramble to keep up, producing three to four games in a single year (a feat unheard of in 2001, when you thought in terms of shipping two to three games in your entire *career*). This rapid pace comes at a high cost: engineers often have to build entire virtual empires of code, only to scrap them a mere six weeks later to design an entirely different gameplay dynamic. Designers churn through hordes of ideas in a week in order to find the smallest portion of fun that they can extract from any one idea. Artists also construct terabytes of content for gameplay features that never see the light of day.

A lot of tribal knowledge and solutions get lost in this frantic process; many techniques, mental models, and data just evaporate into the air. Tapping into the brains of game developers, cataloging their processes, and recording their techniques is the only real way to grow as an industry. This is especially relevant in today's game development ecosystem, where the number of "indie" developers greatly outnumbers the "professional" developers.

Today we're bombarded with messaging about how "it's never been easier to *make* a game," which is true to some extent. The entry barrier to *creating* a game is pretty low; eight-year olds can do it. The real message here is what it takes to make a *great* game. Success comes from iteration; you can't just point yourself in a direction, move toward it, and expect your game to be great. You have to learn. You have to grow. You have to *evolve*. Moreover, with less and less time between product shipments, the overhead available to grow as a developer is quickly getting smaller and smaller. Developers can't do it on their own; they need to learn, ask questions, and see what everyone else is doing. As a developer, you have to find mentors in design, marketing, and distribution. You have to connect with other people who feel your pain, and who are trying to solve the same problems and fight the same battles. Evolve as a community, or die as an individual.

Making games *is* hard. That's why we wrote this book; even the best of us must find time to learn.

—Colt McAnli

HTML5 has come a long way.

It might be hard to believe today, but getting publisher support for *Pro HTML5 Programming*, the book I co-authored with Brian Albers and Frank Salim in 2009, and released as one of the first books on the subject in 2010, was quite hard. Publishers were just not sure if this new HTML5 thing had a future or if it was just a passing fad.

The launch of the iPad in April 2010 changed all that overnight and drove the curiosity and excitement about HTML5 to a whole new level. For the first time, many developers started to look seriously at the new features and APIs, such as canvas, audio, and video. The possibility of many kinds of new web applications with real native feature support seemed almost too good to be true. And, to a certain extent, it was.

When developers seriously started to dig into the new APIs, they discovered many missing pieces. Features that had long been staples of other platforms were now lacking, or were implemented in such a way that they were not very useful. This disappointed many developers, and yet they were eager to improve on the HTML5 feature set. That cycle is, of course, the nature of development and the impetus for innovation.

Game software, perhaps more than any other genre, tends to stress its host platform to the max, so it was not surprising that there was some backlash to the initial hype that HTML5 was the be-and-end-all for every application on the web. However, that was never the intention of HTML5. In fact, one of the core design principles behind HTML5 is "evolution not revolution," and it is the slow but steady progress of features, spanning many years, that has changed the HTML landscape.

Nevertheless, browser vendors and spec authors have not been sitting still. Instead, they have developed many new and more powerful APIs. One example is the Web Audio API, now shipping in many of the major browsers. This API offers fine-grained audio manipulation, which the regular audio element could not provide. With this and other new APIs, it is now much easier to develop applications and web-based games that, until recently, would have been hard to imagine, let alone code.

That is why I believe we're just at the beginning of a future full of great possibilities in web-based game software. Of course, we'll never be "done." There will always be room for improvement but, as my esteemed co-authors clarify in this book, you can now build compelling games that leverage the power and flexibility of the web platform in ways that were unheard of even a few years ago.

Code, learn, improve, and repeat. Be a part of software evolution at its best.

—Peter Lubbers

■ ■ ■

CHAPTER 1

JavaScript Is Not the Language You Think It Is

Sean Bennett, Course Architect, Udacity

JavaScript is a deceptively familiar language. Its syntax is close enough to C/C++ that you may be tricked into thinking it behaves similarly.

However, JavaScrit has a number of gotchas that trip up developers coming from other languages. In this chapter, I'll go over some of the more egregious offenders, teach you how to avoid them, and showcase the hidden power in the language.

This chapter is for game programmers who are coming from other languages and who are using JavaScript for the first time. It's the tool I wish I'd had when I first started using JavaScript.

Variables and Scoping Rules

You wouldn't think that declaring variables would be at all hard or error prone. After all, it's a fundamental part of any language, right? The problem is that with JavaScript, it's

- very easy to accidentally declare variables after they're used, which leads to accidentally accessing undefined variables
- deceptively difficult to restrict access to variables, leading to naming collisions as well as memory allocation issues

I'll discuss the issues with and limitations of JavaScript scoping and then present a well-known solution for modularizing your JavaScript code.

Declaration Scoping

The first thing you need to realize about JavaScript is that there are only two different scopes: global and function level. JavaScript does not have any further lexical or block scoping.

A variable is declared on the global scope like so:

```
zombiesKilled = 10;
```

A variable is declared on the function scope as follows:

```
var antiPokemonSpray = true;
```

That's not entirely true, actually. Using the var keyword attaches the variable to the nearest closing scope, so using it outside any function will declare the variable on the global scope as well.

Note that the lack of any block-level scoping can cause bugs that are pretty hard to track down. The simplest example of this is the use of loop counters; for instance,

```
for (var i = 0; i < 10; i++) {
    console.log(i);
}
console.log(i);
```

That last logging statement won't output null or undefined, as you might expect. Because of the lack of block scope, i is still defined and accessible. This can cause problems if you don't explicitly define the value of your loop counter variables on every reuse.

Global scope is something to be avoided in JavaScript. Not only do you have all the usual reasons, such as code modularity and namespacing issues, but also JavaScript is a garbage-collected language. Putting everything in global scope means that nothing ever gets garbage collected. Eventually, you'll run out of memory, and the memory manager will constantly have to switch things in and out of memory, a situation known as memory thrashing.

Declaration Hoisting

Another concern with variable declarations is that they're automatically hoisted to the top of the current scope. What do I mean by that? Check this out:

```
var myHealth = 100;

var decrementHealth = function() {
    console.log(myHealth);

    var myHealth = myHealth - 1;
};

decrementHealth();
```

So, you would think that this would

- output 100

- declare a new, function-scoped variable, myHealth, shadowing the globally scoped variable myHealth

- set the function-scoped myHealth to 99

And, it would be totally reasonable to think that. Unfortunately, what you actually output is undefined. JavaScript will automatically lift the declaration of myHealth to the top of the function, but not the assignment.

After the JavaScript engine gets done with that, here is the code you're actually left with:

```
var myHealth = 100;

var decrementHealth = function() {
    var myHealth;
    console.log(myHealth);

    myHealth = myHealth-1;
```

· Suddenly, that undefined output makes sense. Be careful! Declare all your variables up front so that this scenario doesn't catch you unawares, and make sure they have sane default values.

As a further illustration, let's take a look at the following example:

```
var myHealth = 100;

var decrementHealth = function(health) {
    var myHealth = health;
    myHealth--;
    console.log(myHealth);
};

decrementHealth(myHealth);
console.log(myHealth);
```

This will output 99 first, then 100, because you're setting myHealth to the value of health inside the function rather than setting by reference.

JavaScript Typing and Equality

Now that you understand the basics of variables, let's talk about what types of values those variables can take.

JavaScript is a loosely typed language, with a few base types and automatic coercion between types (for more information, see the section "Type Coercion").

Base Types

JavaScript only has a few basic types for you to keep in mind:

1. Numbers
2. Strings
3. Booleans
4. Objects
5. Arrays
6. null
7. undefined

Numbers

Numbers are fairly self-explanatory. They can be any number, with or without a decimal point or described using scientific notation, such as 12e-4.

Most languages treat at least integers and floating-point numbers differently. JavaScript, however, treats all numbers as floating point.

It would take too long to go into the potential problems with floating-point numbers here. Suffice it to say that if you're not careful, you can easily run into floating-point errors. If you want to learn more about the pitfalls of floating-point arithmetic, I'd recommend checking out the Institute of Electrical and Electronics Engineers (IEEE) spec *IEEE 754: Standard for Binary Floating-Point Arithmetic*.

The two additional values numbers can take on are Infinity and NaN. That's right, NaN is a number. (for more information, see the section "Equality Checking").

Strings

Strings are quite a bit simpler. As in most languages, you can treat a string like an array of characters. However, strings are also objects, with numerous built-in properties and methods, such as length and slice:

```
> "example string"[0]
"e"
> "example string".length
14
> "example string".slice(7)
" string"
```

I should point out that what I'm doing in the previous example is particularly bad. The memory behavior of where hard-coded strings are allocated isn't part of the language specification. Being allocated on the global heap is actually one of the better scenarios. Depending on the browser, each individual use could be allocated separately on the heap, further bloating your memory.

Booleans

Booleans, as in most languages, can take on the values true and false. Both are reserved keywords in JavaScript. The main difference here between JavaScript and many other languages lies in which values can be coerced to either true or false (for further details, see the section "Truthiness," later in this chapter).

Objects

Objects are the bread and butter of JavaScript, but they behave a bit differently from those in several other languages. In many ways, objects are similar to dictionaries in modern interpreted languages:

```
 = {};
```

Curly braces indicate that you're defining an object. Nothing inside suggests that this is the empty object. You can assign key-value pairs to an object like so:

```
layer = { health: 10 };
```

Pretty simple, really. You can assign multiple key-value pairs to an object by separating them with a comma:

```
layer = {
    health: 10,
    position: {
        x: 325,
        y: 210
    }
 ;
```

Note in this example that you're assigning another object to the position property of player. This is entirely legal JavaScript and incredibly simple to do.

To access the object, you can use either dot or bracket notation:

```
> player.health
10
> player['position'].x
325
> player['position']['y']
210
```

Note that when using bracket notation, you need to enclose the key in quotes. If you don't do this, then the key will instead be treated like a variable:

```
> x = "unknownProperty";
"unknownProperty"
> player['position'][x]
undefined
```

This code returns undefined, because the interpreter can't find player['position']['unknownProperty']. As a side note, you should minimize use of bracket notation whenever possible. Dot notation uses fewer bytes to represent the same thing and can be more effectively minified over the wire (for more information, see the section "Inheritance the JavaScript Way").

Arrays

Arrays act similarly to other languages you may be familiar with:

```
> x = [1, 10, 14, "15"]
[1, 10, 14, "15"]
> x[0]
1
> x[3]
"15"
> x.length
4
> x.push(20, "I'm last!")
Undefined
> x
[1, 10, 14, "15", 20, "I'm last!"]
```

As you can see, arrays are heterogenous, meaning that you can have arbitrary types in a single array. Note that this is a bad idea; the internal representation for heterogenous arrays causes some serious performance headaches. Always try to keep a single type in a given array.

Arrays have a number of convenience functions as well, such as push, pop, and slice. I'm not going to go into much detail on these here. To learn more about them, check out the coverage of the Array object by the Mozilla Developer Network (MDN) (https://developer.mozilla.org/en-US/docs/Web/JavaScript/Reference/Global_Objects/Array).

I do, however, want to sound a note of caution regarding the memory performance of these convenience functions. Most, if not all, act by allocating an entirely new array from the heap rather than modifying things in place.

In general, garbage collection and memory management are going to be huge performance concerns in JavaScript, so you want to avoid allocating new arrays and causing object churn as much as possible.

Yet, there isn't a good way to modify arrays in JavaScript without creating newly allocated objects on the heap. You can do some things to mitigate this, and, to that end, a great resource is *Static Memory JavaScript with Object Pools* (www.html5rocks.com/en/tutorials/speed/static-mem-pools/). Unfortunately, it won't completely solve your problems, but keeping these performance considerations in mind will go a long way toward mitigating your biggest memory performance issues.

null

The null type is a special value similar to None in Python. null signifies when a value has been emptied or specifically set to nothing. Note that this is distinct from the value that unknown variables are equal to or that declared but unassigned variables are set to. For that, we have undefined.

undefined

Variables are initially set to undefined when declared. Remember from declaration hoisting that declarations are automatically hoisted to the top of the function but that any accompanying assignments are not. This means that any variables will be set to undefined between where they're declared at the top of a function and where they're assigned to.

Let's take a look at the difference between undefined and null:

```
var player = {
    health: 100,
    damage: 5,
    hit: function() {
        console.log('poke');
    }
};
console.log(enemy);

var enemy = {
    health: 100,
    damage: 50,
    hit: function() {
        console.log('SMASH');
    }
};
console.log(enemy.health);
console.log(player.shields);
```

This code will output as follows:

```
undefined

100
undefined
```

The typeof Operator

JavaScript has a handy operator, typeof, which can tell you, as you'd guess, the type of its operator. Let's examine a few of these:

```
> typeof 2
"number"
> typeof 2.14
"number"
> typeof Infinity
"number"
> typeof NaN
"number"
```

So far so good; as you might expect, all of these return the string "number".

```
> typeof ""
"string"
> typeof "coconuts"
"string"
> typeof '2.4'
"string"
> typeof true
"boolean"
> typeof false
"boolean"
```

Strings and booleans also behave as expected. The challenge comes when looking at objects, undefined, and null.

```
> typeof {}
"object"
> typeof { key: "value" }
"object"
> typeof undefined
"undefined"
> typeof null
"object"
```

The issue is that null is treated as an object rather than its own type. This can be a problem when using the typeof operator, so make sure only to use null in situations in which this isn't a concern.

Note as well that typeof makes no distinction between different kinds of objects; it just tells you whether a value is an object. To distinguish between different types of objects, we have the instanceof operator.

The instanceof Operator

instanceof compares two objects and returns a boolean indicating whether the first inherits from the second. Let's look at a few examples:

```
> String instanceof Object
true
> Object instanceof String
False
```

```
> var a = {};
> a instanceof Object
true
> a instanceof String
false
```

In JavaScript all objects inherit from the base Object, so the first result, comparing String, makes sense, as does the third, comparing a, the empty object. In contrast, neither Object nor a inherits from String, so this should return false (for details on how to structure inheritance and object-oriented (OO) code in JavaScript, see the section "Inheritance the JavaScript Way").

Type Coercion

JavaScript is a dynamically typed language, with automatic type conversion, meaning that types are converted as needed, based on the operations being performed. Now, this type conversion is a little . . . misbehaved. Let's take a look at the following example:

```
> x = "37" + 3
"373"
> x = 3 + "7"
"37"
> x = 10 - "3"
7
```

Wait, what?

JavaScript will automatically convert between numbers and strings, but the way it does so depends on the operators involved. Basically, if the + operator is involved, it will convert any numbers to strings and assume that + means "concatenate."

However, any other operators will instead convert strings to numbers and assume that the operators involved are arithmetic.

What about an expression with more operators?

```
> x = "10" + 3 / 4 - 2
98.75
```

Can you tell what steps JavaScript took to get the result 98.75? Personally, it took me a few seconds to step through and figure it out.

In general, you should avoid automatic coercion between types, and instead be explicit. JavaScript has a couple of handy built-in functions to convert from strings to numbers, parseInt and parseFloat:

```
parseInt("654", 10)
654
parseInt("654.54", 10)
654
parseInt("654", 8)
428
parseFloat("654")
654
parseFloat("654.54")
654.54
```

The first parameter for both functions is the string you want to convert to a number. Note that `parseInt` automatically truncates anything after the decimal point rather than rounding.

`parseInt` also takes an optional second parameter, which is the radix, or base of the number system being converted to. The default is the standard base-10 number system.

It's worth pointing out the reverse process, converting a number to a string. The primary way to do this is to call `String(value)`, where `value` is what you want converted to a string.

Equality Checking

One of the greatest challenges for new JavaScript developers is, without a doubt. equality checking. Thankfully, the key to avoiding getting tripped up can be summed up very easily:

Always use === and !== to do equality checking rather than == and !=.

But, why must you do that? What's the deal with this `===` nonsense, and why are there two different equality operators?

The answer has to do with our friend automatic type coercion. `==` and `!=` will automatically convert values to different types before comparing them for equality. The `===` and `!==` operators do not and will return `false` for different types.

However, what are the rules for how `==` converts types?

- Comparing numbers and strings will always convert the strings to numbers.

- `null` and `undefined` will always equal each other.

- Comparing booleans to any other type will always cause the booleans to be converted to numbers.

- Comparing numbers or strings to objects will always cause the numbers or strings to be converted to objects.

- Any other type comparisons are automatically `false`.

Once the types have been converted, the comparison continues the same as with `===`. Numbers and booleans are compared by value, and strings, by identical characters. `null` and `undefined` equal each other and nothing else, and objects must reference the same object.

Now that you know how `==` works, the earlier advice never to use it can be relaxed, at least a little bit. `==` can be useful, but you must be absolutely sure you know what you're doing.

Truthiness

Using various types in conditional statements is similarly problematic. Because of type coercion, you can use any type in a conditional, and that type is converted to a boolean.

The rules for converting other types to booleans are actually relatively straightforward:

- `undefined` and `null` are always `false`.

- Booleans are just treated as booleans (obviously).

- Numbers are `false` if they equal 0 or `NaN`; otherwise, they're `true`.

- Strings are `true`, except for the empty string `""`, which is `false`.

- Objects are always `true`.

The biggest thing to watch out for is that, whereas the empty string is `false`, the empty object is `true`. Be aware of this when using objects in comparisons, and you'll have solved 90 percent of your problems with truthiness.

Inheritance the JavaScript Way

If you're coming from traditional game development, you're probably very familiar with object-oriented programming (OOP) and specifically, class-based OOP, the model that C++ and Java use.

JavaScript uses a different OOP model, prototypical inheritance, which is derived from `self`'s object model.

I'll close out this chapter by discussing what prototypical inheritance is and how to use it instead of the more classical inheritance you may be used to.

Prototypical Inheritance

Prototypical inheritance, at its core, is concerned with only two things:

1. How do you create a new object?

2. How do you extend a new object from an existing one?

Creating a bare new object is simple, using object literal notation. Let's say you wanted to create the following ship:

```
var myAwesomeShip = {
    health: 100,
    shields: 50,
    guns: [{
        damage: 20,
        speed: 5
    },{
        damage: 5,
        speed: 9000
    }],
    fire: function() {
        console.log('PEW PEW');
    }
};
```

Simple enough. But, what if you wanted to create a new ship, using myAwesomeShip as a template, but with better shields? Obviously, you could just copy and paste things, but that's no good. Instead, you can create a clone of yAwesomeShip, using prototypical inheritance, like so:

```
var myMoreAwesomeShip = Object.create(myAwesomeShip);
myMoreAwesomeShip.shields = 100;
```

And, you're done. Now, if you wanted, you could roll this into a ship template object, as follows:

```
var ship = {
    manufacture: function(shields) {
        var newShip = Object.create(this);
        newShip.shields = shields;
        return newShip;
    },
```

```
    health: 100,
    shields: 50,
    guns: [{
        damage: 20,
        speed: 5
    },{
        damage: 5,
        speed: 9000
    }],
    fire: function() {
        console.log(PEW PEW');
    }
};

var myWayMoreAwesomeShip = ship.manufacture(150);
```

Voilà: you have a ship template that you can build off of, using any given ship as the template.

Of course, there is still one very important question that must be answered: Can you somehow combine these steps in order to extend the base ship with arbitrary properties?

It turns out that you can do this by writing an extend function and attaching it to all objects. The code for this is short, but dense:

```
Object.prototype.extend = function(extendPrototype) {
    var hasOwnProperty = Object.hasOwnProperty;
    var object = Object.create(this);

    for (var property in extendPrototype) {
        if(hasOwnProperty.call(extendPrototype, property) || typeof object[property] ===
'undefined') {
            object[property] = extendPrototype[property];
        }
    }
    return object;
};
```

Whew! There's a lot going on there. Here's what's happening:

1. You create a function, extend, attached to the base Object.

2. The function hasOwnProperty checks whether the object has the passed-in property or whether it's inherited from somewhere else, for example, the base Object.

3. You create a clone of this; in the previous example, this would be ship.

4. Now, you loop through all the properties in the extension; for each property, you perform these tasks:

   a. You check whether the base Object does not have the given property or whether the extension has the property directly.

   b. You then you assign the value from the extension to the cloned object.

5. Once you're done, you return the completed object.

Reread that a few times if you need to; it's a lot to digest. Now that you know the steps, however, you can create a new ship template, with any additional property changes you want, as shown:

```
var newShipModel = ship.extend({
    health: 200,
    shields: 100,
    fire: function() {
        console.log('TRIPLE PEW!!!');
    }
});
```

You can think of this as a new model of ship that you're going to have your shipyards build:

```
var oldShip = ship.manufacture(100);
var newShip = newShipModel.manufacture(150);
```

this

You may be a little confused by the use of the this keyword in the prior extend function. this behaves somewhat differently in JavaScript than it does in many other languages, primarily because JavaScript is not a class-based language. this can behave differently, depending on where it's called, and can even change from function call to function call in the same function.

Let's walk through the different values this can take on:

- If you call this globally, then it refers to the global object, which is the window object, if running inside a browser.

- If you call this inside a function that is not attached to an object, this refers to the global object, because, by default, functions are attached to the global object.

- If you call this inside a function that is attached to an object, such as in the fire method of ship, then it refers to the object the function is attached to (in this case, ship).

- If you call this inside a constructor function, then a new object is created when you call it with new, and this refers to that object.

- If you call this in a function that is then called from an event handler, then this refers either to the document object model (DOM) element in the page that triggered the event or to the global object, if there is no such DOM element.

Note that this last value is where you're most likely to run into trouble, because the behavior concerning event handlers specifically overrides the behavior you would otherwise expect.

Fortunately, you can get around some of this behavior with the call and apply functions. These are attached to every function object and are used to explicitly set what this refers to. For instance, if you called myAwesomeShip.fire.call(myMoreAwesomeShip), then this would refer to myMoreAwesomeShip.

In general, it's useful to explicitly declare what you expect this to be whenever you call a function that uses it.

Note Often, developers coming from a class-based OOP language rail against the lack of proper OOP in JavaScript. The truth is that JavaScript has a very flexible OOP model that can be used in much the same way as a more classical language if required. If you don't need it, then the flexibility of JavaScript's prototypical inheritance can actually be a huge boon, making it far simpler to build up the complex inheritances necessary for a game.

Conclusion

This has been a whirlwind tour of JavaScript, detailing all the pieces you need to start building a basic game architecture and pointing out some of the pitfalls along the way.

JavaScript gets a bad rap for some of its quirks and idiosyncrasies. I've detailed a few of the more nuanced issues here, and awareness of these should keep you from making some of the more painful mistakes I made when first starting out.

CHAPTER 2

■ ■ ■

Optimal Asset Loading

Ian Ballantyne, Software Engineer, Turbulenz Limited

Designing an efficient method of loading game asset data for HTML5 games is essential in creating a good user experience for players. When games can be played immediately in the browser with no prior downloading there are different considerations to make, not only for the first time play experience but also for future plays of the game. The **assets** referred to by this chapter are not the usual HTML, CSS, JavaScript, and other media that make up a web site, but are the game assets required specifically for the game experience. The techniques mentioned in this chapter go beyond dealing with the standard image and sound data usually handled by the browser and aim at helping you consider assets such as models, animations, shaders, materials, UIs, and other structural data that is not represented in code. Whether this data is in text or binary form (the "Data Formats" section will discuss both) it somehow needs to be transferred to the player's machine so that the JavaScript code running the game can turn it into something amazing that players can interact with.

This chapter also discusses various considerations game developers should make regarding the distribution of their game assets and optimizations for loading data. Structuring a good loading mechanism and understanding the communication process between the client's browser and server are essential for producing a responsive game that can quickly be enjoyed by millions of users simultaneously. Taking advantage of the techniques mentioned in the "Asset Hosting" section is essential for the best first impressions of the game, making sure it starts quickly the first time. The tips in the "Caching Data" section are primarily focussed on improving performance for future runs, making an online, connected game feel like it is sitting on the player's computer, ready to run at any time. The final section on "Asset Grouping" is about organizing assets in a way that suits the strengths and weaknesses of browser-based data loading.

The concepts covered by each section are a flavor of what you will need to do to improve your loading times. Although the concepts are straightforward to understand, the complexity lies in the details of the implementation with respect to your game, and which services or APIs you choose. Each section outlines the resources that are essential to discover the APIs in more detail. Many of the concepts have been implemented as part of the open source Turbulenz Engine, which is used throughout this chapter as a real world example of the techniques presented. Figure 2-1 shows the Turbulenz Engine in action. The libraries not only prove that the concepts work for published games, but also show how to handle the capabilities and quirks of different browsers in a single implementation. By the end of the chapter you should have a good idea of which quick improvements to make and what new approaches are worth investigating.

Figure 2-1. *Polycraft is a complete 3D, HTML5 game built by Wonderstruck Games (http://wonderstruckgames.com) using the Turbulenz Engine. With 1000+ assets equating to ~50Mbs of data when uncompressed, efficiently loading and processing assets for this amount of data is essential for a smooth gaming experience. The recommendations in this chapter come from our experiences of developing games such as Polycraft for the Web. The development team at Turbulenz hope that by sharing this information, other game developers will also be able to harness the power of the web platform for their games*

Caching Data

Caching content to manage the trade-off between loading times and resource limitations has always been a game development concern. Whether it be transferring information from optical media, hard disks, or memory, the amount of bandwidth, latency, and storage space available dictates the strategy required. The browser presents another environment with its own characteristics and so an appropriate strategy must be chosen. There is no guarantee that previous strategies will "just work" in this space.

In the world of browser-based gaming, caching can occur in the following locations: server side and client side. On the server side, the type of cache depends on the server configuration and the infrastructure behind it, for example whether a content distribution network (CDN) is being used to host the files. On the client side, it depends on the browser configuration and ultimately the game as it decides what to do with the data it receives. The more of these resources you have control over, the more optimizations you can make. In some occasions, certain features won't be available so it's always worth considering having a fallback solution. Figure 2-2 shows a typical distribution configuration. The server-side and request caches on the remote host servers, either on disk or in memory, ensure that when a request comes in, it is handled as quickly as possible. The browser cache and web storage, typically from the local disk, reduce the need to rely on a remote machine. The asset cache, an example of holding data (processed or unprocessed) in memory until required, represents the game's own ability to manage the limited available memory, avoiding the need to request it from local disk or remote host server.

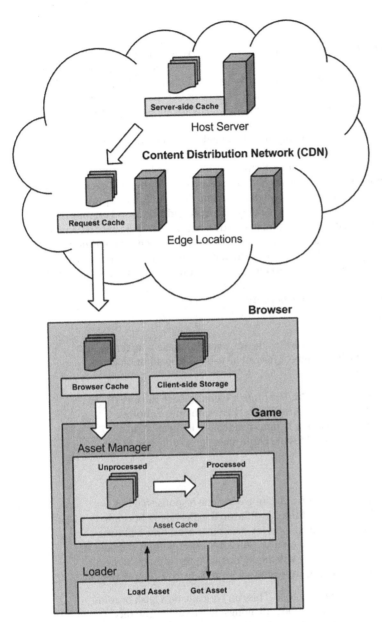

Figure 2-2. *Possible locations on the server and client side where game assets can be cached, from being stored on disk by a remote host server to being stored in memory already processed and ready to use by the game*

HTTP Caching

The most prevalent client-side caching approach is HTTP caching in the browser. When the browser requests a file over HTTP, it takes time to download the file. Once the file has been downloaded, the browser can store it in its local cache. This means for subsequent requests for that file the browser will refer to its local cached copy. This technique eliminates the server request and the need to download the file. It has the added bonus that you will receive fewer server requests, which may save you money in hosting costs. This technique takes advantage of the fact that most game assets are static content, changing infrequently.

When a HTTP server sends a file to a client, it can optionally include metadata in the form of headers, such as the file encoding. To enable more fine-grained control of HTTP caching in the browser requires the server to be configured to provide headers with caching information for the static assets. This tells the browser to use the locally cached file from the disk instead of downloading it again. If the cached file doesn't exist or the local cache has been cleared, then it will download the file. As far as the game is concerned, there is no difference in this process except that the cached file should load quicker. The behavior of headers is categorized as **conditional** and **unconditional**. Conditional means that the browser will use the header information to decide whether to use the cached version or not. It may then issue a conditional request to the server and download if the file has changed. Unconditional means that if the header conditions are met and the file is already in the cache; then it will return the cached copy and it won't make any requests to the server. These headers give you varying levels of control for how browsers download and cache static assets from your game.

The HTTP/1.1 specification allows you to set the following headers for caching.

- Unconditional:

  - **Expires: HTTP-DATE**. The timestamp after which the browser will make a server request for the file even if it is stored in the local cache. This can be used to stop additional requests from being made.

  - **Cache control: max-age=DELTA-SECONDS**. The time in seconds since the initial request that the browser will cache the response file and hence not make another request. This allows the same behavior as the Expires header, but is specified in a different way. The max-age directive overrides the Expires header so only one or the other should be used.

- Conditional:

  - **Last-Modified: HTTP-DATE**. The timestamp indicating when the response file was last modified. This is typically the last-modified time of the file on the filesystem, but can be a different representation of a last modified date, for example the last time a file was referenced on the server, even if not modified on disk. Since this is a conditional header, it depends on how the browser uses it to decide whether or not a request is made. If the file is in cache and the HTTP-DATE was long ago, the browser is unlikely to re-request the file.

  - **ETag: ENTITY-TAG**. An identifier for the response. This can typically be a hash or some other method of file versioning. The ETag can be sent alongside a request. The server can use the ETag to see if the version of the file on the client matches the version on the server. If the file hasn't changed, the server returns a HTTP response with a status code of 304 Not Modified. This tells the client that a new copy of the file is not required. For more information on ETags, see http://en.wikipedia.org/wiki/HTTP_ETag.

The ability to control caching settings is not always available from every server and behaviors will differ depending on the server. It is worth referring to the documentation to discover how to enable and set these headers.

HTTP Caching Example

Since the caching works per URL, you will need to serve your asset files in a way that can take advantage of these headers. One approach is to uniquely name each file and set the expires header/max-age to be as long as possible. This will give you a unique URL for each version of the asset file, allowing you to control the headers individually. The unique name could be a hash based on the file contents, which can be done automatically as part of an offline build process. If this hash is deterministic, the same asset used by different versions of your games can be given the same unique URL. If the source asset changes, a new hash is generated, which can also be used to manage versioning of assets.

This approach exhibits the following behaviors:

- You can host assets for different versions of your game (or different games entirely) in the same location. This can save storage space on the server and make the process of deploying your game more efficient as certain hashed assets may have previously been uploaded.

- When a player loads a new version of your game for the first time, if the files shared between versions are already in the local cache, no downloading is required. This speeds up the loading time for game builds with few asset changes, reducing the impact of updating the game for users. Updates are therefore less expensive and this encourages more frequent improvements.

- Since the file requested is versioned via the unique name, changing the request URL can update the file. This has the benefit that the file is not replaced and hence if the game needs to roll back to using an older version of the file, only the request URL needs to change. No additional requests are made and no files need to be re-downloaded, having rolled back (provided the original file is still in local cache).

- Offline processing tools for generating the asset files can use the unique filename to decide if they need to rebuild a file from source. This can improve the iterative development process and help with asset management.

Loading HTTP Cached Assets

Once a game is able to cache static assets in this way, it will need a process to be able to manage which URLs to request. This is a case of matching the name of an asset with a given version of that asset. In this example, you can assume that the source path for an asset can be mapped directly to the latest required version of that asset. The asset contents can be changed, but the source path remains the same, so no code changes are required to update assets. If the game requires a shader called shaders/debug.cgfx, it will need to know the unique hash so it can construct the URL to request. At Turbulenz, this is done by creating a logical mapping between source path and asset filename, and storing the information in a mapping table. A mapping table is effectively a lookup table, loaded by the game and stored as a JavaScript object literal; see Listing 2-1.

Listing 2-1. An Example of a Mapping Table

```
var urlMapping = {
    "shaders/debug.cgfx" : "2Hohp_autOWOWbutP_NSUw.json",
    "shaders/defaultrendering.cgfx" : "4HdTZBhuheSPYHe1vmygYA.json",
    "shaders/standard.cgfx" : "5Yhd75LjDeV3WEvRsKnGSQ.json"
};
```

Each source path represents an asset the game can refer to. Using the source path and not the source filename avoids naming conflicts and allows you to structure your assets like a file system. If two source assets generate identical output, the resulting hash will be the same, avoiding the duplication of asset data. This gives you some flexibility when importing asset names from external tools such as 3D editors.

In this example, the shaders for 3D rendering are referenced by their source path, which maps to a processed JSON formatted object representation of the shader. Since the resulting filename is unique, there is no need to maintain a hierarchical directory structure to store files. This allows the server to apply the caching headers to all files in a given directory, in this case a directory named staticmax, which contains all files that should be cached for the longest time period; see Listing 2-2.

Listing 2-2. A Simplified Example of Loading a Static Asset Cached as Described Above

```
/**
 * Assumed global values:
 *
 * console - The console to output error messages for failure to load/parse assets.
 */

/**
 * The prefix appended to the mapping table name.
 * This is effectively the location of the asset directory.
 * This will eventually be the URL of the hosting server/CDN.
 */
var urlPrefix = 'staticmax/';

/**
 * The mapping of the shader source path to the processed asset.
 * If an asset is not yet loaded this mapping will be undefined.
 */
var shaderMapping = {};

/**
 * The function that will make the asynchronous request for the asset.
 * The callback will return with the status code and response it receives from the server.
 */
function requestStaticAssetFn(srcName, callback) {

    // If there is no mapping, a URL request cannot be made.
    var assetName = urlMapping[srcName];
    if (!assetName) {
        return false;
    }

    function httpRequestCallback() {
        // When the readyState is 4 (DONE), call the callback
        if (xhr.readyState === 4) {
            var xhrResponseText = xhr.responseText;
            var xhrStatus = xhr.status;
            if (callback) {
                callback(xhrResponseText, xhrStatus);
            }
            xhr.onreadystatechange = null;
            xhr = null;
            callback = null;
        }
    }
}
```

```
    // Construct the URL to request the asset
    var requestURL = urlPrefix + assetName;

    // Make the request using XHR
    var xhr = new window.XMLHttpRequest();
    xhr.open('GET', requestURL, true);
    if (callback) {
        xhr.onreadystatechange = httpRequestCallback;
    }
    xhr.send(null);
    return true;
}

/**
 * Generate the callback function for this particular shader.
 * The function will also process the shader in the callback.
 */
function shaderResponseCallback(shaderName) {
    var sourceName = shaderName;
    return function shaderResponseFn(responseText, status) {
        // If the server returns 200, then the asset is included as responseText and can be
processed.
        if (status === 200) {
            try {
                shaderMapping[sourceName] = JSON.parse(responseText);
            }
            catch (e) {
                console.error("Failed to parse shader with error: " + e);
            }
        }
        else {
            console.error("Failed to load shader with status: " + status);
        }
    };
}

/**
 * Actual request for the asset.
 * The request should be made if there is no entry for shaderName in the shaderMapping.
 * The allows the mapping to be set to null to force the shader to be re-requested.
 */
var shaderName = "shaders/debug.cgfx";
if (!shaderMapping[shaderName]) {
    if (!requestStaticAssetFn(shaderName, shaderResponseCallback(shaderName))) {
        console.error("Failed to make a request for: " + shaderName);
    }
}
```

For a live server, the urlPrefix will be something like "http://asset.hostserver.com/game/staticmax/". This example shows how it may work for a text-based shader, but this technique could be applied to other types of assets. It is also worth noting that this example doesn't handle the many different response codes that are possible during asset loading, such as 404s, 500s, etc. It is assumed that this code will be part of a much more complex asset handling and automatic retry system. Figure 2-3 shows an example of how the process may play out: loading and running the game, loading the latest mapping table, requesting a shader that is sent from the server, and finally, requesting a shader that ends up being resolved by the browser cache. For a more complete example of this, see the Request Handler and Shader Manager classes in the open source Turbulenz Engine (https://github.com/turbulenz/turbulenz_engine).

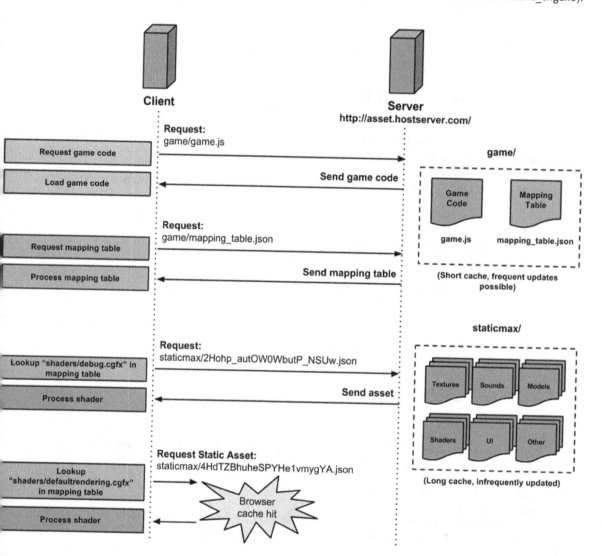

Figure 2-3. *An example of the communication process between a server and the client when using a mapping table. Game code and mapping table data served with short cache times provide the ability to request static assets served with long cache times that take advantage of HTTP caching behaviours*

Client-Side Storage

At this point it is worth mentioning a little bit about client-side storage. The techniques described for HTTP caching are about using a cache to avoid a full HTTP request. There is another option for storing data that sits between server requests and memory that could potentially achieve this if used correctly. Client-side storage usually refers to a number of different APIs that allow web sites to store data on a local machine; these are Web Storage (sometimes referred to as Local Storage), IndexedDB, Web SQL Database, and FileSystem. They ultimately promise one thing: persistent storage between accesses to a web site. Before you get excited and start preparing to save all your game data here, it is important to understand what each API provides, the limitations, the pros and cons, and the availability. Two very good articles that explain all of this very well are at www.html5rocks.com/en/tutorials/offline/whats-offline/ and www.html5rocks.com/en/tutorials/offline/storage/.

What is important is how these APIs are potentially useful for games. Web Storage allows the setting of key/value pairs on a wide range of devices, but has limited storage capacity and requires data to be stored as strings. At the other end of scale, file access via the Filesystem API allows applications to request persistent storage much larger than the limitations of Web Storage with the ability to save and load binary content, but is less widely supported across browsers. If you have asset data that makes sense to be cached by one of these APIs, then it may potentially save you loading time.

Ideally a game would be able use client-side storage to save all static asset data so that it can be accessed quickly without server requests, even while offline, but the ability to do this across all browsers is not consistent and at the time of writing it is difficult to write a generic storage library that would be able to utilize one of the APIs depending on what is available. For example, if you wanted to store binary data for quick access, then it would be possible via "Blobs" for IndexedDB, Web SQL Database, and FileSystem API, but would require data to be base64-encoded as plain text for Web Storage. The amount of storage available and the cost of processing this data would differ depending on which API was used; for example, Web Storage is synchronous and will block during loading, unlike the others, which are asynchronous. If you are happy to acknowledge that only users of browsers that support a given API would have the performance improvements, then client-side storage may still be useful for your game.

One thing client-side storage is potentially useful for across all available APIs is the storing and loading of small bits of non-critical data, such as player preferences or storing temporary data such as save game information if the game gets temporarily disconnected from the cloud. If storing this data locally means that HTTP requests are made less frequently or at not all, then this can certainly speed up loading and saving for your game. In the long term, client-side storage is essential in being able to provide offline solutions to HTML5 games. If your game only partially depends on being able to connect to online services, then players should be able to play it without having a persistent Internet connection. Client-side storage solutions will be able to provide locally cached game assets and temporary storage mechanisms for player data that can be synchronized with the cloud when the player is able to get back online.

Memory Caching

Having loaded an asset from an HTTP request, cache, or client-side storage, the game then has the opportunity to process the asset appropriately. If the asset is in JSON form, then at this point you might typically parse the data and convert it to the object format. Once parsed, the JSON is no longer needed and can be de-referenced for the garbage collector to clean up. This technique helps the application minimize its memory footprint by avoiding duplicating the data representation of an object in memory. If, however, the game frequently requests common assets in this way, the cost of reprocessing assets, even from local cache, can accumulate. By holding a reference to commonly requested assets, the game can avoid making a request entirely at the cost of caching the data in memory. The trade-off between loading speed and memory usage should be measured per asset to find out which common assets would benefit from this approach.

An example of such an asset might be the contents of a menu screen. During typical gameplay, the game may choose to unload the processed data to save memory for game data, but to have a responsive menu, it may choose to process the compressed representation because it is faster than requesting the asset again. Another case where this is convenient is when two different assets request a shared dependency independently of each other, such as a texture used by two different models. If assets are referred to in a key (in this example, the path to an asset, such as "textures/wall.png"), then the game could use a generic asset cache in memory that has the ability to release assets if they are not being used. Different heuristics can be used to decide if an asset should be released from such a cache, such as size. In the case of texture assets, where texture memory is limited, that cache can be used as a buffer to limit the storage of assets that are used less frequently. Releasing these assets will involve freeing it from the texture memory on the graphics card. Listing 2-3 shows an example of such a memory cache.

Listing 2-3. A Memory Cache with a Limited Asset Size That Prioritizes Cached Assets That Have Been Requested Most Recently

```
/**
 * Assumed global values:
 *
 * Observer - A class to notify subscribers when a callback is made.
 *            See https://github.com/turbulenz/turbulenz_engine for an example.
 * TurbulenzEngine - Required for the setTimeout function.
 *                   Used to make callbacks asynchronously.
 * requestTexture - A function responsible for requesting the texture asset.
 * drawTexture - A function that draws a given texture.
 */


/**
 * AssetCache - A class to manage a cache of a fixed size.
 *
 * When the number of unique assets exceeds the cache size an existing asset is removed.
 * The cache prioritizes cached assets that have been requested most recently.
 */
var AssetCache = (function () {
    function AssetCache() {}

    AssetCache.prototype.exists = function (key) {
        return this.cache.hasOwnProperty(key);
    };

    AssetCache.prototype.isLoading = function (key) {
        // See if the asset has a cache entry and if it is loading
        var cachedAsset = this.cache[key];
        if (cachedAsset) {
            return cachedAsset.isLoading;
        }
        return false;
    };

    AssetCache.prototype.get = function (key) {
        // Look for the asset in the cache
        var cachedAsset = this.cache[key];
        if (cachedAsset) {
            // Set the current hitCounter for the asset
            // This indicates it is the last requested asset
            cachedAsset.cacheHit = this.hitCounter;
            this.hitCounter += 1;
```

```
            // Return the asset. This is null if the asset is still loading
            return cachedAsset.asset;
    }
    return null;
};

AssetCache.prototype.request = function (key, params, callback) {
    // Look for the asset in the cache
    var cachedAsset = this.cache[key];
    if (cachedAsset) {
        // Set the current hitCounter for the asset
        // This indicates it is the last requested asset
        cachedAsset.cacheHit = this.hitCounter;
        this.hitCounter += 1;
        if (!callback) {
            return;
        }
        if (cachedAsset.isLoading) {
            // Subscribe the callback to be called when loading is complete
            cachedAsset.observer.subscribe(callback);
        } else {
            // Call the callback asynchronously, like a request response
            TurbulenzEngine.setTimeout(function requestCallbackFn() {
                callback(key, cachedAsset.asset, params);
            }, 0);
        }
        return;
    }

    var cacheArray = this.cacheArray;
    var cacheArrayLength = cacheArray.length;

    if (cacheArrayLength >= this.maxCacheSize) {
        // If the cache exceeds the maximum cache size, remove an asset
        var cache = this.cache;
        var oldestCacheHit = this.hitCounter;
        var oldestKey = null;
        var oldestIndex;
        var i;

        // Find the oldest cache entry
        for (i = 0; i < cacheArrayLength; i += 1) {
            if (cacheArray[i].cacheHit < oldestCacheHit) {
                oldestCacheHit = cacheArray[i].cacheHit;
                oldestIndex = i;
            }
        }

        // Reuse an existing cachedAsset object to avoid object re-creation
        cachedAsset = cacheArray[oldestIndex];
        oldestKey = cachedAsset.key;
```

```
        // Call the onDestroy function if the cachedAsset is loaded
        if (this.onDestroy && !cachedAsset.isLoading) {
            this.onDestroy(oldestKey, cachedAsset.asset);
        }
        delete cache[oldestKey];
        // Reset the cachedAsset for the new entry
        cachedAsset.cacheHit = this.hitCounter;
        cachedAsset.asset = null;
        cachedAsset.isLoading = true;
        cachedAsset.key = key;
        cachedAsset.observer = Observer.create();
        this.cache[key] = cachedAsset;
    } else {
        // Create a new entry (up to the maxCacheSize)
        cachedAsset = this.cache[key] = cacheArray[cacheArrayLength] = {
            cacheHit: this.hitCounter,
            asset: null,
            isLoading: true,
            key: key,
            observer: Observer.create()
        };
    }
    this.hitCounter += 1;

    var that = this;
    var observer = cachedAsset.observer;
    if (callback) {
        // Subscribe the callback to be called when the asset is loaded
        observer.subscribe(callback);
    }
    this.onLoad(key, params, function onLoadedAssetFn(asset) {
        if (cachedAsset.key === key) {
            // Check the cachedAsset hasn't be re-allocated during loading
            cachedAsset.cacheHit = that.hitCounter;
            cachedAsset.asset = asset;
            cachedAsset.isLoading = false;
            that.hitCounter += 1;

            // Notify all callbacks that the asset has been loaded
            cachedAsset.observer.notify(key, asset, params);
        } else {
            if (that.onDestroy) {
                // Destroy assets that have been removed from the cache during loading
                that.onDestroy(key, asset);
            }
            // Notify the original observer that asset was not saved in the cache
            observer.notify(key, null, params);
        }
    });
};
```

```
    AssetCache.create = // Constructor function
    function (cacheParams) {
        if (!cacheParams.onLoad) {
            return null;
        }

        var assetCache = new AssetCache();

        assetCache.maxCacheSize = cacheParams.size || 64;
        assetCache.onLoad = cacheParams.onLoad;
        assetCache.onDestroy = cacheParams.onDestroy;

        assetCache.hitCounter = 0;
        assetCache.cache = {};
        assetCache.cacheArray = [];

        return assetCache;
    };
    AssetCache.version = 2;
    return AssetCache;
})();

/**
 * Usage:
 *
 * A textureCache is created to store up to 100 textures in the cache.
 * The onLoad and onDestroy functions give the game control
 * of how the assets are created and destroy.
 *
 * In the render loop the texture is fetched from the cache.
 * It will be rendered if it exists, otherwise will be requested.
 *
 * The render loop is unaware of how the texture is obtained, only that
 * it will be requested as soon as possible.
 */

var textureCache = AssetCache.create({
    size: 100,
    onLoad: function loadTextureFn(key, params, loadedCallback) {
        requestTexture(key, loadedCallback);
    },
    onDestroy: function destroyTextureFn(key, texture) {
        if (texture) {
            texture.destroy();
        }
    }
});
```

```
function renderLoopFn() {
    var textureURL = "textures/wall.png";
    var texture = textureCache.get(textureURL);
    if (texture) {
        drawTexture(texture);
    }
    else if (!textureCache.isLoading(textureURL)) {
        textureCache.request(textureURL);
    }
}
```

In this example, an asset cache is created with a limited size of 100. Imagine that you only have the memory allowance to store 100 textures uncompressed in graphics memory at a given time. The game may require more than this number over its lifetime, but not at a single point in time. The aim is to provide the game with the set of textures it requires most often, which are available as it needs them. In addition, you want to avoid re-requesting a texture where possible. By allowing an asset cache to manage the texture storage, the game is able to access the texture quickly while it is in memory and make a request if it is not.

In this example, the textureCache.get function will be called in the render loop every time a texture is required to draw on screen. If the function returns "null", then the texture is not yet in the cache (or not available). If the texture is not already loading, then the game will request it. The request function will in turn call the onLoad function that the game provides for the AssetCache. This gives the game control over how it loads the asset that the cache will store. In this case, it simply calls a requestTexture function, which will request and allocate memory for the texture. It is assumed that this function will locate the texture using the quickest method, whether that be from an HTTP request, the browser cache, or client-side storage. The onLoad function also provides a callback to the requestTexture function to return the loaded asset. In the case where a request to the textureCache is made but exceeds the 100-texture limit, then the cache will find the least accessed texture and call the onDestroy function, destroying the texture and releasing the memory. If the game attempts to get a texture that has since been removed from the cache, a request will be made and the process will start again.

This allows the game to access many different textures without having to worry about filling up texture memory with unused textures. Other heuristics such as texture size could be used in conjunction with this approach to ensure the best use of texture memory. The "Leaderboards" sample, which can potentially require hundreds or thousands of textures for avatar images, is a more complete example. It is included as part of the open source Turbulenz Engine see https://github.com/turbulenz/turbulenz_engine).

Data Formats

When building complex HTML5 games with an ever-increasing demand for content, inevitably the amount of asset data required will increase. The previous topic discussed methods to quickly access this data, but what about the cost of the data itself? How it is stored in memory and the processing costs play a part in how quickly the game will be able to load. Memory limitations restrict you from storing all data uncompressed and ready for use, and processing costs have a direct impact on the time to prepare the data.

The processing of data can be a native functionality provided by the browser features of the hardware, such as the CPU, or written in JavaScript and executed by the virtual machine itself. Choosing the appropriate format for the data in a given browser/platform can help utilize the processing and storage functionality available by avoiding long load times and reducing storage cost.

Texture Formats

Anyone who has written web content will be familiar with browser support for file formats such as JPEG, PNG, and GIF. In addition, some browsers support additional file formats such as WebP, which provides smaller file sizes for equivalent quality. The browser is usually responsible for loading these types of images, some of which can be used by the Canvas (2D) and WebGL (2D/3D) APIs. By using WebGL as the rendering API for your game, you may have the option to load other image formats and pass the responsibility of processing and storing the data to the graphics card. This is possible with WebGL if certain compressed texture formats are supported by the hardware. When passing an unsupported format such as JPEG to WebGL via the gl.texImage2D function, the image must first be decompressed before uploading to the graphics card. If a compressed texture format such as DXT is supported, then the gl.compressedTexImage2D function can be used to upload and store the texture without decompressing. Not only can you reduce the amount of memory required to store a texture on the graphics card (and hence fit more textures of equivalent quality into memory), but you can also defer the job of decompressing the texture until the shader uses it. Loading textures can be quicker because they are simply being passed as binary data to the graphics card.

In WebGL spec 1.0, the support for compressed texture formats such as DXT1, DXT3, and DXT5 that use the S3 compression algorithm is an extension that you must check for. This simplified example shows you how to check if the extension is supported and then check for the format you require. If the format is available, you will be able to create a compressed texture from your image data. See Listing 2-4 for a simplified example of how to achieve this. The assumed variables are listed in the comment at the top.

Listing 2-4. Checking if the Compressed Textures Extension Is Supported and How to Check if a Required Format is Available

```
/**
 * gl - The WebGL context
 * textureData - The data that will be used to create the texture
 * pixelFormat - The pixel format of your texture data that you want to use as a compressed texture
 * textureWidth - The width of the texture (power of 2)
 * textureHeight - The height of the texture (power of 2)
 */


/**
 * Request the extension to determine which pixel formats if any are available
 * The request for the extension only needs to be done once in the game.
 */
var internalFormat;
var ctExtension = gl.getExtension('WEBGL_compressed_textures_s3tc');
if (ctExtension) {
    switch (pixelFormat) {
    case 'DXT1_RGB':
        internalFormat = ctExtension.COMPRESSED_RGB_S3TC_DXT1_EXT;
        break;
    case 'DXT1_RGBA':
        internalFormat = ctExtension.COMPRESSED_RGBA_S3TC_DXT1_EXT;
        break;
    case 'DXT3_RGBA':
        internalFormat = ctExtension.COMPRESSED_RGBA_S3TC_DXT3_EXT;
        break;
```

```
    case 'DXT5_RGBA':
        internalFormat = ctExtension.COMPRESSED_RGBA_S3TC_DXT5_EXT;
        break;
    }
}

if (internalFormat === undefined) {
    // If the pixel format is not supported, fall back to an option that creates an uncompressed
    texture.
    return "Compressed pixelFormat not supported";
}

var texture = gl.createTexture();
gl.bindTexture(gl.TEXTURE_2D, texture);
gl.texParameteri(gl.TEXTURE_2D, gl.TEXTURE_MAG_FILTER, gl.LINEAR);
gl.texParameteri(gl.TEXTURE_2D, gl.TEXTURE_MIN_FILTER, gl.LINEAR);
gl.compressedTexImage2D(
    gl.TEXTURE_2D,
    0,
    internalFormat,
    textureWidth,
    textureHeight,
    0,
    textureData);
```

This simple example does not cover all aspects of using the extension (including checking browser-specific names for the extension and robust error handling), but it should give an indication of how the extension is used. For more information about best practices for using compressed textures, see the Graphics Device implementation as part the open source Turbulenz Engine (https://github.com/turbulenz/turbulenz_engine). It is also worth noting that in the future more compression formats may be supported, so check up-to-date documentation.

There are a few key considerations from looking at this example. The first is what to do when a given pixel format is not supported. As mentioned throughout this chapter, the best way to load an asset is to not load it at all, so checking the available formats should happen before the data is even loaded. This allows the game to select the best option for the given platform. In the event that the WebGL extension or any of the required formats are not supported, the game will have to provide a fallback option. This could be by choosing to load one of the browser-supported file formats and accepting the cost of decompressing or, alternatively, if the file format is not supported by the browser, reading the file and decompressing the data in JavaScript. This may not be as bad as it sounds if the task is executed by Web Workers running in the background while other data loads. Remember that the result will be an uncompressed pixel format, which will take up more memory. If you have control of the compression/decompression, you may be able to choose to use a lower bit depth per pixel (e.g. 16-bit instead of 32-bit), which may affect quality but reduce storage. The advice is to experiment with different combinations for your game and instrument the loading time in different browsers on different platforms. Only then will you be able to get a true idea of what best suits your content as a fallback option.

Another consideration is how texture data is loaded onto the client if the browser doesn't support the file format and the cost of doing this. DDS is typically used as a container format for DXT compressed textures and will need to be loaded and parsed to extract the texture data. The files are usually requested using XHR as binary data using the arraybuffer response type and can use the Uint8Array constructor to create a byte array that can be manipulated. Once the loader has parsed the container format, the pixel data, which exists as a byte array, can be passed directly to

WebGL to use as texture data. The Turbulenz Engine includes a JavaScript implementation of such a DDS loader to provide this functionality. In most cases, the binary data is just being passed to WebGL so there is little processing cost in JavaScript, which makes this a quick way to load texture data.

For some textures in your game, you may want to include mipmaps. This common practice adds processing costs for image formats that don't include mipmap data, such as PNG and JPEG. If the game requires mipmapped textures created from these formats, they will be generated on the fly, adding to the total load time. The advantage of loading a file format that supports mipmaps such as DDS is that they can be generated offline with more control over the level of quality. This does add to the total size of the file (around 33%, as each mipmap is a quarter the size of the previous level); however, these files tend to compress well with gzip, which can be enabled as a server compression option (discussed later).

The decision for the exact format to use for texture data is often subjective when it comes to quality. The more compression, the smaller the file size and faster load times, but the more visual artifacts that can be seen. Think carefully about options for pixel formats, the use of an alpha channel, the pixel depth, and the compression depending on the image content. The choice of which S3 compressed algorithm (DXT1, DXT3, DXT5) is like choosing between PNGs for images with alpha and JPEGs for images where artifacting is less obvious: it depends on what they support best. Quick loading is the goal, while still attempting to maintain an acceptable level of quality.

Audio Formats

Similar to texture formats; balancing data size and quality of audio files will affect the overall load time. Games are among the power-users of audio on the Web when it comes to effects, music, experience, and interactivity. The many variations of sound effects and music tracks can easily add up and eclipse the total size of the other types of data combined (even mesh data). This of course depends on the game, and you should keep track of how much audio data you are transferring during development. It is therefore important to consider different options for loading sounds that best fit your game.

If you are using sound within your game, you should be familiar with HTML5 Audio and the Web Audio API as the options available for browser audio support. The history of support for both the APIs and audio codecs has been hampered due to the complex issue of patents surrounding some audio formats, which has resulted in an uneven landscape of support across different browser vendors. The upshot is that audio support in games is not just a matter selecting the optimal format for your sound data, but also choosing based on availability and licensing. Familiar formats such as MP3 and AAC are supported by the latest versions of the majority of browsers, but cannot be guaranteed due to some browser manufacturers intentionally avoiding licensing issues. Formats such as OGG and WAV are also supported, but again not by all browser manufacturers. At the time of writing, the reality is that documenting the current support of audio formats would quickly be out of date and wouldn't help address the practicalities of efficiently loading audio for games. The best advice is to look at the following references to help understand the current support for desktop and mobile browsers and to apply the suggestions in this section to your choice of formats: (http://en.wikipedia.org/wiki/HTML5_Audio and https://developer.mozilla.org/en-US/docs/HTML/Supported_media_formats).

Transferring audio data is similar to other types of binary data. It can either be loaded directly by the browser by specifying it in an <AUDIO> tag or via an XHR request. The latter gives the game control of when the sound file is loaded and the option of what to do with it when it is received. The availability of the Web Audio API in browsers means that most games should have a fallback to HTML5 Audio. As with texture formats, testing for support, then deciding which format to use, is preferable to loading all data upfront. This does mean that you will probably be required to have multiple encodings of the same audio data hosted on your server. This is the price of compatibility, unlike textures where the choice is based mainly on performance. See Listing 2-5.

Listing 2-5. A Simplified Example of Loading an Audio File

```
/**
 * soundName - The name of the sound to load
 * getPreferredFormat - A function to determine the preferred format to use for a sound with a given
name.
 *                       The algorithm for this decision is up to the game.
 * audioContext - The audio context instance for the Web Audio API
 * bufferCreated - The callback function for when the buffer has been successfully created
 * bufferFailed - The callback function for the audio decode has failed
 */

// Check once at the start of the game which audio types are supported
var supported = {
    ogg: false,
    mp3: false,
    wav: false,
    mp4: false
};
var audio = new Audio();

if (audio.canPlayType('audio/ogg')) {
    supported.ogg = true;
}
if (audio.canPlayType('audio/mp3')) {
    supported.mp3 = true;
}
if (audio.canPlayType('audio/wav')) {
    supported.wav = true;
}
if (audio.canPlayType('audio/mp4')) {
    supported.mp4 = true;
}


// Audio element is thrown away after the support query
audio = null;

var soundPath = getPreferredFormat(soundName, supported);

var xhr = new window.XMLHttpRequest();
xhr.onreadystatechange = function () {
    if (xhr.readyState === 4) {
        var xhrStatus = xhr.status;
        var response = xhr.response;
```

```
        if (xhrStatus === 200) {
            if (audioContext.decodeAudioData) {
                audioContext.decodeAudioData(response, bufferCreated, bufferFailed);
            } else {
                var buffer = audioContext.createBuffer(response, false);
                bufferCreated(buffer);
            }
        }
        xhr.onreadystatechange = null;
        xhr = null;
    }
};
xhr.open('GET', soundPath, true);
xhr.responseType = 'arraybuffer';
xhr.send(null);
```

In Listing 2-5, the getPreferredFormat function is specified by the game to best decide which format to use. The choice should be based on the knowledge the game has about the required sound and how it is used. For example, if the file is a short sound effect (a few seconds in length) that needs to be played quickly, such a bullet fire sound, then selecting an uncompressed WAV file might be the best option, because unlike most MP3/OGG/AAC files it doesn't need to be decoded before use. It depends on the size and length of the sound. This example is unlikely to hold true for music files, which are usually minutes, not seconds, in length and hence are much larger when uncompressed.

Since the Web Audio API requires compressed audio files to be decompressed before use, storage of the uncompressed audio can quickly become an issue, especially on mobile where resources are more limited. Depending on the hardware, this decoding can be expensive for large files, so loading all large data files, such as music, upfront and then decoding is considered a bad idea. One option is to only load the music immediately required and wait until later to load other music.

If the sound needs to be played immediately, then an alternative approach is required for larger audio files. It is possible to combine streaming HTML5 Audio sounds with the Web Audio API, but at the time of writing, support is limited and unstable but should get better with improvements to media streaming in the future. In the absence of such features, one possible approach to speed up loading times is to load a smaller lower quality version of an audio file and start playing, only to replace it with a higher quality version after it has been loaded. The ability to seek and cross-fade two sources in the Web Audio API should make this a seamless transition. This type of functionality could be written at an audio library level. Figure 2-4 shows an example of loading and playing audio data with respect to user-driven events within the game.

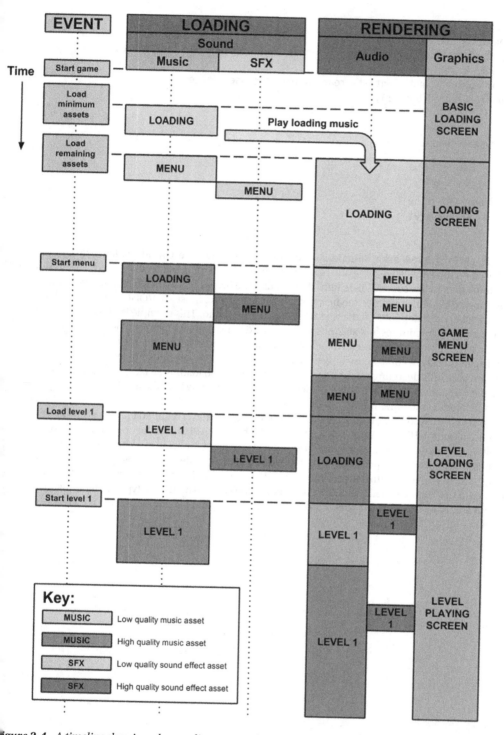

Figure 2-4. *A timeline showing when audio assets are loaded and when they are played. By loading lower-quality audio assets first, sound effects and music can be played sooner and long load times can be avoided. Loading higher-quality sound effects and music can be deferred, leaving the game to decide when is the most appropriate time to process them*

Having dealt with the issues of quality, format support, and encoding, the main choice that impacts loading is how late to defer it, assuming that a connection to the asset data server will still be available. Games providing a combination of MP3, OGG, and WAV audio files should cover the question of browser compatibility. A time will come where the available choices outweigh the limitations and at that point selecting an optimal audio format will be more important.

Other Formats

On the web, JSON is commonly used as a data-interchange format for sites. JSON data has the benefit that, once parsed, it can easily be manipulated as a JavaScript object. This makes it a simple way to transfer text data such as "string tables" for localization, where looking up the data is convenient because it is already in the appropriate format for use. It lends itself to defining extensible data formats where manipulating parts of the data is easy to do by setting properties on objects.

The downside is although JSON.parse is a native function in modern browsers, the cost of processing large assets with complex data structures is high, so much so that it can take anything from a few milliseconds to a few seconds to process, depending on the data. This has an impact on loading time, but also on the performance of the game. If the processing takes longer than 16.6ms on a 60fps game, then it can affect the frame-rate of the game, which makes the process of background loading problematic. It is possible to use Web Workers to ensure that the processing is done in a separate thread, which can help reduce the impact of parsing.

Some data, however, lends itself to using a binary format. Accessing this is possible in JavaScript with the help of the arraybuffer XHR transfer type and typed arrays such as Uint8Array, Int32Array, Float64Array, and Float32Array. This allows you to intentionally transfer floating-point values at a given precision or define a fixed size for your data. If you use a Uint8Array view on a transferred arraybuffer, you effectively have a byte array for your file format to manipulate as you require. This allows you to write your own binary data parsers in JavaScript. The DataView interface is designed specifically for doing this and to handle the endianness of the data. For more information for how to use these interfaces for manipulating binary data, see www.html5rocks.com/en/tutorials/webgl/typed_arrays/.

In addition to structuring your own binary file data to be used in JavaScript, proposals are emerging to standardize many of the common formats that are used by games. One example is the Khronos proposal for **glTF**, a format for transferring and compressing 3D assets that is designed to work with WebGL (www.khronos.org/news/press/khronos-collada-now-recognized-as-iso-standard). Another example is the **webgl-loader** project that aims to provide mesh compression for WebGL (https://code.google.com/p/webgl-loader/). Proposals like these combine text and binary data and aim to provide a strategy to deliver complex mesh data in a format optimized for web delivery. At the time of writing there is no standardized approach, but it is worth being aware of the data formats that are specifically designed to help deliver certain file content to the Web.

Asset Hosting

When running your game on your local machine, the performance of loading the asset data from a file or in most cases from a locally run web server can appear to be very quick. As soon as you start loading from a server hosted on a local network and then eventually from where your game will be hosted online, it becomes apparent that what you considered an acceptable load time is no longer acceptable in the real world. There are many factors involved when downloading assets; considering how best to host them is key to having consistent behavior for all players of your game. The decisions are not only about where they are hosted, but how they are hosted. Web sites employ many strategies for delivering content quickly to millions of users all over the globe. Since HTML5 games operate as web sites/web apps, the same strategies can be applied to make loading your assets as quick as possible. There are many other considerations for asset hosting, such as cost and storage size, that should not be ignored, but for now let's consider performance.

Server Compression

The transfer time of a file is longer the larger the file, given a fixed bandwidth, so anything that can be done to reduce the file size that doesn't modify the data within the asset can be a benefit. The previous section discussed compression techniques specific to the type of data, but there is also the option of generalized compression algorithms. The majority of browsers support receiving content gzip compressed, such as HTML, CSS, and JavaScript, so compressing large text-based data, such as JSON objects, in the same way is a good idea.

There are many choices of web server technology available to use for hosting, such as Apache, IIS, and nginx. Most servers support enabling gzip as a configuration option and usually allow you to specify which file types to apply it to when a request comes in with the header `Accept-Encoding: gzip`. If a server has it turned on, it should serve the asset gzipped with the header `Content-Encoding: gzip`. There is usually an associated CPU cost of encoding and decoding the gzip on server and client side, but this assumes that the cost is less than the transfer cost of a larger file. Server-side compression costs can usually be eliminated if the response is cached with the gzipped file. Also, not all gzip compression utilities are considered equal. At Turbulenz, we have found that 7-Zip provides very good gzip compression, which can be done offline before uploading the assets to the server. In this case, the server should be configured to serve up the pre-compressed version of the file when gzip is requested. It is worth trying different compression tools to find which one works best for you. For more information about enabling HTTP compression, see `http://en.wikipedia.org/wiki/HTTP_compression`.

Gzip compression is considered essential for uncompressed text formats, but for compressed formats such as PNG it can result in files that are larger than the original compressed file. However, some types of compressed data do benefit from additional gzip compression, such as DXT texture data. The preferred approach should be to compress the file offline and compare with and without compression. If the resulting file sizes are similar, then the added decompression overhead may make loading times slower, and it is probably not worth compressing. If the compressed file size is much smaller, it might be worth considering. If you have limited hosting space, it is worth doing a few tests before choosing which version to upload and serve.

Geolocating Assets

The latency of a request (the time it takes the server to receive, process, and respond) has an impact on how quickly the game will load, regardless of whether the asset is actually transferred or not. Assuming a player is accessing the game for the first time and can't take advantage of any of the client-side caching techniques previously described, what can be done to reduce this latency? Since the latency is related to how far the client is away from the server, the logical solution is to reduce the distance from the player to the host server. As an example, assume that the latency to the server is 100ms (not including transfer time) and assume your game needs to transfer 100 assets. Worst case, that's 10000ms (10 seconds) to query the host server to even find out about each asset (assuming a single server with a single sequential request). In reality, browsers can make more than one request at a time to a given server, but there is a limit to how many requests can be made. If, however, the base latency can be reduced, then savings can be made for every asset request. If the player's bandwidth available to transfer a given asset is the same for two different servers, then the performance benefit will be with the one with lower latency. Having host servers in multiple locations around the world helps reduce the start time for all your players. It's easy to forget this if you only test run the game from a single location.

Using a Content Distribution Network

Providing geolocated assets in multiple locations around the world would require you to run multiple servers and distribute assets among those locations. Luckily, CDNs exist to provide this type of service. The infrastructure provided by companies running these networks can serve internet content up to millions of users with more hosting servers than would be feasible for an individual games company to provide. Pricing, performance, and interfaces vary depending on the provider, so it is worth investigating before making a decision.

As a model for game asset hosting, CDNs can effectively be configured to cache requests made for certain assets server-side, with a given set of request headers to edge locations around the world, which are closer to the players. The advantage is you don't need to distribute your assets to these locations; that task is usually handled by the CDN. Another advantage to CDNs is that they can help provide geolocated DNS lookups. If you request an asset from cdn.company.com, some CDN services will use Anycast to connect you to the host that is identified as being closest to the machine that made the request. This is usually managed by the provider's DNS service and the route with the lowest latency may not always be the geographically closest. This allows all requests for an asset to be made to a single URL, but then handled by different servers. It is worth noting that the behaviours of CDNs in terms of configuration differ between providers, so this is just one example of how a CDN can be used.

Imagine, similar to the local server approach, which you are able to set the cache time to be a long period of time for assets that you consider static and are rarely modified. When you first upload the asset to your server and request it via the CDN, which is configured to respect the cache times of the asset in the same way the client would, the CDN edge locations make a request for the file and from that point onwards any identical requests (with the same request headers) will be served from the CDN and not from your asset server. Your server should now have a manageable number of requests from the CDN edge locations and the actual players will only be loading assets from edge locations with the lowest latency for them. If you want to force the CDNs to re-request the asset, you would need a different type of request to be made or the length of cache time to be smaller. By hashing the files as described in the mapping table section, a new hash will indicate a change of file and hence there is no need to update the CDN edge locations. This assumes that the cost of storage for more data is low, but the cost to invalidate the cache and ask the CDN to re-request the files is high.

To replace an existing file with a modified version, a unique id is generated and the new file is uploaded with the id in the URL. The mapping file is also modified to include a reference to the id and uploaded. Unlike the static asset, the mapping table has a shorter cache time before the CDN will re-request it from the game asset server. This allows it to quickly propagate to each of the edge locations when clients request it. Once a client receives a new mapping table, it will request the new asset from the nearest edge location, which will in turn request it from the game asset server. This will need to happen for all edge locations. Once the new asset has been requested and propagated to all edge locations, then all players can access the new asset. The time it takes for this to happen is effectively the "server-side cache" length (i.e., the time from having uploaded the new asset and mapping table to the time when all users can get the new version of the game asset). Because the old mapping table can still be accessed, both versions can be requested. This has the advantage that it can be used to stagger the roll-out of a new update, by selecting to only serve the new mapping table to a percentage of clients. In this scenario, some players will be given the new game with new assets and some the old game with old assets.

Figure 2-5 shows an example scenario in which clients are requesting different mapping tables and assets from a range of edge locations. It also shows the data that needs to be requested by the clients and the edge locations to satisfy the requirements of the game. Client 1 wants to load version 2 of the game. From the mapping table m2, it requires the group of assets known as a2 and aC. Since the client has already played version 1 of the game, it has both a1 and aC in its cache. This means that it will only need to request a2 in order to play the game. It does so by requesting the assets from Edge Location 1. That server has already downloaded the assets from the Host Server, and therefore no additional requests to the host are required. Client 2 wants to load version 1 of the game. From mapping table m1, it requires the group of assets known as a1 and aC. Since the client has not played the game it will have to request both a1 and aC. It requests these from its preferred server, Edge Location 1. Again, the server already has a1 and aC cached, so it does not need to make any requests to the Host Server. Client 3 wants to load version 2 of the game. From mapping table m2, it requires a2 and aC, which it must request because there are no cached assets. This time, the preferred server is Edge Location 2. This server does have the common assets aC, but does not have a2. The server can quickly respond with aC, but it needs to request a2 from the Host Server. This will only happen once for a single client per edge location. After that, all other clients requesting from that server will be served with the cached assets. This simplified example shows how shared content and the distribution among edge locations can reduce the number of requests when serving multiple versions of a game, resulting in less required data transfer.

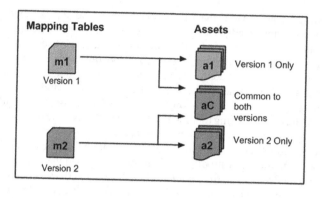

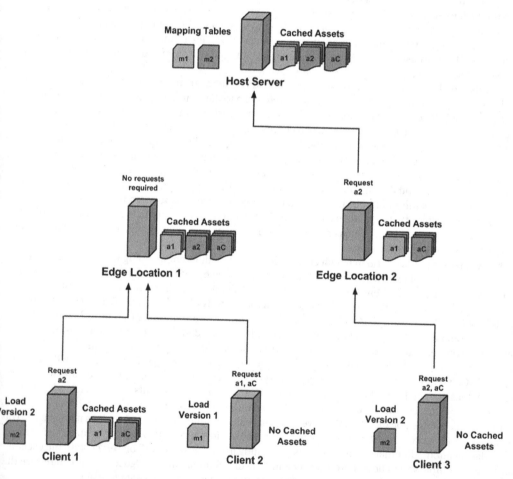

Figure 2-5. *A mapping table strategy combined with a CDN allows you to serve multiple versions of a game with minimal transfer cost between machines. The examples show different scenarios where each client requests assets as referenced by a given version of a mapping table. The requests made vary on the local availability of assets in cache*

Servers play an important role in getting content to your players. You don't need to be a large game developer to experience a runaway success with your game. The last thing you will want is to have hosting and performance issues impeding the playability of your game. A good hosting strategy will allow another service to do the heavy lifting while you focus on providing exciting content.

Effective Asset Grouping

Understanding how files are loaded by the browser and how best to process them is important to have a quick loading game, but reasoning at a higher level about whether to load them is the most effective way of reducing load times. As the game developer, you know when you need an asset, how frequently it is used, and what its dependencies are. For example, to render a simple model you will likely require shaders for all the materials used, one or more textures for the material, and possibly other associated meshes with their own shader and texture requirements. If you are aware of the dependencies between the assets, you can consider grouping them into a single request instead of making separate HTTP requests for each asset. This can reduce the total number requests the browser has to handle and ensures that all asset content is available at the same time. Once again there is a trade-off with the ability to process assets in parallel, but this section assumes that the cost of retrieving the assets separately is higher.

One option is to group assets by type (e.g. sounds, textures, shaders). The advantage is that if you can identify a commonality between them, you may be able to group them in a way that reduces redundant data. The most obvious example is the use of spritesheets to group a number of 2D character animations. In a single texture there would be no duplication of start frame of the animation, for example. Depending on the compression method, you may also see improvements in compressing assets together compared to compressing separately. Another advantage is the ability to easily replace one set of assets with another, for example a texture pack for a model that provides a different skin for the same mesh without having to replace the mesh. This might be useful if you have customizable characters. One disadvantage of grouping by type is that you can easily end up waiting for a single asset type to be processed before the game can progress. Players may end up waiting longer for the game to load before they have a visual/audible indication that progress is being made.

Another option is to group by dependency (e.g. any assets that need to co-exist to be used). One example is grouping a model with associated assets specific to that mesh (e.g. shaders, textures, animation data, sounds). The advantage is that you could be animating the model while loading other models in the background. It is important to make sure that background loading of assets doesn't have an impact on the performance of rendering the model, but that topic deserves its own chapter. One disadvantage of this approach is that shared assets may need to be duplicated or the dependency tree ends up encapsulating the majority of the game assets, losing the granularity of loading in small chunks. To avoid duplicating shared assets, it might make sense to group common assets together, which can then be loaded first before any other group.

Another option is to group by association. One example would be grouping by game level. If the game only requires certain sounds, textures, and other data for a specific level, then it might make sense to only load the data when the level is being loaded. This is especially true if players have to unlock levels or buy additional content. Grouping in this way assumes that levels are mainly independent of each other and that the game will have the ability to access that data at a later point. These high level associations depend massively on the design of the game and how it is played, but by thinking about grouping at this granularity you can make more impactful decisions on load time. Figure 2-6 presents a few scenarios in which grouping may occur.

By Dependency		
Player	**Enemy**	**Weapon**
models/player.dae.json	models/enemy.dae.json	models/weapon.dae.json
animations/player_idle.json	animations/enemy_idle.json	animations/weapon_idle.json
textures/player_diffuse.dds	textures/enemy_diffuse.dds	animations/weapon_raise.json
By Type		
Sounds	**Textures**	**Models**
sounds/sfx/hit.ogg	textures/player/diffuse.dds	models/player.dae.json
sounds/sfx/blast.ogg	textures/enemy/diffuse.dds	models/weapons/sword.dae.json
sounds/music/intro.ogg	textures/walls/brick.dds	models/map/city/statue.dae.json
By Association		
Common	**Menus**	**Level 1**
textures/sky/clouds.dds	ui/menus/main_menu.json	models/boss1.dae.json
sounds/music/background.ogg	sounds/sfx/menu_disabled.ogg	sounds/music/level1.ogg
models/player.dae.json	textures/menus/main_menu.dds	models/map/level1/hut.dae.json
Combined		
Common	**Player Common**	**Player Skin 1**
models/world_shield.dae.json	models/player.dae.json	models/player_cloak.dae.json
textures/shield/diffuse.dds	animations/player_idle.json	sounds/sfx/cloak_swoosh.ogg
sounds/sfx/hit_steel.ogg	sounds/sfx/player_jump.ogg	textures/player_diffuse.dds

Figure 2-6. *An example of grouping assets by various scenarios. Combining the options based on your own assets can help reduce the total number of requests required to load your game*

Grouping Using Tar Files

If you are interested in grouping assets together as a single file but maintaining some structure, then using the tar archive format is one option. Tar files allow you to archive files of different types by concatenating them together in a single bitstream, which can later be compressed. This process allows you to group assets while preserving the file structure into a single HTTP request, and allows you the choice of compression techniques to transfer it. Since the resulting file is binary data, it can be transferred and processed as an arraybuffer. Tar files contain header information for each file which if processed as binary data gives information about the files contained, for example the filename and filetype. This gives the loading code the option to choose which files to process if and when required. There is an example implementation of a JavaScript based tar loader in the open source Turbulenz Engine (https://github.com/turbulenz/turbulenz_engine).

Conclusion

You should now be familiar with different areas that affect the loading times of HTML5 games. By considering the techniques mentioned for caching, data compression, hosting, and data arrangement applied to your game content, we hope it helps you achieve performance improvements in your HTML5 game.

The Turbulenz team has worked hard in the area of optimization to make sure that not only our own games, but games of other developers, including those using the Turbulenz Engine, take advantage of these techniques. Surely there will be many more cost-saving measures in the future as the technology progresses, which we hope to exchange with other developers to ensure that HTML5 and the Web continues to be a powerful and exciting medium for distributing games.

Acknowledgements

I would personally like to thank Michael Braithwaite, David Galeano, Joe Kilner, Blake Maltby, and Duncan Tebbs for their insights into the inner workings of the Turbulenz Engine, their in-depth knowledge of browser technologies, and their feedback. I would also like to thank the rest of the Turbulenz engineering team and Wonderstruck team for constantly pushing the boundaries of what is possible with HTML5 and for making great browser games, which are the driving force for much of the content of this chapter.

CHAPTER 3

■ ■ ■

High-Performance JavaScript

Florian d'Erfurth, Freelance Game Developer

For a game to be enjoyable, smoothness is critical. A smooth game can feel lifelike and amazing; without smoothness, a game will be sluggish and annoying, even with the best art.

Smoothness is also important for user retention. Facebook recently revealed the results of an A/B test in which scrolling was slowed from 60FPS to 30FPS (http://youtu.be/3-WYu_p5rdU?t=36m): engagement collapsed.

In this chapter, I will discuss the essential techniques for making a simple, two-dimensional HTML5 game feel and perform like a native one.

The first two techniques are the low-hanging fruit and will give you a lot, while taking only a couple of hours each to implement. It is worth noting that these techniques are useful even if you are using one of the many game frame works available.

You may have heard that premature optimization is the root of all evil, and although this is true, planning for optimizations in advance of your game architecture is a smart move. If you have a game in the planning stages, that is the time to consider how optimizations would fit, and in the event that you decide to apply the following techniques to your game, make sure, using profiling, that it would benefit from their implementation.

Profiling your game with Google Chrome DevTools will help you identify bottlenecks; these tools have improved considerably in last year, especially in the area of profiling. I'd recommend checking the documentation for updated information on the subject: https://developers.google.com/chrome-developer-tools.

About the Demo

I will use the example of a particle system throughout this chapter to illustrate how the aforementioned techniques can be applied. You can find the demo at the book's home page on the Apress web site (www.apress.com), along with the code this chapter is based on. This particle system wasn't made to be efficient as a particle system *per se*, but instead was made to resemble a two-dimensional game, in the sense that the system moves objects around and then renders them every frame.

The demo uses the Web Graphics Library (WebGL) to render two-dimensional sprites; however, you don't need to know WebGL to understand the techniques I outline.

As Figure 3-1 shows, the coordinate system is the same as that of Canvas 2D, with x: 0, y: 0 at the top-left corner and x: width, y: height at the bottom-right corner, so you should feel at ease, even if you are more comfortable with Canvas 2D.

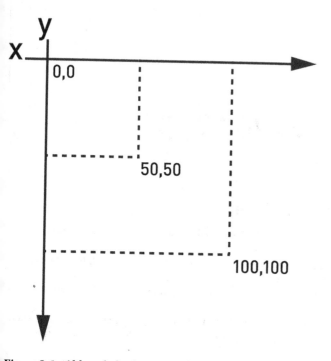

Figure 3-1. Although the demo uses WebGL, its coordinate system is the same as that of Canvas 2D

Object Pools

As discussed in the introduction, steady frame rate is definitely the goal, and you cannot have a steady frame rate if your memory usage looks like what you see in Figure 3-2.

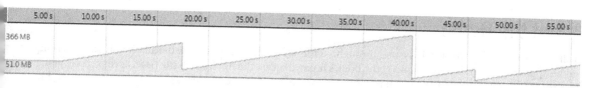

Figure 3-2. Memory spikes in the particle system demo suggest that your games can benefit from an object pool

This illustration, taken from Chrome DevTools, displays the memory usage of the demo when spawning 60,000 objects per second, without turning on object recycling. You can see that the memory usage varies widely, from 0MB to 360MB.

If your game exhibits the same memory behavior, it may greatly benefit from an object pool. Use Chrome DevTools, and check your memory timeline! You may also use the heap profiler, as well as the object allocation tracker, to get a precise view of your memory usage. Refer to the Chrome DevTools documentation for how-tos and up-to-date information.

When a particle reaches the end of its life, you dereference the particle object by removing it from the particles array:

```
// This is the kind of code you want to avoid!
// not only we are creating garbage from dereferencing particles
// but also by splicing arrays.
for (i = 0; i < particles.length; i++) {

    var particle = particles[i];

    if( particle.life === 0 ){
        // our particle reached the end of its life
        // splicing like pushing should be avoided
        particles.splice(i, 1);
        i--;
    }

    else
        demo.integrate( particle );

    particle.life--;
}
```

The memory occupied by all discarded objects isn't freed as you dereference them, but later, when the garbage collector (GC) decides to do it. That's when memory usage drops in Figure 3-1.

The bad news is that during the garbage collection, the program is stopped for the time needed to complete the task and only resumes when the GC has done its job. This may take a long time, especially on mobile, which may miss several frames.

The result of leaving memory management to the GC is that the game performs badly for a period of time whenever the garbage is to be collected.

To have a steady frame rate, you need to take care of memory management yourself and recycle dead particles instead of throwing them away; this avoids memory churn and the garbage collection taxes that come with it. Figure 3-3 illustrates what the memory usage looks like when recycling is turned on in the demo:

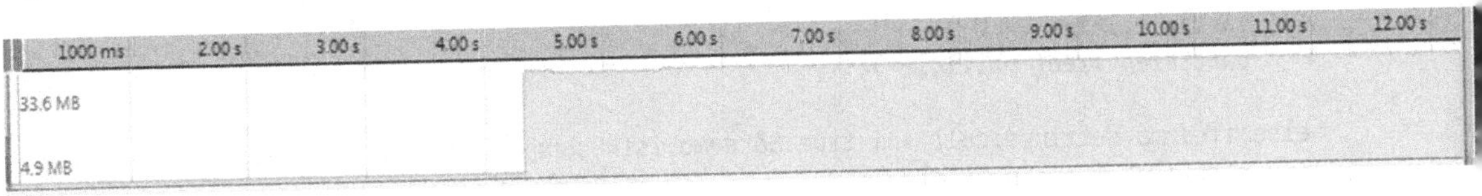

Figure 3-3. *Memory usage climbs to 33.6MB and never goes down*

You can see the memory usage climb when the number of particles per second is bumped from 60 to 60,000. But memory usage is stable now that you are using an object pool. By managing the churn of memory objects, you are avoiding the largest contributor to the occurrence of GC events, meaning that your game's performance is going to be much more consistent; you won't see performance loss from garbage collection.

How to Make an Object Pool

The goal of a pool is to avoid memory churn by reusing objects instead of allocating and freeing them, thus improving performance.

Object pools maintain a collection of reusable objects and track their usage. As you will see, object pools are easy to build and only require a few modifications to your existing objects' classes.

As the chapter demo source code demonstrates, using a pool is pretty straightforward and doesn't call for a lot of changes:

```javascript
//
// Our step function called on each Request Animation Frame (RAF)
//

// in this step we recycle our particle
demo.recyclingStep = function( particles ) {

    var i;

    for (i = 0; i < demo.settings.rate; i++) {

        var min = -10,
            max = 10,
            velx = min + Math.random() * (max - min),
            vely = min + Math.random() * (max - min),
            w = demo.settings.size,
            h = demo.settings.size,
            life = demo.settings.life;

        particles.getFree()
            .setup( demo.settings.width * 0.5, demo.settings.height * 0.5, w, h, life )
            .setVel( velx, vely );
    }

    for (i = 0; i < particles.elements.length; i++) {

        var particle = particles.elements[i];

        if( particle.allocated === true ){

            if( particle.life === 0 )
                particles.free( particle );

            else if(demo.settings.cull === true && demo.isInBounds(particle) === false)
                particles.free( particle );

            else
                demo.integrate( particle );

            particle.life--;
        }
    }

    if( demo.settings.render === true )
        demo.draw( demo.particles.elements );
```

```javascript
// in this step we create new particles instead of recycling them
demo.notRecyclingStep = function( particles ) {

    var i;

    for (i = 0; i < demo.settings.rate; i++) {

        var min = -10,
                max = 10,
                velx = min + Math.random() * (max - min),
                vely = min + Math.random() * (max - min),
                x = demo.settings.width * 0.5,
                y = demo.settings.height * 0.5,
                w = demo.settings.size,
                h = demo.settings.size,
                life = demo.settings.life;

            // continuously pushing new objects in an array cause high memory churn and should be
avoided
            particles.push( new demo.Particle( x, y, w, h, life ).setVel( velx, vely ) );
    }

    for (i = 0; i < particles.length; i++) {

        var particle = particles[i];

        if( particle.life === 0 ){
            // splicing like pushing should be avoided
            particles.splice(i, 1);
            i--;
        }

        else if(demo.settings.cull === true && demo.isInBounds(particle) === false){
            // splicing like pushing should be avoided
            particles.splice(i, 1);
            i--;
        }

        else
            demo.integrate( particle );

        particle.life--;
    }

    if( demo.settings.render === true )
        demo.draw( demo.particles );
};
```

Pool Structure

Listing 3-1 displays the pool recipe for the demo: an array of objects and an array that holds the free objects' indexes.

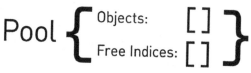

Listing 3-1. A Simple Object Pool

```
demo.ParticlePool = function(){
this.elements = [];      // will be filled with particles
this.freeElements = new DoublyLinkedList();//hold free particles indices
    // Fill the pool
    this.grow();
};
```

As you can see, a linked list holds the free elements' indexes. Free-object pointers are kept in a dedicated data structure so that the getFree method (see Listing 3-3) will yield a free particle quickly. I prefer using a custom linked-list class to an array in order to avoid the memory churn that would be caused by using the Array.push() and Array.pop() methods repeatedly (see Chapter 1): JavaScript is not the language you think it is. For more on linked lists in JavaScript, visit www.nczonline.net/blog/2009/04/13/computer-science-in-javascript-linked-list.

Recyclable Objects

A recyclable object can look like the one that follows. The important thing to note is that an object can be either alive or dead, so the game ignores the dead ones.

```
// Recyclable particle
demo.RecyclableParticle = function(poolindex) {
    this._poolindex = poolindex; // used by the pool
    this.allocated = false;     // true means alive, false means dead
```

Right after creating the pool, you initialize it by filling it with objects (see Listing 3-2). The process of increasing the number of allocated objects may also be used later in the life of the pool in the event that you run out of free objects.

$$Pool \left\{ \begin{array}{l} \text{Objects:} \quad [\ 0\ |\ 1\ |\ 2\ |\ 3\ |\ 4\ |\ 5\ |\ 6\ |\ 7\ |\ 8\ ] \\ \text{Free Indices:} \ [0,1,2,3,4,5,6,7,8] \end{array} \right\}$$

Listing 3-2. A Pool Containing Eight Recyclable Objects

```
demo.ParticlePool.prototype.grow = function( growth ){
    growth = growth || demo.settings.rate * 130;

    var oldsize = this.elements.length, // previous array size
        newsize = oldsize + growth;     // size after growth
```

```
    // Resize our elements array
    this.elements.length = newsize;

    for( var i = oldsize; i < newsize; i++ ){

        // Add a new element to our pool
        this.elements[i] = new demo.Particle( i );

        // Add its index to the free elements array
        this.freeElements.push( i );
    }

    console.log( 'Pool grown from ' + oldsize + ' to ' + newsize + ' particles.' );
};
```

Requesting a Free Object from the Pool

When you need a free object, instead of creating a **new** object, you ask the pool for one. If no free objects are left, the pool has to be grown.

The object is also reset. As for your particles, you reset their position, velocity, and acceleration; otherwise, the particles will spawn with increasing speed as the simulation runs. If you forget to reset the object properties, you may have unexpected bugs in your game. These bugs can be hard to figure out, so double-check, triple-check, and unit test that your objects are reset properly.

Here's the particle reset code, straight from the demo:

```
RecyclableParticle.prototype.reset = function() {
    this.setup( 0, 0, 0, 0, 0 ); // reset size and position
    this.setVel( 0, 0 );         // reset velocity
    this.acc.x = 0;              // reset acceleration x
    this.acc.y = 0;              // reset acceleration y
    return this;                 // so our particle API is chainable
}
```

The pool will quickly find a free object by looking to the free-indexes array. If an array is empty, it will grow itself again. The pool will both remove the index of its internal-indexes array and mark the object as allocated before returning it, as shown in Listing 3-3.

Listing 3-3. Following a Request for a Free Object, Object 8 Has Been Returned and Marked as Allocated, and Its index, Removed from the Free-Indexes Array

```
demo.ParticlePool.prototype.getFree = function(){
        if( this.freeElements.length === 0 ){
            // no free particles left, grow the pool
            this.grow()
        }
```

```
        // get and remove head from freeElements linked-list
        var index = this.freeElements.remove(0);
        // retrieve the particle from the elements array
        var particle = this.elements[index];
        // mark the particle allocated so we use it when iterating on the pool
        particle.allocated = true;

        // reset particle position, velocity etc.
        particle.reset();

        // done
        return particle;
    };
```

Returning Objects to the Pool

When the game doesn't need an object anymore (see the section "Updating Only What's Important"), it can return the object to the pool (see Listing 3-4). To do this, push the object index to the free-indexes array, and mark the object as unallocated so that your loop will skip it.

Pool { Objects: [0 | 1 | 2 | 3 | 4 | 5 | 6 | 7 | 8] }
Free Indices: [0,1,2,3,4,5,6,7,8] }

Listing 3-4. Object 8 Has Been Returned to the Pool and Marked as Free, and Its Index, Added to the Free-Indexes Array

```
demo.ParticlePool.prototype.free = function( particle ){
    if( particle.allocated === true ){
        // mark the particle as not allocated
        particle.allocated = false

        // add the particle's index to the free elements array
        this.freeElements.push( particle._poolindex )
    }
};
```

Iterating on a Pool

After a while, your pool will look like the one shown in Listing 3-5. You can see here the benefit of both having an array of free indexes and embedding in each object its own index; otherwise, you would have to iterate over the objects array to get objects from the pool as well as to free them.

Pool { Objects: [0 | 1 | 2 | 3 | 4 | 5 | 6 | 7 | 8] }
Free Indices: [0,1,4] }

Listing 3-5. Your Pool after Many Requests and Returns

In the demo, you loop over the pool objects array twice, first to move particles around, in the physics step, then to render them. In the loops the particles are processed only if their allocated flag is set to `true`, so you ignore unallocated particles instead of discarding them. In this way, you are holding references to the unallocated particles rather than generating garbage, as you would if you were not using a pool (see listing 3-6).

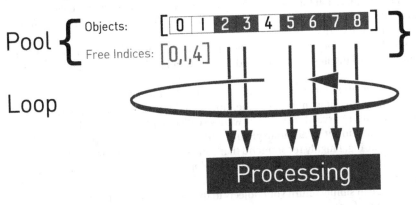

Listing 3-6. Looping over Only Allocated Objects

```
for (i = 0; i < particles.elements.length; i++) {

    var particle = particles.elements[i];

    if( particle.allocated === true ){

        if( particle.life === 0 )
            particles.free( particle );

        else
            demo.integrate( particle );

        particle.life--;
    }
}
```

Using an Object Pool

As in real life, filling a pool takes time and can be expensive. You must avoid having the object pools fill while the player is playing your game by preallocating the necessary number of objects during the initialization of the game, effectively moving the cost of creating objects up front.

You may also prefer not to allow some of your pools to grow. For instance, you may want to have only a fixed number of particles in your game. In this case, when you need to display a particle, and there is no free one left, you can choose not to spawn a particle at all or to remove the oldest one to spawn it in a new place. Do you remember trying to write your name with bullet holes in Half-Life, and the ones you shot first disappeared as you were writing? Well, now you know what was happening.

During the development process, you should monitor your pool usages to determine the levels at which your pools should initially be filled.

For more information on static memory JavaScript and object pools, you may want to consult HTML5Rocks.com (www.html5rocks.com/en/tutorials/speed/static-mem-pools).

Updating Only What's Important

It may be worth noting that not every item in the world needs to be alive and in memory. For instance, a two-dimensional side-scrolling game doesn't need to simulate enemies at the end of the level; also, more important, any particles that are offscreen shouldn't be rendered. If the player only moves forward, you may discard everything behind the player past a certain point to save both memory and central processing unit (CPU) cycles. Just make sure the player cannot walk backward and fall into the void!

Depending on your game, the cost of keeping objects rather than discarding them may be high. For example, not discarding enemies may cause physics-, artificial intelligence- (AI-), and rendering-related functions to be called way more than is necessary.

To get an idea of your game functions' execution times, you may use the Chrome DevTools CPU Profiler, which will give you a good idea of where your game is spending most of its time. Note that this profiler is a sampling profiler, meaning that it collects data periodically (at 1ms intervals), so you may want to collect samples over a relatively large period of time (for example, a few seconds) to get an accurate picture. There is also a structural profiler in Chrome, which you can find at `chrome://tracing`. I highly recommend that you check the great Chrome DevTools documentation for more information on those tools as well as this Google Developers Live show about profiling in Chrome: `https://developers.google.com/live/shows/7327030-5001`.

Also, now that you are using a pool, you can simply return your objects to their respective pools for reuse later on. For instance, if your game is like Sonic Jump (`www.sega.com/games/sonic-jump`), you may want to return both platforms and enemies to their respective pools when they are below a certain point in order to retrieve them at a later time to place above your hero.

Culling for Simulation

Discarding particles as soon as they are offscreen is the simplest task in the demo. Figure 3-4 shows a drop in CPU usage when culling is turned on.

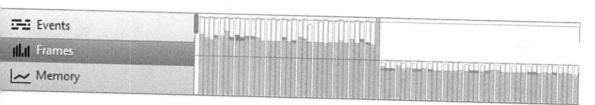

Figure 3-4. *Discarding offscreen particles decreases CPU usage*

In your loop, you call the following function and discard the particle if it returns `false`:

```
sInBounds = function( particle ){
        var x = particle.pos.x,
             y = particle.pos.y,
             w = particle.size.y,
             h = particle.size.x,
             areaW = demo.settings.width,
             areaH = demo.settings.height;

        return !(x > areaW || x + w < 0 || y > areaH || y + h < 0);
    }
```

Not exactly rocket science, and that's the point. This function must be cheap to be worth it, as it will be used as many times as there are live particles in the pool.

Discarding objects as soon as you can is the easiest way to save performance. It is far more time-consuming to optimize a physics engine so that it becomes 10 percent faster than it is to discard 10 percent of your objects. By not discarding objects, you are not only making the game perform worse than it should, but also wasting user CPU time and battery life.

Culling for Rendering

Chances are that, the demo notwithstanding, you may actually care about offscreen objects. For instance, if your hero were moving freely on a large map, you wouldn't discard enemies as soon as they were offscreen. In this case, you would use boundaries that are much larger than the viewable area.

If your game boundaries are larger than the viewable area (see Figure 3-5), you should check during the rendering loop that each object is effectively in the viewable area before trying to render it. Otherwise, you will overdraw (draw more than necessary) and end up burning precious graphics processing unit (GPU) power.

Out of bounds

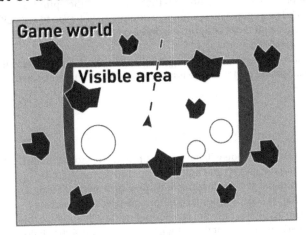

Figure 3-5. *The world may be larger than what the player sees*

Note that if you use a framework, you should check to see if it does the culling for you.

Warming Up the Virtual Machine

Chances are that your game is far more complex than the demo. And, it's likely that on mobile, you get a rather choppy frame rate during the first 10s–30s, while your code is being optimized on the fly.

Because those first seconds are crucial to the player experience, it's important to get a smooth frame rate from the start. Otherwise, your game will be perceived as slow and laggy, and the player may very well quit and never come back.

Your Code Will Be Compiled and Optimized on the Fly

What happens to your JavaScript code is rather fascinating: first it is compiled in machine language in order to run on the CPU, and then it may be compiled again, but in a more optimized way if the browser's JavaScript engine judges this necessary and possible.

The initial compilation generates slow code, then the following compilations generate fast, optimized code, and whereas on desktop, compilation time is unnoticeable, on mobile, slowdowns are occurring as optimizations are made and tested by the JavaScript engine.

Your code will run fast only when optimized, and only the functions that are called many times will be optimized (the engine marks these as hot and optimizes them).

The consequence of this approach is that the JavaScript engine will make optimizations while your game is running.

Deoptimizations

Optimizations performed by the compiler are speculative; they are made under the assumption that the JavaScript state is stable. If the state changes, then the compiler changes the evaluation of your function, which can cause a deoptimization to occur (called a global deopt).

You can also get deoptimizations if there's some specific part of your function that invalidates the optimization process, such as a try/catch block (called a local deopt). The engine will continue to attempt to optimize to a specific threshold and then will give up. Until that time, you can get a plethora of optimize/deopt combos every frame as the engine tries to understand itself and find a local minimum of execution.

Finding and fixing all this is madness and varies from engine to engine. I suggest that you check out the literature for each virtual machine (VM) if you see that deopts are causing performance issues (for more information, see the section "Digging Deeper.")

Rev Up the Engine

To have your game running at a steady 60FPS from the start, your code will have to be optimized before the start. Or, to put it differently, the player shouldn't be able to play before the JavaScript engine has optimized your game.

The obvious solution is to have a warm-up phase while the game is loading or displaying a menu. During this phase, you would run your game in the background so that its code is optimized before the user starts playing.

If you run only a subset of the game during the warm-up phase, only the JavaScript engine will optimize this subset. Sometimes, it may be enough to call only the most expensive functions, for example, a physics simulation, at a fast rate during the warm-up phase. But, I would say that the best warm-up is to run the entire game at a fast rate; however, it may be impractical to do so.

Figure 3-6 displays how Foxes and Shotguns (www.foxesandshotguns.com) warms up behind the scenes while loading assets.

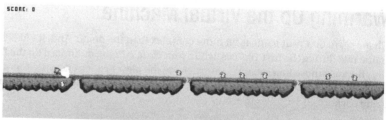

Figure 3-6. *Behind the loading screen a special level is generated*

Instead of generating spaced platforms, platforms are lined up, and the hero jumps and shoots randomly. Meanwhile, the loading screen is displayed. None of this is rendered, and the user will see only the loading scene. The result for this particular game is a silky smooth frame rate right from the start, instead of a rate punctuated by random slowdowns caused by JavaScript engine optimizations times.

As you can see, the warm-up phase depends on your game. Creating a special level to be used only for that purpose may be an easy way to move the compilation time up front.

Benchmarking

There's no direct way of knowing when the browser JavaScript engine is done optimizing a function, and although using a warm-up phase is good, warming up longer than necessary makes the user wait longer than is desirable.

The only way to get a hint from your code about what's going on is to measure the execution time of your loop, like so:

```
var t = window.performance.now();
function tick() {
        requestAnimationFrame( tick );

    var n = window.performance.now(),
        raf_delta = n - t,
        current_fps = 1000 / raf_delta;
    t = n;

    // read input, move things, render them
    game.step()

    // use step_duration to guess if the game code has been optimized
    var step_duration = window.performance.now() - t;
}
```

As you can see, the time it takes the loop to execute step_duration decreases and stabilizes after a while. By benchmarking your loop on various devices, you'll get a good sense of the minimum execution time your loop should target to be to be considered good enough to exit the warm-up phase. However, keep in mind that you cannot assume a fixed number of iterations for your code to be optimized, as the heuristics used are nondeterministic and vary from browser to browser.

Now, it's up to you to use your benchmark data to decide the best course of action for your game. For instance, you could employ a dynamic solution that uses average execution times on the fly, or a short, special level that runs for a fixed number of frames, and check the elapsed time to determine if your code has been optimized by reaching a target execution time.

Digging Deeper

To get a glimpse of what's happening behind the scenes, you can run Chrome or Chromium with flags to print out when functions are optimized, as follows:

```
chrome.exe --no-sandbox --js-flags="--trace-opt --trace-deopt" -user-data-dir=<empty dir path>
http://localhost/awesomegame.html
```

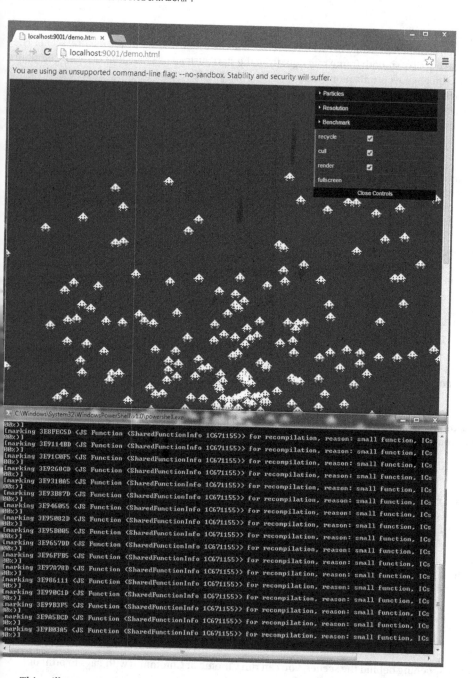

This will output in the console optimizations as they are happening, as pictured in this screenshot. Hopefully, you'll get a better idea of what the browser is doing to make your code run fast, and maybe you'll start optimizing your most demanding functions for V8 or find out what prevents some part of your code from being optimized. But, beware that this is a time-consuming process and probably of no value unless you find out that deopt code is a bottleneck.

For more on V8, visit `https://docs.google.com/document/d/1hOaE7vbwdLLXWj3C8hTnnkpEOqSa2P--tDvwXXEeDO/pub`.

For more on optimizing for V8, check out: `http://floitsch.blogspot.de//search/label/V8-optimizations`.

Conclusion

In this chapter, I've covered the common pitfalls that cause a game to perform poorly as well as the techniques to address them.

By avoiding garbage collection and unnecessary computations and forcing early optimizations, your game can compete with native ones, in terms of performance. In Chapter 15, I will discuss techniques to make your game look native, while maintaining performance on mobile devices.

■ ■ ■

CHAPTER 4

Efficient JavaScript Data Structures

Duncan Tebbs, Senior Software Engineer, Turbulenz Limited

Efficient use of system resources is essential to most game applications, to ensure that the game runs correctly and as smoothly as possible across a range of devices and browsers. Here, the term "resources" can refer to available memory, CPU execution time, or other processing or storage units in the system. Although JavaScript can be considered a rather high-level language, the data structures employed by JavaScript application code can significantly impact upon resource usage.

Much of the information here is taken from the significant amount of research and engineering manpower that the Turbulenz team has invested in high performance HTML5. As an open-source, proven engine that boasts a portfolio including several fully playable 2D and 3D games, the Turbulenz engine (turbulenz.com) represents a valuable resource for developers seeking to learn more about HTML5 and understand what is possible with modern web technology.

For many experienced HTML5 engineers the material presented may need little or no explanation. However, the authors hope this chapter will serve as an introduction for newcomers, and as a reference and explanation of some fundamental optimization concepts.

As with all optimization, it is important to measure the effect of code and data changes on memory and execution time. This is something of a universal mantra when writing and maintaining high-performance code, and it is even more important in the case of JavaScript and the browsers. Execution performance and memory usage characteristics can vary wildly across JavaScript engines and HTML5 implementations, and all of the major browsers are changing rapidly as their developers continue to aggressively address the bottlenecks experienced by high performance interactive applications.

For this reason, it is highly recommended that developers measure performance over a range of target browser and versions, and keep track of how new browser releases affect their code. As another consequence of the variety and changing nature of browser performance characteristics, this article intentionally avoids mentioning specific JavaScript engines or browsers, and concentrates on general strategies for efficiently handling application data in HTML5 applications.

The Importance of Data Structures

Almost all variables stored in the JavaScript engine require more memory than the equivalent native data structure. The JavaScript engines implement numbers as either 32-bit signed integers (where frequently only 31-bits are used for the integer value) or 64-bit floating-point numbers. JavaScript Objects must behave like dynamic key-value dictionaries, with all of the (non-trivial) memory and execution overhead required to support this system.

All Object properties are referenced by string name. Modern JavaScript engines use a variety of techniques to reduce the cost of retrieving and storing data by name, and in many cases these can be highly effective. Particularly in the case where the engine can correctly predict the "type" of object being dereferenced, the cost of storing and retrieving data can be comparable to native code. Here "type" may refer to a set of known properties that make up an Object "template" or a specific underlying native implementation of the Object. However, in the general case, the engine may need to hash strings, perform hash-table lookups, and traverse prototype hierarchies and scopes in order to find a given piece of stored data.

Garbage collection has traditionally been a source of "long" (up to several hundred milliseconds) pauses that can be noticeable in interactive JavaScript applications. This situation is now all but resolved as all "major" JavaScript engines have addressed this issue rather effectively, using strategies such as "generations" to avoid freezing execution and traversing all active objects on the heap. The evolution of solutions to this problem provides a good example of the varied and changing nature of the HTML5 implementations. The different JavaScript engines introduced solutions at different times in their development history, but as of today garbage collection is much less of an issue in modern browsers.

However, make sure that it has minimal impact on older browsers and browsers running to on low-end platforms, it is generally advisable to keep total Object count as low as possible and to minimize the number of temporary Objects being dynamically created at runtime.

As you shall see, Object count has a pronounced effect on memory usage and as a general rule, structures that use fewer Objects to store the same amount of data are likely to result in more efficient code execution. This principle, along with an understanding of how data is stored and accessed for some common object types, is fundamental to designing data structures that support optimal execution across various HTML5 implementations.

Object Hierarchies

The process of flattening data structures can be a very effective way of reducing object count, and thereby memory overhead and the cost of looking up data. "Flattening" here involves replacing hierarchies or subhierarchies of objects with single Objects or Arrays. For example, consider the object structure in Listing 4-1.

Listing 4-1. A Naïve Particle Structure

```
Particle
{
    position:
    {
        x: <number>
        y: <number>
        z: <number>
    }
    velocity:
    {
        x: <number>
        y: <number>
        z: <number>
    }
}
```

An immediate gain in memory efficiency (and runtime performance) can be achieved by flattening this structure, as shown in Listing 4-2.

Listing 4-2. A Flat Particle Structure

```
Particle
{
    position_x: <number>
    position_y: <number>
    position_z: <number>
    velocity_x: <number>
    velocity_y: <number>
    velocity_z: <number>
}
```

The code in Listing 4-2 is clearly very simplified, but illustrates an effective way of reducing the object count (and thereby memory usage) and the number of property lookups required to access various properties (improving performance).

A simple particle simulation based on these structures (particles accelerating under gravity) shows that flattening the structure in this way yields a memory saving of between 25% and 35%, and execution of a trivial particle simulation (updating position based on velocity, and velocity based on a fixed acceleration vector) showed a speed increase of roughly 25% on all browsers, with one browser showing roughly a 30% reduction in execution cost.

We can explain the memory savings by noting that each particle is now represented as a single Object with a list of six properties, rather than three Objects: particle, position, and velocity with a combined property count of eight and, more significantly, all of the extra properties and infrastructure required by the JavaScript runtime. Execution cost savings likely result because fewer property lookup and dereferencing operations are required to reach a given piece of data.

Arrays

As a storage mechanism, JavaScript Arrays can often be more efficient than Objects in several scenarios. Most JavaScript engines have optimized implementations of Arrays, with very low overhead for access to indexed properties, efficient storage of sparse data, and flags to inform that garbage collector when the Array does not need to be traversed (e.g. if it only contains primitive data such as numbers).

The process of looking up indexed properties on Arrays is generally cheaper than accessing named properties on generic Objects. This is particularly true when the indices or keys are fully dynamic (and thereby the JIT compiler cannot predict them at compile time), as well as for code that iterates through all items in a structure.

Structures such as those discussed in the simple particle example in Listing 4-1 are very commonly stored in Arrays (a so-called "array of structures"). In this case, a very effective way to save memory is to completely flatten an array of Particle structures into a "structure of arrays," as shown in Listing 4-3.

Listing 4-3. A List of Particles as a Structure of Arrays

```
// Each particle consists of 6 numbers
var particles_posx = new Array(numParticles);
var particles_posy = new Array(numParticles);
var particles_posz = new Array(numParticles);
var particles_velx = new Array(numParticles);
var particles_vely = new Array(numParticles);
var particles_velz = new Array(numParticles);
```

In this way, code accesses and uses the data as shown in Listing 4-4.

Listing 4-4. Simulation Code Using a Structure of Arrays

```
var velocity_x;
var velocity_y;
var velocity_z;

for (var i = 0 ; i < numParticles; ++i)
{
    velocity_x = particles_velx[i];
    velocity_y = particles_vely[i];
    velocity_z = particles_velz[i];

    particles_posx[i] += deltaTime * velocity_x;
    particles_posy[i] += deltaTime * velocity_y;
    particles_posz[i] += deltaTime * velocity_z;

    // continue simulation ...
}
```

In Listing 4-4, all data is stored in just six Objects. Compared to the Array of flattened Objects, some simple experiments showed this to yield a memory savings of between 35% and 45%. That is a 40% to 60% savings compared to the original hierarchical version. This memory savings is a result of drastically reducing the number of Objects required to maintain the data, and allowing the JavaScript engine to store it as a few large contiguous lists of values rather than a large list of references to structures, each with some named properties.

Note that although the way the data is referenced has changed, the impact on the maintainability of the code is small. The effort required to add or remove properties from individual particles is roughly the same as it would be for the original data structure.

You can reduce object count even further if you are willing to sacrifice some readability (see Listing 4-5).

Listing 4-5. A Single Interleaved Array

```
// Each particle consists of 6 numbers
// Single Array containing the all particle attributes.
// [ posx, posy, posz, velz, vely, velz,  // particle 0
//   posx, posy, posz, velz, vely, velz,  // particle 1
//   posx, posy, posz, velz, vely, velz,  // particle 2
//   . . .
// ]
var particles = new Array(6 * numParticles);
```

The code in Listing 4-5 maintains a single Array containing all properties of all objects. Individual properties of a given particle must be addressed by their relative indices, as shown in Listing 4-6.

Listing 4-6. Simulation Code Using a Single Interleaved Array

```
var velocity_x;
var velocity_y;
var velocity_z;

var endIdx = 6 * numParticles;
for (var i = 0 ; i < endIdx ; i = i + 6)
```

```
{
    velocity_x = particles[i+3];
    velocity_y = particles[i+4];
    velocity_z = particles[i+5];

    particles[i+0] += deltaTime * velocity_x;
    particles[i+1] += deltaTime * velocity_y;
    particles[i+2] += deltaTime * velocity_z;

    // continue simulation ...
}
```

The set of all particles now requires only one object, instead of six. In this case, the memory savings will be trivial compared to using an Array per property, although in more complex cases involving a large number of independent systems, changes of this kind can have an impact.

In our experiments, switching to a single flat Array did indeed show no significant memory difference, but gave between a 10% and 25% speed increase depending on the browser. One explanation for both the speed increase and the discrepancy across browsers is that using a single object in this way presents the JIT compiler with several opportunities for optimization (which, of course, it may or may not take advantage of).

Some JIT compilers can take a "guess" at the type of certain variables and emit fast code to directly access object properties. In this case, the generated native code must check that incoming objects are indeed of the correct type before enabling their fast-path. Where the data is spread across several Arrays, the type-check must be made for each object. Furthermore, a single Array allows the code to maintain only a single index and address all data elements as fixed offsets from that single register. Note also that memory access for our particular example will very likely be cache-coherent.

This completely flattened structure has been commonly used by Turbulenz to optimize engine and game code for more demanding 3D games and games that must run efficiently on mobile platforms. Unfortunately, this approach does sometimes involve sacrificing maintainability, since changes to the original Particle structure require extremely error-prone changes across a disproportionately large amount of code. Naturally, it is important to be sure that this extra maintenance cost is justified.

Of course, there are a variety of compromises that can be reached to balance performance with readability, depending on how critical a given bit of code is determined to be. For example, in the Particles case in Listing 4-6, one obvious middle ground would be to use an Array for each of position and velocity, as shown in Listing 4-7.

Listing 4-7. Splitting Data into Logical Groups

```
// One Array for position x,y, and z of all particles.
// particles_pos = [
//      posx, posy, posz,  // particle 0
//      posx, posy, posz,  // particle 1
//      . . .
// ]
//
// Array for velocity x,y, and z of all particles.
// particles_vel = [
//      velz, vely, velz,  // particle 0
//      velz, vely, velz,  // particle 1
//      . . .
// ]
var particles_pos = new Array(3 * numParticles);
var particles_vel = new Array(3 * numParticles);
```

In Listing 4-7, only two Arrays are required, but changes to the data structure (such as adding new Particle properties) can be made without unnecessarily large code changes.

Performance Data

The data for memory usage and performance given above should be interpreted with caution. Apart from the rapidly changing HTML5 implementations, which can render any performance data out-of-date, it can be rather difficult to get an accurate measurement of true execution cost and memory usage. Memory usage in particular can be difficult to measure. Some browsers provide tools to take a snapshot of the JavaScript heap, whereas others do not expose this information.

However, for completeness, the results of our approximate measurements during the preparation of this content are given in Figures 4-1 and 4-2 for a simulation involving 1,000,000 particles. We intentionally omit browser names and versions, and further details of the experiment to underline the fact that this data is purely for illustrative purposes.

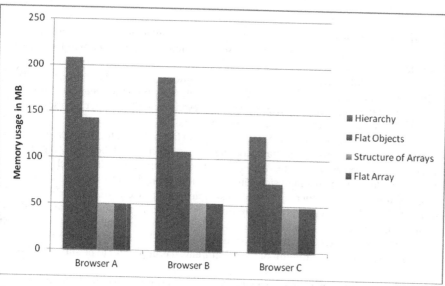

Figure 4-1. Approximate memory usage of the various data structures

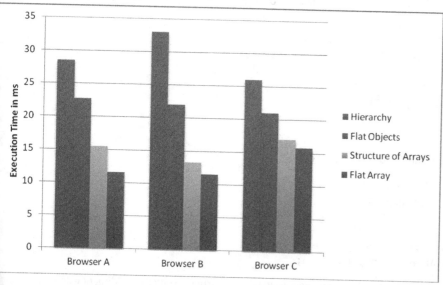

Figure 4-2. Approximate execution time of simulation for various data structures

Some noteworthy patterns appear. Firstly, memory usage follows roughly the trend one would expect. The solutions involving flat arrays introduce very little overhead, occupying almost as little memory as the equivalent native representation, which we would expect to be 48,000,000 bytes == 6 * 8 * 1,000,000 (== properties per particle * size of property * number of particles). Particularly in the case of memory usage, the more optimal solutions appear to have more consistent and predictable costs across browsers.

Although the effectiveness of each optimization can be seen to vary across the browsers, all the techniques introduced so far have a measurable positive effect on both memory and execution time over all the browsers tested. The technique we will discuss next had a measurable, but less uniform, impact on the measurements.

ArrayBuffers and ArrayBufferViews

The TypedArray standard describes an interface that allows JavaScript code to access raw memory buffers by reading and writing native types (at the level of signed or unsigned bytes, shorts, ints, as well as float and double values). Intended in part for manipulating graphics data (such as vertex, index, or texture buffers) in a format that can be directly consumed by graphics hardware, ArrayBuffers and ArrayBufferViews also introduce many opportunities for optimization in the JavaScript engine.

Broadly, an ArrayBuffer represents a contiguous memory buffer with no type information, and an ArrayBufferView (such as Int8Array or Float32Array) represents a "window" onto some subregion of that buffer, exposing the memory as an array of specific native types. Multiple ArrayBufferViews of different types can point to regions of the same ArrayBuffer, and can overlap with each other. A slightly more complex particle structure that uses floating point and lower precision integer data is illustrated by Listing 4-8.

Listing 4-8. Combining Different Native Data Types into a Single Memory Buffer

```
// Implementation of this native structure:
//
// struct Particle
// {
//     float      position_x, position_y, position_z;
//     float      velocity_x, velocity_y, velocity_z;
//     uint16_t   timeToLive, flags;
// };
//
// Particle stride in bytes: 6*4 + 2*2 = 28
// Particle stride in words: 7
// Particle stride in half words: 14

// The underlying memory buffer
var particlesBuffer = new ArrayBuffer(numParticles * 28);

// Access the buffer as float32 data
var particlesF32 = new Float32Array(particlesBuffer);

// Access the buffer as uint16_t data, offset to start at
// 'timeToLive' for the first particle.
var particlesU16 = new Uint16Array(particlesBuffer, 6*4);

// 'position' and 'velocity' for the i-th particle can be accessed:
//    particlesF32[(7*i) + 0] ... particlesF32[(7*i) + 5]

// 'timeToLive' and 'flags' for the i-th particle is accessed as:
//    particlesU16[(14*i) + 0] and particlesU16[(14*i) + 1]
```

Care must be taken to specify offsets and strides correctly, but it should be clear that a small number of objects can be used to finely control the type and layout of data in memory. See the TypedArray specification at `http://www.khronos.org/registry/typedarray/specs/latest` for full details.

The first obvious advantage of TypedArrays over regular Arrays is the potential memory saving. Much game code only requires 32-bit floating-point numbers, rather than the 64-bit values that JavaScript uses by default. In the particle example of the previous section, replacing Arrays with Float32Arrays does indeed reduce memory usage of the data structure by roughly 50%. Further memory savings can be made where lower precision integers can be used in place of generic JavaScript numbers.

The major JavaScript engines all have an internal concept of ArrayBuffer and ArrayBufferView that allows them to make important code optimizations. When the engine can correctly predict that an Object is a specific ArrayBufferView, it can dereference the data directly from memory, bypassing the usual property lookup process. Furthermore, because the retrieved data is of a known type, in some special cases it may not need to be converted to the usual 64-bit floating-point representation before operations can be performed.

For example, replacing Array with Float32Array in the code in Listing 4-8 and ensuring that all constants are stored in Float32Arrays means that most of the simulation can (in the ideal case) be translated by the JIT compiler into simple memory reads and writes, and primitive operations on 32-bit floating-point numbers. In general, this will be much faster than the equivalent operations on values of which the compiler cannot predict the type. However, it can be very difficult to predict how many of these optimizations a given engine will perform. Optimizations at this level naturally require several conditions to be met, for example the destination of the operation must be known to be of the correct type to ensure that calculation results are not affected.

The `Math.fround` function, included in the sixth edition of the ECMAScript specification, provides a way to explicitly tell the JavaScript engine that a given operation can use 32-bit precision. It is not yet widely supported at the time this article is published, but is an example of how the programmer can provide optimization hints to the JavaScript engine.

It should be made clear at this stage that TypedArrays do have some drawbacks. At the time of writing, they can be much more expensive than Arrays to create, and the JIT compilers still do not take advantage of all possible optimizations. In some cases, Arrays can actually result in faster execution, particularly where temporary Objects are created and destroyed frequently (although in general it is advisable to minimize the number of transient objects required by a given algorithm).

In our simple particle system in Listing 4-tk, we saw a speed increase of about 10% on some browsers when all variables use Float32Arrays; however, we saw a slight speed decrease on other browsers compared to the flat JavaScript Array.

Complex Structures as Single ArrayBufferViews

In the Turbulenz engine, we have written and tested several implementations of a Math library to operate on Matrix, Vector, and Quaternion Objects, including a set of native implemented functions. At the time of writing, we have settled on a solution where all objects (Vector3, Vector4, Matrix33, Matrix34, ...) are single Float32Array objects of the appropriate size.

To avoid creation of temporary objects, all math operations optionally take a destination argument, which allows temporary or scratch variables to be reused to avoid too much Object creation and destruction.

In some cases, such as our 3D animation library, or 2D and 3D physics engine, structures, or arrays containing several math primitives are implemented as single Float32Arrays containing, say, a sequence of Quaternion objects representing animation bones.

In other situations, Float32Arrays can be used to represent structures that include non-float data, so properties such as flags or indices, which might otherwise be stored as integers, are also kept in a single Float32Array along with numerical data. It is important to be aware of the trade-off that has been made with code clarity here, but for key areas that can very easily become an execution bottleneck, we are giving the JavaScript engines the best possible opportunity to save memory and optimize JIT-generated code.

Custom tools represent an opportunity to improve code maintainability while using flat structures in this way. For example, in the case of flattening an array of structures into a single Array or Float32Array, a simple code transformation could generate the code in Listing 4-4 from source code of the form, as shown in Listing 4-9.

Listing 4-9. Maintainable Source Code That Could Be Used to Generate Listing 4-4

```
for (var i = 0 ; i < endIdx ; i = i + PARTICLES_STRIDE)
{
    var velocity_x = particles[i+PARTICLES_VEL_X];
    var velocity_y = particles[i+PARTICLES_VEL_Y];
    var velocity_z = particles[i+PARTICLES_VEL_Z];
...
```

This allows properties to be added and removed with relative ease. More complex tool-based solutions are conceivable that could generate the same output from even higher level code, particularly where more accurate type information is available at compile time (as is often the case for languages such as TypeScript, which the Turbulenz engine has adopted throughout the core engine). Tooling of this kind may also represent a trade-off if it introduces a build step where one was previously not necessary.

Late Unpacking

Data cannot always easily be flattened, and sometimes the runtime representation is necessarily a memory-hungry hierarchy of objects. In these cases, it is sometimes possible and preferable to encode data into custom byte-code or strings, and decode the data on the fly, as required.

There is an obvious trade-off made with CPU resources here. The encoded data must be unpacked into its equivalent object hierarchy, and potentially this process must be repeated each time the hierarchy is destroyed. However, since the TypedArray interfaces give full access to raw memory buffers, it is possible to decode (and encode) even binary compression formats to save memory effectively.

Best Practices

The concepts discussed above are relatively simple, and imply some straightforward best practices. Here we describe a few of these, as well as some recommendations based on the experience of our engineers developing engine technology and porting and creating high-performance 3D HTML5 games.

The importance of measurement has already been mentioned above, but this cannot be understated. The behavior of JavaScript and HTML5 implementations is not just varied, but rapidly changing. The true effectiveness of a given optimization on execution speed and memory consumption is very rarely quantifiable in terms of a single number. In the worst case, diversity of HTML5 implementations may mean that developers are required to maintain several code paths and determine which to enable based on browser version.

The browsers themselves often provide useful tools, including memory and code profilers as well as convenient debugging environments. In general, these may have some limitations (for example, JavaScript heap profilers may not take into account raw memory used by ArrayBuffers, or graphics resources such as textures or vertex buffers), but they form a useful part of the toolbox for measuring code behavior. Keep in mind that different profiling tools may have different side effects, so it is usually most effective to compare the results from several of them (ideally from two or three major browsers) before drawing conclusions.

At the code level, we have found that it is important to maintain clear relationships between data structures, including keeping the responsibility for creation and destruction well defined. As well as making code easier to understand and maintain, clear ownership policies allow applications to accurately and consistently "null-out" references to unused objects. This helps to avoid memory leaks, which in JavaScript refers to unnecessary objects on the heap, wasting both memory and CPU resources, but kept alive by dangling references.

Conclusion

An impressive level of performance and efficiency can already be achieved using HTML5, and the pace of improvements of modern browsers is high. The gap between native code and optimized JavaScript is closing, and indications are that further improvements are still possible. The comments and examples given here cover some simple cases, and hopefully illustrate some easy ways to ensure a good level of efficiency when developing performance-sensitive applications with JavaScript.

The research efforts, experience, and talents of several people from the Turbulenz engineering team were leveraged in the creation of this chapter. In particular, Michael Braithwaite and David Galeano deserve special thanks for sharing their extensive knowledge of the technology and their real-world experience creating fully featured high quality HTML5 games.

CHAPTER 5

Faster Canvas Picking

Colt "MainRoach" McAnlis, Developer Advocate, Google

If you're writing a 2D game in HTML5, chances are that you'll want the user to have the ability to pick an object on the screen. More specifically, at some point, the user will need to select some item on the screen, or in your game, which may represent part of the world. We call this "picking" as the user is selecting what object they are interacting with. Consider, for instance, your standard social time-management game. The user is presented with a 2.5D play area where bitmaps (or "sprites") are rendered with some perspective distortion on the screen. For the more advanced users, you can quickly saturate the play area with these sprites, often stacking many of them together, only leaving a few pixels visible between overlapping objects. In this environment, determining the picking result of a mouse click is quite difficult. The canvas API doesn't provide any form of pixel-based selection and the large number of objects makes it difficult to brute-force the technique. This section will cover how to address performance and accuracy problems in canvas picking using a few old-school techniques that most of us have forgotten about.

Creating Pickable Objects

For the sake of simplicity, I'll first introduce the most basic form of 2D picking I can, which is simply doing a point-to-rectangle test for each object in the scene. This type of *brute force* technique will yield accurate results, but not the most *precise* results (I will cover how to get "precise" picking later), especially where two sprites are overlapping. But before we tackle that topic, let's first start off with a few definitions of objects we'll use throughout this section, the *SpritePrototype* and *SpriteInstance*.

Defining a Sprite Prototype

As with most 2D canvas games, your world will not be populated with millions of unique bitmaps, but rather millions of objects where large groups of them share similar bitmaps between them. As such, it makes no sense to load a given image into memory for each sprite that uses it; you'd have duplicate versions of the images, for each *instance* of the sprite that exists, sitting around in main memory, which could quickly become a problem.

A much more performant solution is to simply load your images a single time and create references to them as each instance is created. You effectively cache the *prototype* images into a large array, which can be referenced by the individual instances later. The sample *SpriteProto* class that follows is pretty simplistic. It contains a filename field, alongside width and height (important later for picking, or in the future when using atlases; see http://en.wikipedia.org/wiki/Texture_atlas for more information). The most interesting part of this class is the *load* function, which given a filename will invoke JavaScript to load the image into memory. Once loaded, a *SpriteProto* object will then retain a handle to the loaded image in the *imgHandle* member (see Listing 5-1).

Listing 5-1. The SpriteProto definition

```
function SpriteProto(){
    this.filename="";
    this.imgHandle=null;
    this.size={w:0,h:0};
    this.load= function(filename,w,h)
    {
        var targetSpriteProto = this;
        this.size.w = w;
        this.size.h = h;
        var img = new Image();
        img.onload = function(){
            targetSpriteProto.imgHandle = img;
        }
        img.src = filename;
    }
}
```

For most game build-chains, you'll generally create some sort of designer or artist-centric view of the world ahead of time. That is, before this level is actually loaded by the user, you have a pretty good idea what assets will be needed to load, simulate, and display this level. As such, you don't define a complex asset dependency hierarchy here, but rather brute-force the loading of your basic proto-sprites so that they can be used by object instances later. During your initialization, you fill the globally accessible *protoSprites* array using the *loadProtos* function (see Listing 5-2).

Listing 5-2. Loading a set of prototype images

```
var protoSprites = new Array();
//---------------
function loadProtos()
{
    //technically, this should be an atlas definition!
    var imgs=[
        {nm:"0.png",w:66,h:42},
        {nm:"1.png",w:66,h:52},
        {nm:"2.png",w:66,h:46},
        {nm:"3.png",w:70,h:65}
    ];
    for(var i =0; i < imgs.length; i++)
    {
        var sp = new SpriteProto();
        sp.load(imgs[i].nm,imgs[i].w,imgs[i].h);
        protoSprites.push(sp);
    }
}
```

Note that for your purposes, you don't just list the path to the image, but also the width and height of the bitmap in pixels. These image-specific bounding conditions are important for gross-level picking that we'll discuss a bit later in the bounding boxes section.

Representing Objects

Now that you have your images loaded and in a form you can reference, you need to generate the actual objects that will populate your canvas and be targets for picking. To this end, you create a new *SpriteInstance* class.

You'd expect the basic two parameters of this class, *position* and *size*, which you will use for picking later. You also add a few other parameters: a unique *ID* value, alongside a *ZIndex*, which is useful for sorting during rendering, and collision resolution. And of course, you need a reference to what *ProtoSprite* object you'll be using to render (see Listing 5-3).

Listing 5-3. Definition of a SpriteInstance

```
function SpriteInstance(){
    this.id=0;                  //the unique ID for this object
    this.zIndex=50;             //needed for rendering and picking resolution, range [0,numObjects]
    this.pos={x:0,y:0};
    this.size={w:0,h:0};
    this.spriteHandle=null; //what sprite we'll use to render
```

For your simple uses, you need to populate the world with pickable objects, and to do so, you simply flood the given canvas with randomly placed objects. Note that you store the generated sprites in a global array for other systems to access later on (see Listing 5-4).

Listing 5-4. Populating the scene with randomly located SpriteInstances

```
var spriteInstances = new Array(); //global list of active sprites
//--------------
function generateInstances()
{
    var numSprites = 4096; //magic number
    for(var i = 0; i < numSprites; i++)
    {
        var sp = new SpriteInstance();
        sp.id = i;
        sp.zIndex = i; //just to keep my sanity...
        sp.pos.x = Math.floor(Math.random() * (500)); //random point on canvas
        sp.pos.y = Math.floor(Math.random() * (500));
                    //choose a random sprite to render this with
        var idx = Math.floor(Math.random() * (protoSprites.length));
        sp.spriteHandle = protoSprites[idx];
        sp.size = sp.spriteHandle.size;

        spriteInstances.push(sp);
    }
}
```

When you'd like to draw the sprites, you simply iterate over each instance, fetch its corresponding *spriteHandle*, and use that to draw to the canvas with the correct position data (see Listing 5-5).

Listing 5-5. Drawing the sprites in the scene

```
function drawSprites()
{
    //note that zIndex = i here, so this rendering is correct according to depth
    for(var i =0; i < spriteInstances.length;i++)
    {
        var sp = spriteInstances[i];
        var ps = sp.spriteHandle;
        ctx.drawImage(ps.imgHandle,sp.pos.x, sp.pos.y);
    }
}
```

See Figure 5-1 for an example of this code in action. Note that this is NOT the way you should be doing rendering in your production code. Real games have various types of restrictions and orderings for depth from their sprites. It's a complex dance between artist-generated content and runtime performance achieved by sorting of sprites. This simple example avoids all this, since a discussion of that size is beyond the scope of this chapter.

Figure 5-1. The results of rendering sprites onto the canvas

Basic Picking with Bounding Boxes

Since your *SpriteInstance* object supports both position and size information, the most straightforward way to determine what sprite has been picked is to test the given point against the bounding box of the sprite. In this simplistic model of picking, all that's needed is a simple loop over all the sprites in the scene, and to test which of their bounding-boxes intersect with the given x,y point on the canvas (given from the mouse); see Listing 5-6.

Listing 5-6. Find the desired sprite by looping through all instances, and determining which one contains the XY pair. Note that this function returns the FIRST instance it finds

```
function findClickedSprite(x,y)
{

 //loop through all sprites
 for(var i =0; i < spriteInstances.length; i++)
 {
  var sp = spriteInstances[i];
  //pick is not intersecting with this sprite
  if( x < sp.pos.x || x > sp.pos.x + sp.size.w ||   y < sp.pos.y || y > sp.pos.y + sp.size.h)
   return sp;
}
return null;
}
```

In Listing 5-6, you're completely ignoring z-ordering and complex depth stacking, and just returning the first sprite that contains this selection point. Don't worry; we'll get to that later.

Caveats

As mentioned, the brute-force, bounding-box method of picking is quite effective for scenes with low object count. However, once the number of objects in your scene increases, this technique will quickly reveal performance problems, especially on underpowered devices. Another particular issue is scene depth complexity—that is, how many overlapping sprites you have. Once you start adopting more aggressive versions of depth complexity, you'll quickly find that this method is unacceptable to user input and expectations, and you'll need a more fine-grain solution.

Faster Picking via Bucketing

Let's say you're building a complex app and you have thousands of images in flight when a user clicks. You'll quickly see that the performance burden lies in the inner loop of the sprite-to-point collision test, and although a simple bounding-box test will be the quickest to implement, you still end up touching a lot of items that aren't even remotely *near* the point in question.

The solution to this is to introduce a *spatial acceleration structure* to your canvas. This data structure organizes/separates your sprites spatially, such that you speed up spatial tests by only referencing items that are reasonably co-located. There's lots of variants for SAS (for example, scene graphs, bounding volume hierarchies, quadtrees, and octrees), each having a unique set of pros, cons, and trade-offs, the analysis of which is outside the scope of this section.

For your purpose, you will use a very simplistic 2D binning algorithm, which will divide your canvas into a grid of cells (of fixed sizes); each cell will contain a list of objects that touch that cell, allowing a sprite to be listed in multiple cells (see Figure 5-2).

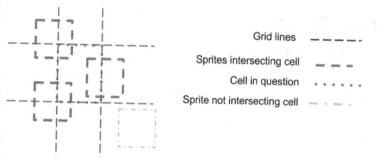

Figure 5-2. *Given a 2D grid, you can determine what sprites overlap with what cells. Later, when a pick event occurs, you can determine what cell the point resides in, and reduce the number of per-sprite checks you need to perform*

Your *BucketGrid* class will effectively create a 2D array of *arrays*, such that when a sprite is spawned, you calculate what grid cells it overlaps, and add a pointer to this instance to each of those cell's lists; see Listing 5-7.

Listing 5-7. Definition of a BucketGrid

```
function BucketGrid(){
    this.tileSize=32;
    this.numXTiles=0;
    this.numYTiles=0;
    this.tileData=null;

    this.init=function()
    {
        this.tileData = new Array();
        this.tileSize = 16;
        this.numXTiles= 512/this.tileSize;
        this.numYTiles= 512/this.tileSize;

        this.tileData.length = this.numXTiles*this.numYTiles;
        for(var k =0; k < this.tileData.length;k++)
            this.tileData[k] = new Array();
    }
```

Marking a sprite instance on the grid is pretty simple. You just run some math on the corners of the sprite to calculate the min/max boundaries of it, and what tiles those boundaries fall into; and for each grid cell, you add the sprite to the containing list (see Listing 5-8).

Listing 5-8. Given a sprite, mark which grid cells it overlaps in

```
this.markInstanceInAccelGrid=function(sp)

    var gridminX = Math.floor(sp.pos.x / this.tileSize);
    var gridmaxX = Math.floor((sp.pos.x + sp.size.w) / this.tileSize);
    var gridminY = Math.floor(sp.pos.y / this.tileSize);
    var gridmaxY = Math.floor((sp.pos.y + sp.size.h) / this.tileSize);
```

```
        if(gridmaxX >= this.numXTiles) gridmaxX = this.numXTiles-1;
        if(gridmaxY >= this.numYTiles) gridmaxY = this.numYTiles-1;

        for(var y = gridminY; y <=gridmaxY; y++)
        {
            var idx = y*this.numXTiles;
            for(var x = gridminX; x <=gridmaxX; x++)
            {
                this.tileData[idx+x].push(sp);
            }
        }
};
```

This makes finding entities extremely quick, because you've already pre-sorted the environment. When a mouse-click comes in, you simply find the bucket it resides in, and return the list of entities for that bucket, which you've already calculated.

```
this.getEntsForPoint=function(x,y)
    {
        var gridminX = Math.floor(x / this.tileSize);
        var gridminY = Math.floor(y / this.tileSize);
        var idx = gridminX + gridminY*this.numXTiles;
        var ents = this.tileData[idx];
        return ents;
    };
}
```

This makes modification to your existing code very nice and tidy:

```
function findClickedSprite(x,y)
{

 //loop through all target sprites
 var tgtents = acclGrid.getEntsForPoint(x,y);
 for(var i =0; i < tgtents .length; i++)
 {
  var sp = tgtents [i];
  //pick is not intersecting with this sprite
  if( x < sp.pos.x || x > sp.pos.x + sp.size.w ||   y < sp.pos.y || y > sp.pos.y + sp.size.h)
    return sp;
 }
 return null;
 }
```

The acceleration grid reduces performance overhead by reducing the number of times the *inner loop* is called; regardless of how many sprites you have universally, this bucketing will only care about what sprites reside in a grid cell. An easy trade-off in bang-for-the-buck; you didn't have to derail yourself by worrying how JavaScript is handling the math for convex hulls or the array-access times for pixel-perfect picking (both covered later in this chapter). It's a simple technique that can be used for static and dynamic environments.

Note that to use the grid, an entity needs to be responsible for updating its markings on the grid. For your simple purpose, you only need to update the entity spawning code to mark the location of the object in the grid (see Listing 5-9)

Listing 5-9. Inserting the BucketGrid into the existing code

```
//--------------
var protoSprites = new Array();
var spriteInstances = new Array();
var acclGrid = new BucketGrid();
//--------------
function generateInstances()
{
    acclGrid.init();

    var numSprites = 4096; //magic number
    for(var i = 0; i < numSprites; i++)
    {
        //.......

        spriteInstances.push(sp);
        acclGrid.markInstanceInAccelGrid(sp);
    }
}
```

Caveats

This type of spatial acceleration structure is always in demand for games. It's primary goal is to reduce the number of *potential* intersections to a defined list that is always smaller than the entire set. And to be clear, your BucketGrid structure did nothing to increase the *precision* of your picking, but only increased the *performance* of your picking. We will discuss precision issues more in the following sections.

One large issue to keep an eye on is that as your game evolves, your spatial structure will need to adapt to take into account objects that move, objects that have been scaled/rotated, etc. Without proper gardening, it's easy to generate bugs with object spawn/update/die lifecycles. In these cases, it may be wise to generate versions of spatial grids, each one specialized to the objects that need it. For example, a static 2D binning grid is fine for static objects, but dynamic ones may need a more aggressive quadtree hierarchy, or perhaps a k-dimensional tree.

Take care of your spatial grid, and it'll remain a strong data structure for your games.

Pixel Perfect Picking

For games that utilize picking for desktop applications, pixel-perfect response to a mouse click is crucial. Multiple images can be overlaid against each other, and each one can have varied alpha footprints which in no way match their conservative bounding box estimates. As such, to do a pixel-perfect pick of an object on the screen, you'll need to be able to determine what pixel from what image was clicked on and what object instance that image belongs to.

In order to do this in HTML5, you need to introduce two separate data structures, a *sprite prototype*, which represents a single loaded image sprite, and a *sprite instance*, which represents an instance of the prototype on the canvas—that is, you assume that a single image is used multiple times on a canvas.

1. The process for pixel-perfect picking is really straightforward. You need to load an image, somehow get access to its pixel data, and keep that around in memory for access later.

2. As objects are created and drawn to screen, you need a reference back to what image it's using.

3. When the user clicks, you need to find what objects intersect with that click, and then per-object, check if the click has hit a transparent or opaque section of the image representing that object.

Step 3 is where the real magic happens: being able to check for intersection against transparent or opaque pixels allows your game to overlay images on top of each other, and you can still determine, at pixel granularity, which image/object was selected (see Figure 5-3).

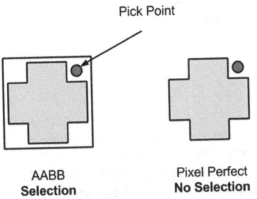

Figure 5-3. *Valid areas for bounding-box picking vs. pixel-perfect picking. Since the bounding-box for an object is larger than its discrete bounds, a selection does not need to be pixel perfect*

Loading Pixel Data

The cornerstone of your picking process is assuming that your images *contain* alpha values, and that you can access those pixels during a pick operation to determine if the selected point is in a transparent or opaque part of the image, which you generally assume is loaded this way:

```
var img = new Image();
img.onload = function(){alert('loaded!");}
img.src = filename;
```

The problem here is that in JavaScript you don't directly handle the pixel data; it's handled behind the scenes on your behalf.

To get the data then, you need to do some extra work. You could start by writing a JavaScript PNG decoder, but that would be massive overkill, considering PNGs support lossless compression, meaning you'd have to implement the entire DEFLATE codec by hand. Since you're really only concerned with the *alpha* values of an image, you could store the alpha channel in a separate .RAW file that you fetch in parallel; however, this would increase the transfer and asset size of the app.

For the sake of your purpose, you ignore those two options, and instead decide to keep the code footprint and transfer sizes low by using the *canvas* element to fetch the data. To do this, you create an off-screen canvas, render your image to it, and *fetch the pixels* of the canvas object back to memory (see Listing 5-10).

Listing 5-10. Fetching the image data by using an off-screen canvas

```
var offScreenCanvas= document.createElement('canvas');
var fetch_ctx = offScreenCanvas.getContext('2d');

// set a max size for our offscreen fetch canvas
offScreenCanvas.width = 128;
offScreenCanvas.height = 128;
function fetchImageData(imgObject, imgwidth,imgheight)
```

```
{
    fetch_ctx.clearRect(0,0,128,128);
    fetch_ctx.drawImage(imgObject, 0, 0);
    var last = Date.now();
    //CLM note this keeps an additional in-memory copy
    var imgDat = fetch_ctx.getImageData(0,0, imgwidth, imgheight);
    var current = Date.now();
    var delta = (current - last)
    console.log("getImageData " + delta  + "ms");

    return imgDat;
}
```

■ **Note**   For some odd security reason, you aren't able to use *getImageData* to fetch the pixels for an image file that isn't being served off the same origin as the code. As such, if you try the code in Listing 5-10 by simply loading your file in a browser, it will fail. You need to serve the code from some simple web server and browse to it appropriately. The pixel-perfect picking example in the source code comes supplied with a simple Python script to create a web server to load the example from. For more information on this type of thing, try searching for "Same Origin Policy getImageData."

This allows you to transfer a smaller asset footprint, keep using your PNGs/ GIFs or whatever other compression footprint you want, and still get the RGBA data available in main memory during load time (see Listing 5-11).

Listing 5-11. Updating the SpriteProto definition to handle pixel data

```
function SpriteProto(){
    this.filename="";
    this.imgHandle=null;
    this.imgData=null;
    this.size={w:0,h:0};
    this.load= function(filename,w,h)
    {
        var targetSpriteProto = this;
        this.size.w = w;
        this.size.h = h;
        var img = new Image();
        img.onload = function(){
            targetSpriteProto.imgHandle = img;
            targetSpriteProto.imgData = fetchImageData(targetSpriteProto.imgHandle,w,h);
        }
        img.src = filename;
    }
}
```

Testing a Mouse Click

Now that you have your per-sprite image data, as well as in-game instances of *referencing* that data, you can continue with the process of determining which of those objects intersect a given point on the screen, taking into account pixel transparency.

CHAPTER 5 ■ FASTER CANVAS PICKING

Firstly, the *findClickedSprite* function will loop through all the sprite instances in memory and do a bounding box test against the picking point; you assume that array lookup is a performance limiting action in JavaScript, and this bounding-box test allows an early out for items that don't potentially intersect with the pick position.

Once you find a sprite instance whose bounding box intersects with the picking point, you grab the sprite prototype and translate the canvas-relative mouse position to a sprite-instance-relative position that you use to test against.

■ **Note** that you're still utilizing the bounding-box picking style covered earlier. Per-pixel picking is quite an intensive inner-loop operation: the lookup and calculation of pixel data will easily cause performance problems. As such, using a bounding-box specific test first allows you to create a list of "potential" selected sprites (omitting objects that don't intersect with the target in any way) which you can then continue forward with to do pixel-perfect testing on.

These values are passed to a function on the sprite prototype to determine if the target pixel is transparent or not. If you're clicking an opaque pixel for this sprite, you set this as the selected sprite (see Listing 5-12).

Listing 5-12. Updating the findClickedSprite function to take into account pixel-based picking

```
function findClickedSprite(x,y)
{
    var pickedSprite = null;
    var tgtents = spriteInstances;
    //loop through all sprites
    for(var i =0; i < tgtents.length; i++)
    {
        var sp = tgtents[i];
        //pick is not intersecting with this sprite
        if(    x < sp.pos.x || x > sp.pos.x + sp.size.w ||
               y < sp.pos.y || y > sp.pos.y + sp.size.h)
            continue;

        var ps = sp.spriteHandle;
        //get local coords and find the alpha of the pixel
        var lclx = x - sp.pos.x;
        var lcly = y - sp.pos.y;
        if(!ps.isPixelTransparent(lclx,lcly))
        {
            pickedSprite = sp;
        }
    }
}
```

Again, in this particular example, you're somewhat naive about z-index collisions and visible ordering to the user The fix for this is somewhat simplistic: if you've found a pick collision, you test the zIndex of the new sprite with the zIndex of the existing picked sprite to see which one is closer to 0 (which represents closer to the camera), as shown ir Listing 5-13.

Listing 5-13. Updating the picking logic to take into account zIndex depth

```
if(!ps.isPixelTransparent(lclx,lcly))
{
    //do depth test (if applicable)
    if(pickedSprite && sp.zIndex < pickedSprite.zIndex)
        continue;
    pickedSprite = sp;
}
```

The *isPixelTransparent* function for the proto-sprite does very simple logic. It effectively fetches the pixel of the image in RGBA (that is, Red, Green, Blue, Alpha) form, and tests if the alpha channel of that pixel is greater than some threshold. The threshold is important, as most artists can add gradient falloffs, drop shadows, and other items which increase the visual of the item, but shouldn't be considered for picking purposes; see Listing 5-14.

Listing 5-14. isPixelTransparent is an important function which determines if a given pixel should be considered for collision or not

```
function SpriteProto(){
    //other stuff here
    this.isPixelTransparent=function(lclx,lcly)
    {
        var alphaThreshold = 50;
        var idx = (lclx*4) + lcly * (this.imgData.width*4);

        var alpha = this.imgData.data[idx + 3];

        //test against a threshold
        return alpha < alphaThreshold;
    };
}
```

Results and Caveats

The results, as shown in Figure 5-4, are quite nice. You can select the right object out of a very complex pixel coverage area.

Figure 5-4. The results of a pixel-perfect picking. Users can select sprites which may be complex or hidden under other objects in Z-ordering

While this method works, and produces pixel-perfect results, it presents two primary issues.

1. Image data, which is normally stored in your JavaScript layer behind the scenes, now has to be duplicated in your scripts. As such, this results in a larger memory footprint, often more than double the size since your in-memory copy is uncompressed.

2. It's currently unclear how an array look-up affects performance in JavaScript under the hood. In C++ you have the ability to avoid CPU addressing issues like L2 Cache optimization for array traversal, which is completely missing in JavaScript. On my 12-core work machine, a single pick against 4096 images takes around ~2ms. I'd imagine on a phone it would be *significantly* longer.

And finally, it's unclear if you *really* need pixel-perfect picking for *every part* of your game. For instance, the user may benefit from a more loosely defined picking area that allows an extension of the valid picking area beyond the pixel boundaries around the object, in an attempt to reduce user picking frustration.

Convex Hull Picking

While pixel-perfect picking represents the most resolution-specific solution you can produce for selecting objects, it has a large downside of increased memory footprint and potential performance burden for slower devices. For example, if you had a 1024x1024 image, that may only be 64k in PNG form, but once you fetch it to main memory, it's now 4MB. There's really no (good) way around this, since the `getImageData` function on canvas returns RGBA data uncompressed; even if you pass in a grayscale image, you'd get the full pixel footprint.

Ideally, it would be great to get a lower-memory *representation* of the image without having to store the whole thing in memory. And to that end, I'm going to introduce the concept of using convex hulls for picking.

Effectively, a convex hull is a minimum representation of the *shape* of your sprite, without curving inward towards itself (i.e. being concave). See Figure 5-5 for a representation of a convex hull versus a traditional bounding box.

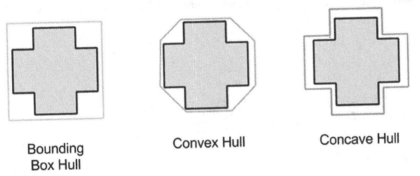

Bounding
Box Hull
Convex Hull
Concave Hull

Figure 5-5. *Visualizing the difference between a bounding box (which is always some form of rectangle), a convex hull (which is not allowed to "curve inward" on itself) and a concave hull (which allows itself to curve towards the source object boundaries)*

Convex hulls have been used for years in game development as a rough estimation of shape for 2D and 3D objects; they're especially useful in physics engines, where calculating the intersection of concave objects is roughly 2x slower than intersection of convex ones. Figure 5-6 shows a convex hull of one of the example sprites.

Figure 5-6. *A convex hull in action. Advanced data structures can accelerate your picking code, while in some cases sacrificing resolution perfection*

Once the mouse selection is pressed, you'll test the mouse-point against the convex hull of sprite instances to determine if it's inside or outside a target object.

You will lose some resolution on this process; that is, your results won't be pixel-perfect any longer, but there's a whole separate discussion about *how precise* your picking code needs to be, especially on mobile, where pixels are (generally) smaller than peoples' fingers. Figure 5-7 illustrates the difference in precision for the different selection methods.

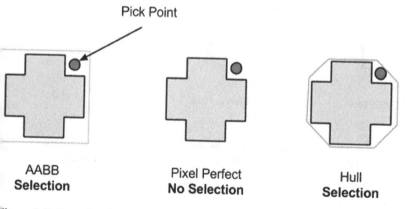

igure 5-7. *Bounding box, pixel-perfect, and convex hull regions for the same image. Notice that convex hulls are maller than bounding boxes, but larger than pixel-perfect. This trade-off allows it to be both semi-fast and ›mi-accurate when needed*

Generating the Convex Hull

Generating a convex hull should be done offline, ahead of time, so that you can reduce the loading time for your HTML5 game. As such, I threw together a simple C++ app that loads a sprite, calculates its convex hull, and outputs JSON data that you include in the HTML file. Your mileage may vary.

I'll spare you walking through the C++ details here, as the code itself is simple. It opens an image and calculates for each scan-line the min/max pixels that represent alpha boundaries (see Figure 5-8). From there, it uses a modified QHull algorithm (which you can get at www.qhull.org) to determine what the maximum convex hull is for the set of spatial points.

Figure 5-8. *Hull generation process. Per scan-line, you find the min-max pixels for that row and toss those at a convex hull generator*

The hull points are dumped to individual files, which for simplicity, I've manually added the hull data to the HTML file.

```
var cHullData=[
```

```
{"name":"0.png", "hull":[{"x":0,"y":16}, {"x":1,"y":15}, {"x":31,"y":0}, {"x":34,"y":0},
{"x":64,"y":15}, {"x":65,"y":16}, {"x":65,"y":25}, {"x":64,"y":26}, {"x":34,"y":41},
{"x":31,"y":41}, {"x":1,"y":26}, {"x":0,"y":25}, {"x":0,"y":16}]},
```

```
//See source code for the full list of hulls defined by our tool
```

Once again, it's worth pointing out that this method of spitting out per-file information may not be the correct way to handle the issue of getting hull information into your data chain (your mileage may vary). It's merely provided as an example to help you understand the process and determine the right integration paths that best suit your needs.

Doing Picking Against the Convex Hull

To transition from per-pixel picking to hull picking, you need to make a few small changes. Firstly, a sprite prototype needs to load the hull data, rather than fetching the image pixel data. This is an easy task, as the hull building app will spit out the image name for a hull, so that when an image loads, you can look up the proper hull for the image (see Listing 5-15).

Listing 5-15. Updating the SpriteProto definition to support convex-hull picking

```
function SpriteProto(){
//...

this.load= function(filename,w,h)
    {
        var targetSpriteProto = this;
        this.size.w = w;
        this.size.h = h;
        var img = new Image();
        img.onload = function(){

            targetSpriteProto.imgHandle = img;
            for(var u =0; u < cHullData.length; u++)
            {
                var thull = cHullData[u];
                if(thull.name == filename)
                {
                    targetSpriteProto.hullData = cHullData[u].hull;
                    break;
                }
            }
        }
        img.src = filename;
    };
})
```

To determine if a mouse click (i.e. point) is inside your new convex polygon hull, you utilize a method of *point-in-polygon testing* known as *ray casting*, which performs its test by casting a line through the 2D polygon, through the point in question (see Figure 5-9 for an example). For each line that your ray intersects, you toggle a Boolean value to determine if you're in or out of the polygon; see Listing 5-16.

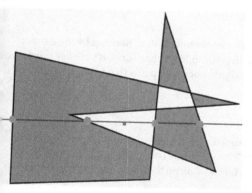

Figure 5-9. *An example of ray casting to determine if a point is in a polygon. The line runs through the polygon an even number of times, signaling that the point is not inside the polygon boundaries*

Listing 5-16. isPixelContained will determine if a given point resides inside the convex hull for this sprite

```
function SpriteProto(){
//...
//--------------
    this.isPixelContained=function(lclx,lcly)
    {
        var inPoly = false;
        var numPoints = this.hullData.length;
        var j = numPoints-2;
        var latLng={x:lclx,y:lcly};
        //from http://www.ecse.rpi.edu/Homepages/wrf/Research/Short_Notes/pnpoly.html
        for(var i=0; i < numPoints; i++)
        {

            var vertex1 = this.hullData[i];
            var vertex2 = this.hullData[j];

            if ((vertex1.x < latLng.x && vertex2.x >= latLng.x) ||
 (vertex2.x < latLng.x && vertex1.x >= latLng.x) )
            {
                if (vertex1.y + (latLng.x - vertex1.x) / (vertex2.x - vertex1.x) *
 (vertex2.y - vertex1.y) < latLng.y)
                {
                    inPoly = !inPoly;
                }
            }
            j=i;
        }
        return inPoly;

    }
} // end of SpriteProto function
```

Caveats

As mentioned, this method will reduce the overall memory footprint for your data significantly (compared to per-pixel testing), and on some platforms can have the added benefit of faster execution for a given pick operation.

The real "gotcha" with convex hulls is that it takes a bit of management in order to properly fit into your asset build pipeline the correct way. This poses a particularly large issue for those games using texture atlases, as you'll need to calculate the convex hull of each sprite *before* inserting it into the atlas.

Moving Forward

This chapter has discussed a set of techniques which, when used independently, can decrease processing time for picking and increase precision at the same time.

Industrial strength implementations of this type of code, however, will find the right and smart way to *combine* these techniques for the best results. Before you ship this technique in your title, consider some of the following modifications:

- For example, having a separate spatial grid for dynamic vs. static objects will help create early-out logic for frequently updating objects that tend to complicate your binning selection.

- Only allow visible objects to be pickable. It doesn't help your performance to check objects which are off-screen and not visible to the user, especially in large levels, where the majority of objects are outside the view bounds.

- Per sprite, define what type of picking collision it should use. Some images are fine with box-only picking; for others, convex hull should be enough; and for the rare few that need it, use pixel-perfect solutions.

- Don't forget that as your scene changes, so does the complexity of picking. For example, a tall building may hide multiple objects behind it, which may not need to be selectable any longer. Updating your scene representation to take this into account is ideal.

- Animated images complicate picking quite easily. Your art chain will need some way to output pixel/hull/bounding information per frame of animation and update your sprite representation to produce picking information for the current frame of the animation.

- Transforms and scales of bitmaps also complicate things. Most of the simplistic logic presented in this article quickly becomes error-prone when you rotate and scale bitmaps.

- One of the most annoying results of picking is pick complexity, or rather when the user clicks on objectA, meaning to get to objectB below it. If this is a common complaint, consider adding code paths to allow a multi-click within a tolerance (so if the user clicks the same location twice) to select the second or third stacked object. (In this article I only discussed returning the CLOSEST object to the pick.)

■ ■ ■

CHAPTER 6

Autotiles

Ivan Popelyshev, Game Developer, bombermine.com

Tile-based maps are the easiest way to construct dynamic worlds for 2D games. Such maps are described by a grid, where each cell belongs to one possible type. Most map formats allow the concept of layers in their rendering engine. A single cell can have multiple graphics that render to the same location of the map. In this chapter, I will discuss and solve the following common problems:

- Visually, there are types of tiles that quickly become redundant and an eyesore. An entire screen painted with the same grass tile quickly becomes boring. Artists often have to produce additional artwork and layers in order to hide such repetitive visuals.

- Memory usage is another problem. If a map is big, you can't create objects for each cell without significant memory loss. A number must describe most cells, which is an index of their tile. If you store only the numbers of tiles instead of objects, then any change in the list of possible tiles can ruin an already-drawn map.

- For large, complex worlds, the asset creation pipeline can quickly become an issue. Problems with graphics files and tile organization quickly present themselves as technical problems for large team 3D voxel games. If you want to make a Minecraft clone, this tutorial has to be in your favorites list.

The first problem is solved with an autotiles technique, where an algorithm, depending on the types of all surrounding tiles, generates each rendering sprite for a tile.

This chapter is based on the editor code from Chapter 11, where the basic functionality for editing maps is created. In this chapter, you will do something serious that extends your epic engine.

Shadows

Let's create a separate type of object tiles: a solid. Solids are necessary to create closed spaces; the characters can't go through them. Solids can be of different types: some are destroyed easily, and some are indestructible. The configuration to accomplish this is shown in Listing 6-1.

Listing 6-1. Solids

```
var ShadowConfig = {
init: function(game) {
        var tiles = game.tiles, sprites = game.sprites
        tiles.addMany(SolidTile, ["brick", "wall", "bush", "block", "metal"])
} }
```

Every solid can have two sprites to describe it: with wall and without wall. The magic number will be 0 or 1, depending on if there is a solid at the bottom (see Listing 6-2).

Listing 6-2. Solids and Sprites

```
var SolidTile = extendTile(Tile, {
        type:3, layer: 1,
        auto: function(map, i, j) {
                return map.getObject(i, j+1).type == 3
        },
        render: function(renderer, hasBottom, x, y) {
                var sprite = hasBottom?this.sprite2:this.sprite;
                var context = renderer.context;
                if (sprite)
                        context.drawImage(sprite.source, sprite.x, sprite.y, TILE_SIZE, TILE_SIZE,
                                x, y, TILE_SIZE, TILE_SIZE);
        },
        bind: function(sprites) {
                this.sprite = sprites.get(this.name);
                this.sprite2 = sprites.get(this.name+"-plain") || this.sprite;
        }
})
```

The height of each solid object will be the same, so there will be no shadows between them. You should draw a thin 1-px shadow around every solid, except in places that separate two solids. Put the light source at the left-bottom corner, and an extra shadow will appear at the right of each solid. If there is no solid below, the shadow won't be a rectangle.

For each cell that has an object tile, you have to calculate mask of its neighbors. The i-th bit will be ON if the neighboring cell at the i-th direction contains a solid tile. Since objects can store something else in a magic number, let's use its last 8 bits (from 24 to 31) to store it (see Listing 6-3).

Listing 6-3. Calculating the mask of the neighbors for each cell with an object tile

```
var dx = [1, 1, 0, -1, -1, -1, 0, 1], dy = [0, 1, 1, 1, 0, -1, -1, -1];

function getTileShadow(map, i, j) {
        var shadow = 0
        for (var bit=0;bit<8;bit++)
                if (map.getObject(i + dx[bit], j+dy[bit]).type == 3) shadow |= (1<<bit)
        return shadow<<24


function drawTileShadow(renderer, mask, x1, y1) {
        var shadow = (mask >> 24)&0xff;
        if (shadow == 0) return;
        var context = renderer.context;
        context.strokeStyle = "rgba(0,0,0,0.4)"
        context.beginPath();
        var x2 = x1 + TILE_SIZE, y2 = y1 + TILE_SIZE
        if ((shadow&1)!=0) {
                context.moveTo(x2-0.5, y1); context.lineTo(x2-0.5, y2);
        }
```

```
     if ((shadow&4)!=0) {
             context.moveTo(x1, y2-0.5); context.lineTo(x2, y2-0.5);
     }
     if ((shadow&16)!=0) {
             context.moveTo(x1+0.5, y1); context.lineTo(x1+0.5, y2);
     }
     if ((shadow&64)!=0) {
             context.moveTo(x1, y1+0.5); context.lineTo(x2, y1+0.5);
     }
     context.stroke();

     if ((shadow&24) != 0) {
             var t = 4;
             context.fillStyle = "rgba(0,0,0,0.3)"
             context.beginPath();
             if ((shadow&24) == 24) { // rectangle shadow
                     context.rect(x1, y1, t, TILE_SIZE); //rectangle + triangle
             } else if ((shadow&24) == 16) {
                     context.moveTo(x1 + t, y1);
                     context.lineTo(x1, y1);
                     context.lineTo(x1, y2);
                     context.lineTo(x1 + t, y2 - t);
                     context.lineTo(x1 + t, y1);
             }
             context.fill();
     }
}

ObjectTile.prototype.auto = getTileShadow

ObjectTile.prototype.render = function(renderer, mask, x1, y1) {
        Tile.prototype.render.call(this, renderer, mask, x1, y1);
        drawTileShadow(renderer, mask, x1, y1);
}
<!-- MODS -->
        <script src="mods/mod-shadows.js"></script>
        <!-- CONFIGURATION -->
        <script src="cfg/basic.js"></script>
        <script src="cfg/shadows.js"></script>
...
window.app = new App([BasicConfig, ShadowConfig])
```

Save the code in Listing 6-3 into the configuration and modification files, respectively; then add ShadowConfig in the App constructor, and you will see the results shown in Figure 6-1.

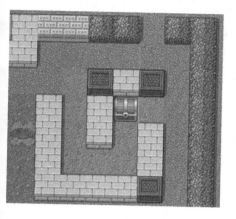 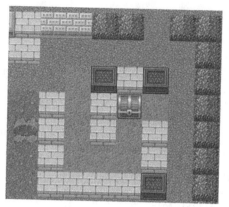

Figure 6-1. Shadows and walls

The Abyss

The abyss is an endless pit for those who don't watch their step. You have to describe the wall of the pit by a magic number. Let's add all possible walls to new TileList and call it deep, binding sprites to them. The magic number will be equal to the index of a tile in this list, depending on what tile you have above the pit. Since the abyss is a surface and you can modify surfaceTile later, you have to call its renderer after you draw the wall of the pit.

Listing 6-4 contains the code to perform the abyss modification.

Listing 6-4. Abyss Modification

```
var AbyssTile = extendTile(SurfaceTile, {
        type:4, layer: 0,
        auto: function(map, i, j) {
                var mask = SurfaceTile.prototype.auto.call(this, map, i, j);
                var id = map.getSurface(i, j-1).type != 4 ?    map.getObject(i, j-1).deepTile.id : 0xff;
                return mask | id;
        },
        render: function(renderer, mask, x, y) {
                var id = mask&0xff;
                if (id != 0xff) {
                        renderer.tiles.deep.byId[id].render(renderer, 0, x, y);
                }
                SurfaceTile.prototype.render.call(this, renderer, mask, x, y);
        }
}
)
```

The configuration code is as follows:

```
var AbyssConfig = {
init: function(game) {
        var tiles = game.tiles
        tiles.deep = new TileList();
        Tile.prototype.deepTile = tiles.deep.add( new Tile("deep_default"));
        tiles.addMany(ObjectTile, ["bridge_v", "bridge_h"], {
```

```
                deepTile: tiles.deep.add(new Tile("deep_bridge"))
        })
        tiles.add(new AbyssTile("abyss"));
},
afterInit:  function(game) {
        var tiles = game.tiles, sprites = game.sprites
        tiles.deep.bind(sprites);
}}
```

Add new script tags to the HTML file, and view the result, as seen in Figure 6-2.

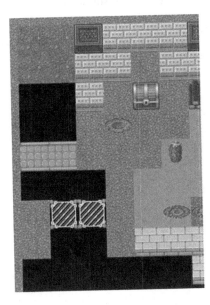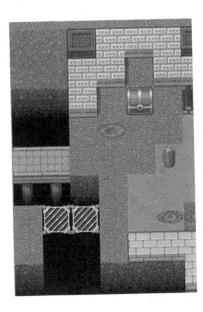

Figure 6-2. *Endless pit*

Smooth Transitions

This is the most interesting part of this chapter: how to make smooth transitions between surfaces (see Figure 6-3).

Figure 6-3. *Surfaces*

Here's an explanation of how to make such sprites in the simplest way. This method yields a decent result if you have no professional artists on your team. Additionally, these bundles are stored in an easy way for browsing and editing.

First, make sure you have turned on a grid that fits the tile size. In Photoshop, it's in the Edit ➤ Preferences ➤ Guides ➤ Grid&Slices menu. Set the Gridline Every parameter of the tile size (32 in your case) and the Subdivisions parameter to 2. Close the window, and turn on the grid (View ➤ Show ➤ Grid).

Now you must choose a ligament, which is a kind of tile that links other tiles among themselves. In your case, it's gravel. Make the canvas 3*4 tiles, and fill it with a linking basis. Next, select the surface that you want to smooth.

Make two upper tiles on separate layers, and four bottom links in one layer. Now you need to cut the useless elements from the grass layer including the large empty space in the center of the bottom four tiles and the edging in the upper-right tile. Then cut the second tile in the third row. It has to be filled with gravel. Erase a narrow line around central square (expand it a bit). After that, erase a narrow frame around the upper-right tile. Your result should look like Figure 6-4.

Figure 6-4. Surface step 1

Now let's see how the future image is constructed. You construct the resulting sprite from quarters. As an example, let's take the upper-left quarter. Depending on the neighbors of that corner, it can take up five positions of the texture. In Figure 6-5, neighbors are schematically shown; a dot corresponds to your tile, V are tiles that are equal to yours, X are different tiles, and a ? can be any tile.

1		2		3		4		5	
V	V	?	X	X	V	?	V	?	X
V	•	V	•	V	•	X	•	X	•

Figure 6-5. Neighbors of a corner. V means equals your tile, X means different than your tile, and a dot is your tile

All possible positions of the upper-left corner are matched in Figure 6-6.

Figure 6-6. *Five possible positions for the upper-left corner of the tile*

Other corners will be drawn following the same principle, as shown in Figure 6-7.

Figure 6-7. *Surface symmetry*

In the end, you have the variant shown in Figure 6-8, where you can see that some corners are not used.

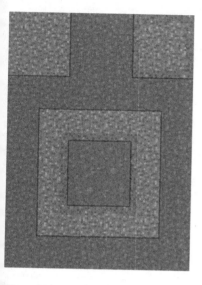

Figure 6-8. *Surface useless corners*

If corners are not used, then they are not worth of storing (see Figure 6-9).

Figure 6-9. *Surface resulting tile unprocessed*

This is the compact variant that you are going to use. It's better to give it to an artist, but there are ways to make it viable with simple tools. Use a 1-pixel eraser on the edges to achieve simulated grass. If you are familiar with Photoshop, it's more convenient to apply a raggy eraser. After that, you perform the same process on the upper tile.

The final step is to add some shadows. Click twice on the grass layer, and select drop shadow. Set Size and spread to 0 and Distance to 1. Tune the opacity to make it not very sharp. Repeat these steps on the upper tile (see Figure 6-10).

Figure 6-10. Surface production in four steps

Obviously, you shouldn't repeat this procedure each time using a 3×4 tiles set, because you can do it on a 2×3 tiles set from the beginning. Also, don't forget that in the 2×3 variant, the bottom 2×2 square is constructed from sprites shifted by 16 pixels in each direction.

If an object tile is allowed to create a smooth edge (noSurface is equal to false), and a surface tile has a special spritesheet for it (autoSurface is equal to true), then the magic number will describe which 16 × 16 parts of the spritesheet you have to render in each of the quarters of tile on the canvas. Since there are 4 * 6 = 24 possible indices, you store each of them in 6 bits (see Figure 6-11). First, you need 24 bits of the magic number (see Listing 6-5).

0	1	2	3
4	5	6	7
8	9	10	11
12	13	14	15
16	17	18	19
20	21	22	23

Figure 6-11. Indices for quarter of tile

Listing 6-5. Determining the 24 bits of the magic number

```
var test = [0, 0, 0, 0, 0, 0, 0, 0, 0];
Tile.prototype.noSurface = false
SurfaceTile.prototype.autoSurface = false
SolidTile.prototype.noSurface = true

SurfaceTile.prototype.auto = function(map, i, j) {
        //AUTOTILE #1
        if (!this.autoSurface || map.getObject(i, j).noSurface) return 0;
        var noEdges = true;
```

```
        for (var dx = -1; dx<=1; dx++)
                for (var dy = -1; dy<=1; dy++) {
                        var v = test[dx+ 3*dy+4] = map.getSurface(i+dx, j+dy) != this
                                && !map.getObject(i+dx, j+dy).noSurface
                        if (v) noEdges = false;
                }
        if (noEdges) return 0;
        var res = 0;
        for (var i=0;i<4; i++) { // THIS IS THE MAGIC WITH INDICES
                var dx = i&1, dy = i>>1;
                var dx2 = dx*2-1, dy2 = dy*2-1;
                var r;
                if (test[4+dx2]) {
                        if (test[4+dy2*3]) {
                                r = 2; // position 5
                        } else r = 13 - dx2*2; // position 2
                } else if (test[4+dy2*3]) {
                        r = 13 - dy2*8; // position 4
                } else if (test[4 + dx2 + dy2*3]) {
                        r = 13 - dx2*2 - dy2*8; // position 3
                } else r = 0; // position 1
                r+= dx + dy*4;
                res |= (r<<(8+i*6));
        }
        return res;
}

SurfaceTile.prototype.render = function(renderer, mask, x, y) {
        var sprite = this.sprite
        var context = renderer.context
        if (!sprite) return
        var dx, dy;
        mask>>>=8;
        var T2 = TILE_SIZE/2; // 16 pixels
        if (mask!=0) {
                dx = (mask&3)*T2;          // 2 bits - X coordinate of quarter
                dy = ((mask&63)>>2)*T2; // then 4 bits - Y coordinate of quarter
                context.drawImage(sprite.source, dx+sprite.x, dy+sprite.y, T2, T2, x, y, T2, T2);
                mask>>>=6;
                dx = (mask&3)*T2;
                dy = ((mask&63)>>2)*T2;
                context.drawImage(sprite.source, dx+sprite.x, dy+sprite.y, T2, T2, x+T2, y, T2, T2);
                mask>>>=6;
                dx = (mask&3)*T2;
                dy = ((mask&63)>>2)*T2;
                context.drawImage(sprite.source, dx+sprite.x, dy+sprite.y, T2, T2, x, y+T2, T2, T2);
                mask>>>=6;
                dx = (mask&3)*T2;
```

```
                dy = ((mask&63)>>2)*T2;
                context.drawImage(sprite.source, dx+sprite.x, dy+sprite.y, T2, T2, x+T2, y+T2, T2, T2);
        } else context.drawImage(sprite.source, sprite.x, sprite.y, TILE_SIZE, TILE_SIZE, x, y,
TILE_SIZE, TILE_SIZE);
}
```

The configuration here is easy. Add a new tileset, separating surface spritesheets by empty lines because they are twice as wide as single tiles. You don't want smooth transitions between the bridge and the abyss (it looks awful), so let's mark them by the noSurface flag, as shown in Listing 6-6.

Listing 6-6. Smooth Transitions

```
var SurfaceConfig = {
init: function(game) {
        var tiles = game.tiles, sprites = game.sprites
        tiles.apply(["grass", "sand", "dirt", "abyss"], {autoSurface: true});
        tiles.apply(["bridge_v", "bridge_h"], { noSurface: true});
        sprites.addSpriteSheet("img/surfaces.png", [
                ["grass", "", "abyss", "", "sand", "", "dirt"]
        ]);
} }
```

Now add files to index.html, and note the difference, as seen in Figure 6-12.

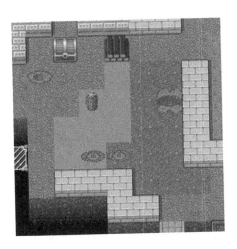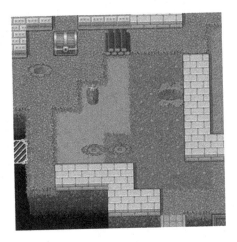

Figure 6-12. *Perfection!*

You can further enhance this tiny autotile engine to serve your design purposes as follows:

- Add irregular tiles and supplementary patterns.

- Create tile transitions that can be fully automated if there's no need for pixel-perfect art on each tile.

So take this approach and try some tiling! You'll be revisiting the techniques learned in this chapter in Chapter 22.

CHAPTER 7

■ ■ ■

Importing Flash Assets

Bruno Garcia, co-founder, 2DKit

The first generation of HTML5 games was simply about fighting to reach an acceptable frame rate. These games were mainly developed by individual hackers or tiny, programmer-led teams and featured mainly static artwork.

These days, we're seeing a coming of age in HTML5 games. Devices and browsers are fast enough to push more pixels, teams are growing to include more artists, and there's an increasing focus on visual quality to rival native applications (apps).

But, what tools are there to create HTML5 animations? As it turns out, there are very few, and many game artists are already trained in using Flash. Can we leverage those skills in the production of HTML5 games?

In this chapter, I will be presenting three different approaches to exporting assets from Flash into HTML5 games: sprite sheets, vectorization, and cutout animation.

Sprite Sheets

By far the simplest and most common approach is to render each frame of the animation to an image and then pack those images into a single texture atlas, or sprite sheet, as shown in Figure 7-1. Metadata, such as frame size and playback rate, are also typically exported in a separate JavaScript Object Notation (JSON) or XML file.

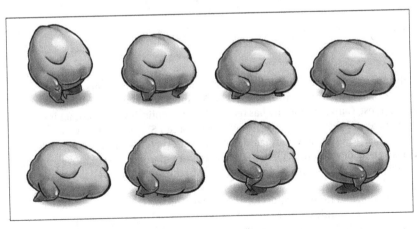

Figure 7-1. *A sprite sheet containing eight frames of a walk animation*

Tools that can export this format include TexturePacker, Zoë, and Flash itself. Besides the tools' being ubiquitous, the main advantage of sprite sheets is how simple they are to implement. If you're rolling your own game engine, it's only a matter of parsing the metadata and using them to draw the correct image each frame. Depending on the animation, this can also be pretty efficient, as each frame is a single rectangle, with no overdraw (pixels painted more than once).

One big drawback, especially with games that run on mobile or that are loaded over the Web (which is to say, most HTML5 games), is texture atlas memory usage. For more complex animations this means quickly hitting the dreaded memory limit on mobile and slow download times. Because the size of the texture atlases is directly correlated with the duration and frame rate of the animation, the only way to reduce the size is to make shorter, choppier animations, which is not always ideal.

If you can accept the memory footprint, sprite sheets can be a good choice for small or short animations. For longer animations, there are luckily other approaches.

Vectorization

Instead of storing images pixel by pixel, vector assets contain only a list of shapes and effects used to compose the final image. For simple, cartoonlike scenes, this works pretty well. One large benefit of vector images is that they retain their quality when scaled and rotated (see Figure 7.2). Another benefit over sprite sheets is that playback frame rate and duration aren't directly tied to memory usage.

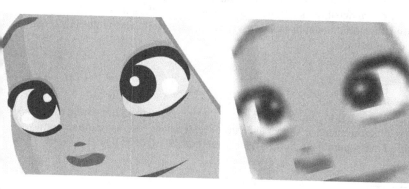

Figure 7-2. *An extreme close-up of a character; the vector version (left) retains quality, whereas the cutout version (right) shows artifacts*

Scalable vector graphics (SVG) is the de facto vector graphics file format for the Web, with renderers built into almost every modern browser. Unfortunately, SVG performs worse than HTML5 Canvas across the board. One reason for this is that, owing to game developer interest, Canvas rendering has received a lot of optimization. Another is that SVG was simply not designed for performance and games. Moreover, browser support for SVG animation is very spotty.

Flash's SWF format is light on memory usage, especially compared with SVG, but vector rendering still suffers in drawing speed. Common practice in Flash game development circles is to use vectors sparingly and to move images to bitmaps as much as possible. Especially on mobile, vector graphics performance does not scale well to complex assets with lots of tiny, intricate shapes and gradients.

Flash itself is a vector-based authoring tool, and its SWF export format contains all the vector data needed to render an animation in the Flash player. SWF is a complex, binary format, but once parsed, the vector graphics methods in HTML5 Canvas are well suited to rendering it. Mozilla Shumway is an experimental project whose aim is to develop a SWF renderer (along with an entire Flash player) in HTML5. The way in which Flash renders SWF files is largely undocumented, so any game engine that implements SWF rendering necessarily takes on a lot of complexity.

Implementing a complete SWF renderer is a tall order, but a renderer that supports a subset of the format may be feasible. The SWF library for Open Flash Library (OpenFL) is an example of this. Despite the complexity and performance issues with vectors, it may be worth it for assets that need to be wildly scaled and rotated.

Cutout Animation

This third approach is similar to traditional paper cutout animation and is popular for character animation. An asset is split into individual "cutouts," which, for characters, usually consists of an assemblage of body parts; each cutout is rendered to an image and packed into a texture atlas (see Figure 7-3). To play back the animation, each cutout is independently translated, rotated, and scaled on a timeline.

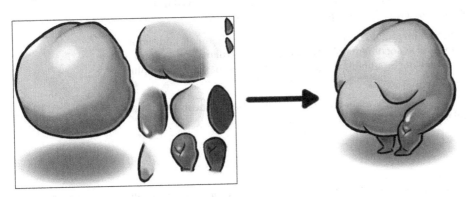

Figure 7-3. A texture atlas containing body parts is used to assemble a character

Because only the cutouts are saved to the atlas, and not entire frames, this technique uses far less memory than sprite sheets. The cutouts are tweened on a keyframe timeline, so the animation can play back at a smooth 60FPS and do so much more efficiently than vectors. The tools for exporting cutouts and the accompanying metadata are freely available, such as Dragon Bones and Flump.

A downside is that not all animations can be easily split into cutouts. An animation such as a writhing tentacle, which makes heavy use of shape tweens, is not easy to split up into individual parts. Unlike the other two approaches, cutouts also require that artists structure their assets a certain way.

Furthermore, overdraw can be a concern with cutouts. Scenes made up of several large, overlapping pieces can add up to a lot of painting and perform poorly on devices with low fill rates (see Figure 7-4).

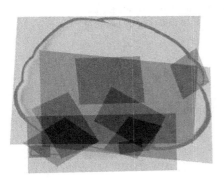 

Figure 7-4. Overdraw comparison between cutout animation (left) and the equivalent, using a sprite sheet (right); darker regions have more overdraw

Despite a few drawbacks, cutouts represent a good middle ground between sprite sheets and full vectorization and can be efficiently applied to a wide range of scene types.

New Tools

The Flash plug-in is on the way out, but the Flash authoring tool will still be used in game production on platforms for years to come. There are some possible alternatives popping up, though:

Spriter: An editor for cutout animation, targeted explicitly to games. Cutouts can be attached to a fully posable skeleton, which is great for characters that need to switch between multiple animations fluidly. Spriter exports to an open format and has implementations available in multiple languages. Unlike Flash, Spriter is only for animation; artists will need to author images in another editor.

Google Web Designer: Mainly suited to creation of banner advertisements and simple motion graphics. Exports to document object model (DOM) elements and Cascading Style Sheets (CSS), so this may not be suitable for games using Canvas or the Web Graphics Library (WebGL).

Adobe Edge Animate: Adobe's answer to HTML5 publishing. Not yet nearly as complete as Flash, and limited to DOM and CSS exporting.

Other Assets

This chapter focuses on animated image assets, but Flash can also manage other asset types, all of which need special consideration when taking to HTML5:

Sounds: The Flash plug-in comes with an MP3 decoder, so there has never been any question about which format to choose. In HTML5, audio format support across browsers is more fragmented. To support all modern browsers, encode copies of the same sound in both MP3 and OGG, and load the correct format at runtime.

Fonts: TrueType font rendering is fairly slow in HTML5 Canvas, and prerendering lines of text to cached surfaces can eat up a lot of memory. A great alternative is to use bitmap fonts, in which each glyph is prerendered to a texture atlas. The BMFont editor and file format are commonly used in the games industry for bitmap fonts.

Nine-Slice images: These are images that are divided into a 3 × 3 grid (nine cells) that can be scaled independently. Rendering these images is no problem in Canvas. The tedious part is copying the grid coordinates from Flash. It may be possible to automate this task by parsing the FLA, which is actually just a zip containing several XML files.

Conclusion

To recap, Table 7-1 is a handy reference comparing the three different animation methods.

Table 7-1. *The Most Common Tablet Resolutions and Their Aspect Ratios*

	Pros	Cons
Sprite sheets	Simple and easy to implement Fast	High memory usage: even moderate animations use tons of memory and take a long time to download. Opaque: scene structure is not exposed to code, so tasks such as swapping parts are not easily done.
Vectorization	Assets can be nicely scaled and rotated. Scene structure is fully exposed to code; recoloring and swapping parts are easy to do. Low memory usage	Very difficult to implement correctly and efficiently Slow; does not scale well to complex assets
Cutouts	Scene structure is exposed to code, though not as completely as vectors. Low memory usage Fast	Scenes must be structured in a certain way by the artist. Not suitable for every type of scene

Like a lot of things in HTML5 game development, there is no best method; it's all about trade-offs and compromises. Which method(s) you use entirely depends on the type of game and assets you're creating. Moreover, you may employ a variety of methods in a single game. An asset that will need to be scaled way up could be vector, whereas characters could be cutouts, and short, hand-drawn explosions could be sprite sheets. The ideal game engine would allow all three types to be used interchangeably.

CHAPTER 8

■ ■ ■

Applying Old-School Video Game Techniques in Modern Web Games

Mario Andrés Pagella, founder, Warsteed Studios

In computer graphics, frames are processed and painted on the screen by what some people refer to as the "animation," "main," "game," or "update" loop. Personally, I prefer to call it "main," "game," or "update loop" for the sole reason that it's standard practice in the industry to use this routine to perform other tasks besides painting pixels on the screen.

A good example of this is the accuracy of physics calculations. If your update loop is called 60 times per second, it means that the variables in your physics formulas will get updated every 16.67 ms (1000 ms/60 FPS). If you work with small objects and rapid movements, the movements and calculations won't be as accurate and realistic than if you work with a higher framerate.

The reason why I mention this is because, while the framerate may be higher than the refresh rate of the monitor that is displaying the images, the three variables are not dependent on each other. To put it simply, the number of times your update loop is being called per second is completely independent from the number of times you're refreshing the pixels on the screen, which is also independent from the refresh rate of the monitor itself. For example, the update loop could be called 1000 times per second, but the images could only be refreshed (on purpose, by the program) every 33.3 ms (30 FPS) and at a maximum of 16.67 ms (60 FPS), which is dictated by the refresh rate of the monitor. In the same way, a game could be running at 3 FPS but the monitor would still refresh images at 60 Hz. The only caveat is that the framerate that you're using to display images on the screen can never be faster than the number of times the update loop is called per second (unless you keep them separate, which in my experience is never a good idea, at least with web games).

Nevertheless, games such as Bungie's Halo were designed to run at 30 FPS, while others such as Epic's Unreal Tournament or id Software's Quake III Arena worked better if they ran at more than 60 FPS (for example, in Q3A, a higher framerate made bullets and model movements more accurate). As with most things, it always depends on what you're trying to achieve and how you've developed the software.

However, we haven't always depended on calculating time differences in order to perform animations. In the early days of game development, developers tied their update loops to the clock speed of CPUs, which is why later on some computers had a "Turbo" button that could be pressed to reduce the clock speed and make applications such as games run at the speed for which they were designed.

The reason why computer graphics developers and game developers are so obsessed with the framerate is because it dictates two extremely important pieces of information. The first one is the processing budget that you need to work within, and the other is the accuracy and precision of certain calculations.

10

The processing budget dictates how much processing time is available until the next frame is called. You need to consider that if your game is running and displaying graphics at 60 FPS, you have 16.67 ms to handle the following:

- Pixels being painted on the screen

- Calling the next tick on the physics engine

- Updating variables, game state, and other objects

If for some reason you're unable to process all those things in that amount of time, you will be skipping a frame, which could incur jerkiness or slowdowns in the animations. Which is why, for example, some developers choose to display graphics at 30 FPS. Instead of having just 16.67 ms, they have 33.3 ms to take care of everything, leaving some leeway to handle more demanding scenes or calculations. Others may choose to call the update loop at 120 FPS to have increased precision in physics calculations, but to display graphics at a constant 30 FPS.

So, the question arises, what happens if you want to be able to display graphics at a constant 60 FPS with no stuttering or slowdowns? That is, you want to be able to process all these things in less than 16.67 ms, leaving some leeway for when your optimization efforts are not enough.

The truth is that optimization of update loops has been, and will most likely always be, a hot topic of discussion. There will always be some sort of limitation, restriction, or problem that you'll need to work out to make your games run better, or that allows you to create richer and more exciting experiences for your users. There is always room to make things faster, and sometimes the gains can be enough to make us say, "Wow, now there's enough processing power to add this new feature I've wanted to add" or "Hey, this can now run on my smartphone!" So in my experience, they are always worth pursuing.

In the past, game developers had to work with even tougher constraints. Not only were processors slower, but graphics and storage capabilities were extremely limited as well, which is why they had to come up with incredibly clever "performance hacks" to make their games better. Competition has been, and will most likely be in years to come, fierce. For this reason, I propose that you study how "old" games were made.

High-Performance Update Loops

Unlike in other languages such as C or C++, creating a recursive function without an exit condition will create a UI-blocking infinite loop, exhausting the computer's memory; therefore, it's necessary to use another method.

In the past, there were two methods that allowed you to accomplish this: setTimeout and setInterval. Both functions work similarly, by accepting two parameters: a function or string with the code that you want to execute, and another with the delay (in milliseconds). For example, two possible implementations of update loops using JavaScript follow. The first one, shown in Listing 8-1, uses setTimeout.

Listing 8-1. Using setTimeout

```
// Define the amount of times the loop is going to get called
var maxCount = 3;

// Call the function for the first time
update(0);

function update(current) {

    // Execute the function 3 times
    if (current < maxCount) {

        console.log('this is a test!');

        setTimeout(function() {
```

```
            // Increase the value of current by one
        update(current + 1);

            // Execute every 500 ms.
    }, 500);

  }

}
```

Listing 8-2 uses setInterval.

Listing 8-2. Using setInterval

```
// Define the amount of times the loop is going to get called,
// initialise the counter and define an empty variable for our timer.
var maxCount = 3,
    current = 0, //
    intervalId = null;

function update() {

    // Execute the function 3 times
    if (current < maxCount) {

        // Do Something
        // Increase the value of the counter by one
        current += 1;

    } else {

        // If the function has been called 3 times, stop the timer.
        clearInterval(intervalId);

    }

}

// Define the interval and save the timerId to a variable. Call every 500 ms.
intervalId = setInterval(update, 500);
```

The second parameter of both functions is the delay. Common reason would dictate that if you want to make the loop run as many times as possible per second, you could set it to zero. Unfortunately, that'd produce a similar result to doing an infinite while loop. For this reason, the delay (referred to as DOM_MIN_TIMEOUT_VALUE in the spec) used to be clamped to a minimum value of 10 ms.

However, both methods suffered (and still do) from a very serious problem: if the window or tab is inactive, or (in the case of a mobile application) if you switch to another application, both functions will continue to be called at 10 ms, consuming valuable processing and battery power.

In modern browsers, both setTimeout and setInterval have a DOM_MIN_TIMEOUT_VALUE of 4 ms. They also include a new function that not only behaves similarly to setTimeout and setInterval, but that also solves the "inactive window" problem. This function is defined in the document "Timing control for script-based animations" (http://www.w3.org/TR/animation-timing/) and it's called requestAnimationFrame.

Calling requestAnimationFrame

One of the best features of requestAnimationFrame is that it will be scheduled to run before the web browser performs a repaint, which in most browsers happens approximately 60 times per second (that is, 60 FPS). This basically means that requestAnimationFrame cannot be called more times than the number of repaints in the browser. When the browser window (or tab) goes inactive, the number of times that the function is called per second will be reduced automatically to a minimum.

Browsers as recent as IE9 didn't support requestAnimationFrame, but luckily there's a very easy way to polyfill it (which means creating a way to make it work similarly in older browsers) by using a RequestAnimationFrame Polyfill, as shown in Listing 8-3.

Listing 8-3. Using a RequestAnimationFrame Polyfill

```
// handle multiple browsers for requestAnimationFrame()
window.requestAnimFrame = (function () {
    return window.requestAnimationFrame ||
            window.webkitRequestAnimationFrame ||
            window.mozRequestAnimationFrame ||
            window.oRequestAnimationFrame ||
            // if all else fails, use setTimeout
            function (callback) {

                // shoot for 60 fps
                return window.setTimeout(callback, 1000 / 60);

            };

})();
```

Therefore, you can implement an update loop as shown in Listing 8-4.

Listing 8-4. Implementing an Update Loop

```
// Define the amount of times the loop is going to get called
var maxCount = 3;

// Call update() for the first time
update(0);

function update(current) {

    // Execute the function 3 times
    if (current < maxCount) {

        // Do Something

        // Call requestAnimFrame
        requestAnimFrame(function() {

            // Increase the value of current by one
            update(current + 1);

        });
    }
}
```

As mentioned, requestAnimationFrame is capped at 60 FPS (or rather, it's limited by the refresh rate of your web browser), but as you have probably noticed there's no way to specify a delay. So what happens if you want to display graphics at less than 60 FPS?

One possible solution to this problem involves calculating the delta between two timestamps. If the delta is bigger that a given interval, which would basically dictate the framerate, you can draw the frame, leaving you with enough processing power to perform more complex (and time-consuming) calculations.

Luckily, when you specify the callback to requestAnimationFrame, it will attempt to pass an additional parameter with a timestamp that is relative to when the page has finished loading; that is, instead of being a DOMHighResTimeStamp, it will attempt to pass a DOMTimeStamp. You can use this to your advantage by creating an update loop that displays graphics at 30 FPS, as shown in Listing 8-5.

Listing 8-5. An Update Loop that Displays Graphics at 30 FPS

```javascript
var fps = 30,                    // Define the maximum number of FPS
    interval = 1000 / fps,  // Calculate the interval in milliseconds
    delta = 0,                   // Variable initialisation
    previousTs = 0;              // Variable initialisation

// Call the update loop for the first time
requestAnimationFrame(update);

function update(ts) {

    // Calculate the delta between the previous timestamp and the new one
    delta = ts - previousTs;

    // Performing a calculation here means that it will be
    // executed every 16.67 ms. at 60 frames per second

    // Paint routine
    if (delta > interval) {

        // This bit will be executed only if it's bigger than the
        // interval and therefore will be executed every 33.33 ms.
        // at 30 frames per second (or the value of the "fps" variable)

        // Set the previous timestamp, which will be used
        // in the "next" loop.
        // Subtract the difference between the delta and the interval
        // to account for the time that it took the computer to
        // process the function.

        previousTs = ts - (delta % interval);

    }

    // Call requestAnimationFrame again
    requestAnimationFrame(update);

}
```

However, in some games (such as card, match-3, or strategy games) there are periods of time where the scene doesn't suffer any modifications, so it's not necessary to redraw it. That's why the International Association of Responsible Game Developers recommends, "Just because you can, it doesn't mean you should constantly consume the resources of the user's system." (This is obviously made up and meant to be sarcastic.)

Knowing this, you can make an extremely small addition to your code that will result in memory and processing savings when you don't need to redraw the scene. The optimization consists of creating a special flag that you'll call shouldRepaint that will dictate whether you need to repaint the scene, as shown in Listing 8-6.

Listing 8-6. Special Flag shouldRepaint

```
var fps = 30,                   // Define the maximum number of FPS
    interval = 1000 / fps,      // Calculate the interval in milliseconds
    delta = 0,                  // Variable initialisation
    previousTs = 0,             // Variable initialisation
    shouldRepaint = true;       // Set the repaint flag to true by default

// Call the update loop for the first time
requestAnimationFrame(update);

function update(ts) {

    // Calculate the delta between the previous timestamp and the new one
    delta = ts - previousTs;

    // Performing a calculation here means that it will be
    // executed every 16.67 ms. at 60 frames per second

    // Check whether or not something needs to be repainted in the scene

    // Only execute the paint routine if the delta is bigger
    // than the interval and the shouldRepaint flag is set to true
    if (delta > interval && shouldRepaint) {

        // This bit will be executed only if it's bigger than the
        // interval and therefore will be executed every 33.33 ms.
        // at 30 frames per second (or the value of the "fps" variable)

        // Set the previous timestamp, which will be used
        // in the "next" loop.
        // Subtract the difference between the delta and the interval
        // to account for the time that it took the computer to
        // process the function.

        previousTs = ts - (delta % interval);

    }
    // Call requestAnimationFrame again
    requestAnimationFrame(update);
```

Bottlenecks in an Update Loop

Most commonly, when it comes to performance, the biggest bottlenecks in an update loop can be found in two places. The first one is the painting routine because painting pixels on the screen is an extremely expensive process, as you'll remember from the last chapter. The second one is the physics calculations.

The reason why you have spent a considerable amount of time learning the definition of framerate and how to define a proper update loop is because both will aid you in the implementation of a rock-solid and extremely performant update routine that separates the paint process from other calculations.

That being said, let's shift focus to the topic at hand. Minimizing or completely eliminating the impact of a performance bottleneck is not an easy task. Many times it requires several days of intense profiling or searching (or even inventing) the right algorithm. Keep in mind that micro-optimizations will only result in micro-improvements. Real performance gains can only be made when you tackle the elephant in the room: the slowest and most CPU/GPU demanding parts of the routine.

Back in the day, computers came with CGA cards, which included a color depth of 4-bits (16 different colors) at a maximum of 640×200 pixels, and 16 kilobytes of video memory. Even though they were revolutionary at the time, they lacked the necessary features to support scrolling in hardware, which meant that scenes had to be redrawn in software, frame by frame. Additional limitations of processing power meant that making side-scrolling games was practically impossible.

In order to overcome this limitation, John D. Carmack (one of the Founders of ID Software and creator of games such as Wolfestein, Doom, and the Quake series) invented a technique called Adaptive Tile Refresh (ATR) that combined the "extra" space in EGA cards and used them as double-buffers in combination with an extremely popular technique that we nowadays refer to as dirty rectangles.

Dirty Rectangles

From web browsers to video streaming algorithms to videogames, the use of dirty rectangles has been and continues to be one of the most efficient graphical algorithms that can be used to repaint small changes within a bigger image. Best of all, the algorithm itself is quite simple to understand and implement.

The concept behind dirty rectangles is that usually on certain types of applications there is no need to repaint the entire image when there is a small variation (such as a character moving, or an object appearing or disappearing). In order to deal with this problem, you can think of an image as a grid. When something changes, you flag the affected cells as modified; when it's time to repaint, you only have to repaint the flagged cells. Obviously, the reason why there is a possibility of using algorithms like dirty rectangles in HTML5 Canvas applications is because the canvas object works in immediate mode; whatever you draw on the screen will stay there until you draw something else on top of it, or you clear the screen.

One possible way to implement this algorithm consists of subdividing the screen into many columns and rows, and then when all of them are drawn on the screen, you mark them as "unmodified." When some other object within the screen moves, you need to calculate which of the cells are affected and mark them as "modified" or add them to a list of "modified cells." When the update loop is triggered again, the only thing you have to do is to cycle the list of modified cells and re-draw those cells. Figure 8-1 explains how this would work in practice.

11

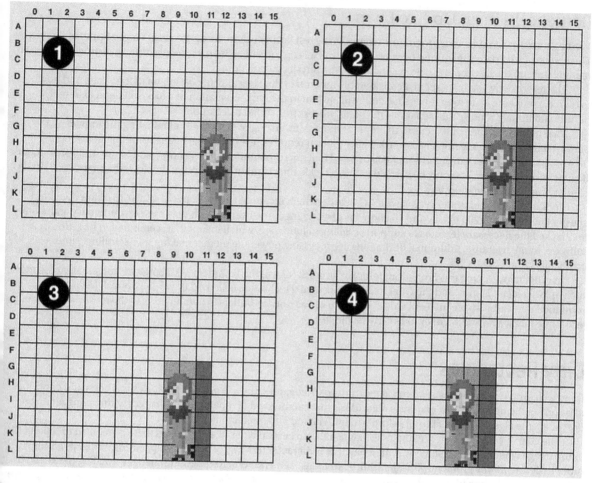

Figure 8-1. As the character moves, only the tiles that the character was on top of are being repainted

In order to show how this concept works in a practical application, you're going to develop a very simple application that draws a somewhat complex background and a small red dot that you'll be able to control using the arrow keys or keys W, A, S, and D. See Listing 8-7.

Listing 8-7. Canvas Application Demo

```
window.addEventListener('keydown', function(e) {

    switch(e.keyCode) {
        case 65: // A
            console.log('Go left!');
            break;
        case 68: // D
            console.log('Go right!');
            break;
```

```
            case 87: // W
                console.log('Go up!');
                break;
            case 83: // S
                console.log('Go down!');
                break;
        }
    }
}
```

Listing 8-8 shows how to display and control the small red circle using your keyboard.

Listing 8-8. Display and Controlling the Small Red Dot

```
;(function() {

    var fps = 30, // Define the maximum number of FPS
        interval = 1000 / fps, // Calculate the interval in milliseconds
        delta = 0, // Variable initialisation
        previousTs = 0,// Variable initialisation
        shouldRepaint = true, // Set the repaint flag to true by default
        Grid = [], // Initialize an array where we're going to be storing the grid values
        gridCols = 15, // Setup the number of columns of the grid
        gridRows = 10, // Setup the number of rows of the grid
        viewportWidth = 640, // Setup the width of the viewport (the canvas)
        viewportHeight = 480, // Setup the height of the viewport (the canvas)
        cellWidth = (viewportWidth / gridCols) >> 0, // The width of each cell is calculated
dynamically with the width of the canvas. Floor the result.
        cellHeight = (viewportHeight / gridRows) >> 0, // The height of each cell is calculated
dynamically with the height of the canvas. Floor the result.
        playerRadius = 10, // Our player is going to be a circle. Set the radius.
        playerPositionX = (cellWidth * gridCols) - playerRadius, // Position the player within the map
        playerPositionY = (cellHeight * gridRows) - playerRadius, // Position the player within the map
        playerVelocityX = 0, // Velocity of the player's movements in the X axis
        playerVelocityY = 0, // Velocity of the player's movements in the Y axis
        playerVelocityLimit = 2, // Limit the acceleration
        canvas = document.querySelector('canvas'), // Grab a reference to the canvas object...
        ctx = canvas.getContext('2d'), // ...and its context
        i = 0, // Declare counters for the for loop we'll be using below
        j = 0; // Declare counters for the for loop we'll be using below

    // Set the size of the canvas
    canvas.width = viewportWidth;
    canvas.height = viewportHeight;

    // Initialise the grid. By default, it will be empty,
    // so we'll need to "paint" all the cells
    for ( ; i < gridRows ; ++i ) {

        for ( j = 0 ; j < gridCols ; ++j ) {

            if (Grid[i] === undefined) {
                Grid[i] = [];
            }
```

11

```
            // Flag all the cells as "modified"
            Grid[i][j] = 1;
        }

    }

    // Call the update loop for the first time
    requestAnimationFrame(update);

    // Listen for keydown
    window.addEventListener('keydown', function(e) {

        var diff = 0.2;

        switch(e.keyCode) {
            case 37: // Left
            case 65: // A
                playerVelocityX -= diff;
                break;
            case 39: // Right
            case 68: // D
                playerVelocityX += diff;
                break;
            case 38: // Up
            case 87: // W
                playerVelocityY -= diff;
                break;
            case 40: // Down
            case 83: // S
                playerVelocityY += diff;
                break;
        }

        // Make sure the acceleration in the X axis is limited
        if (Math.abs(playerVelocityX) > playerVelocityLimit) {
            playerVelocityX = (playerVelocityX < 0) ? (playerVelocityLimit * -1) :
playerVelocityLimit;
        }

        // Make sure the acceleration in the Y axis is limited
        if (Math.abs(playerVelocityY) > playerVelocityLimit) {
            playerVelocityY = (playerVelocityY < 0) ? (playerVelocityLimit * -1) :
playerVelocityLimit;
        }

    }, false);

    function update(ts) {
```

```
// Calculate the delta between the previous timestamp and the new one
delta = ts - previousTs;

// Performing a calculation here means that it will be
// executed every 16.67 ms. at 60 frames per second

// Check whether or not something needs to be repainted in the scene

// if the velocity of the player is different than 0,
// we'll need to repaint the frame
if (playerVelocityX !== 0 || playerVelocityY !== 0) {
    playerPositionX += playerVelocityX;
    playerPositionY += playerVelocityY;
    shouldRepaint = true;
}

// Only execute the paint routine if the delta is bigger
// than the interval and the shouldRepaint flag is set to true
if (delta > interval && shouldRepaint) {

    // This bit will be executed only if it's bigger than the
    // interval and therefore will be executed every 33.33 ms.
    // at 30 frames per second (or the value of the "fps" variable)

    // Paint the "background"
    var i = 0,
        j = 0;

    for ( ; i < gridRows ; ++i ) {

        for ( j = 0 ; j < gridCols ; ++j ) {

            if (Grid[i][j] === 1) {

                paintCell(ctx,
                        j * cellWidth,
                        i * cellHeight,
                        cellWidth,
                        cellHeight);

                // Set that position as painted
                Grid[i][j] = 0;

            }

        }

    }
```

```
        // Paint the "player"
        paintPlayer(ctx, playerPositionX, playerPositionY);

        // There's no need to go through all this logic on every frame
        shouldRepaint = false;

        // Set the previous timestamp, which will be used
        // in the "next" loop.
        // Subtract the difference between the delta and the interval
        // to account for the time that it took the computer to
        // process the function.

        previousTs = ts - (delta % interval);

    }

    // Call requestAnimationFrame again
    requestAnimationFrame(update);

}

function paintCell(ctx, x, y, w, h) {

    // Set the colour to blue
    ctx.strokeStyle = '#00F';

    // Instead of drawing straight lines, draw dashed lines instead
    w -= (cellWidth / 2);
    h -= (cellWidth / 2);

    ctx.beginPath();
    ctx.moveTo(x, y);
    ctx.lineTo(x + w, y + h);
    ctx.stroke();

    // Set the colour to gray
    ctx.strokeStyle = '#ccc';

    // Draw an outline
    w += (cellWidth / 2);
    h += (cellWidth / 2);

    ctx.strokeRect(x, y, w, h);

}

function paintPlayer(ctx, x, y) {

    // Set the colour to a dark red
    ctx.fillStyle = '#CC0000';
```

```
    // Draw the circle
    ctx.beginPath();
    ctx.arc(x, y, playerRadius, 0, 2 * Math.PI);
    ctx.fill();

    }

}());
```

However, you will notice that whenever you move the dot, it leaves a trail. The reason why this happens is because you're not "cleaning up after yourself" by repainting the cells. In order to take care of this problem, first of all you need to figure out where you are—that is, upon which cells the circle is sitting.

A naive solution to the problem would consist of cycling every cell asking, "Is the circle on top of me?" but that would be an extremely time- and resourcing-consuming operation. Luckily, there's a much simpler solution that consists in dividing the position in the X-axis by the width of the cell, and flooring the result. Keep in mind that you'll need to do the same with Y-axis, by dividing it by the height of the cell.

You can try this concept by making a very small modification to the `paintPlayer()` function, as shown in Listing 8-9.

Listing 8-9. Modifying the `paintPlayer()` Function

```
function paintPlayer(ctx, x, y) {

    var col = (x / cellWidth) >> 0,
        row = (y / cellHeight) >> 0;

    // Set the colour to a semi-transparent blue
    ctx.fillStyle = 'rgba(0, 0, 255, 0.05)';
    ctx.fillRect((col * cellWidth),
                 (row * cellHeight),
                 cellWidth,
                 cellHeight);

    // Set the colour to a dark red
    ctx.fillStyle = '#CC0000';

    // Draw the circle
    ctx.beginPath();
    ctx.arc(x, y, playerRadius, 0, 2 * Math.PI);
    ctx.fill();
}
```

But if you try this example in a web browser, you'll find situations like the ones in Figure 8-2 where even though the circle is on top a cell, the cell is not being painted. The reason why this happens is because the X and Y are being calculated from the center of the circle, and you're not taking the radius of the circle into account.

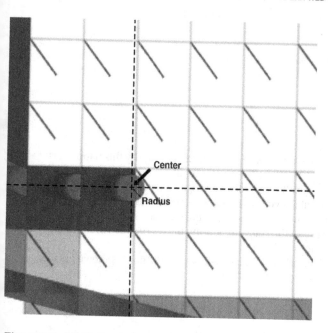

Figure 8-2. *While the circle seems to be on top of a new cell, the cell remains white instead of changing to blue (which means that it's marked as "dirty")*

One easy way to handle the problem is to create a *bounding rectangle*—that is, to turn the sphere into a box, as seen in Figure 8-3.

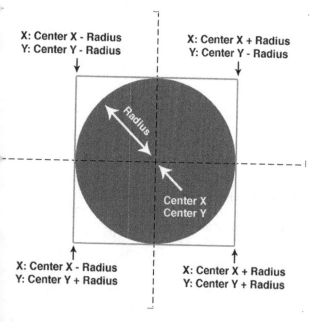

igure 8-3. *How to calculate the bounding box of a circle properly*

Additionally, you need to keep in mind what happens when the circle is bigger than four cells. In Listing 8-10, you increase the radius of the sphere from 10 pixels to 60, which means that it occupies a total area of nine cells. In order to get the area of the bounding rectangle, you just need to calculate the top left corner and bottom right corner.

Listing 8-10. Increasing the Radius

```
function paintPlayer(ctx, x, y) {

    var l = ((x - playerRadius) / cellWidth) >> 0,   // Grab the left corner
        r = ((x + playerRadius) / cellWidth) >> 0,   // Grab the right corner
        t = ((y - playerRadius) / cellHeight) >> 0,  // Grab the top corner
        b = ((y + playerRadius) / cellHeight) >> 0,  // Grab the bottom ccorner
        i = l,
        j = t;

    // Set the colour to a semi-transparent blue
    ctx.fillStyle = 'rgba(0, 0, 255, 0.05)';

    // Cycle between left-right and top-bottom, adding 1 for error correction
    for ( ; i < r + 1 ; ++i ) {

        for ( j = t ; j < b + 1 ; ++j ) {

            // Paint the square
            ctx.fillRect((i * cellWidth),
                         (j * cellHeight),
                         cellWidth,
                         cellHeight);

        }

    }
    // Set the colour to a dark red
    ctx.fillStyle = '#CC0000';

    // Draw the circle
    ctx.beginPath();
    ctx.arc(x, y, playerRadius, 0, 2 * Math.PI);
    ctx.fill();

}
```

Now that you can reliably detect which cells the circle's movements are affecting, you can proceed with the full implementation of the dirty rectangles algorithm.

In Listing 8-10, you implemented a routine within the update loop that checked whether the cells had to be repainted or not. So, instead of painting a square, all you need to do now is to set those cells as "modified." The flag check on the loop will take care of the rest. Listing 8-11 shows the relevant part to modify.

Listing 8-11. Setting Cells as Modified

```
function paintPlayer(ctx, x, y) {

    var l = ((x - playerRadius) / cellWidth) >> 0,   // Grab the left corner
        r = ((x + playerRadius) / cellWidth) >> 0,   // Grab the right corner
        t = ((y - playerRadius) / cellHeight) >> 0, // Grab the top corner
        b = ((y + playerRadius) / cellHeight) >> 0, // Grab the bottom corner
        i = t,
        j = l;

    // Adding 1 more row/col for error correction
    // Also, make sure that they are not bigger than gridCols and gridRows
    r = ((r + 1) > gridCols) ? r : (r + 1);
    b = ((b + 1) > gridRows) ? b : (b + 1);

    // Set the colour to a semi-transparent blue
    ctx.fillStyle = 'rgba(0, 0, 255, 0.05)';

    // Cycle between left-right and top-bottom
    for ( ; i < b ; ++i ) {

        for ( j = l ; j < r ; ++j ) {

            Grid[i][j] = 1;

        }

    }

    // Set the colour to a dark red
    ctx.fillStyle = '#CC0000';

    // Draw the circle
    ctx.beginPath();
    ctx.arc(x, y, playerRadius, 0, 2 * Math.PI);
    ctx.fill();
```

While this new code has been massively improved as compared to the last example, you will quickly notice that there are two bottlenecks in your update loop. The first one is caused by the loop that checks each cell's flag, and the other loop is found within the paintPlayer() function. On small grids you wouldn't even notice the bottleneck, but imagine what would happen if your grid were to be substantially larger, which leads to the next topic within this chapter.

Rendering Massive Grids

So far, your grids are not very big, so for now the performance seems to be good. However, how would this work with a bigger grid?

A beginner might attempt to improve the performance by doing something like the code in Listing 8-12.

Listing 8-12. Improving Grid Performance

```
var i = 0;

for ( ; i < gridRows ; ++i ) {

    for ( j = 0 ; j < gridCols ; ++j ) {

        if (withinScreen()) {

            if (Grid[i] === undefined) {
                Grid[i] = [];
            }

            // Flag all the cells as "modified"
            Grid[i][j] = 1;

        }

    }
}
```

While this approach might improve the performance, you will realize later what happens when the values of gridRows and gridCols surpass 1,000,000, 100,000, or as little as 10,000. In such cases, you would quickly notice that the real problem lies in the loops themselves, which are cycling the entire range of values between zero and gridRows/gridCols.

From Mario Bros to Megaman, Sonic the Hedgehog, or SimCity 2000, having a performant grid-rendering algorithm is a must-have in any game with a sufficiently large grid of values. Luckily, you have already figured out the "hardest" part of the problem, which is how to discover which cells are dirty and should be repainted; the rest is accounting for the missing stuff, such as the initialization loop, or how values are accessed in the rendering routine.

But let's see how you can make this even better. You're going to start by displaying a simple grid, as shown in Listing 8-13.

Listing 8-13. Displaying a Simple Grid

```
;(function() {

    var fps = 30, // Define the maximum number of FPS
        interval = 1000 / fps, // Calculate the interval in milliseconds
        delta = 0, // Variable initialisation
        previousTs = 0, // Variable initialisation
        shouldRepaint = true, // Set the repaint flag to true by default
        Grid = [], // Initialize an array where we're going to be storing the grid values
        gridCols = 1000, // Setup the number of columns of the grid
        gridRows = 1000, // Setup the number of rows of the grid
        viewportWidth = 640, // Setup the width of the viewport (the canvas)
        viewportHeight = 480, // Setup the height of the viewport (the canvas)
        cellWidth = 60,
        cellHeight = 30,
        canvas = document.querySelector('canvas'), // Grab a reference to the canvas object...
        ctx = canvas.getContext('2d'), // ...and its context
        i = 0, // Declare counters for the for loop we'll be using below
        j = 0; // Declare counters for the for loop we'll be using below
```

```
// Set the size of the canvas
canvas.width = viewportWidth;
canvas.height = viewportHeight;

// Initialize the grid. By default, it will be empty,
// so we'll need to "paint" all the cells
for ( ; i < gridRows ; ++i ) {

    for ( j = 0 ; j < gridCols ; ++j ) {

        if (Grid[i] === undefined) {
            Grid[i] = [];
        }

        // Flag all the cells as "modified"
        Grid[i][j] = 1;

    }

}

// Call the update loop for the first time
requestAnimationFrame(update);

function update(ts) {

    // Calculate the delta between the previous timestamp and the new one
    delta = ts - previousTs;

    // Performing a calculation here means that it will be
    // executed every 16.67 ms. at 60 frames per second

    // Check whether or not something needs to be repainted in the scene

    // Only execute the paint routine if the delta is bigger
    // than the interval and the shouldRepaint flag is set to true
    if (delta > interval && shouldRepaint) {

        // This bit will be executed only if it's bigger than the
        // interval and therefore will be executed every 33.33 ms.
        // at 30 frames per second (or the value of the "fps" variable)

        // Paint the "background"
        var i = 0,
            j = 0;

        for ( ; i < gridRows ; ++i ) {

            for ( j = 0 ; j < gridCols ; ++j ) {
```

```
            if (Grid[i][j] === 1) {

                paintCell(ctx,
                            j * cellWidth,
                            i * cellHeight,
                            cellWidth,
                            cellHeight);

                    // Print the current values of i and j for each cell
                ctx.fillStyle = '#000';
                ctx.font = '10px Arial';
                ctx.textAlign = 'center';
                ctx.fillText(i + ' ' + j,
                                j * cellWidth,
                                i * cellHeight);

                    // Set that position as painted
                Grid[i][j] = 0;

            }

        }

    }

    // There's no need to go through all this logic on every frame
    shouldRepaint = false;

    // Set the previous timestamp, which will be used
    // in the "next" loop.
    // Subtract the difference between the delta and the interval
    // to account for the time that it took the computer to
    // process the function.

    previousTs = ts - (delta % interval);

}

// Call requestAnimationFrame again
requestAnimationFrame(update);

}

function paintCell(ctx, x, y, w, h) {

    // Set the background colour to white
    ctx.fillStyle = '#fff';

    // Draw the background
    ctx.fillRect(x, y, w, h);
```

```
    // Set the border colour to gray
    ctx.strokeStyle = '#ccc';

    // Draw an outline
    ctx.strokeRect(x, y, w, h);

  }

}());
```

If again you run this in a web browser, you will quickly notice that this one will take considerable more time to initialize and render, but at the same time note that you have increased the number of rows and cells to 1,000. At this point, the reason why things are so slow is obvious: you're trying to cycle through every single one of the 1,000,000 cells.

To find out quickly how much time both processes (grid initialization and rendering) are taking, you can use the console.time(<string>) and console.timeEnd(<string>) functions, as shown in Listing 8-14.

Listing 8-14. Timing the Grid Initialization and Rendering Processes

```
// Initialize the grid. By default, it will be empty,
// so we'll need to "paint" all the cells
console.time("Grid Initialisation");
for ( ; i < gridRows ; ++i ) {

    for ( j = 0 ; j < gridCols ; ++j ) {

        if (Grid[i] === undefined) {
            Grid[i] = [];
        }

        // Flag all the cells as "modified"
        Grid[i][j] = 1;

    }

}


console.timeEnd("Grid Initialisation");
```

For example, on my computer the console reported the values shown in Figure 8-4.

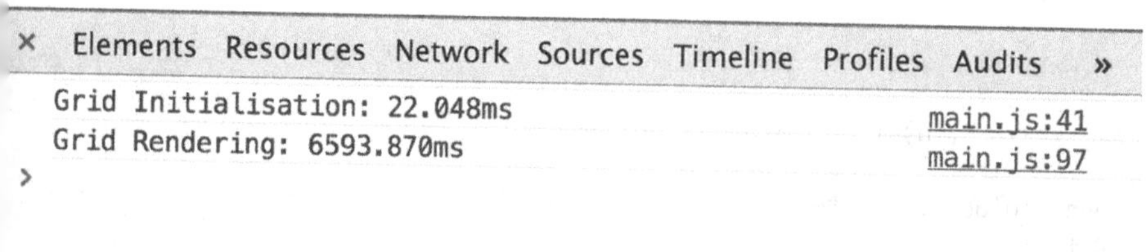

✕	Elements	Resources	Network	Sources	Timeline	Profiles	Audits	»

```
  Grid Initialisation: 22.048ms                          main.js:41
  Grid Rendering: 6593.870ms                             main.js:97
>
```

Figure 8-4. *A quick snapshot of how long it's taking the program to initialise and paint the grid*

As you can see in Figure 8-4, the initialization took approximately 22 ms, which is a lot of time but it's not worrying. The rendering, however, took more than 6.5 seconds. And keep in mind that that's on every frame.

I previously mentioned that an easy optimization would be to call only the paintCell() function if the current cell was within the viewport, so let's do that. All you need to do is to modify the code in Listing 8-14 to check that the cell is within function, which gets you the code in Listing 8-15.

Listing 8-15. Checking that a Cell Is Within a Function

```
console.time("Grid Rendering");
for ( ; i < gridRows ; ++i ) {

    for ( j = 0 ; j < gridCols ; ++j ) {

        if (Grid[i][j] === 1) {

            if ((j * cellWidth) >= 0 && (j * cellWidth) < viewportWidth &&
                (i * cellHeight) >= 0 && (i * cellHeight) < viewportHeight) {
                paintCell(ctx,
                        j * cellWidth,
                        i * cellHeight,
                        cellWidth,
                        cellHeight);

                // Print the current values of i and j for each cell
                ctx.fillStyle = '#000';
                ctx.font = '10px Arial';
                ctx.textAlign = 'center';
                ctx.fillText(i + ' ' + j,
                            j * cellWidth,
                            i * cellHeight);

                // Set that position as painted
                Grid[i][j] = 0;
            }

        }

    }
}
console.timeEnd("Grid Rendering");
```

Run this example and open the console. Note that you have made a remarkable improvement to the performance. For my part, I sped up the rendering routine from ~6.5 seconds to a mere ~8.5 ms.! See Figure 8-5.

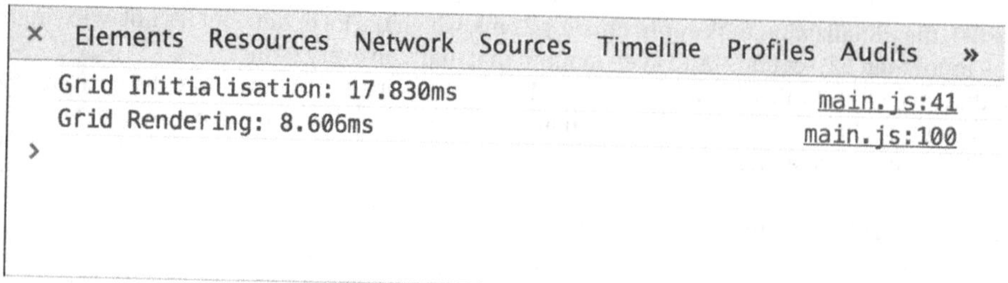

```
×   Elements  Resources  Network  Sources  Timeline  Profiles  Audits    »

    Grid Initialisation: 17.830ms                        main.js:41
    Grid Rendering: 8.606ms                              main.js:100
 >
```

Figure 8-5. *The modification resulted in a dramatic improvement to the grid rendering routine*

While this looks like a massive improvement (and it is) and you could stop here, you still have a long way to go until you reach a point where you can render your grid at 60 or 30 FPS. To make things even harder, let's increase the number of rows and columns to 100,000. Or better yet, let's go for the gold, and do it with 1,000,000 rows and columns for a grand total of 1,000,000,000,000 (trillion) cells. (Note: While it's highly unlikely that you'll ever need to store and render a trillion cells, it's nevertheless a nice exercise.)

So far, you know that your rendering routine will only paint the cells that can be displayed within the viewport. If that's the case, why is it taking so long? Where are those ~8.5 ms. coming from?

Let's do a detailed walkthrough of the update routine to understand what's going on. Start with the first few lines, shown in Listing 8-16.

Listing 8-16. Analyzing the Update Routine

```
function update(ts) {

    // Calculate the delta between the previous timestamp and the new one
    delta = ts - previousTs;
```

Declare the update() function, which takes a timestamp as a parameter, and refresh the value of the delta variable that is used later on to see if it's bigger than the interval (which is the number of milliseconds given by doing the operation 1000 ms/# FPS, which in this case is 30 FPS); see Listing 8-17.

Listing 8-17. Declaring the update() function

```
// Check whether or not something needs to be repainted in the scene

// Only execute the paint routine if the delta is bigger
// than the interval and the shouldRepaint flag is set to true
f (delta > interval && shouldRepaint) {
```

As mentioned, if the delta is bigger than the interval and the shouldRepaint flag is set to true, you're going to execute the code block in Listing 8-18.

Listing 8-18. Executing the Code Block when the Delta Is Bigger than the interval and the shouldRepaint flag Is Set to True

```
/ This bit will be executed only if it's bigger than the
/ interval and therefore will be executed every 33.33 ms.
/ at 30 frames per second (or the value of the "fps" variable)
```

```
// Paint the "background"
var i = 0,
    j = 0;

console.time("Grid Rendering");
```

You then declare two counters that you'll be using in two for() loops, as shown in Listing 8-19.

Listing 8-19. Declaring Two Counters that to Use in the Two for() Loops

```
for ( ; i < gridRows ; ++i ) {

    for ( j = 0 ; j < gridCols ; ++j ) {

        if (Grid[i][j] === 1) {

            // Only render the cell if it's within the viewport
            if ((j * cellWidth) >= 0 && (j * cellWidth) < viewportWidth &&
                (i * cellHeight) >= 0 && (i * cellHeight) < viewportHeight) {

                paintCell(ctx,
                        j * cellWidth,
                        i * cellHeight,
                        cellWidth,
                        cellHeight);

                // Print the current values of i and j for each cell
                ctx.fillStyle = '#000';
                ctx.font = '10px Arial';
                ctx.textAlign = 'center';
                ctx.fillText(i + ' ' + j,
                        j * cellWidth,
                        i * cellHeight);

                // Set that position as painted
                Grid[i][j] = 0;
            }

        }

    }

}
console.timeEnd("Grid Rendering");

// There's no need to go through all this logic on every frame
shouldRepaint = false;
```

Currently, the value of gridCols and gridRows is 1000. This basically means that your for() loops are iterating through every single one of the cells, checking if they are within the viewport one by one. Surely there must be a way to make things faster. And obviously, there is.

As you can see in Figure 8-6, both loops are also processing all of the cells that are outside the visible area. If you're not going to be displaying the cell, then it's not necessary to process it in the for() loop.

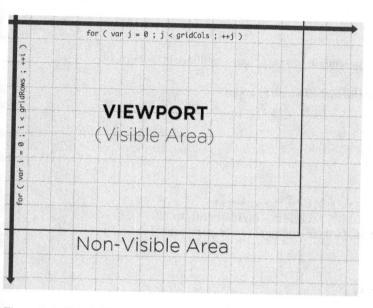

Figure 8-6. *The visible area of the viewport vs. the non-visible area*

As seen in Listing 8-20, one way to force your rendering routing to paint only the visible area of the viewport is to limit both loops to the dimensions of the viewport. In essence, the idea is to see what cell is being shown on the bottom right hand corner of the viewport, which will reveal what column and what row are the last ones.

Listing 8-20. Limiting Loops to the Dimensions of the Viewport

```
// Paint the "background"
var i = 0,
    j = 0,
    lastRow = (canvas.height / cellHeight) >> 0, // Grab the last row
    lastCol = (canvas.width / cellWidth) >> 0;    // Grab the last column

console.time("Grid Rendering");
for ( ; i < lastRow ; ++i ) {

    for ( j = 0 ; j < lastCol ; ++j ) {

        // ...

    }

}

console.timeEnd("Grid Rendering");
```

Additionally, you need to find a way to do something similar with the initialization routine, or to make it even more efficient; you can add a check within the update loop that if the cell is not initialized, you set a default value (see Listing 8-21).

Listing 8-21. Adding a Check to the Update Loop

```
console.time("Grid Rendering");
for ( ; i < lastRow ; ++i ) {

    for ( j = 0 ; j < lastCol ; ++j ) {

        // Handle the initialisation of new cells, in case they are not created
        if (Grid[i] === undefined) {

            // Has the row been declared?
            Grid[i] = [];

        }

        // Has the column been declared?
        if (Grid[i][j] === undefined) {

            // Flag all the cells as "modified" by default
            Grid[i][j] = 1;

        }

        // ..
    }

}
console.timeEnd("Grid Rendering");
```

And what's even better is that if you open the console, you'll notice that both initialization and rendering are now being done in just ~3 ms (see Figure 8-7).

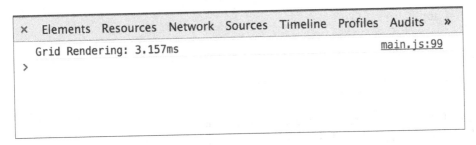

Figure 8-7. *A massive improvement in the performance of your rendering routine*

Now that you can potentially initialize and render a trillion cells efficiently, you need to add a way to scroll through the grid. One way to approach this problem is to add scrollX and scrollY variables that allow you to offset the starting and ending points of the loop, then you can add an event listener that would allow you to increase or decrease the values of scrollX and scrollY, as seen in Listing 8-22.

Listing 8-22. Adding Variables to Allow You to Offset the Starting and Ending Points of a Loop

```
var scrollX = 0, // Offset in the X axis
    scrollY = 0; // Offset in the Y axis

// Listen for keypresses
window.addEventListener('keydown', function(e) {

    switch (e.keyCode) {
        case 37: // Left
        case 65: // A

            // Make sure that we can't scroll past our minimum value (0)
            if (scrollX > 0) {
                scrollX -= 10;
            }

            break;
        case 39: // Right
        case 68: // D

            // Make sure that we can't scroll past our maximum value
            // (Width of the Cell * Number of Columns)
            if (scrollX < (cellWidth * gridCols)) {
                scrollX += 10;
            }

            break;
        case 38: // Up
        case 87: // W

            // Make sure that we can't scroll past our minimum value (0)
            if (scrollY > 0) {
                scrollY -= 10;
            }

            break;
        case 40: // Down
        case 83: // S

            // Make sure that we can't scroll past our maximum value
            // (Height of the Cell * Number of Rows)
            if (scrollX < (cellHeight * gridRows)) {
                scrollY += 10;
            }

            break;
    }
, false);
```

Now that you have worked out a method to scroll around the map by offsetting things in the X-axis and Y-axis, let's see how you can adapt that to your current code. If you go back to the last code that you used in your update loop, you'll notice that the starting row and column is hard-coded to 0, meaning that it will ignore the value of the offset. As a reference, here's what you were doing before:

```
// Paint the "background"
var i = 0,
    j = 0,
    lastRow = (canvas.height / cellHeight) >> 0, // Grab the last row
    lastCol = (canvas.width / cellWidth) >> 0;    // Grab the last column
```

"Fixing" the lastRow and lastCol values is easy enough, all you need to do add the values of scrollX and scrollY in the following way:

```
lastRow = ((canvas.height + scrollY) / cellHeight) >> 0, // Grab the last row
lastCol = ((canvas.width + scrollX) / cellWidth) >> 0;   // Grab the last column
```

But what about the starting values for i and j? In that case, you can divide the value of scrollX and scrollY by cellWidth and cellHeight, like this:

```
i = (scrollY / cellHeight) >> 0,
j = (scrollX / cellWidth) >> 0;
```

However, you also need to keep in mind that as you modify the offset, you might have to show cells that weren't showing up before, which means that you'll need to mark them as "modified" so that in the next loop they get redrawn, as shown in Listing 8-23.

Listing 8-23. Marking Cells as Modified

```
// Listen for keypresses
window.addEventListener('keydown', function(e) {

    switch (e.keyCode) {
        case 37: // Left
        case 65: // A

            // Make sure that we can't scroll past our minimum value (0)
            if (scrollX > 0) {
                scrollX -= 10;
            }

            break;
        case 39: // Right
        case 68: // D

            // Make sure that we can't scroll past our maximum value
            // (Width of the Cell * Number of Columns)
            if (scrollX < (cellWidth * gridCols)) {
                scrollX += 10;
            }
```

```
                  break;
            case 38: // Up
            case 87: // W

                // Make sure that we can't scroll past our minimum value (0)
                if (scrollY > 0) {
                    scrollY -= 10;
                }

                  break;
            case 40: // Down
            case 83: // S

                // Make sure that we can't scroll past our maximum value
                // (Height of the Cell * Number of Rows)
                if (scrollX < (cellHeight * gridRows)) {
                    scrollY += 10;
                }

                  break;
        }

    // Set those cells as "modified", therefore we need to redraw them
    var i = (scrollY / cellHeight) >> 0,
        j = (scrollX / cellWidth) >> 0,
        lastRow = ((canvas.height + scrollY) / cellHeight) >> 0, // Grab the last row
        lastCol = ((canvas.width + scrollX) / cellWidth) >> 0;   // Grab the last column

    for ( ; i < lastRow ; ++i ) {

        for ( j = ((scrollX / cellWidth) >> 0) ; j < lastCol ; ++j ) {

            // Handle the initialisation of new cells, in case they are not created
            if (Grid[i] === undefined) {

                // Has the row been declared?
                Grid[i] = [];
            }

            Grid[i][j] = 1;

        }

    }

    shouldRepaint = true;

, false);
```

One other thing that you need to keep in mind is that when you draw the cells, you'll need to take scrollX and scrollY into account, which means that the following code

```
paintCell(ctx,
        j * cellWidth,
        i * cellHeight,
        cellWidth,
        cellHeight);

// Print the current values of i and j for each cell
ctx.fillStyle = '#000';
ctx.font = '10px Arial';
ctx.textAlign = 'center';
ctx.fillText(i + ' ' + j,
            j * cellWidth,
            i * cellHeight);
```

will now look like this (notice the addition of the scrollX/scrollY variables):

```
paintCell(ctx,
        (j * cellWidth) - scrollX,
        (i * cellHeight) - scrollY,
        cellWidth,
        cellHeight);

// Print the current values of i and j for each cell
ctx.fillStyle = '#000';
ctx.font = '10px Arial';
ctx.textAlign = 'center';
ctx.fillText(i + ' ' + j,
            (j * cellWidth) - scrollX,
            (i * cellHeight) - scrollY);
```

The results speak for themselves. See Figure 8-8.

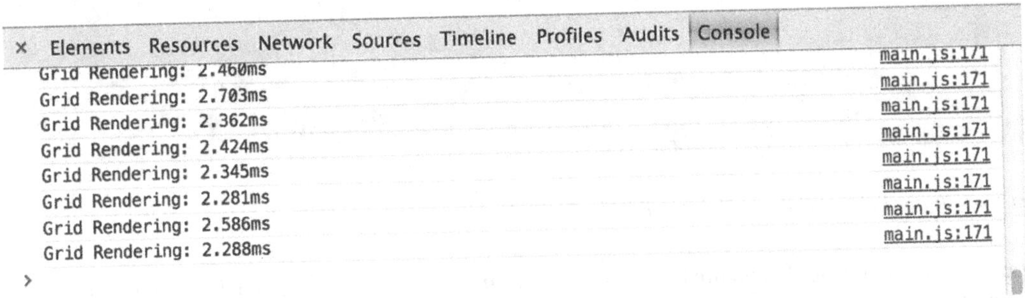

| × | Elements | Resources | Network | Sources | Timeline | Profiles | Audits | Console |

```
Grid Rendering: 2.460ms                                    main.js:171
Grid Rendering: 2.703ms                                    main.js:171
Grid Rendering: 2.362ms                                    main.js:171
Grid Rendering: 2.424ms                                    main.js:171
Grid Rendering: 2.345ms                                    main.js:171
Grid Rendering: 2.281ms                                    main.js:171
Grid Rendering: 2.586ms                                    main.js:171
Grid Rendering: 2.288ms                                    main.js:171
>
```

Figure 8-8. *Results of Listing 8-23 and Modifications*

You can find the fully animated player example, complete with a dirty rectangles-enabled rendering routine, in the chapter folder.

One of the main benefits of using grids is that they are extremely easy to use, and have an almost infinite number of potential applications. This is especially true in video game development. They can be used to draw arcade games, platformers, board games, RTSs, and RPGs or to do complex collision detection, among many other uses.

Nevertheless, sometimes you may find yourself trying to solve a similar situation in a scenario that doesn't use grids at all. In such case, you might find the next technique to be extremely useful.

Displaying Animations in Extremely Large Viewports

So far you've learned how to efficiently cycle and paint massive grids, but this begs the question: What happens if you need to do something similar on an extremely large screen? Consider the example shown in Figure 8-9.

Figure 8-9. Just a big image being painted on a canvas object

The background image being used in Figure 8-9 has a size of 1920 x 1080, which means that it would take most devices a fair amount of time to paint it on the screen. For example, on my computer (a fairly high-end Retina MacBook Pro with 16GB of RAM and a 1024MB video card), it took Chrome 22.113 ms to paint that image within the canvas. You already know that if you want to render the program at 60 FPS, you need to execute the update loop in less than 16.67 ms (1000 milliseconds/60 frames per second), so this basically means that you won't be able to repaint the scene at 60 FPS.

You can try it yourself to see how much time it'd take your computer to render an image that big. The example in Listing 8-24 loads a massive image and attempts to paint it on the canvas every 33.33 ms.

Listing 8-24. Painting a Large Image

```
;(function() {

    var fps = 30, // Define the maximum number of FPS
        interval = 1000 / fps, // Calculate the interval in milliseconds
        delta = 0, // Variable initialisation
        previousTs = 0; // Variable initialisation
        shouldRepaint = true, // Set the repaint flag to true by default
        viewportWidth = 640, // Setup the width of the viewport (the canvas)
        viewportHeight = 480, // Setup the height of the viewport (the canvas)
        canvas = document.querySelector('canvas'), // Grab a reference to the canvas object...
        ctx = canvas.getContext('2d'), // ...and its context
        backgroundTexture = new Image(); // Declare a new image object that we'll be using to store
our background texture

    // Set the default size of the canvas (it will be resized when the background image is loaded)
    canvas.width = viewportWidth;
    canvas.height = viewportHeight;

    // Load the background texture
    backgroundTexture.src = 'texture.jpg';
    backgroundTexture.addEventListener('load', function() {

        // Resize the canvas to the size of the image
        canvas.width = backgroundTexture.width;
        canvas.height = backgroundTexture.height;

        // Call requestAnimationFrame as soon as we make sure the image is loaded
        requestAnimationFrame(update);

    }, false);

    function update(ts) {

        // Calculate the delta between the previous timestamp and the new one
        delta = ts - previousTs;

        // Performing a calculation here means that it will be
        // executed every 16.67 ms. at 60 frames per second

        // Check whether or not something needs to be repainted in the scene

        // Only execute the paint routine if the delta is bigger
        // than the interval and the shouldRepaint flag is set to true
        if (delta > interval && shouldRepaint) {
```

```
        // This bit will be executed only if it's bigger than the
        // interval and therefore will be executed every 33.33 ms.
        // at 30 frames per second (or the value of the "fps" variable)

        console.time("Painting Scene");

        // Paint the image on the canvas
        ctx.drawImage(backgroundTexture,
                      0,
                      0);

        console.timeEnd("Painting Scene");

        // There's no need to go through all this logic on every frame
        shouldRepaint = false;

        // Set the previous timestamp, which will be used
        // in the "next" loop.
        // Subtract the difference between the delta and the interval
        // to account for the time that it took the computer to
        // process the function.

        previousTs = ts - (delta % interval);

    }

    // Call requestAnimationFrame again
    requestAnimationFrame(update);

    }

}());
```

Obviously, in order to repaint this background 60 times per second you would need one of two possible options, either a faster machine or a better painting algorithm.

But what if you were using a much slower device (such as a smartphone)? While many people would consider that to be impossible, it's always nice to have one more trick up your sleeve.

Let's suppose that besides the background, you also wanted to display a bouncing ball on your canvas. In that case, there are two potential solutions. The first solution consists of handling the background and the animations in two different viewports; therefore you would only need to clean and update the foreground canvas, leaving the background canvas unchanged, as explained in Figure 8-10. While it's certainly not very elegant, this solution is fit for used in a scenario where the background won't be suffering any modifications. In such case, the background canvas doesn't even need to be a canvas at all; it could be any other markup element that allows you to display an image such as a <div>).

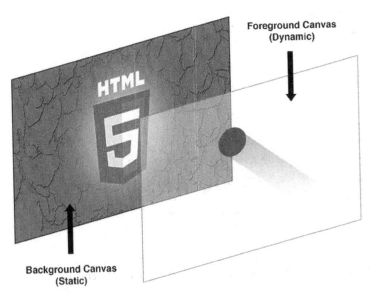

Figure 8-10. *One easy method to avoid having to repaint the big image on every frame is to keep it "static" and completely separate from the actual, dynamic canvas where you'll be painting the animation*

Like in the "Dirty Rectangles" section, the second solution consists of only repainting the portion of the image that was overwritten by the moving object (in this case, the ball). The biggest advantage of this second approach is that it will allow you to not only paint the ball, but also to replace small bits of the background as well. A good example is a background of a forest where some of the trees are moving while the rest of the image remains static.

Usually, there are two ways to handle this scenario. The first approach, which is the one you've been using so far, consists of painting an image directly into the canvas in your DOM tree. Then, in order to grab a portion of the image, you would just need to use a reference to your image object. But what happens if your background is composed of more than one image? For example, let's suppose that your background is composed of three different images, one that has a sky texture, another one that has clouds, and another one with trees (the trees, for example, could be generated and placed procedurally). In such a case, one of the best approaches is to work with an in-memory canvas that allows you to compose the full background in an in-memory Canvas, and then treat that canvas as a regular image, as displayed in Figure 8-11.

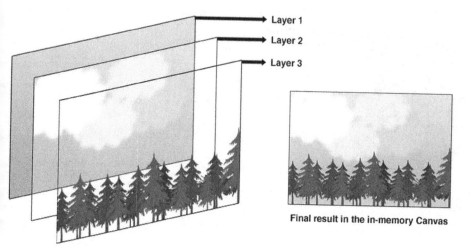

Layer 1

Layer 2

Layer 3

Final result in the in-memory Canvas

Figure 8-11. *If you have three different images, you can merge them together in memory and handle them as a single, unified, layer*

In order to show how this would work, let's start by defining some variables that you'll be using to demonstrate how to implement the bouncing ball example (see Listing 8-25).

Listing 8-25. Defining Variables to Implement the Bouncing Ball Example

```
var ballRadius = 20,                      // Set the radius of the ball
    ballVelocityX = 15,                   // Velocity of the ball in the X axis
    ballVelocityY = 15,                   // Velocity of the ball in the Y axis
    ballPositionX = canvas.width / 2,     // Position of the ball in the X axis
    ballPositionY = canvas.height / 2;    // Position of the ball in the Y axis
```

Now you're going to create a paintBall() function that paints the ball in the canvas; see Listing 8-26.

Listing 8-26. paintball() Function

```
function paintBall(ctx, r, x, y) {

    // Set the background colour to yellow
    ctx.fillStyle = '#ff0';

    // Draw the circle
    ctx.beginPath();
    ctx.arc(x, y, r, 0, 2 * Math.PI);
    ctx.fill();

    // Make sure to trigger a repaint
    shouldRepaint = true;
```

And finally, you're going to integrate the function within your update loop, as shown in Listing 8-27.

Listing 8-27. Integrating the paintBall() Function in the Update Loop

```
function update(ts) {

    // Calculate the delta between the previous timestamp and the new one
    delta = ts - previousTs;

    // Performing a calculation here means that it will be
    // executed every 16.67 ms. at 60 frames per second

    // Check whether or not something needs to be repainted in the scene

    // Only execute the paint routine if the delta is bigger
    // than the interval and the shouldRepaint flag is set to true
    if (delta > interval && shouldRepaint) {

        // This bit will be executed only if it's bigger than the
        // interval and therefore will be executed every 33.33 ms.
        // at 30 frames per second (or the value of the "fps" variable)

        // There's no need to go through all this logic on every frame
        shouldRepaint = false;

        console.time("Painting Scene");

        // Paint the image on the canvas
        ctx.drawImage(backgroundTexture,
                    0,
                    0);

        // If the position of the ball in the X axis minus its radius
        // multipled by 2 is less than 0, or it's bigger than the width
        // of the canvas, invert the velocity
        if (ballPositionX - (ballRadius * 2) < 0 ||
            ballPositionX + (ballRadius * 2) > canvas.width) {
            ballVelocityX *= -1;
        }

        // If the position of the ball in the Y axis minus its radius
        // multipled by 2 is less than 0, or it's bigger than the width
        // of the canvas, invert the velocity
        if (ballPositionY - (ballRadius * 2) < 0 ||
            ballPositionY + (ballRadius * 2) > canvas.height) {
            ballVelocityY *= -1;
        }
```

```
    // Add the velocity to the position in the X and Y axis
    ballPositionX += ballVelocityX;
    ballPositionY += ballVelocityY;

    // Paint the ball
    paintBall(ctx, ballRadius, ballPositionX, ballPositionY);

    console.timeEnd("Painting Scene");

    // Set the previous timestamp, which will be used
    // in the "next" loop.
    // Subtract the difference between the delta and the interval
    // to account for the time that it took the computer to
    // process the function.

    previousTs = ts - (delta % interval);

  }


  // Call requestAnimationFrame again
  requestAnimationFrame(update);

}
```

So far, the background is being rendered on every frame; if you place it outside the update loop (therefore, it will only be painted once), you will notice that something like what you see in Figure 8-12.

Figure 8-12. As the yellow ball moves around the canvas and bounces against its limits, it leaves a trail

Like in previous "Dirty Rectangles" section, the reason why this happens is because you're not cleaning up after yourself when you draw the ball in a new position. Luckily, there's an easy and highly efficient way to solve this problem, which consists of grabbing the previous portion of the image that was covered by the ball.

The magic behind this approach is provided by an alternative use of the drawImage() method of the Canvas object. So far, when you've used drawImage(), you just specified three parameters: the image object itself, and the coordinates in the X- and Y-axis. However, this method also accepts two additional uses:

- One method allows you to scale up or down the image by specifying the target width and height, like this:

```
drawImage(imageObject,
          sourceX,
          sourceY,
          newWidth,
          newHeight);
```

- The final method allows you to draw a portion of the image object by specifying

```
drawImage(imageObject,
sourceX,
sourceY,
sourceWidth,
sourceHeight,
destinationX,
destinationY,
destinationWidth,
destinationHeight);
```

Therefore, this will allow you to do the following, as shown in Listing 8-28.

Listing 8-28. Applying the drawImage() Method of the Canvas Object

```
// Before changing the values of ballPositionX and ballPositionY:
// Redraw the previous portion of the background that
// was overdraw by the ball
ctx.drawImage(backgroundTexture,
              ballPositionX - ballRadius,
              ballPositionY - ballRadius,
              (ballRadius * 2),
              (ballRadius * 2),
              ballPositionX - ballRadius,
              ballPositionY - ballRadius,
              (ballRadius * 2),
              (ballRadius * 2));

// Add the velocity to the position in the X and Y axis
ballPositionX += ballVelocityX;
ballPositionY += ballVelocityY;

// Paint the ball
paintBall(ctx, ballRadius, ballPositionX, ballPositionY);
```

But what if you wanted to somehow display an animation in your background? One possible way to approach this task would be to use the technique described in the next section of this chapter.

Color Cycling

A very particular problem in video game development is how to display animations over large areas. As you have seen earlier in this chapter, it's neither practical nor efficient to create a spritesheet of a large sprite because of the cost associated with having to repaint the entire background. Another big problem with the spritesheet-based approach is the massive memory requirements to store it.

In the past, game development companies such as Maxis or LucasArts relied on a technique called color cycling (also known as palette shifting) to display animations in backgrounds in games such as SimCity 2000 or The Secret of Monkey Island.

As the name implies, the technique consists of cycling colors of certain pixels through a given palette to give the impression that something is moving on the background. In order to implement it, you'll be using a texture similar to that shown in Figure 8-13.

Figure 8-13. *The word "HTML5" seems to be painted with five different colors, which you'll use as your palette*

In order to implement color cycling using the texture shown in Figure 8-13, the portion of the texture that will be changing is painted with six particular colors. Usually, color cycling requires a custom file that not only allows you to store color information, but also additional metadata. The metadata is used to indicate which pixels are grouped together, in what order, what palette to use, and how that palette should be cycled. For example, in Figure 8-14, each number corresponds to a given color in your palette.

Method 1

1	2	3	4	5	6	1	2	3	4	5	6

Method 2

1	2	3	4	5	6	5	4	3	2	1

Figure 8-14. *In this figure, each number corresponds to a given colour in your palette*

For the sake of simplicity (discussing the creation of a custom image format is outside the scope of this chapter), you're going to generate the metadata dynamically by cycling through every pixel of your texture. As such, it needs to be said that one of the biggest downsides with this technique is that it's only fit to be used with 8-bit images (256 colors). Another word of caution is that, as you need to dynamically discover and change the palette, your approach will be considerably slower than with using a custom image format.

You're going to start by defining four variables:

- `backgroundTexture = new Image()` will be used to store your image

- `pixelGroups = {}` will be used to group pixels of a same color together

- `colourIndexes = ['4766b5', '3e589a', '354c87', '2e4276', '2a3c6c', '22325a']` will be your palette, as shown in Figure 8-13

- `currentColourOrder = colourIndexes.slice(0)` will be used to cycle through all the colors in your palette

Then, as soon as your image is loaded, you'll need to read all the pixels of the image to group them together in the `pixelGroups` variable, like this:

```
// Load the background texture
backgroundTexture.src = 'texture.gif';
backgroundTexture.addEventListener('load', function() {

    var i = 0,
        j = 0,
        backgroundTextureData = null;
```

In order to read the colors of a given pixel, you'll need to resort to using a method of the Canvas object called `getImageData()`, but before doing that, you'll need to paint the texture in the canvas first, as shown in Listing 8-29.

Listing 8-29. Painting the Texture in the Canvas Object

```
// Paint the image on the canvas for the first time)
ctx.drawImage(backgroundTexture,
              0,
              0);

  // Grab the image data using the getImageData() method
backgroundTextureData = ctx.getImageData(0, 0, backgroundTexture.width, backgroundTexture.height);
backgroundTextureData = backgroundTextureData.data;

// Resize the canvas to the size of the image
canvas.width = backgroundTexture.width;
canvas.height = backgroundTexture.height;
```

Here comes the interesting part; you'll need to cycle through each pixel of the image to get the color data, as shown in Listing 8-30.

Listing 8-30. Cycling Through each Pixel

```
// Group pixels by colour
// (keep in mind that there's a much faster way to cycle through
// all these pixels using typed arrays, I'm keeping it "simple" for
// the sake of clarity
for ( ; i < backgroundTexture.height ; ++i ) {

    for ( j = 0 ; j < backgroundTexture.width ; ++j ) {
```

14

```
        var red = backgroundTextureData[((backgroundTexture.width * i) + j) * 4],
            green = backgroundTextureData[((backgroundTexture.width * i) + j) * 4 + 1],
            blue = backgroundTextureData[((backgroundTexture.width * i) + j) * 4 + 2],
            hex = numberToHexadecimalValue(red) + numberToHexadecimalValue(green) +
    numberToHexadecimalValue(blue);


        if (pixelGroups[hex] === undefined) {
            pixelGroups[hex] = [];
        }


        pixelGroups[hex].push({ x: i, y: j });


    }


}
```

What you're really doing here is using the hex code of the color as a key, and then you're storing each pixel as a small object with x and y coordinates. This will be extremely useful later on when you need to cycle through it. Finally, you'll need to paint the texture on the canvas again, and call the update loop, as shown in Listing 8-31.

Listing 8-31. Painting the texture in the Canvas object and calling the Updalet Loop

```
// Paint the image on the canvas again
ctx.drawImage(backgroundTexture,
                0,
                0);


// Call requestAnimationFrame as soon as we make sure the image is loaded
requestAnimationFrame(update);

}, false);
```

Within your update loop, you're going to shift the colors by one, placing the first item as the last one, as shown in Listing 8-32.

Listing 8-32. Shifting Colors in the Update Loop

```
// Shift the order by one item (grab the first value and put it last)
var firstValue = currentColourOrder[0];

// Remove the first value of the order array
currentColourOrder.splice(0, 1);

// And place it last
currentColourOrder.push(firstValue);
```

Once you've done that, you'll need to replace the pixels in the last order, with the new colors. In order to do this, you're going to prepare a utility function called paintPixels() that does just that, as shown in Listing 8-33.

Listing 8-33. paintPixels() Function

```
function paintPixels(newColour, pixels) {

    var i = 0;

    for ( ; i < pixels.length ; ++i ) {

        ctx.fillStyle = '#' + newColour;

        ctx.fillRect(pixels[i].y,
                     pixels[i].x,
                     1,
                     1);

    }
}
```

As you can see, the paintPixels() function accepts two arguments, the first one with the new color, and the second one with the array of pixels that need to be repainted. All you need to do now is to cycle the new order and call the function, as shown in Listing 8-34.

Listing 8-34. Calling the paintPixels() Function

```
for ( ; i < currentColourOrder.length ; ++i ) {

    paintPixels(currentColourOrder[i], pixelGroups[colourIndexes[i]]);

}
```

This entire example can be found within the chapter folder.

Conclusion

In this chapter, I've only covered a handful of the performance-improvement techniques used in old-school video games. It was my intention not only to share some of these things with the readers of this book, but, as an author, also to inspire you to think outside the box when you believe that something can't be done.

■ ■ ■

CHAPTER 9

Optimizing WebGL Usage

Don Olmstead, Software Engineer, Sony Network Entertainment

As hardware evolved, games went from two-dimensional affairs into the third dimension. This evolution also happened in the browser. Although two-dimensional rendering could be done through the use of the Canvas application programming interface (API) it wasn't until the Web Graphics Library (WebGL) debuted that the graphics hardware was actually exposed to a lower level within the context of the browser. This API has now been implemented by every major browser vendor, making it possible to create a fully three-dimensional game without relying on a plug-in.

Game developers are power users of the platform. To push what's possible, they need to get as much work done as is possible within the context of a frame. To do this, they optimize their code for the platform it's running on top of. The browser is no different in this regard. To optimize a game on this platform, it's important to understand the inner workings of the hardware and play to its strengths.

With WebGL it's especially important to understand what's going on under the hood. The API, although providing a low-level interface, has an overhead that is much more significant than the equivalent native code. By mastering its usage, the amount of time spent in the API can be minimized, leaving more time for the other game systems to do their work.

To show how to optimize the rendering side of a WebGL application effectively, this chapter will present the following information:

- What happens when a WebGL call is invoked, including the overhead behind various security checks and the browser's rendering model

- How WebGL works internally and how this can be used to minimize the number of calls to the API

- The sketching out of a rendering framework on top of WebGL that ensures optimal usage

- Tools that can be used to prove that the rendering is ideal

- Additional functionality present in extensions that can further reduce the number of calls to WebGL

- General techniques that can be used when presenting a scene to the renderer

The Anatomy of a WebGL Call

To learn how to optimize an application's usage of WebGL, it's important to understand what happens within the browser whenever a call is made. Although at its core, WebGL is a way of exposing Open Graphics Library for Embedded Systems (OpenGL ES) to the Web, the implementation is more complicated than just providing low-level bindings to the graphics API. WebGL has to slot into the general rendering of web content within the browser, and it has to ensure that security is not compromised through its usage. Thus, the operation within the browser is more elaborate than it would seem at first glance.

To illustrate the steps that take place during the execution of a WebGL call, the behavior of Blink, the rendering engine that powers Google Chrome, can be highlighted (see Figure 9-1). The implementation presented is current at the time of writing; however, the internals of Blink are subject to change at any time. Even if the internals did change, or if another browser's functionality were examined, the gist would be roughly the same.

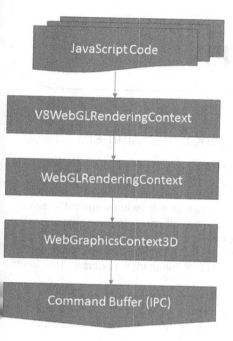

Figure 9-1. *Blink data flow*

For those interested in perusing the actual implementation, there is the Chromium code search, which can be queried for the classes in question.

Listing 9-1 sketches out a general logic to rendering a geometry to the screen. Now, what happens within the browser when the drawArrays call is made? To answer that, the call's flow through the browser will be traced through each layer.

Listing 9-1. Drawing a Model

```
function drawModel() {
  bindShaderProgram();
  bindTextures();
  bindVertexBuffer();

  // Invoke the draw call
  gl.drawArrays(gl.TRIANGLE_STRIP, 0, 16);
```

The lifetime of a WebGL call begins within the context of the scripting language's virtual machine; in the case of Blink, this is fulfilled within the V8 JavaScript engine. Any API the browser supports requires there to be glue between the script's execution context and the browser. The cohesion between the two is specified by the Web **Interface Definition Language** (Web IDL) format, a standard that describes interfaces, which are to be implemented within a web browser, as shown in Listing 9-2.

Listing 9-2. WebGLRenderingContext, IDL Portion

```
interface WebGLRenderingContext {
  void drawArrays(GLenum mode, GLint first, GLsizei count);
  void drawElements(GLenum mode, GLsizei count, GLenum type, GLintptr offset);
}
```

The Web IDL specification outlines the interface available to the scripting language. This specification is used by the browser to determine how data should be marshalled between them and the virtual machine. In general, this layer is generated automatically during the build process, though some bindings are created by hand. The result of this operation within Blink is the V8WebGLRenderingContext, the first layer that the WebGL call passes through.

WebGL puts additional restraints on top of the OpenGL ES specification to ensure a secure environment, and the purpose of the WebGLRenderingContext is to verify that this contract is not broken. In the case of a drawArray call, the browser will verify that the arguments passed in are correct by checking that a valid offset and count were supplied and that the current render state is legitimate. If everything checks out, then it's off to the next layer, the WebGraphicsContext3D.

From here on, the explanation gets very Blink specific, as it has its own ideas on how compositing should be accomplished within a browser. Because of this, some of the finer points will be glossed over;for more information, refer to the Google document *GPU Accelerated Compositing in Chrome* (http://www.chromium.org/developers/design-documents/gpu-accelerated-compositing-in-chrome), which goes into considerable detail on the compositing architecture.

As mentioned earlier WebGL is not the only portion of the browser that utilizes hardware acceleration; Blink may promote portions of the page to render on the graphics card. The GraphicsContext3D class handles the needs of any portion of the browser requiring hardware accelerated rendering, furnishing an interface very similar to OpenGL.

At some point in the rendering process, the underlying OpenGL implementation has to be hit, yet that does not actually occur on the same process that the WebGL command originated in. Instead, the interaction with the graphics processing unit (GPU) is architected to occur on a completely different process. The aptly named GPU process handles the hardware-accelerated rendering, which receives its marching orders through the renderer process. The WebGraphicsContext3D populates a command buffer in a shared memory location that can be accessed by both processes, thereby giving the GPU process the required steps to render the scene properly.

Over on the GPU process side, the populated command buffer is vetted yet again. This is for security purposes, as the GPU process does not trust the renderer process, because the GPU process has no way to determine if it was compromised when loading a site. Once verified, each command is shipped off to the OpenGL implementation of the platform. For platforms other than Windows the command reaches the graphics card's driver. On Windows the command goes through an additional transformation by the Almost Native Graphics Layer Engine (ANGLE) library, which converts the OpenGL commands into their DirectX counterparts. Only after all these steps does the WebGL command reach the actual graphics card.

These steps occur whenever a WebGL call is made. This overhead cannot be avoided and is essentially the penalty you have to pay for doing three-dimensionality in the browser. However, this cost is not a deal breaker; it just means that one has to be mindful of how the API is being used in order to maximize performance. What that boils down to is minimizing the number of calls made to the API while rendering the scene. To accomplish this at this low level, the inner workings of WebGL need to be illuminated.

How WebGL Works

The most important thing to know about WebGL is that it is a state machine. The vast majority of the commands available will modify either the entire state of the rendering or the internal state of an object provided through WebGL. This knowledge is key to minimizing the number of calls made by the application.

To illustrate this point a simple scene can be profiled. One of the easiest examples, a "hello world" of sorts for WebGL, is the spinning cube rendered with a texture (see Listing 9-3). Although not a solid, real-world example, the cube showcases how calls can be reduced, owing to state being retained.

14

Listing 9-3. Rendering a Cube

```
function drawScene() {
  // Clear the buffers.
  gl.clearColor(0.0, 0.0, 0.0, 1.0);
  gl.clearDepth(1.0);
  gl.clear(gl.COLOR_BUFFER_BIT | gl.DEPTH_BUFFER_BIT);

  // Set the depth test
  gl.enable(gl.DEPTH_TEST);
  gl.depthFunc(gl.LEQUAL);

  // Create the perspective matrix
  perspectiveMatrix = makePerspective(45, 640.0/480.0, 0.1, 100.0);

  // Create the model view matrix
  loadIdentity();
  mvTranslate([-0.0, 0.0, -6.0]);
  mvPushMatrix();
  mvRotate(cubeRotation, [1, 0, 1]);

  // Set the program and its uniforms
  gl.useProgram(shaderProgram);

  var pUniform = gl.getUniformLocation(shaderProgram, "uPMatrix");
  gl.uniformMatrix4fv(pUniform, false, new Float32Array(perspectiveMatrix.flatten()));

  var mvUniform = gl.getUniformLocation(shaderProgram, "uMVMatrix");
  gl.uniformMatrix4fv(mvUniform, false, new Float32Array(mvMatrix.flatten()));

  gl.uniform1i(gl.getUniformLocation(shaderProgram, "uSampler"), 0);

  // Specify the texture.
  gl.activeTexture(gl.TEXTURE0);
  gl.bindTexture(gl.TEXTURE_2D, cubeTexture);
  gl.texParameteri(gl.TEXTURE_2D, gl.TEXTURE_MAG_FILTER, gl.LINEAR);
  gl.texParameteri(gl.TEXTURE_2D, gl.TEXTURE_MIN_FILTER, gl.LINEAR_MIPMAP_NEAREST);

  // Set the position for the vertices
  gl.bindBuffer(gl.ARRAY_BUFFER, cubeVerticesBuffer);
  gl.enableVertexAttribArray(gl.getAttribLocation(shaderProgram, "aVertexPosition"));
  gl.vertexAttribPointer(vertexPositionAttribute, 3, gl.FLOAT, false, 0, 0);

  // Set the texture coordinates attribute for the vertices
  gl.bindBuffer(gl.ARRAY_BUFFER, cubeVerticesTextureCoordBuffer);
  gl.enableVertexAttribArray(gl.getAttribLocation(shaderProgram, "aTextureCoord"));
  gl.vertexAttribPointer(textureCoordAttribute, 2, gl.FLOAT, false, 0, 0);
```

```
// Set the index buffer
gl.bindBuffer(gl.ELEMENT_ARRAY_BUFFER, cubeVerticesIndexBuffer);

// Draw the elements
gl.drawElements(gl.TRIANGLES, 36, gl.UNSIGNED_SHORT, 0);

// Restore the original matrix
mvPopMatrix();

// Update the rotation of the cube
updateRotation();
}
```

The naive implementation goes through the following steps:

1. Sets the values for clearing the screen's frame buffer

2. Clears the screen's frame buffer

3. Enables the depth test

4. Binds the shader program

5. Sets the uniforms for the matrices

6. Sets the texture unit for the sampler

7. Binds the texture to the specified unit

8. Sets the texture properties

9. Binds the vertex buffers

10. Sets up each vertex's attributes

11. Binds the index buffer

12. Issues a draw call

This results in 25 calls to WebGL. In reality only three of these calls are needed with each frame: the clearing, setting the model-view-projection matrix (MVP matrix) uniform as the cube's rotation is animating, and the draw call. The rest of the calls can be done once, during initialization. This is because the state of those calls is retained, so making them again with each frame results in redundant operations.

All calls contained in Table 9-1 will modify the state of an object or the rendering context as a whole.

Table 9-1. *Functions That Modify State*

State	Functions		
Global	blendColor blendEquation blendEquationSeparate blendFunc blendFuncSeparate depthFunc stencilFunc stencilFuncSeparate stencilOp stencilOpSeparate enableVertexAttribArray	clearColor clearDepth clearStencil colorMask depthMask stencilMask stencilMaskSeparate depthRange scissor viewport disableVertexAttribArray	useProgram activeTexture bindTexture bindBuffer enable disable bindFramebuffer cullFace frontFace lineWidth polygonOffset
Programs	uniform[1234][fi] uniform[1234][fi]v uniformMatrix[234]fv	vertexAttrib[1234]f vertexAttrib[1234]fv vertexAttribPointer	
Textures	texParameterf	texParameteri	texImage2D
Framebuffers	framebufferRenderBuffer	frameBufferTexture2D	

WebGL also allows the state of itself or its objects to be queried. These calls should be avoided, as they can be very costly, and, at their worst, they can cause the pipeline to stall completely.

The only real exception to this rule, with regard to global state, is during the startup process, as the application can use this time to determine what features are available with the implementation, such as the number of texture units present.

With shader programs it's perfectly valid to query the uniform information after creation; however, this should only happen once, as the value returned will be unchanged. The information for setting the value later can easily be stored by the application for future use.

During development it's highly recommended that you check for any errors, using getError after every call. Yet, this should not go into production. The Khronos Group, the consortium that oversees the WebGL specification, provides a debug context for WebGL applications using JavaScript, and doing the same sort of wrapper is trivial in Dart through noSuchMethod invocations.

Any calls enumerated in Table 9-2 will query the state of WebGL.

Table 9-2. *Functions That Query State*

State	Functions		
Global	getParameter getError	isEnabled	readPixels
Programs	getActiveAttrib getAttribLocation isProgram	getActiveUniform getUniform getProgramParameter	getVertexAttrib getVertexAttribOffset getProgramInfoLog
Textures	isTexture	getTexParameter	
Buffers	isBuffer	getBufferParameter	
Renderbuffers	isRenderbuffer	getRenderbufferParameter	
Framebuffers	checkFramebufferStatus	getFramebufferAttachmentParameter	isFramebuffer

Rather than relying on WebGL to enumerate the current state, the application itself should keep track of its status by mirroring WebGL's own state machine. By so doing, redundant calls can be prevented.

Building the Renderer

When building a large application, it's best to partition different subsystems into layers that handle specific functionality. This separates concerns and offers a singular component that can be tested and verified. Building the graphics subsystem involves wrapping the WebGL API into something friendlier to work with higher up within the program. This is also the level at which the API usage can be optimized.

Although the creation of a renderer that binds the whole of WebGL is a topic worthy of an entire tome, a smaller piece of the puzzle can be examined to learn how to go about building the larger whole. How the renderer deals with textures internally can provide that insight.

At a very high level, WebGL allows

- creation and deletion of objects

- manipulation of the underlying objects

- setting of the rendering pipeline

The code in Listing 9-4 begins to sketch out an implementation of this layer.

Listing 9-4. Graphics Library

```
function GraphicsDevice(gl) {
  this.gl_ = gl;
  this.context_ = new GraphicsContext(gl);
}

GraphicsDevice.prototype.createTexture2D = function() {
  var binding = this.gl_.createTexture(),
      texture = new Texture2D(this);
  texture.setBinding(binding);

  // The texture is not complete, and therefore not usable until
  // after the parameters have been set
  this.context_.initializeTexture(texture);
  return texture;
}

GraphicsDevice.prototype.deleteTexture = function(texture) {
  var binding = texture.getBinding();

  this.gl_.deleteTexture(binding);
  texture.setBinding(null);
}
//----------------------------------------------------------------
function GraphicsResource(device) {
  this.device_ = device;
  this.binding_ = null;
}
```

```
GraphicsResource.prototype.getBinding = function() {
  return this.binding_;
}

GraphicsResource.prototype.setBinding = function(binding) {
  this.binding_ = binding;
}
//-----------------------------------------------------------
Texture2D.prototype = new GraphicsResource();
Texture2D.constructor = Texture2D;

function Texture2D(device) {
  GraphicsResource.call(this, device);
}

Texture2D.prototype.getType = function() {
  // Corresponds to WebGLRenderingContext.TEXTURE_2D
  return 0x0DE1;
}
```

The layer is built to reflect those concerns. A GraphicsDevice class handles the creation and deletion of resources. Those resources are descended from the GraphicsResource class, which serves as a mechanism for binding the underlying objects WebGL provides. Resources such as textures and buffers would descend from the resource class and communicate an interface that allows the object's internal state to be modified. The GraphicsContext class handles the state of the pipeline, containing a snapshot of its current condition, which is used to prevent redundant calls from being made.

The OpenGL is a C API, so it doesn't have the clear separation of concerns that DirectX offers (see Listing 9-5). This means that the GraphicsContext class and GraphicsDevice class are more intertwined than is desirable, as initializing a texture requires calling to the context.

Listing 9-5. Texture Binding

```
function GraphicsContext(gl) {
  this.gl_ = gl;

  this.activeTexture_ = 0;
  this.boundTextures_ = new Array(8);
}


GraphicsContext.prototype.setTextureAt = function(index, texture) {
  // See if the texture is already bound
  if (this.boundTextures_[index] !== texture) {
    var gl = this.gl_;

    // See if the active texture unit is at the given index
    if (this.activeTexture_ !== index) {
      gl.activeTexture(gl.TEXTURE0 + index);

      this.activeTexture_ = index;
    }
```

```
  // Bind the texture
  gl.bindTexture(texture.getType(), texture.getBinding());

  this.boundTextures_[index] = texture;
  }
}

GraphicsContext.prototype.initializeTexture = function(texture) {
  // Bind the texture to the pipeline
  this.setTextureAt(0, texture);

  var gl = this.gl_,
      type = texture.getType();

  // Set the default sampler data
  gl.texParameteri(type, gl.TEXTURE_MAG_FILTER, gl.LINEAR);
  gl.texParameteri(type, gl.TEXTURE_MIN_FILTER, gl.TEXTURE_LINEAR_MIPMAP_NEAREST);
}
```

The GraphicsContext retains information that is contained within the underlying state machine. WebGL allows multiple textures to be bound to the pipeline at the same time, with each one residing in a separate texture unit. This information can be kept track of by holding an array of textures with the value held corresponding to the specific texture unit. The way to specify that texture unit is to make a call to the API, activeTexture, which specifies the index. This information also has to be retained.

When setting a texture to a given unit, the first thing to check is if that texture is already bound to the given location. This is done first, as the current texture unit only needs to be changed if the texture will actually be replaced. The check of the texture unit is performed when the texture is due to be replaced, because the texture unit may have been modified. During the process, whenever the internal WebGL state is modified, that same modification is applied to the context. This ensures that the underlying states are kept in lockstep with each other.

When building up the renderer further, it's just a matter of extrapolating the same concepts to encompass other objects: only a single program can be bound to the pipeline at a time, the layout of the vertex buffer can be retained, and a uniform's value should be changed only when a different input has been provided. All this, and more, needs to be reflected within the rendering context. Once these issues are handled, the interaction with WebGL is optimal at this level.

Debugging WebGL Usage

To verify that the API is being used properly, there are multiple techniques that can be implemented. Those interested in unit testing the graphics layer can do a mock of the WebGLRenderingContext and record the calls being sent. If a call passes through that shouldn't have occurred, then the test should fail. Which framework to use is really dependent on developer choice, as there are a ton of frameworks available in JavaScript. The Closure Library provides a unit-testing and mocking framework, whereas QUnit is a popular unit-testing framework that can be coupled with Sinon.js for mocks. With Dart the choice is easier; it comes with a robust unit-testing library that also handles mocks. Writing unit tests is outside the scope of this chapter but is a great way to verify that no redundant calls are being made in an automated fashion.

What is more useful during the actual application development is to view the calls being made during a frame, by taking snapshots of what is actually happening. The most robust way to accomplish this is through the WebGL Inspector, a Chrome extension that allows the entire WebGL context to be viewed (see Figure 9-2). When WebGL content is available, a GL icon appears in the address bar, which is used to toggle the extension on and off.

Figure 9-2. The WebGL Inspector

The extension allows the entire state of a single frame to be examined. Each call made to the API is recorded and can be played back in the window, making it simple to see what the rendering looks like step by step. The extension can also show what redundant calls were made to the API, which can be used to diagnose how the renderer is doing. Another feature of the extension is its ability to observe the contents of various buffers within the context. This includes textures, vertex buffers, and index buffers. Shader programs, including the source code that makes up the vertex and fragment stages, can also be studied. Finally, the state of the API, such as what is enabled or disabled on the pipeline, can be seen within the user interface (UI).

There is another option that just relies on Chrome itself, the Canvas Profiler, which introspects not only WebGL usage, but Canvas 2D Context API usage as well. At the time of writing, the profiler is not as robust as as WebGL Inspector, but it is likely to gain the same sort of functionality as its development continues. To signal that the tool is still under development, it is currently hidden behind the Experiments tab in Chrome DevTools and has to be enabled before it will appear under the Profiles section of the tools. If the Experiments tab is not present within the DevTools settings, then it needs to be enabled through chrome://flags by turning on the Developer Tools Experiments option. Once deemed ready for mass consumption, it should be available without any further configuration within the browser.

Once up and running, the profiler can capture calls to the API. The biggest piece of functionality available in Canvas Profiler that is not present in WebGL Inspector is the ability to capture multiple frames and thus a block of time. In terms of the UI, the profiler groups calls into batches, based on when the actual draw calls occur. This allows the individual geometries being drawn to be tracked in a simple manner.

To see how redundant calls can negatively affect the performance of an application, sample code is included that makes varying degrees of redundant calls. The number of objects being drawn can be modified, and these tools can be used to determine how the application is making use of WebGL. From there on, other three-dimensional content can be examined to see how different applications use the API.

Using Extensions

As graphics APIs evolve, they open up additional parts of the pipeline and offer new ways to perform more work with fewer calls. In the OpenGL world this functionality is exposed through extensions. OpenGL extensions allow developers to try new functionality and provide a path for promotion into the core specification. WebGL follows this same model and contains a number of extensions that can reduce the number of calls to the API.

It is important to note that there are no guarantees that an extension will be available, so relying on their presence can erode the number of potential users for the application. Unless the extension is widely supported, a fallback will be required for those users. A site such as WebGL Stats (http://webglstats.com), can give a good indication of what WebGL implementations in the wild have available. On the plus side all the extensions that will be examined here are present in the WebGL 2.0 specification.

Vertex Array Objects

When preparing to draw geometry, the buffers holding the vertex data need to be bound. During this process, the attributes, such as the positions and texture coordinates, must be specified for the vertex shader. Optionally, an index buffer can be specified. All this results in a number of calls to WebGL. With the vertex array object (VAO) extension, these calls can be minimized.

A VAO object keeps the vertex buffers bound and all the attributes specified. It even hangs on to the index buffer in use. The best way to visualize the functionality is to think of a sound recorder. The VAO is bound to the pipeline, the commands are issued, and the results are held in the object. When needed again, the VAO is pressed into service, and the commands are played back. Thus, to render geometry, only a single call is required to set up the vertex and index buffers.

The VAO extension is the easiest extension to support, as its presence is never integral to rendering. If it's there, the number of calls can be reduced, but if it's not, the user isn't missing any graphical goodies.

Draw Buffers

Modern rendering techniques rely on making multiple passes over the same data, with each pass accumulating a different set. An example of this is deferred shading, a screen-space shading technique. In deferred shading the lighting is decoupled from the rendering of a model. The algorithm renders to a geometry buffer (G-buffer), which contains, at minimum, the position, the color information, and normal data for a pixel. If only one render target can be specified at a time, then the scene needs to be rendered once for each target. This involves a lot of overhead. With the draw buffers extension, multiple render targets are supported in WebGL.

WebGL allows the creation of framebuffer objects (FBOs), which can be backed by textures. With the draw buffers extension the framebuffer can be specified with multiple attachments. In the case of deferred shading, there would be a target for position, normal, and color. The fragment shader would then specify an index into gl_FragColor to target the output at the different components. Once the scene is done, these textures are used to create the final image by applying lighting, based on the information within the textures.

Although the draw buffers extension allows amazing effects in the browser, handling a case in which the extension isn't supported on the device is fairly complex. As mentioned earlier, each geometry will have to be drawn once for each target, and shaders will have to be authored to handle outputting each component. Also, note well that rendering the scene multiple times may not be possible within the allotted time frame.

Instanced Arrays

In a three-dimensional scene it is quite likely that there are multiple objects within the scene sharing the same geometry. Commonly, this involves things such as vegetation, trees, and grass but also extends to characters. However, each of these instances has different parameters to give some amount of uniqueness, for example, different colors. Rather than rendering each mesh one at a time, the hardware allows many geometry instances to be rendered with one call. This functionality is afforded through the instanced arrays extension.

With instanced rendering, per-instance data, such as colors and positions, are transferred through vertex buffers rather than uniforms (see Listing 9-6). First, one or more vertex buffers need to be created to hold the individual instance data. From there on, the extension is used to notify the implementation that the buffer itself holds instanced data and to render the geometries.

Listing 9-6. Instanced Array Setup

```
// Create the instance data
gl.bindBuffer(gl.ARRAY_BUFFER, colorBuffer);
gl.enableVertexAttribArray(colorLocation);
gl.vertexAttribPointer(colorLocation, 4, gl.FLOAT, false, 16, 0);
ext.vertexAttribDivisorANGLE(colorLocation, 1);

// Draw the instanced meshes
ext.drawElementsInstancedANGLE(gl.TRIANGLES, indexCount, gl.UNSIGNED_SHORT, 0, instanceCount);
```

To use instancing, the shaders have to be modified, as the values are now coming from a vertex buffer rather than a uniform. This just means that any values that were in uniforms but that are now coming from the instanced vertex buffer have to be modified. The fix is simply to change occurrences of uniform with attribute. Also, if the uniform now being passed in as instance data was only in the fragment shader, it must be moved to the vertex shader and then passed over to the fragment shader as a varying variable, because fragment shaders cannot access vertex attributes.

The instanced arrays extension allows many geometries to be drawn with a single call. But, supporting devices without this extention requires a bit of work as well. Any shaders that act on instanced geometry will require a fallback version. Additionally, the renderer will need to handle setting uniform values directly instead of using a vertex buffer, which could be complicated, depending on the how the renderer is set up. Another word of caution: the number of API calls is based on the number of instances and the number of values per instance and thus could go up drastically. If the scene is bound by the number of draw calls being submitted, the number of instances will have to be slashed when the extension is not available.

WebGL 2

There are some optimizations possible besides the promoted extensions for the next iteration of WebGL. At the time of writing, the specification has been released in draft form, so there is a possibility that things could change. WebGL 2 provides a wrapper over OpenGL ECMAScript 3 functionality, which is already available for use, so it's doubtful that the finalized specification will deviate too far from what has already been proposed. Because at this time no browser vendors have implemented the specification, no example code is given here.

In WebGL 1.x all the information on how a texture is sampled is contained within the texture object itself. In WebGL 2.x this state is replicated within a sampler object. This allows the state of the texture to be easily changed and the same texture to be bound to multiple texture units with different sampling options.

When switching between geometries to draw, the uniform values will need to be updated. This can result in a lot of calls to set uniform data, even though the data may remain constant for the object. Uniform buffer objects offer a new way to set uniform data. Instead of setting a value within the shader program, data are set directly on the uniform buffer. From there on, the data are bound to the shader program, allowing multiple uniform values to be set with a single call.

Rendering the Scene

With the renderer ensuring that no redundant calls are occurring, it's time to focus on how the scene is being submitted. Even with the underlying optimizations present, the API usage may not be optimal when rendering the scene. For example, imagine that 100 cubes are visible and that each one can be one of three colors. Let's also assume that there's a uniform for the diffuse color and another uniform for the MVP matrix. The worst case scenario for the renderer diffuse value is that, modified for each cube, there are 200 uniform calls. This is almost 100 more than the best case scenario, in which the cubes are rendered by color, resulting in 3 calls to set the diffuse color and 100 calls setting the matrix. So, even though the underlying renderer is smart enough to prevent redundant calls, there can still be bottlenecks because of how the renderer is being fed the scene.

When optimizing, it's important to think about the how the application works and to choose algorithms that fit the specific use. Generalization is usually in opposition to execution speed, so really think about how the scene should be rendered, and adjust accordingly. Additionally, profiling should be added from the start, as there is no way to prove that one algorithm is more effective than another without having any metrics to back that up. Also, remember that some optimizations may have a bigger effect on different hardware, so make sure to profile on a good sampling of devices that may run the program.

With graphics programming there are multitudes of published algorithms available to help speed the rendering. For this reason, it's impossible to cover them all. However, there are a few optimization techniques that should be present in a software engineer's toolbox.

Frustum Culling

Sometimes, the entire scene is not completely within the view of the user. In this case, it's important to submit only geometry that can affect the final rendering. To determine what is visible, the bounds of the geometry can be compared with the viewing volume, and if the geometry is contained within the extents, it can be passed to the renderer.

The viewing volume (also called the viewing frustum) can be represented as a set of six planes: near, far, left, right, top, and bottom (see Figure 9-3). The bounding volume is then compared against those planes to determine whether it is contained within the frustum.

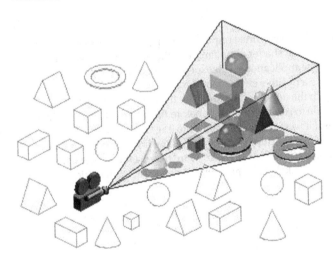

Figure 9-3. *Frustum culling*

The algorithm depends on the bounding volume used. The tighter the bounding volume, the higher the computational cost. The simplest is the bounding sphere (see Listing 9-7 for a simple implementation), which can easily be compared against the plane but which is highly unlikely to provide a snug fit around the geometry. An axis-aligned bounding box (AABB) is more likely to have a close fit than a sphere, resulting in less geometry's being inadvertently set to the renderer, but the computation cost is greater. There are other potential bounding volumes— cylinder, capsule, object-oriented (OO) bounding box—but the sphere or AABB are the ones most likely to be encountered when working on the graphics side.

Listing 9-7. Naive Frustum Culling

```
/// Could be sped up by batching a number of spheres and removing branches.
Frustum.prototype.containsSphere = function(sphere) {
  var plane, dist, radius = sphere.getRadius();

  for (var i = 0; i < 6; ++i) {
    plane = this.planes_[i];

    dist = Vector3.dot(sphere.getCenter(), plane.getNormal()) + plane.getDistance();

    if (dist < -radius)
      return Frustum.Out;
    else if (Math.abs(dist) < radius)
      return Frustum.Intersect;
  }

  return Frustum.In;
}
```

For a bounding sphere the distance from the center point to the plane is compared, along with the radius of the sphere, to determine which side of the plane the sphere is on. If the sphere is outside any of the six planes making up the bounding volume, its geometry can be discarded from the visible set.

Rendering Order

The order in which geometry is sent to the graphics card can have a direct impact on the performance of the rendering. For example, the hardware will not run the fragment shader upon failure of the depth test. This is an optimization known in OpenGL as the Early Depth Test. For applications with expensive fragment shaders, or multiple passes over the same geometry, this test can have a positive effect on performance.

The OpenGL specification defines a pipeline in which the depth test occurs after the fragment shader is run (see Figure 9-4). However, in certain scenarios it is possible to run the depth test before the fragment shader, which meets this stipulation, as the depth test still functions as if it were being done after the fragment shader. Whether this optimization is available depends on the underlying OpenGL implementation and the fragment shader being used. The optimization is likely to be turned off if the source uses the discard keyword. Also, if the shader uses gl_FragDepth, which isn't present in WebGL 1.x but which is likely to be present in WebGL 2.x, the technique will not be available.

ES2.0 Programmable Pipeline

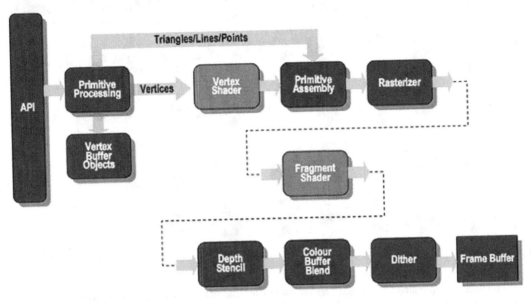

Figure 9-4. *OpenGL ES 2.0 pipeline*

A way to exploit this functionality is to render all opaque geometry from front to back. This can be done by measuring the distance from the camera to the geometry and sorting, based on the calculation. From there on, the geometry is submitted according to that ordering, which will likely result in use of the Early Depth Test.

Batching

Although it's often useful to think of a geometry as a singular object with its own data, there is nothing preventing multiple geometries from sharing the same underlying vertex buffer; in fact, this can drastically reduce the number of calls to the underlying API. Packing multiple sets of geometry in the same vertex buffer, known as batching, is a common technique for geometry that contains a small number of vertices, such as sprites.

Assume that a scene has 100 of the same sprite being displayed on-screen. To draw the sprites in the best way, such that the vertex buffer is shared between all instances, will necessitate setting a uniform for the transformation and a draw call for each instance, requiring a total of 200 calls. However, if batched together through a shared vertex buffer, all the sprites can be sent to the GPU with a single draw call.

Batching goes hand in hand with another technique, texture sheeting (see Figure 9-5). In a texture sheet (also called a sprite sheet or texture atlas), multiple smaller textures are combined into a single texture. The individual sprites are displayed by setting texture coordinates that correspond to the position of the texture data within the larger sheet. This allows a greater number of sprites to be rendered in a single call.

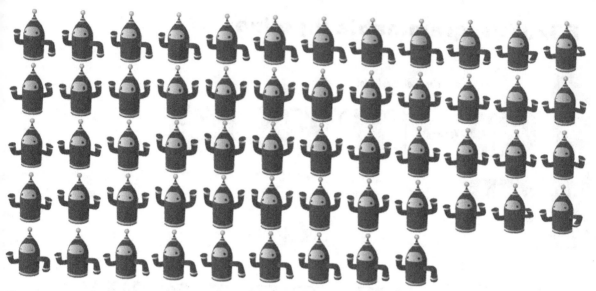

Figure 9-5. *A texture sheet*

Batching gets a bit more complicated when the sprites are mobile instead of being statically placed within the world, as with a tile map. In this case, the vertex data need to be updated whenever the sprite's position changes. This means keeping a separate copy of the position data, as WebGL does not have a way to get back the data held in the buffer. Once all the vertex data have been updated, they must then be applied to the vertex buffer, as shown in Table 9-3.

Table 9-3. *Buffer Usage Enumeration*

Enumeration	Behavior
(i) STREAM_DRAW	The data store contents will be modified once and used at most a few times.
(ii) STATIC_DRAW	The data store contents will be modified once and used many times.
(iii) DYNAMIC_DRAW	The data contents will be modified repeatedly and used many times.

When setting up vertex buffers, it's important to think about how they are going to be used. In this case, the position data are likely to change often, whereas the texture coordinates are going to be constant. For this reason, it's best to place them in two separate buffers. When populating the data, there are enumerations, which tell the underlying driver how the data are going to be used. This functions as a hint to the underlying implementation on how it should store the data internally. The position buffer should be passed the DYNAMIC_DRAW enumeration, whereas the texture coordinate buffer receives the STATIC_DRAW usage. This lets the underlying implementation optimize accordingly.

Conclusion

Effectively using WebGL is integral for three-dimensional applications on the Web. Spending more time than is required within the API results in less time for the rest of the application to do its work. Hitting a smooth 60 frames per second, or at the very least 30, is integral to the user experience and is a goal that needs to be met.

By ensuring that the application is not making unwarranted calls to the API, the battle is largely won. The application should leverage any extensions available to further reduce the number of calls. And, finally, the renderer should be fed in a way that is efficient for dealing with the scene being displayed. With all that in place, the rendering path is optimized, maximizing the amount of frame time available for the rest of the application.

■ ■ ■

CHAPTER 10

Playing Around with the Gamepad API

Andrzej Mazur, HTML5 Games Developer, Founder, Enclave Games

There is a great focus on making HTML5 games for mobile devices, which is good, of course, but core progamers are usually visualized as having a gamepad in their hands. So why not use it and deliver the full experience of a game using the Full Screen, Mouse Lock, and Gamepad APIs? The last API provides the ability to use a console's controller to play HTML5 games—how cool is that? With the W3C specification presently being written, we will have an API that is easy to implement, does not require any plug-ins to run in your browser, and is as simple as just plugging in your device and playing the game right away.

Draft Stage

Please remember that the Gamepad API is still in the early stages of development. The document describing its implementation indicated Editor's Draft status at the World Wide Web Consortium. This means that the API can change in the process, so the implementations and demos working right now may not work in the future when the specification is closed and published as an official document. Though experimental, you can dive into it right now and see how it will work in the future, and that's just what you will be doing in this chapter. You'll be using it at your own risk, so it's not the best idea to use it for a big commercial project just yet, but it's perfect for a demo and as a way to impress your game development friends. Plus you'll have an advantage over the competition when it is fully supported.

Browser Support

It is important to know about browser support of the Gamepad API, as you'll be testing it yourself in one browser or another. For now, only two browsers support the API implementation: Mozilla Firefox and Google Chrome.

The first one, Firefox, had a special build done by Ted Mielczarek where the API could be tested, even though it wasn't available officially. After some work had been done, gamepad support was delivered in version 24 and above of the Firefox browser. It was not available by default—you still had to set special flags in the config file.

If you're using Firefox 24-27, simply enter about:config in your browser address bar. You will get the warning shown in Figure 10-1.

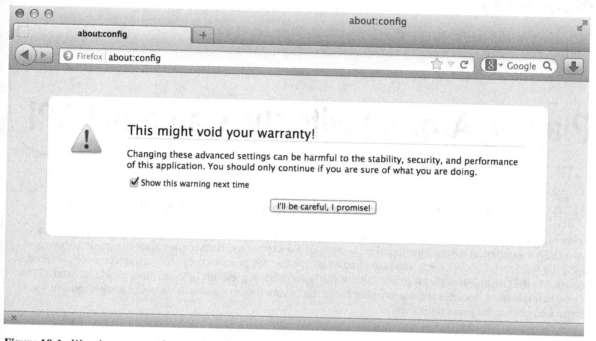

Figure 10-1. *Warning message shown when setting special flags within Firefox to enable gamepad support*

Click the button to see the list of available options. Search for the word "gamepad" to find the two values in which you're interested: dom.gamepad.enabled and dom.gamepad.non_standard_events.enabled (see Figure 10-2). Double-click both of them to enable gamepad support in your browser.

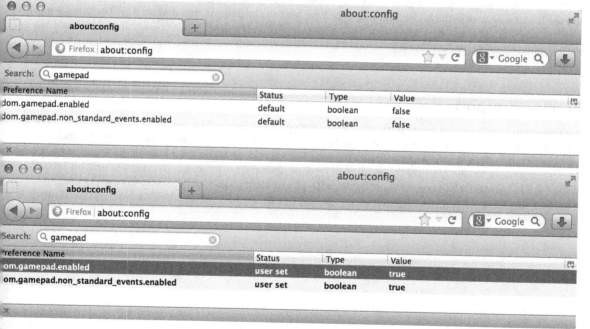

igure 10-2. *Enabling gamepad support in Firefox*

The first setting will actually enable gamepad support and the second setting will give you access to events that are not yet in the specification draft: gamepadbuttonup, gamepadbuttondown, and gamepadaxismove. It won't be necessary to enable gamepad support in the near future as the Firefox browser from version 28 on will have this enabled by default.

A second browser, Chrome, supports the Gamepad API from version 21 and above out of the box. This means that you don't have to search for any flags in your browser settings. You can just plug in your device and it will work right away.

Both browsers support the Gamepad API on the Windows, Mac, and Linux platforms. Other browsers, like Opera, Safari, and Internet Explorer, have not implemented the API to date, but this may change in the near future.

Supported Devices

When you want to test the Gamepad API, it's important to know which devices are supported. There are plenty of gamepads out there, and some have a better chance of working with the API than others. The best devices to use are the wired XBox (older ones from XBox 360 and the newer ones from XBox One) and the Play Station (PS3 and PS4) controllers, both on Windows; although I've tested the wireless XBox 360 and PS3 on Mac OS X and they all worked just fine. The easiest way to see if it works is to visit a test web site with Gamepad API support and just plug in the device to test it out.

Gamepad API Implementation

Now you know the browsers that have implemented Gamepad API and the supported devices that you can use, so let's dive into code! The first thing to do will be to plug in the device and then detect its presence. The XBox wireless device, for example, has a receiver that you plug into the USB port. After connecting the gamepad with the receiver, you will be able to detect it in your browser.

Project Setup

Usually when you work on more complicated projects there's a strict structure of folders, such as separate ones for JavaScript, CSS, and images. As you want to have a working demo quickly cooked up, let's just put everything in a single HTML file.

Use you favorite text editor to create new text file and name it index.html. Populate it with the following HTML code to have the starting structure of your basic test web site:

```
<!DOCTYPE html>
<html>
<head>
    <meta charset="utf-8">
    <title>Gamepad API Test</title>
</head>
<body>
<p>Check the browser's JavaScript console for output.</p>
<script>
    /* The JavaScript code we'll write goes here */
</script>
</body>
</html>
```

All of the code you will be writing should be added between the `<script>` tags where the comment is right now. You're going to have a working demo to actually see the output of the buttons pressed in the browser's JavaScript console (see Figure 10-3).

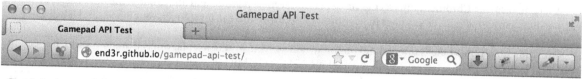

Figure 10-3. Browser's JavaScript console output

Connecting the Gamepad

There's a special object that is exposed with the list of all connected gamepads, so theoretically you'll be able to connect more than one and play the game with your friends sitting beside you. Now let's see how to do it. You will first create a JavaScript object that will store the information about the connected gamepads:

```
var gamepadAPI = {
    controllers: {},
    active: false
};
```

Thanks to this code, you will have access to the connected gamepads and will set the Boolean variable saying that at least one device is active. To do this, you will set up an event listener called gamepadconnected:

```
window.addEventListener("gamepadconnected", function(e) {
    var controller = e.gamepad;
    gamepadAPI.controllers[e.gamepad.index] = controller;
    gamepadAPI.active = true;
});
```

The event will be fired, and the function inside will be executed as soon as any device compatible with the Gamepad API is connected. You're assigning the gamepad object to the controller variable and then adding it to the controller's table under the unique index where all of the connected gamepads reside. The last line is about setting the Boolean variable to let you know that the gamepad is actually active and that you are ready to read the input from the player.

You can print out the gamepad unique ID in the JavaScript console if you write it down in your index.html file inside the <script> tags:

```
window.addEventListener("gamepadconnected", function(e) {
    var gamepadID = e.gamepad.id;
    console.log("Connected Gamepad ID: "+gamepadID+".");
});
```

You can extract any data from the gamepad object and do whatever you want with it.

Prefixes

For some time, as in the CSS world, there was an issue with vendor prefixes. When using an API, one had to use the names of the methods or attributes with the prefix that was unique to the browser in which it was executed. When Firefox implemented the Gamepad API from the unfinished draft, the event gamepaddisconnected had to be prefixed for that browser as follows:

```
window.addEventListener('MozGamepadConnected', gamepadConnectedFunction);
```

The same goes for the Chrome browser. Thus if you wanted to support it, you had to use WebkitGamepadConnected. To have the Gamepad API code working in both browsers, you had to check to see if any of those methods existed. Also, don't forget about the unprefixed version: GamepadConnected. Tricky, right? To see if a browser supports the Gamepad API, you had to use something like this:

```
var gamepadSupportAvailable = navigator.mozGamepads || navigator.webkitGamepads || navigator.gamepads;
```

When you launch the code in Firefox, the attribute with the moz prefix will be used; for Chrome, it will be webkit. For future-proof code when the API is fully implemented, the attribute without any prefix will be used.

Now let's think about other browser vendors that would implement their own support in the meantime: o prefix for Opera and ms for Internet Explorer. That's a mess! The good thing is that the prefixes are being dropped, so now the code will work without them and you won't have to remember all of those crazy hacks to check for support. Now that's a relief!

Detecting Disconnection

You know how to detect the gamepad connection, so now let's manage the state when it gets disconnected. Usually, it would be good to have alternative controls, for example, the keyboard. Of course, you can just show a box saying that the user has to reconnect their device in order to play the game if you really need it.

Here's the code to manage the state of a disconnecting a device:

```
window.addEventListener("gamepaddisconnected", function(e) {
    delete gamepadAPI.controllers[e.gamepad.index];
    if(!gamepadAPI.controllers.length) {
        gamepadAPI.active = false;
    }
    console.log('Gamepad disconnected.');
});
```

You're adding an event listener to the event named gamepaddisconnected. Thanks to this step, when the device is no longer available, you will delete the row containing your gamepad object with all of its data. If this was the last available device, you will also set the active variable to false. You can do other things here, or just use the gamepadAPI.active variable anywhere in your code to control the game depending on whether the device is connected or not.

Detecting Button Presses

To know what button was pressed, you can listen for a particular event: gamepadbuttondown. This will provide the information that you want.

```
window.addEventListener("gamepadbuttondown", function(e) {
    gamepadAPI.buttonPressed(e);
});
```

If you define a function called buttonPressed, you can see which button was pressed.

```
buttonPressed: function(event) {
    var button = event.button;
    console.log("Button "+button+" was pressed.");
}
```

There's also the gamepadbuttonup event, which tells you that the given button was released. You can change the buttonPressed function to reflect that and then fire at those two events.

```
buttonPressed: function(event, pressed) {
    var button = event.button;
    if(pressed) {
        console.log("Button "+button+" was pressed.");
    }
    else {
        console.log("Button "+button+" was released.");
    }
}
```

Now all you have to do is to bind this function to those two events.

```
window.addEventListener("gamepadbuttondown", function(e) {
    gamepadAPI.buttonPressed(e, true);
});
window.addEventListener("gamepadbuttonup", function(e) {
    gamepadAPI.buttonPressed(e, false);
});
```

Axis Events

You have the buttons covered, but what about the analog sticks? They are different from buttons, as buttons have only two possible values, 1 or 0, as they are either pressed or not. It's more complicated, however, with analog sticks as they can have different pressure applied at different angles. For example, if you move your left analog stick halfway to the bottom-left corner, you'll end up with the top-down axis holding a value of 0.5 and the left-right one with a value of -0.5. Let's see how to handle this.

```
window.addEventListener("gamepadaxismove", function(e){
    gamepadAPI.axisPressed(e);
});

axisPressed: function(event) {
    var axis = event.axis,
        value = event.value;
    console.log("Axis: "+axis+", value: "+value+".");
}
```

First comes the event listener for gamepadaxismove, and then the function that is executed. You just take the axis that was moved by the player on the device and its value. This can be applied to any game logic, for example steering a tank or other vehicle.

Axis Threshold

Be aware that analog sticks are not perfect—some of them will not return to 0.0 states, whether it's because of the materials used or simply a problem of a little dirt. They can stay with 0.02 values, and it's important to take that into account. For example, you can move your tank's turret right only when the value from the left-right axis exceeds 0.5, so it's between 0.5 and 1. The values from 0 to 0.5 will be ignored and the turret will be moved only when you exceed the 0.5 threshold.

Gamepad Object

It might be difficult to put all of a game's logic inside a single function responsible for managing the buttons. Fortunately, there is another solution: querying the gamepad object directly. I already covered this at the beginning of the implementation part, remember?

```
window.addEventListener("gamepadconnected", function(e) {
    var controller = e.gamepad;
    gamepadAPI.controllers[e.gamepad.index] = controller;
    gamepadAPI.active = true;
});
```

Earlier, I said that *you can extract any data from the gamepad object and do whatever you want with it*, so let's do it! You will put the code responsible for querying the gamepad object for any buttons that are pressed in a game loop. That way, you will have the actual data about whether the button is pressed or not in every frame, or what was the exact value of the axis used. Here's the code used in the main menu of the game *Hungry Fridge*, which was put into the update loop to allow the player to start the game on a gamepad button press:

```
if(gamepadAPI.active) {
    for(c in gamepadAPI.controllers) {
        var controller = gamepadAPI.controllers[c];
```

```
        for(var b=0, len=controller.buttons.length; b<len; b++) {
            if(controller.buttons[b]) {
                if(b == 1) {
                    startGame();
                }
            }
        }
    }
}
```

The first line is just checking if a gamepad is connected. The second line loops through connected gamepads. On the third line, you're assigning a given gamepad object to a variable that will be used later. The fourth line is another loop, this time going through all of the available buttons in your controller. The fifth line verifies if the button you're actually checking is pressed. The sixth line is checking if the button is the one from the right face of the controller; that is, you're asking for **B** (XBox 360) or **0** (PS3) in particular. If it's the button you're looking for and it's being pressed, then you're starting a new game.

Gamepad Differences

When looping through the buttons, remember that different controllers may have different key mappings, so the button[12] can be a top d-pad on an XBox 360 controller but something totally different on another controller. There are plenty of controllers available, and the Gamepad API specification is not officially released yet, so remember this when you're implementing gamepad keys in your game.

Hooking Up to the Event

There could be even easier solution if you want to use only a few buttons in your game. You can, for example, hook up your own function inside the buttonPressed one and check for the specific button press. Let's assume you will have a GAME object with your game's logic.

```
var GAME = {};
```

You can define startNewGame function that will do just that—start a new game.

```
GAME.startNewGame = function(){
    alert("New game started!");
}
```

Now you can modify the buttonPressed function and add those lines that will check for a specific button being pressed.

```
if(button == 1) { // button[1] is B or 0
    GAME.startNewGame();
}
```

This is how the function looks like after the addition:

```
buttonPressed: function(event, pressed) {
    var button = event.button;
    if(pressed) {
```

```
      console.log("Button "+button+" was pressed.");
      if(button == 1) { // button[1] is B or O
        GAME.startNewGame();
      }
    }
    else {
        console.log("Button "+button+" was released.");
    }
  }
},
```

Thanks to this, when the gamepad is connected, pressing the given button will start the game.

Complete Source Code

Listing 10-1 shows what your gamepad test code looks like when complete.

Listing 10-1. Finished Gamepad API

```html
<!DOCTYPE html>
<html>
<head>
  <meta charset="utf-8">
  <title>Gamepad API Test</title>
</head>
<body>
<p>Check the browser's JavaScript console for output.</p>
<script>
/* Here goes the JavaScript code we'll write */

/* Completed Gamepad API object: */
var gamepadAPI = {
    controllers: {},
    active: false,
    gamepadConnected: function(event) {
        var controller = event.gamepad;
        var controllerID = event.gamepad.id;
        gamepadAPI.controllers[event.gamepad.index] = controller;
        gamepadAPI.active = true;
        console.log("Connected Gamepad ID: "+controllerID+".");
    },
    gamepadDisconnected: function(event) {
        delete gamepadAPI.controllers[event.gamepad.index];
        if(!gamepadAPI.controllers.length) {
            gamepadAPI.active = false;
        }
        console.log('Gamepad disconnected.');
    },
    buttonPressed: function(event, pressed) {
        var button = event.button;
        if(pressed) {
            console.log("Button "+button+" was pressed.");
```

```
                if(button == 1) { // button[1] is B or O
                  GAME.startNewGame();
                }
            }
            else {
                console.log("Button "+button+" was released.");
            }
        },
        axisPressed: function(event) {
            var axis = event.axis;
            var value = event.value;
            console.log("Axis: "+axis+", value: "+value+".");
        }
};

/* Here are all the event listeners: */
window.addEventListener("gamepadconnected", function(e) {
    gamepadAPI.gamepadConnected(e);
});
window.addEventListener("gamepaddisconnected", function(e) {
    gamepadAPI.gamepadDisconnected(e);
});
window.addEventListener("gamepadbuttondown", function(e) {
    gamepadAPI.buttonPressed(e, true);
});
window.addEventListener("gamepadbuttonup", function(e) {
    gamepadAPI.buttonPressed(e, false);
});
window.addEventListener("gamepadaxismove", function(e){
    gamepadAPI.axisPressed(e);
});

/* Let's create a GAME object for our game */
var GAME = {};

/* Here's the function that will start our game */
GAME.startNewGame = function(){
  alert("New game started!");

/script>
/body>
/html>
```

That's it; you have created a fully working test case. Connecting the gamepad and pressing the buttons will print the output in the browser's JavaScript console. You can now add this to your game or start implementing new game on top of this.

Demo Time: Hungry Fridge

Hungry Fridge is an HTML5 game that was created especially for this chapter to show the capabilities of the Gamepad API in action. It was also submitted to the GitHub Game Off II competition. (It's always better to merge few tasks into one if it's possible.) The full source code for Hungry Fridge is open sourced and available on GitHub. The game was created under the brand of Enclave Games. It was coded by Andrzej Mazur, and Ewa Mazur did the graphic design. The code for the game was created using Phaser game framework, which is also free and open source.

The game is very simple: you're a refrigerator, and you have to eat food to survive. It gets trickier when you consider two different approaches to the game controls, depending on whether you're playing on a mobile device or a desktop. The *Hungry Fridge* start screen is shown in Figure 10-4.

Figure 10-4. The Hungry Fridge start screen

Mobile vs. Desktop

On a mobile device, you just have to tap the food to get as many points as possible. The only difficulty comes when there are two different types of food from which you can choose only one at a time. The type of food you have to tap is changes dynamically, so you have to think and act quickly. The good food (cabbage, carrot, and apple) is marked with a green overlay, and the bad food (pizza, beer, and hamburger) is marked with a red overlay. When the background glows green, you have to tap only on the good food; when it glows red, you have to tap only on the bad food (see Figure 10-5).

Figure 10-5. The good food vs. bad food interface in the Hungry Fridge

If you launch the game in a desktop browser and connect your gamepad, you'll get a chance to play *Super Turbo Hungry Fridge*. In this mode, you'll have full control over the fridge, which is actually an armored vehicle with a turret that you can move around and shoot, as shown in Figure 10-6. All of this is covered in the Gamepad API; that is, driving the vehicle around, rotating its turret, and shooting its canon. Thanks to the Gamepad API, this feels a lot better and is a lot more fun to play. It's very close to the console gaming experience, but you're using HTML5 in your browser without any plug-ins!

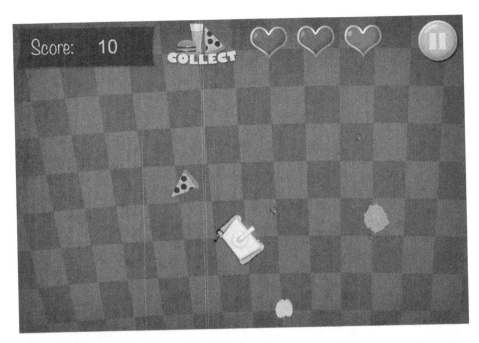

Figure 10-6. *The Super Turbo Hungry Fridge screen*

This is obviously out of scope of this chapter, but you can see the full source code of Hungry Fridge on GitHub and fiddle with it however you like. You can freely fork, modify, and benefit from the source code of the game—especially if you want to see the Gamepad API in action and eventually implement some of the code in your own game.

Conclusion

I hope that after reading this chapter and trying the brief examples, you will want to test the material out by creating a game with Gamepad API support or implement this support in an existing game. You've learned how to listen for gamepad-specific events, how to detect the controller connection, how your program should react upon disconnecting a controller, and how to tell the difference between buttons and analog sticks.

I also covered an example game, Hungry Fridge, which uses the Gamepad API implementation described in the chapter. This gives you a base of knowledge about the Gamepad API that you can use right away, even though the specification hasn't been officially published. All you have to do is to try it out yourself. Good luck and have fun!

■ ■ ■

CHAPTER 11

Introduction to WebSockets for Game Developers

Peter Lubbers, Program Manager, Google Developer Relations

It is a bit hard to imagine, but the Web wasn't always as dynamic as it is today. Before I discuss WebSockets, let's take a trip down memory lane.

Before Asynchronous JavaScript and XML (AJAX) and its cornerstone, XMLHttpRequest (XHR), gained widespread industry adoption, web application updates could only be achieved by refreshing a page. AJAX came of age in the early 2000s and represented the first wave of interactive tools, giving developers the ability to make applications feel more like their desktop counterparts. An AJAX call could be fired off to retrieve the current stock price, update shipping costs, or validate form fields, all without a full-page reload. In addition to AJAX, this need for dynamic data started to be served by what is commonly referred to as *Comet* or *AJAX push*. Comet simulates real-time interactivity by keeping a connection open forever, or at least for a reasonably long time. There are various methods of doing this, including having a hidden persistent inline frame (Iframe) ("forever frame"), long polling, or using Java or Flash plug-ins.

When Comet first became popular, circa 2006, many browsers had a maximum of two concurrent connections, so development was tricky if you wanted to emulate real-time events but needed to draw from many sources. In the quest for page load speed, most modern browsers have significantly raised their concurrent connection limits. This is not to say that you have carte blanche with Comet; it still has the overhead of being transported through HTTP, so there are a lot of extraneous HTTP header data being generated each time, even though the destination URL doesn't change.

The WebSocket protocol is a fully bidirectional data transport mechanism over a Transmission Control Protocol (TCP) connection, and it can traverse proxies. The Internet Engineering Task Force (IETF) codified its standard, RFC 6455, in 2011. WebSockets can be seen as an evolution of the tools used to deliver and respond to real-time events. AJAX and Comet implement a more traditional request-response model that is somewhat symmetrical, whereas a WebSocket, after establishing the connection, is more asymmetrical—basically, "don't call us, we'll call you." WebSocket connectivity is present in most modern browsers and mobile platforms.

As applications such as online games become less tolerant of latency, overhead becomes a problem. WebSockets are great for gaming because it provides a means of achieving real-time multiplayer interaction with greatly reduced overhead.

Setting Up a WebSocket Connection

A WebSocket connection begins with a handshake from the client to the server. The client initiates it over HTTP with a randomly selected Base64-encoded Sec-WebSocket-Key and other data on the desired connection. This all happens under the hood. A sample client connection request is shown in Listing 11-1.

Listing 11-1. *A Sample Client Connection Request*

```
GET /chat HTTP/1.1
Host: server.example.com
Upgrade: websocket
Connection: Upgrade
Sec-WebSocket-Key: x3JJHMbDL1EzLkh9GBhXDw==
Sec-WebSocket-Version: 12
Origin: http://example.com
```

The server takes the Sec-WebSocket-Key and appends the WebSocket "magic string" (258EAFA5-E914-47DA-95CA-C5AB0DC85B11, per the Request for Comments [RFC]), and then SHA-1 and Base64 encode the output. The result is returned in the server response as the Sec-WebSocket-Accept value. This response also marks the last time data will traverse HTTP, as shown in the sample response in Listing 11-2.

Listing 11-2. *A Sample Response*

```
HTTP/1.1 101 Switching Protocols
Upgrade: websocket
Connection: Upgrade
Sec-WebSocket-Accept: HSmrc0sMlYUkAGmm5OPpG2HaGWk=
Sec-WebSocket-Protocol: chat
```

Sending and Receiving Data

Figure 11-1 illustrates the WebSocket handshake.

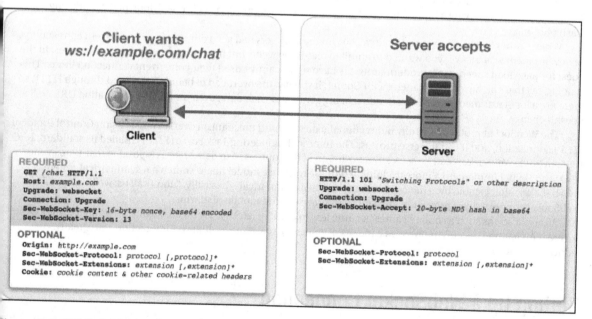

Figure 11-1. *WebSocket handshake*

After the handshake is successfully completed, all messages traverse the TCP connection in frames. Frames contain a small amount of information, including the type of data, some metadata, and the data payload. Messages can be split among multiple frames. The data from client to server are slightly transformed, using a masking key that is randomly generated on each push. If the data are not masked, the server terminates the connection. Data from the server to the client are not masked, but they would also cause the connection to be terminated if they were. The point is not to make the data cryptographically indecipherable, but rather to make the output unpredictable and to avoid proxy poisoning.

In addition to data frames, there are several frame types that are mostly initiated in server or browser code. These control frames include *Close*, *Ping*, and *Pong*. Ping and Pong frames are used for "heartbeat" behavior (testing that the connection is still live). A Ping frame must be answered with a Pong frame so long as the connection is open. Pong frames do not need to be answered, and they can be sent without a preceding Ping. Unless you are building a new WebSocket library, you do not have to worry about generating your own control frames. A library will generally have its own algorithm to determine when to generate Pings or Pongs and when to close a connection if a Ping goes unanswered.

The WebSocket API

The WebSocket interface is simple yet powerful; there are only six functions. The first two, send and close, are used to send a message and close a connection. The other four—onopen, onmessage, **onerror**, and onclose—are callbacks to be executed when a socket is opened, a message is received, an error is generated, and a socket is closed, respectively. A small application-programming interface (API) is easier to learn and build on, and its size allows you to list the signatures in just a couple of dozen lines of code, as shown in Listing 11-3.

Listing 11-3. WebSocket Interface Functions

```
enum BinaryType { "blob", "arraybuffer" };
[Constructor(DOMString url, optional (DOMString or DOMString[]) protocols)]
interface WebSocket : EventTarget {
  readonly attribute DOMString url;

  // ready state
  const unsigned short CONNECTING = 0;
  const unsigned short OPEN = 1;
  const unsigned short CLOSING = 2;
  const unsigned short CLOSED = 3;
  readonly attribute unsigned short readyState;
  readonly attribute unsigned long bufferedAmount;

  // networking
          attribute EventHandler onopen;
          attribute EventHandler onerror;
          attribute EventHandler onclose;
  readonly attribute DOMString extensions;
  readonly attribute DOMString protocol;
  void close([Clamp] optional unsigned short code, optional DOMString reason);

  // messaging
          attribute EventHandler onmessage;
          attribute BinaryType binaryType;
  void send(DOMString data);
  void send(Blob data);
  void send(ArrayBuffer data);
  void send(ArrayBufferView data);
};
```

Creating a Simple Echo Server

You can demonstrate that ease of use by creating a simple echo server. Once it is running, the server will send back whatever data you send it. For the server side of things, you will be using Python. It was chosen because the server-side code is concise and easy to understand. To begin, you will need to have Python (http://python.org) installed on your machine. You will be using the Python web framework Tornado because of its great WebSocket support.

If you don't already have Tornado installed, you can do so with the following command, run from any directory:

```
sudo easy_install tornado
```

Start the server by executing python tornado-demo.py in the same directory as the file; navigate to http://localhost:8888 to see it in action. You do not have to understand fully the Python in Listing 11-4 to see that it closely mirrors the JavaScript WebSocket API. You do some setup when the socket is opened, send a message immediately back to the client when you receive it, and close the connection when the client requests it.

Listing 11-4. Python Example: Open Socket, Send Message, Close Connection

```python
class WebSocketHandler(tornado.websocket.WebSocketHandler):
    def open(self, *args):
        self.id = self.get_argument("Id")
        self.stream.set_nodelay(True)
        clients[self.id] = {"id": self.id, "object": self}

    def on_message(self, message):
        # Print to console when message received
        # Write same message to client
        print "Client %s sent a message : %s" % (self.id, message)
        self.write_message(message)

    def on_close(self):
        if self.id in clients:
            del clients[self.id]
```

On the client, you begin by instantiating a WebSocket connection. The universally unique identifier (UUID) allows each client to have his or her own ID and to receive only the messages targeted to the client. Other libraries, which you will investigate later in the chapter, do this bookkeeping for you. After the WebSocket object is created, you define the handlers that respond to events, as shown in Listing 11-5 and Figure 11-2.

Listing 11-5. Create the WebSocket Object, Define Event Handlers

```javascript
var ws = new WebSocket("ws://localhost:8888/ws?Id="+Math.uuid());

ws.onopen = function() {
    messageContainer.innerHTML += "Preparing to send message";
    ws.send("The time is now "+ new Date());
    messageContainer.innerHTML += "Sent message."
};

ws.onmessage = function (evt) {
    var received_msg = evt.data;
    messageContainer.innerHTML += "Message received: "+received_msg;
};
```

```
ws.onclose = function() {
    messageContainer.innerHTML += "Connection is closed...";
};
```

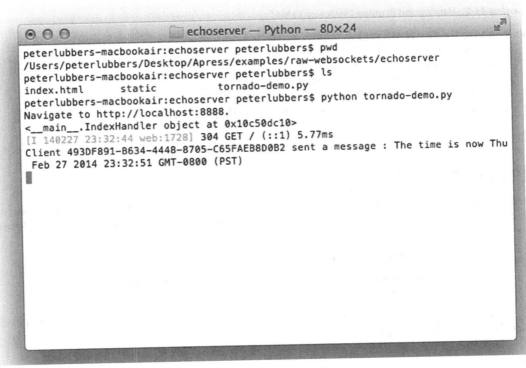

Figure 11-2. *Running the WebSocket echo server*

Encoding Data

As mentioned earlier, WebSockets are bidirectional pipes. A WebSocket does not examine the content of the inbound and outbound streams; it only ensures that the data reach their destination on each end. This is not a problem if the data received are merely being echoed or lightly processed. For anything more complex, you will send discrete packets of information to the server. Not only does this allow you to process the information better, but it also eliminates errors caused by receiving information in the wrong order, a significant benefit.

Luckily, JavaScript already has a built-in type that you can use to send data, an *Object*. To send and receive JavaScript Object Notation (JSON) data on the client, you have to serialize and deserialize it, that is, convert a JSON object to a string and vice versa, with JSON.stringify and JSON.parse.

In the onopen function in Listing 11-6, you create an object and then serialize it to JSON. You need to do this because the WebSocket protocol has no concept of structured data.

Listing 11-6. The onopen Function

```
ws.onopen = function() {
    messageContainer.innerHTML += "Preparing to send message";
    var message = {date: new Date()};
    ws.send(JSON.stringify(message));
    messageContainer.innerHTML += "Sent message."
};
```

Upon receipt of a message, you parse the JSON and print out each key and its value, as shown in Listing 11-7.

Listing 11-7. Parsing and Printing JSON Key Values

```
ws.onmessage = function (evt) {
    var received_msg = evt.data;
    var json = JSON.parse(received_msg);
    messageContainer.innerHTML = "Message received: \n";
    for (var key in json) {
        messageContainer.innerHTML += "key: "+json[key]+"\n";
    }
};
```

Using Socket.IO

Socket.IO is a cross-platform library for Node.js that provides a Websocket-like API for real-time communication in web applications. The library is a mature and de facto standard in the JavaScript community for implementing solutions, using WebSockets. Socket.IO is described as a WebSocket-like API for two reasons:

1. Socket.IO is a superset of WebSockets.

2. WebSockets are one of many transport methods an application can use for communication.

In addition to WebSockets, readily available in modern browsers, Socket.IO has fallback transport methods for older browsers and mobile operating systems:

1. Adobe Flash Sockets

2. AJAX long polling

3. AJAX multipart streaming

4. Forever Iframe

5. JSON with padding (JSONP) polling

The availability of all these techniques means that even Internet Explorer 5.5, which was released in 1999, can use Socket.IO. It is (hopefully) unlikely that users will have a browser that old, but Socket.IO allows you to learn a single API, target the best of the breed, and let things degrade naturally.

Getting Started

Provided that you already have a Node.js install on your machine (for more information, see http://nodejs.org), you can install Socket.IO with node-packaged modules (npm), using the following command:

```
npm install socket.io
```

Echo Server

Let's revisit the echo server example that you completed earlier in the chapter, but this time reimplemented, using Socket.IO. As you can see in Listing 11-8, the Socket.IO code on the client is strikingly similar to that of your previous, raw WebSocket example.

Listing 11-8. Socket.IO Client Code

```
var socket = io.connect('http://0.0.0.0:3000');
socket.on('connect', function() {
    messageContainer.innerHTML += "Socket connected to server<br/>";

});
socket.on('message', function (msg) {
    messageContainer.innerHTML +=  "Message received: " + msg +"<br/>";
});
socket.on('disconnect', function() {
    messageContainer.innerHTML = "Connection is closed...";
});

var sendSocketMessage = function() {
    socket.send("The time is now "+ new Date());
    messageContainer.innerHTML += "Sent message.<br/>";
}
```

Instead of instantiating a WebSocket object directly, you are getting a Socket.IO instance with the io.connect command. The names of the events that are triggered when a socket is opened or closed have changed to connect and disconnect. In sendSocketMessage, you send a message on the socket with code that is almost indistinguishable from that of the earlier WebSocket example.

The full app.js file for setting up an echo server is in Listing 11-9.

Listing 11-9. The Full app.js File

```
var app = require('http').createServer(handler)
  , io = require('socket.io').listen(app)
  , fs = require('fs')

app.listen(3000);

function handler (req, res) {
  fs.readFile(__dirname + '/public/index.html',
  function (err, data) {
    if (err) {
      res.writeHead(500);
      return res.end('Error loading index.html');
    }

    res.writeHead(200);
    res.end(data);
  });
}
```

```
io.sockets.on('connection', function (socket) {
  socket.on('message', function (data) {
    socket.send(data);
  });
});
```

After being bound to an application (app) instance to listen for new connections, the io object attaches a function to any inbound socket to echo back received input. You may have noticed that the form

```
socket.on ('<name of event>', function(args) { })
```

is present in both your front-end and back-end code. It also doesn't require a confusing ws:// or wss:// protocol. Fewer APIs to learn makes for happier developers.

You can run the Node.js example by executing this code:

```
npm install
node app
```

Using Events

In the previous section, I briefly covered events, mostly adhering to the general WebSocket API. In this section, you will work with events further in the completion of a full-fledged application. In this example, we want something that is both easy to code and not obscured by a bunch of Canvas or Web Graphics Library (WebGL) code, so you will use a simple quiz game, with an associated chat box.

When the user navigates to the app, you establish a socket connection and register events for your app to handle. Three custom events, question, answer, and chat, receive questions, send and receive answers, and send and receive chat messages, respectively. The code resides in the app.js file, in the examples/socket.io/quizgame directory. Each event has its own handler function, as shown in Listings 11-10 and 11-11.

Listing 11-10. The Custom Events' Handler Functions

```
App.prototype.setupClient = function() {
  this.socket = io.connect();
  this.socket.on('message', this.handleMessage);
  this.socket.on('question', this.displayQuestion);
  this.socket.on('answer', this.displayAnswer);
  this.socket.on('chat', this.displayChatMessage);
   $('#sendMessage').click(this.sendChatMessage);
  this.time = new Date().getTime();
```

The code for sending a chat message is shown in Listing 11-11.

Listing 11-11. Sending a chat Message

```
pp.prototype.sendChatMessage = function() {
  var text = $('#message').get(0).value;
  if (text == "") return;
  $('#message').get(0).value=""
  app.socket.emit('chat', {message: text});
  app.displayChatMessage({message: text});
```

When the server receives an answer message, it determines a result and then adjusts the score accordingly. For the score, you can use the get and set functions on the socket, as shown in Listing 11-12; these let you store arbitrary data that you want to retain for the lifetime of the socket.

Listing 11-12. The get and set Functions

```
socket.on('answer', function(msg) {
    // Score answer
    var currentScore;
    var result = scoreAnswer(msg);
    socket.get('score', function(err, score) {
      currentScore = score;
    });
    // Emit message only to this client.
    socket.emit('answer', {
        message:result.message,
        score:(currentScore + result.points)
    });
    socket.set('score', currentScore + result.points);
  });
```

Finally, you have a bit of code for retrieving a question at random, masking its answer, and sending it to all connected sockets, as shown in Listing 11-13. The quiz game start screen is displayed in Figure 11-3.

Listing 11-13. Sending a Random Question to All Connected Sockets

```
var sendQuestion = function (questionId) {
    var q = _.clone(findQuestionById(questionId))
    q.correctAnswer = -1;

    io.sockets.emit('question', q);
}
setInterval(function() {
    sendQuestion(getRandomQuestion());
}, 10000);
```

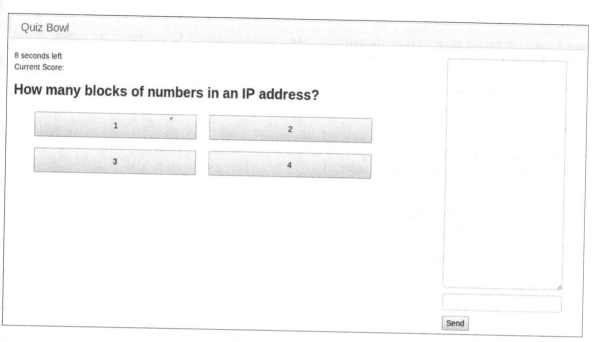

Figure 11-3. *Quiz game start screen*

For this quiz game, you used a single URL to address events for question, answer, and chat messages and general messages, but you could easily have used a separate socket for each event type. There are several other tweaks and enhancements that are beyond the scope of this chapter and whose investigation will remain a follow-up exercise for the reader (for more details, see http://socket.io).

Scaling and Reducing Overhead

When it comes to networking, there are many cases in which what works on a small scale, perhaps between a few local clients on the same computer or local network, fails miserably when attempted on a larger scale. In the following sections, you will explore how to reduce the overhead of passing data to a large number of clients, using various methods.

Reducing the Size of Data Transmitted

In the previous examples, you used either raw text or JSON to transmit data. JSON is great because it is humanly readable, relatively lightweight, and natively supported by JavaScript. However, for a highly connected online game, JSON may not be lightweight enough. The general premise is that the less data transmitted, the faster they transmit and decode. BSON and MessagePack seek to improve transmission rates by discarding one of JSON's key features: readability.

BSON

Binary JSON (BSON) is an exchange format used in the MongoDB database to store data. As the name implies, BSON documents are binary encoded. Many of the core concepts from JSON apply, such as being able to embed complex data structures inside documents (documents inside documents and arrays inside arrays), but BSON adds some new data types that do not exist in the JSON specification. Unlike JSON, BSON has discrete data and raw binary data types.

All numeric types in JSON are stored as 64 bit floating-point numbers. That is fantastic for very large or small numbers in scientific calculations but is overkill for most games. For an unsigned integer, that's a range of 0–18,446,744,073,709,551,615, far too high for most game scores and other numbers, which will be 32 bit or less. So, why use twice the precision that you need?

BSON reduces the numeric overhead by having multiple sizes that it can store. Table 11-1 shows BSON's numeric types.

Table 11-1. *Chart Adapted from bsonspec.org/#/specification*

Type	Bytes	Range (Signed and Unsigned)
Byte	1B (8 bits)	128–127
		0–255
Int32	4B (32 bit)	–2,147,483,648–2,147,483,647
		0–4,294,967,295
Int64	8B (64 bit signed int)	–9,223,372,036,854,775,808–9,223,372,036,854,775,807
		0–18,446,744,073,709,551,615
Double	8B (64 bit IEEE floating point)	4.9E-324–1.7976931348623157E308

If you were developing a side-scrolling game, the number types (and their probable data types) of concern are as follows:

1. Location of the player in the world (two int32s)

2. Location of enemies and obstacles in the world (two int32s per object)

3. Current level (byte)

4. Remaining time (int32)

5. Player's score (int32)

Let's assume there's one enemy in the world, with the aforementioned objects. Using JSON, you'd be transmitting 56B of numeric data per update; using BSON, the total would be just 25B. That's a savings of 55 percent per update.

JSON is supported in every major JavaScript implementation. BSON doesn't lag far behind, with an official JavaScript driver, along with several others for popular languages maintained by MongoDB and third-party drivers. A full listing of implementations can be found at `http://bsonspec.org/#/implementation`. The JavaScript implementation used for the examples is located at `https://github.com/marcello3d/node-buffalo`.

MessagePack

MessagePack expands on the number packing of BSON by providing five integer types, storing 1B, 2B, 3B, 5B, or 9B, respectively, and two floating-point types, storing 5B or 9B each. Using the same parameters as the BSON example, MessagePack further reduces the amount of data required to represent the numbers to 21B ; this is a 16 percent improvement over BSON and a 63 percent savings versus JSON:

- `http://wiki.msgpack.org/display/MSGPACK/Format+specification#Formatspecificatio n-Integers`

- `http://msgpack.org`

So, why not just use MessagePack in all cases if it seems to be faster than JSON and BSON? Microbenchmarks are usually limited in scope and cannot be predictive of all situations. Which method you should choose depends on the conditions of your environment, such as the databases you are using. You generally cannot go wrong with either binary format.

Intelligently Processing and Distributing Packets

Reducing the amount of data transmitted by sending it in a more efficient data exchange format is one way to increase data processing. An equally effective alternative is simply to send less data. In the following sections, I will discuss several ways to send fewer packets over the wire.

Send Mostly Deltas and Infrequent Worldviews

You can prevent cheating by using a "dumb" client/authoritative server model, in which the clients do minimal local calculations and merely display what the server sends them (for more information, see the section "Dumb Clients/ Authoritative Server"). This tactic has the added benefit of allowing the server to optimize further the data that need to be sent to clients.

The amount of "world" that the client can view is generally a subset of the full world. Sending only the parts of the world and enemies with which the player can directly interact reduces the data that must be transmitted.

Another way to reduce the transmitted data is to have the server send less frequent worldviews and more frequent deltas of player and enemy properties.

Autonomous Clients/Echo Server

This kind of setup, in which the clients do everything locally and report their changes to the server, is by far the easiest client-server combination with which to start. However, it is the one that is the most prone to cheating. When you hear about cheating in an online game, it is likely that a client was able to change something maliciously and have that state blindly pushed by the server to all the other clients. This also increases the load on the server, because all actions have to be received and sent to all the clients by it. Assuming that each client sends one update per second, then as the number of clients increases, so, too, does the number of updates, and by a large margin, as seen in Table 11-2.

Table 11-2. Number of Clients vs. Number of Updates

Number of Clients	Updates Sent to Server	Updates Sent by Server
1	1	1
2	2	4
10	10	100
100	100	100,000

That update rate is very close to being n^2. Combine this with the ever-present threat of cheating and variable network latency, and chaos is sure to ensue.

Dumb Clients/Authoritative Server

An alternative to having the server dutifully serve whatever the clients report without question is to have an authoritative server with "dumb" clients. This approach makes cheating less of a problem, while reducing network traffic. Clients receive routine updates from the server, indicating game state. Player commands are issued as requests to the server. If it deems a request possible, the server updates its state and sends it to the clients. If a request is impossible or invalid—for instance, holding down the spacebar to send "rapid-fire" events—the server will drop it. The server will also combine updates so that it can send out fewer of them.

Its parameters similar to those in Table 11-2, , Table 11-3 demonstrates how an authoritative server dramatically reduces load.

Table 11-3. *Reducing Load via an Authoritative Server*

Number of Clients	Updates Sent to Server	Updates Sent by Server
1	1	1
2	2	2
10	10	10
100	100	100

In the two examples presented here, I talked about the two extremes and chose to view them through the lens of network load. There are many intermediate variants that take into account the individual needs of the game being designed. A good place to start is the still relevant Valve paper "Source Multiplayer Networking" (https://developer.valvesoftware.com/wiki/Source_Multiplayer_Networking). Also of interest would be anything on multiplayer networking from the Association for Computing Machinery Digital Library (ACM DL) or the Institute of Electrical and Electronics Engineers (IEEE).

Case Studies

So far, you have only looked at WebSockets in the abstract. In the following sections, you will examine source code from games that use WebSockets.

GRITS

GRITS is a multiplayer, top-down battle game designed by Google engineers to act as an example implementation of an HTML5-based game leveraging best-of-breed HTML5 technology, such as Canvas, WebSockets, Google App Engine, and Google+ integration.

GRITS employs one of the concepts introduced earlier, the authoritative server (see the section "Dumb Clients/Authoritative Server"). Here, clients send requests for specific actions to the server, the server pushes its state to the clients, and the clients see this as the source of truth, overriding any local data. Listing 11-14 displays the setup of GRITS's socket for handling directional input when using an Android device.

Listing 11-14. GRITS's Directional Input Socket for Android

```
var controller_endpoint = '/'+game_id+'!'+id;
console.log('STARTING TO LISTEN ON WASD CHANNEL', controller_endpoint);
io.of(controller_endpoint).on('connection', function(wasdSocket) {
  ref = {};
  console.log('CONTROLLER CONNECTED TO WASD CHANNEL', controller_endpoint);
  wasdSocket.on('disconnect', function(msg) {
    console.log('RECEIVED DISCONNECT FOR WASD CHANNEL', controller_endpoint);
  });
  wasdSocket.on('message', function(msg) {
    // console.log('GOT WASD CONTROLLER MESSAGE', msg,
    //           'ON WASD CHANNEL', controller_endpoint);
    wasdSocket.send('ack ' + msg);
    if (msg.slice(0,4) == 'init') {
      ref = JSON.parse(msg.slice(4));
      return;
    }
    if (!ref['player_name']) {
      console.log('disconnecting', controller_endpoint,
      'wasd controller; received msg', msg, 'while ref has no player_name:', ref);
      wasdSocket.disconnect();
      return;
    }
    W = (msg[0] == 'Y');
    A = (msg[1] == 'Y');
    S = (msg[2] == 'Y');
    D = (msg[3] == 'Y');
    socket.q_wasd({from: ref['player_name'].slice(1), W: W, A: A, S: S, D: D});
  });
});
```

Readers are encouraged to watch the Google IO talk by Colt McAnlis on GRITS at https://developers.google.com/events/io/2012/sessions/gooio2012/210. The previous snippet comes from https://code.google.com/p/gritsgame/source/browse/src/games-server/main.js.

Rawkets

Rawkets is a proof-of-concept, online, multiplayer game developed by Rob Hawkes, the head of developer relations at Pusher and former technical evangelist at Mozilla. The game explores HTML5 Canvas, WebGL, and WebSockets. Rawkets is reminiscent of the classic arcade game Asteroids. A simple line-art ship represents the players; they can move about the world and shoot at other players.

You can peruse the Rawkets code at https://github.com/robhawkes/rawkets. Rawkets uses PHP for some of its code. PHP is outside the scope of this chapter, so I will leave it as an exercise for the reader to work out how to install a LAMP (Linux, Apache, MySQL, PHP [or Perl]) server and get the code running.

Rawkets uses many of the techniques described earlier in this chapter. The interesting portions of code lie in the main.js file at https://github.com/robhawkes/rawkets/blob/422026f0fcd31db7645281568cf5b6d1d7668932/server/main.js.

Listing 11-15 provides all the specific message types in Rawkets. A unit of data for a Rawkets game takes this general form.

Listing 11-15. All Message Types in Rawkets, in the File main.js

```
{type: <MESSAGE TYPE ID>, arg1: value1, arg2: value2, ...}

/**
 * Message protocols
 */
var MESSAGE_TYPE_PING = 1;
var MESSAGE_TYPE_UPDATE_PING = 2;
var MESSAGE_TYPE_NEW_PLAYER = 3;
var MESSAGE_TYPE_SET_COLOUR = 4;
var MESSAGE_TYPE_UPDATE_PLAYER = 5;
var MESSAGE_TYPE_REMOVE_PLAYER = 6;
var MESSAGE_TYPE_AUTHENTICATION_PASSED = 7;
var MESSAGE_TYPE_AUTHENTICATION_FAILED = 8;
var MESSAGE_TYPE_AUTHENTICATE = 9;
var MESSAGE_TYPE_ERROR = 10;
var MESSAGE_TYPE_ADD_BULLET = 11;
var MESSAGE_TYPE_UPDATE_BULLET = 12;
var MESSAGE_TYPE_REMOVE_BULLET = 13;
var MESSAGE_TYPE_KILL_PLAYER = 14;
var MESSAGE_TYPE_UPDATE_KILLS = 15;
var MESSAGE_TYPE_REVIVE_PLAYER = 16;

socket = ws.createServer();
serverStart = new Date().getTime();

players = [];
bullets = [];

// On incoming connection from client
socket.on("connection", function(client) {

    socket.broadcast(formatMessage(MESSAGE_TYPE_REMOVE_BULLET, {i: bulletId}));
    socket.broadcast(formatMessage(MESSAGE_TYPE_KILL_PLAYER, {i: player.id}));
    socket.broadcast(formatMessage(MESSAGE_TYPE_UPDATE_KILLS, {i: bulletPlayer.id,
k: bulletPlayer.killCount}));
    socket.broadcast(formatMessage(MESSAGE_TYPE_UPDATE_BULLET, {i: bullet.id,
x: bullet.x, y: bullet.y}));

    // omitted code
});
```

The helper function formatMessage converts the arguments into a JavaScript object and binary encodes it before passing it to the socket to broadcast to other clients:

```
function formatMessage(type, args) {
        var msg = {type: type};
```

```
    for (var arg in args) {
            // Don't overwrite the message type
            if (arg != "type")
                    msg[arg] = args[arg];
    };


    //return JSON.stringify(msg);
    return BISON.encode(msg);
};
```

BiSON is similar in many respects to BSON and MessagePack; BiSON is more lightweight than JSON and can more efficiently store types. However, BiSON lacks the mindshare of BSON and MessagePack. You can read more about BiSON on its project page at https://github.com/BonsaiDen/BiSON.js.

Off-the-Shelf Solutions and WebSocket-likeProducts

When creating a game, you are not limited to pure WebSockets or a solution like Socket.io. There are several technologies either similar to or based on WebSockets that can be used to create games.

Firebase

Firebase (www.firebase.com) provides a real-time API for syncing and accessing data. Firebase has client libraries and bindings for most mobile and web platforms, while offering the option of a Representational state transfer (REST) API if your favorite language or framework is not supported. Firebase is somewhat like WebSockets plus a data store wrapped up in the same package.

Firebase stores data in a JSON-like format, and it allows you to access the data through one of several options:

- A client library

- Vanilla REST calls

- A browser

Everything that you store is addressable by its object path. For instance, consider a player object stored at the root http://MyGame.firebaseIO-demo.com and represented by the following code:

```
ud7h3if: {
    name: 'John',
    vitals: {
        health: 80,
        attack: 20,
        weapons: ['pistol', 'rifle', 'machete']
    }
}
```

You could display the object by navigating to http://MyGame.firebaseIO-demo.com/ud7h3if, or perhaps only the vitals or weapons by going to http://MyGame.firebaseIO-demo.com/ud7h3if/vitals or ttp://MyGame.firebaseIO-demo.com/ud7h3if/vitals/weapons, respectively.

Unlike WebSockets, in which you listen for message and connectivity events, Firebase events all deal with the underlying object model. They are

1. value

2. child added

3. child changed

4. child removed

5. child moved

Because each property is individually addressable, on http://MyGame.firebaseIO-demo.com/ud7h3if/vitals/weapons, you could trigger the child added or child removed handler functions when the player picks up or drops a weapon or to monitor changes in health. All Firebase clients maintain a copy of the data and fire any attached callbacks locally before the data are synced to the other clients. This system of eventual consistency means that some clients may be in a transitional state for some time until all the data have been propagated. Firebase will merge updates from clients as needed.

As a result, Firebase is great for turn-based games or even some light real-time games, but it doesn't offer enough control for games such as GRITS or Rawkets.

Pusher

Pusher is a software as a service (SaaS) provider of a hosted WebSocket API. Pusher includes fallbacks for noncompliant browsers and libraries (both client and server) in many languages to give the developer a single API to learn. Letting someone else deal with the WebSocket code frees you to offload those responsibilities to Pusher and just work on integration. Many programming languages do have some sort of WebSocket API, but they generally aren't as mature as Socket.io. If your application is not written in Node.js, you have to worry about finding a library or server that supports even a fraction of what Socket.io does. Pusher gives you the best of both worlds: a mature and fully featured solution and no responsibility to maintain a separate socket server.

Channels and Events

Channels are how Pusher implements its publish/subscribe (pub/sub) model. Channels roughly correspond to Socket.io rooms and can be public or private. Private-channel members are authenticated by an endpoint on the application server as part of the subscription process. Pusher also keeps a presence channel that lets an application inquire about the channel's currently subscribed members. The beauty of Pusher's channel model is that there is only one API to learn. Public, private, and presence channels are differentiated only by the default events to which they subscribe and whether they require authentication.

Events are user- or system-defined states that trigger server or client code when that state is attained. All channels are bound with events that are triggered when there is a successful new subscription or a subscription error. Presence channels add events that are triggered when members are added or removed.

Pusher has a free tier and several paid tiers. The lower tiers can fit most small applications but don't offer secure sockets layer (SSL) encryption.

You can read more about Pusher on its web site: http://pusher.com.

Kaazing

Kaazing's commercial WebSocket platform offers the infrastructure and protocol libraries that make it easier to build real-time, in-game experiences, such as peer-to-peer, chat, virtual-goods shopping, auctions, and game-state notifications for players who are away from the game. Kaazing also provides hosted, cloud-based WebSocket servers to take the hassle out of deployment. You can read more about Kaazing and gaming at http://kaazing.com/industries/online-gaming.

Conclusion

In this chapter, I gave a brief overview of WebSockets and how they work. I presented several examples using WebSockets and noted how you could reduce the amount of data going across the wire. I closed with some examples from third-party games and a consideration of alternatives to hosting your own WebSocket server.

In the next chapter, you will learn how to add multiplayer support to a game to increase the range of experiences that a player can have by introducing the elements of human psychology and social interaction to the game agents.

CHAPTER 12

Real-Time Multiplayer Network Programming

Jason Gauci, Research Scientist, Apple

Many of the most popular games have a multiplayer component. All but one of the top ten most popular games on Steam, a digital distribution and communications platform for PCs, are either designed for a multiplayer experience or contain support for multiplayer (see Table 12-1). As you will discover in this chapter, adding multiplayer support to a game increases the range of experiences that a player can have by introducing the elements of human psychology and social interaction to the game agents. However, adding real-time multiplayer can be rather tricky to implement correctly. Although it may seem daunting, by following some principled methods, you can add a new, exciting dimension to your game.

Table 12-1. *Most Popular Games by Player Count (at time of writing)*

Game Name	Multiplayer
Dota 2	Yes
Team Fortress 2	Yes
Terraria	Yes
Civilization V	Yes
Counter-Strike: Global Offensive	Yes
Garry's Mod	Yes
Path of Exile	Yes
The Elder Scrolls V: Skyrim	No
Batman: Arkham Origins	Yes
Total War: Rome II	Yes

This chapter will begin by explaining real-time multiplayer network programming and then discuss what makes this area of software engineering so challenging. The chapter will cover two powerful techniques for implementing real-time multiplayer network programming and offer tips and tricks to make the process as simple as possible. The chapter concludes with a case study, including links to source code and documentation.

Introduction

Clearly, the Internet and HTML5 were designed with multiple clients in mind. According to a survey by Netcraft, as of March 2012 there were more than 600 million active web sites,[1] most designed to serve multiple agents simultaneously. The unique challenge with real-time multiplayer network programming is at the intersection of the term's component parts: "real-time," "multiplayer," "network programming." To illustrate, note how removing one of these terms reduces the complexity substantially.

"Real-time" suggests that the game requires simultaneous, precise coordination among players (either for cooperative or competitive goals). Players must have an accurate, up-to-date description of the shared game state at all times. Providing this description quickly is challenging because of latency (for more information, see the section "Latency"). For games designed to be played gradually (e.g., chess), or games in which only one person is actively modifying the game state at any given time (e.g., poker), latency is not an issue. Implementing these games is actually no different from creating a modern web site. (For more information on building a web platform that can push data from the server to clients when latency is not an issue, check out ShareJS or DerbyJS, which itself is built on ShareJS).

Multiplayer games contain several human agents, who work together or against one another in the same game instance. Note that simply having a global leaderboard in an otherwise single-player game does not make the game multiplayer, because one player's high score does not affect the current game of another player. Also note that most social network games, such as *FarmVille*, are not considered multiplayer in this context, because each player is operating within his or her own sandbox, and sharing content between these sandboxes is limited and not real time. For these and other single-player games, the clients and server can exchange data at their leisure, without time-sensitive synchronization (for more information, see the section "Synchronization").

Network programming in this context involves a constant stream of communication from each single client to all other clients. This is in contrast to many web applications, in which most of the data flow from the server to each client, in sparse intervals. If several people are taking turns on one keyboard or playing at the same computer with different joysticks, the effects of all player actions can be known immediately, and this local multiplayer does not constitute a networked game.

Although this area of game programming is rather specific and presents a unique set of challenges, it also affords an unparalleled level of engagement for your players. The next sections discuss the core challenges of real-time multiplayer network programming.

Challenges

The three main challenges in real-time multiplayer network programming are bandwidth, latency, and synchronization. The following sections cover each of these in detail.

Bandwidth

One of the challenges in real-time multiplayer network programming is bandwidth. Unlike many web applications, networked games require a significant stream of data from each client to every other client. This means that the amount of data each client must transmit to the others increases linearly with the number of players. To illustrate, suppose a player action consumes 256B of data, and a player can make 60 actions a second. In a 2-player game, approximately 15KB will be received per player per second (256 × 60). However, in a 100-player game, approximately 150KB of data per second will be received by each client, which is a significant amount of data for most home Internet connections. This is why massively multiplayer online (MMO) games typically have shards (clones of the game that are isolated from one another) and instances (areas of the game in which a small subset of the players are isolated from the rest of the shard). By isolating smaller groups of players, the actions of these players do not need to be shared with the rest of the world in real time. Also, much of the data do not need to be shared at all. For example, the real-time location of your character in an instance does not need to be known by other players of your guild who aren't in the instance.

---

[1] Julie Bort, "How Many Web Sites Are There?," http://www.businessinsider.com/how-many-web-sites-are-are-there-2012-3, March 8, 2012.

At the dawn of real-time multiplayer network programming, network engineers established peer-to-peer connections among players, whereby all players (peers) are connected to each other and can send their actions to each other directly. Although this reduces the overall network traffic, connecting all peers is problematic, owing to one-way firewalls and routers, which have become commonplace among today's Internet users. As a result, there will be a subset of peers between whom a connection cannot be made, and the server will have to route messages for these peers, regardless. Thus, most modern games use a client-server model, whereby all traffic passes through a central server. This server is typically a dedicated machine with low packet latency and high bandwidth. Because data are flowing through the server, clients need to send their actions to only one destination, dramatically reducing upload bandwidth, but at the expense of increased latency (see Figure 12-1).

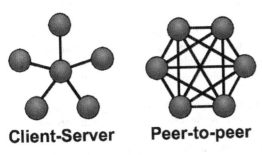

Client-Server   Peer-to-peer

Figure 12-1. Graphical model of peer-to-peer and client-server network topologies (courtesy of Wikimedia)

Latency

Latency is the measure of time delay experienced by a system. Typically, two types of latency concern network programmers.

The first is *input latency*, the time between when the user requests an action (e.g., by pressing a button) and when that action appears to take place. In games such as *WarCraft III*, an early real-time strategy (RTS) game designed when many of the players were on high-latency Internet connections, the game plays an acknowledgment sound immediately after the user takes an action. This audio cue indicates to the user that his or her action has been received, even though the input has not taken effect. This trick and other visual and audio illusions can simulate lower levels of input latency, without making changes to the game engine.

The second form of latency is *state latency* (also called simply latency), which measures the time between when a local action is taken and when that action is received by all the remote clients. This is the true measure of latency in a system, and there are few ways to reduce it. However, it is possible to hide state latency through client-side prediction (for more information, see the section "Client-Side Prediction").

Synchronization

Synchronization is the most challenging problem facing network programmers. When a new client joins a game in progress, or a new game begins, the server must perform an initial sync, whereby the complete state of the game, including any custom assets, or server-specific settings, are sent to the new client. After the initial sync, the server can strictly route client actions and assume that all clients executing the same actions will maintain exactly the same game state. This is known as the lockstep method. The server can also continue to send the complete game state at regular intervals, along with all client actions. This is known as the state broadcast method. When two clients are playing on the same server but contain different game states because of a problem in the network code, they are said to be out of sync. Two out-of-sync clients may each perceive that he or she is winning the game, when in fact the client's opponent is moving, based on his or her own divergent game state. When two clients are experiencing a different game because of a permanent out-of-sync condition, this is called a desync and results in frustrated players and a bad player experience.

These sections have covered several important problems in network programming. The following section discusses two very different approaches that deal with these problems in different ways.

State Broadcast vs. Lockstep

The most intuitive approach to network programming is the *Lockstep method*, whereby the server performs the initial sync and then broadcasts only player actions, with the expectation that all players will simulate exactly the same game. Although the lockstep method is the most bandwidth-efficient approach, it suffers from many issues. First, it requires that each client processes the same actions at the same time. This means that any packet loss or out-of-order packets are unacceptable. Second, the game engine must be entirely deterministic, with no randomness (but note that it is possible to use pseudorandom numbers, so long as all clients share the same seed, or the random numbers are presented in advance from the server). Third, the use of floating point in these systems is problematic, as floating-point computations vary slightly from one machine to another, and these differences can accumulate until the clients are out of sync. Note that the use of floating-point numbers outside the game engine is fine; so long as they have no effect on the game, they can be used in displaying graphics, audio processing, and so on with no problem.

Another approach is the *state broadcast method*, iwhereby the server broadcasts the complete game state to all clients, and each client replaces his or her own game state with the server copy periodically. Although this approach ensures that the server automatically resolves any synchronization issues, it also dramatically increases the amount of bandwidth that the server must use. For example, if the game state is 1KB, and there are 32 players in the game, the server would have to upload 320KB per second to send the ten updates per second necessary to create a smooth experience. For games such as *Minecraft*, which has a game state on the order of megabytes, this approach is intractable. Note that, even when applying the state broadcast method, clients still need to share actions so that they can fast-forward (for more information, see the section "Fast-Forwarding the Game State").

Dealing with Latency

Regardless of which method is used, the problem of latency has to be addressed. Note that a single player's latency is the amount of time it takes for data to travel from his or her computer to the server. For a client-server architecture, the state latency is the time between when a player requests an action on his or her machine and when that action reaches the player with the most latent connection. When a player takes an action, the server delays the action by the state latency. The expectation is that the client's action reaches all other players in time for everyone to execute the action at exactly the same time. If the server delays the action by too much, the game will not feel responsive, making it hard for the player to time his or her actions precisely. If the server delays the action by too little, the game is frozen until players can receive overdue messages, and this can cause stuttering, throwing off the rhythm of the game.

Client-Side Prediction

One of the challenges in real-time multiplayer network programming is *latency prediction*, estimating the latency among all machines in the game. When the prediction is not accurate, latency can cause stuttering in the game play or intermittent pausing. Even with accurate latency prediction, the delay between physically pressing a button and seeing the effect of that press can be disorienting. To address these problems, one can add *client-side prediction*. With client-side prediction, each client stores two copies of the game state: one copy that contains completely accurate information but that is delayed because of latency and another that is current but that assumes that no other clients have sent any new actions. As the client receives new actions or game states from the server, the client updates his or her delayed copy of the game state, replaces the current copy with a copy of the delayed game state, and fast-forwards the newly copied state to the present time (see Figure 12-2). This technique gives the illusion of responding to player actions immediately, while also correcting the state as it goes out of sync.

Client changes direction, takes
effect immediately on client's machine

Server receives action later,
action takes effect on the server.

Client receives the same change from
the server along with when the change
actually took place, adjusts accordingly

Figure 12-2. *Client-side prediction and correction; note that care should be taken when writing the graphics engine to smoothly correct for these transitions (car image courtesy of Wikimedia)*

When using client-side prediction with correction, clients can make new assumptions about when an action should be processed. Without client-side prediction, clients must delay their inputs, basing them on the time it is expected the input will take to reach all other clients. With client-side prediction, clients can reduce input delay to an arbitrary number. As client delay decreases, the number of fast-forwards increases, and the game will feel more responsive, but it will also contain more stuttering. As the delay increases, the number of fast-forwards decreases, but the input latency will increase. The important point to note here is that adding client-side prediction removes the latency constraint on the system and gives the developer more freedom. Adding client-side prediction also keeps the entire game from halting when a particular user experiences packet loss. Note how in RTS games, such as the first *Starcraft*, the entire game must slow down when a single player's connection quality decreases (i.e., when, during play, a box pops up with the heading "Waiting for Players"). This is because many RTSs do not have client-side prediction. The reason they do not is that their game state is so large and that reversing actions is difficult.

Synchronized Time Among Clients

To deal with latency effectively, all clients and the server must have the same absolute time. If a client's operating system clock is different from the server's clock, the client will either send his or her messages too late or try to simulate too far into the future. In both cases, the client's experience will be choppy and could affect the other clients in the system. To address this, a *Network Time Protocol* (*NTP*) synchronization process can be added to calculate a time that all computers can agree on. Two approaches to NTP are to sync with the server's time or to sync with a third-party NTP server. One library that implements a simple NTP client and server is Socket-NTP (`https://github.com/calvinfo/socket-ntp`).

Fast-Forwarding the Game State

With client-side prediction, there can be times when the server sends the client a copy of the game state that is older than the current time. In this case, the client must fast-forward the game state by playing many frames of the game engine in rapid succession. To fast-forward from a past state, it is important that each client keep a history of actions received since the last received game state. During fast-forwarding, the client replays actions experienced in the past.

Figure 12-3 illustrates fast-forwarding. In the first image the client has predicted a car moving in a straight line. The second image depicts a new state from the server, in which the car has made a left turn. Because the left turn event took place before the current time of the predicted state, the client must go back in time, apply the left turn, and then fast-forward in time to catch up to the predicted time. This ensures that the player's perception of time always moves in one direction. Note that, when rewinding or fast-forwarding, the user interface (i.e., graphics, sound, and so on) are not updated, so the player does not experience the rewind or fast-forward, but only the causal effects of these actions.

Remote player appears
to be going straight.

Client receives an input from the
remote player in the past, rewinds to
the time of the action

Client fast-forwards back to the
present time so that the rewind is
not noticed by the player, but the
car will teleport to the new location
in present time.

Figure 12-3. Fast-Forwarding the game state

Tips and Tricks

The following sections illustrate some handy tips and tricks for writing network code.

Keep Client Input Times Monotonically Increasing

If the client predicts that one of his or her inputs will arrive at time t, then the following input from that client should have an expected arrival time greater than t. Note that, because latency between connections changes randomly and as new players arrive and leave, many input delay calculations can cause the time not to be monotonically increasing. In this case, artificially set the input time slightly higher than the previous until the times stabilize. Assuming that inputs from other clients are monotonically increasing in time makes coding the receiving logic simpler and reduces the number of fast-forwards.

Keep the Game State Independent from the Rest of the Game

Consider a hockey game, in which the goalie's position determines whether he or she blocks a slap shot. The goalie's position must be included in the game state. It may be tempting to use the model from the graphics engine to determine whether the slap shot is blocked, but this removes the isolation of the game engine from the rest of the system. Removing this isolation makes fast-forwarding problematic (e.g., graphics engines are often capped at a certain number of frames per second [FPS] and will not run any higher). Do not make the game state depend on the state of the graphics or physics engine. If the game logic depends on physics, then the physics engine needs to be part of the game state (i.e., the physics state should be copied into the game state at every frame).

Avoid Floating Point in the Game State

As mentioned previously, floating-point calculations are not deterministic across machines. This is because some processors have special instructions that allow them to do floating-point math with higher precision than others. Also, some compilers are more aware of these special instructions and will use them at different times from other compilers. With JavaScript in particular, all arithmetic is performed in floating point. Although this technically means that no math can be performed on the game state, in practice all operations on small integers (i.e., less than one million) will yield the same result across processors, operating systems, and interpreters. Note that most physics engines involve many floating-point calculations. In this case, expect that clients will be slightly out of sync, use the state broadcast method, and continuously correct the physics engine as new states arrive. To use client-side prediction, the physics engine must be fast enough to support fast-forwarding and be able to serialize/restore the state of the engine to the game state.

Keep the Game Engine Small

The game state should only include the information necessary to run a headless (i.e., graphic-less) version of your game. Images, textures, music files, your site's URL, and other information that does not directly affect game logic should not be part of the game state. Keeping your game state small has a dramatic effect on the overall bandwidth consumption of the network. Also, maintaining a light game engine will make it easier to fast-forward the game when the client needs to catch up. Separate the game engine from the rest of the system so that it can be updated without updating graphics, sound, or other parts of the game. Physics engines again complicate this, because they often have an unavoidable effect on the game engine. In this case, the physics engine needs to be considered part of the game engine, and the physics world state, part of the game state.

Interpolate Between Game States

Because of bandwidth limitations, the game state can only update ten or fewer times a second, yet most games run at 60 FPS. The way to ensure that your game is smooth is to interpolate the graphics between game states. For example, if the unit is at position 1 in the current game state, and that same unit is known to be at position 2 in the next game state, the graphics engine can slide that unit from 1 to 2 while the game engine is in between states. Interpolation also lessens the effect of server correction by smoothly sliding units into their correct positions.

Do not Assume a Particular Sequence of Game States

Many graphical and sound effects depend on a particular game-state change, such as scoring a point. Note that, because the server is updating the client's game state, and the client is trying to predict future game states that may not be accurate, any subsequent graphical or sound effects may be invalid. Care must be taken to ensure that the graphics and sounds are still smooth, despite jumps in game state. One method for handling this is only to play notification sounds when the server and the client agree on an event.

Send Checksums of the Game State

Because bugs in the network engine typically do not crash the game, it is important to send checksums of the game state frequently. A checksum is a small sequence of characters intended to describe a larger block of data. Although it is possible, in theory, for two clients to have a different game state with the same checksum, it is highly unlikely. Adding and verifying checksums will allow you to catch errors as soon as such errors cause the game state to go out of sync. Checksums make the debugging process much simpler by isolating exactly where there can be a bug in the code. One common method of generating a checksum in JavaScript is to stringify the game-state object and then use a library, such as CryptoJS (https://code.google.com/p/crypto-js/), to hash the string. This small hash can then be passed around as the checksum.

Case Study: *FrightCycle*

FrightCycle is a Halloween-themed light-cycle racing game, in which players try to trap each other with the trail of their light cycle, while also avoiding collision with other trails, their own trail, and the sides of the map. *FrightCycle* fits the description of a real-time multiplayer network game because all players make decisions simultaneously, timing is of importance, and several players can play a game across the Internet. To view the repository for *FrightCycle*, visit the following URL: https://github.com/MisterTea/JSRealtimeNetworking.

The next sections begin with an overview of the technology used in *FrightCycle* and then discuss the specifics of implementing a state broadcast system with time synchronization and client-side prediction.

Getting Started

Although much of the technology in *FrightCycle* is not specific to real-time network programming and is thus outside the scope of this chapter, it is important to spend some time explaining the code base. First, let's look at the dependencies:

- Browserify allows the same "require" syntax (known as CommonJS requires) in node.js to work in browser-based JavaScript. Browserify can also obfuscate and compress client-side JavaScript.

- Socket.IO is an event-based WebSocket client and server library. This library handles the real-time communication in *FrightCycle*.

- Express is a node.js web application framework. It deals with the server-side routing and HTML generation.

- AngularJS is a client-side web application framework. It handles client-side routing and HTML generation.

- Clone deep copies objects.

- Underscore allows object merging, among many other useful functions.

- Fabric.js provides a scene-graph library on top of HTML5 Canvas.

- NTPClient lets the clients and the server agree on a common time.

Next, let's cover the files at a high level. First, the server files:

- server/app.js contains the main server loop and event handlers for client events.

- server/GameManager.js handles spawning/releasing games and registering players to games.

Now, the client files:

- public/js/main.js initializes the network engine that is the entry point for *FrightCycle*.

- common/ai.js offers some simple logic for artificial intelligence (AI) players. Note that the AI players do not use the network engine and are queried for commands at every tick.

- common/game.js is the main loop for the client code. It drives the game, network, input, and rendering engines.

- common/geometry.js holds several functions specific to the *FrightCycle* game logic.

- common/globals.js contains many important constants and global parameters.

- common/input.js provides code for converting player key presses to in-game commands.

- common/network.js is the interface between client and server.

- common/renderer.js has the rendering engine.

Before diving into the code, let's run the game. First, you need the code. You can download a snapshot of the code from the Source Code/Download area of the Apress web site (www.apress.com), or open a shell, and enter the following command for the most recent copy:

```
git clone https://github.com/MisterTea/JSRealtimeNetworking.git
```

Next, you have to compile the client-side code into a single bundle with Browserify. To do this, enter the JSRealtimeNetworking directory, and run the following command:

```
node build.js
```

This creates a file called bundle.js in the public/js folder. The bundle.js file contains the entire client-side source code for the project and is referenced by the playgame HTML fragment, which is in server/views/playgame.ejs:

```
<!DOCTYPE html>
<html xmlns:ng="http://angularjs.org">
    <head>
        <script src="js/bundle.js"></script>
    </head>
```

```
    <body>
        <div ng-controller="WelcomeCtrl">
            <p>Welcome <%= playerId %></p>
        </div>
        <canvas id="c" width="800" height="600"
                    style="border:1px solid #000000;">
        </canvas>
    </body>
</html>
```

Note that the bundle.js file can be minified and obfuscated for added performance and security. The Browserify options are located in the build.js file. Once the client-side code is compiled, start the server with the following command:

```
node server/app.js
```

You should see some logging that ends with this code:

```
Express server listening on port 3000
```

The server is now running. To create a new game, enter the following URL in any modern web browser:

```
http://localhost:3000/playgame?playerid=Player1&gameid=1234
```

This command creates a new game room with the ID 1234 and adds player "Player1" to the room. After the initial handshake and state transfer, the game will start, and you can direct your light cycle with the W, S, A, and D keys. To test the networking capability, open a second browser tab, and visit the following URL:

```
http://localhost:3000/playgame?playerid=Player2&gameid=1234
```

Separate the tabs on your screen so that you can see both at the same time. Note that each tab controls a different player but that the changes from one player are propagated to the other player in rea -time. The remainder of the chapter is dedicated to explaining how this demo application works.

The Game State

As described previously, it is important to keep the game state as small as possible. The game state for *FrightCycle* contains the following elements:

- *Tick*: An integer that is incremented at every game engine update.

- *GameStartTick*: This contains the tick when the game begins (i.e., when the light cycles begin moving); if less than the current tick, the game is active.

- *Players*: An associative array that holds objects for each light cycle (where it is, the trails it has left behind, who is controlling it, and so on).

- *ConnectedClients*: A list of player IDs that were connected to the game server during this state.

Communication Between the Server and Client

The client begins by handshaking with the server. As part of this process, the client and server exchange a token ID that uniquely identifies the browser session with a game Id/player Id pair. As a result, a player can participate in two games simultaneously on two browser sessions but can also reenter the same game in case there is a disconnect. After the handshaking, the server sends the entire state and command histories to the client. Note that, with 100 states generated every second, these objects are rather large. Sending the current state is not sufficient, because a new client may need to reverse time in order to handle input from a lagging client. Even so, a potential optimization would be to send only recent states and ensure a maximum latency on a single input. The following code describes this initial process:

```
On Client (network.js):
var socket = io.connect('http://' + window.location.hostname + ':' + window.location.port);
this.socket = socket;
ntp.init(socket);
socket.emit('clientinit', {
  gameid: gameId,
  tokenid: token
});
```

```
On Server (app.js):
ntp.sync(socket);
socket.on('clientinit', function(data) {
  setTimeout(function() {
    var handler = gameManager.getGameHandler(data.gameid);
    var playerId = handler.tokenPlayerMap[data.tokenid];
    socket.set('playerId', playerId, function() {
      socket.set('gameId', data.gameid, function() {
        var game = handler.game;
        var firstCommandMs = (game.tick * g.MS_PER_TICK) + g.LATENCY_MS;
        gameManager.registerRemotePlayer(
          data.gameid,
          data.tokenid,
          firstCommandMs);
        console.log("Sending join command");
        socket.emit('serverinit', {
          startTime: game.startTime,
          tick: game.tick,
          stateHistory: clone(game.stateHistory),
          commandHistory: clone(game.commandHistory)
        });

        var command = {};
        command[playerId] = [g.PLAYER_JOIN];
        applyServerCommand(data.gameid, command);
      });
    });
  // Wait 3 seconds before accepting the client so the ntp
  // accuracy can improve.
  }, 3000);
});
```

Once this initial phase is complete, the client and the server begin communicating back and forth in real time. The server sends states, player commands, and server commands. The client sends local player commands to be echoed to other clients. The following code snippets walk us through an input from the keyboard to the other clients:

Receiving inputs from the keyboard (input.js):

```
keys: {},
keysToDelete: [],

init: function() {
  if (typeof window === 'undefined') {
    // Only runs client-side
    return;
  }

  var that = this;
  window.addEventListener(
    "keydown",
    function(e) {
      that.keys[e.keyCode] = e.keyCode;
    },
    false);

  window.addEventListener(
    'keyup',
    function(e) {
      // Delay releasing keys to allow the game a chance to read a
      // keydown/keyup event, even if the duration is short.
      that.keysToDelete.push(e.keyCode);
    },
    false);
},

getCommands: function(game) {
  commands = [];
  if ('87' in this.keys) {
    commands.push(g.MOVE_UP);
  }
  if ('68' in this.keys) {
    commands.push(g.MOVE_RIGHT);
  }
  if ('65' in this.keys) {
    commands.push(g.MOVE_LEFT);
  }
  if ('83' in this.keys) {
    commands.push(g.MOVE_DOWN);
  }
```

```
  for (var i = 0; i < this.keysToDelete.length; i++) {
    delete this.keys[this.keysToDelete[i]];
  }
  this.keysToDelete.length = 0;

  return commands;
}
```

Sending command to the server (network.js):

```
lastProcessMs: -1,
sendCommands: function(tick, commands) {
  var processMs = (tick * g.MS_PER_TICK) + g.LATENCY_MS;

  if (this.lastProcessMs >= processMs) {
    // This command is scheduled to run before/during the previous
    // command. Move it just ahead of the previous command.

    // Note that, because of this, some commands may get dropped
    // because they are sandwiched between two other commands in
    // time. As long as all clients drop the same commands, this
    // isn't a problem.
    processMs = this.lastProcessMs + 1;
  }
  this.lastProcessMs = processMs;

  this.socket.emit('clientinput', {
    ms: processMs,
    commands: commands
  });
}
```

Receiving the command on the server (app.js):

```
var applyCommand = function(gameId, playerId, ms, commandlist) {
  var handler = gameManager.getGameHandler(gameId);
  var game = handler.game;
  var playerServerData = handler.playerServerData[playerId];

  if (game.tick * g.MS_PER_TICK >= ms) {
    // This command came in too late, we have to adjust the time
    // and apply the command later than expected.

    // Note that this makes life difficult. Now the command
    // will execute at a different time than was expected by the
    // client when the client sent the command.
    ms = (game.tick * g.MS_PER_TICK) + 1 + g.intdiv(g.LATENCY_MS, 2);
  }
```

```
  if (playerServerData.nextInputMs >= ms) {
    // Note that although we are trying to prevent this scenario
    // client-side, it can still happen because of the if
    // statement above, so we have to be prepared to deal with
    // it. If this happens on the server side, move the command
    // up to accomodate. Note that, as above, the ms of the
    // command has to be modified from the client's original
    // intent.
    ms = playerServerData.nextInputMs + 1;
  }
  playerServerData.nextInputMs = ms;

  // Apply the commandlist on the server
  game.addCommand(ms, playerId, commandlist);

  // Broadcast the commandlist to the other clients
  io.sockets.in(game.id).emit("serverinput", {
    ms: ms,
    commands: commandlist,
    playerId: playerId
  });
};
```

Receiving commands from the server (game.js):

```
addCommand: function(ms, playerId, commandList) {
  this.getCommands(ms)[playerId] = commandList;
  this.updateLastCommandMs(playerId, ms);
  var newTick = g.intdiv(ms, g.MS_PER_TICK);
  if (this.tick > newTick) {
    // A change in the past has happend, we need to rewind.
    this.tick = newTick;
  }
}
}
```

Synchronizing Time

As part of the initial handshaking, the NTP client is initialized and given a few seconds to settle. Note that the NTP client calculates the difference in time between the client and the server. The NTP client does not make any assumption about the server time's correctness and shouldn't be used as a true estimate for the current world clock. With the NTP client library, the client knows the time offset between itself and the server. This offset is important, because the server and all clients should process the same frame of the game at roughly the same time. The NTP client prevents a client from getting too far ahead of or behind the server or the other clients. The getNetworkTime() function in network.js returns the current time, as agreed on by the client and server. The game engine (game.js) uses this function to throttle the game engine Throttling means to put the processor to sleep in between frames so that the game moves at a rate that feels realistic. The following code throttles updates so that all clients are processing the same frame at about the same moment in time:

Throttling code (in game.js):
```
if (g.MS_PER_TICK > 0 && this.tick > 0) {
  // clockTick contains the tick that should be processed
  // based on the current time. In the case of a
```

```
  // fractional tick, the code rounds up.
  var clockTick = g.intdiv(this.network.getNetworkTime() - this.startTime, g.MS_PER_TICK);
  if (this.tick > clockTick) {
    // This means that the game time is ahead of real
    // time, don't process more frames.
    break;
  }
}
```

Server Commands

A server command is a special command that must be processed at the time it is issued in order for the game to progress beyond that time. As mentioned earlier, commands from clients may be dropped if the client is catching up and processing more FPS than the server. To force all clients to process all server commands, clients will not process a game update until the server command list for that tick has been received, and the server will produce exactly one command for every tick. This is similar to the lockstep model described previously but only applies to server commands. To prevent server commands from causing the client to stutter (the main drawback with the lockstep model), an artificially high latency is given to all server commands. This causes a delay in server commands, but this delay is acceptable, because server commands are not time sensitive.

Client-Side Prediction

In *FrightCycle*, client-side prediction is handled by the `CLIENT_SIDE_PREDICTION` variable in `globals.js`. Try setting this variable to `false`, and see the effect. Now, clients will wait until they have inputs from all other clients before processing the next frame. If you have a fast connection to the server, you may not notice the difference, but with a slow connection, you will notice sporadic delays; the game, however, will never be in an inconsistent state.

Conclusion

As *FrightCycle* demonstrates, the complexity of implementing a real-time network multiplayer game is trading off latency for correctness of the current state. At one extreme, a lockstep model without client-side prediction will ensure that all users have complete state information at the expense of high latency. The additional latency makes the game less responsive and can make the game difficult to play. At the other extreme, users submit actions that are effective immediately. This provides instant user feedback but causes jittering, as the game engine is constantly rolled back to apply user commands retroactively and then fast-forwarded to the present time with the additional user inputs.

■ ■ ■

CHAPTER 13

The State of Responsive Design

Tyler Smith, HTML5 Game Developer, Engineer and Tech Evangelist at AgeCheq

Colt "MainRoach" McAnlis, Developer Advocate, Google

Building an HTML5 game in the modern world is rife with difficulties. In addition to technical limitations and variations among browsers, you have the added burden of the current consumer world, which is predominantly driven by a boom in smartphones and tablet devices. What makes developing for this slew of heterogeneous devices difficult is the massive array of resolutions, physical sizes, and performance among them. For your web game to be successful, you'll need to adapt it to take advantage of the many screen resolutions available so that users can experience it on as many devices as possible. To do this, you'll need to adjust your game dynamically, depending on the current resolution, to achieve the desired game layout. This, at its core, is known as *responsive design*.

Understanding the Problem at Hand

Recall that modern screens are represented as a two-dimensional array of pixel values. However, because of the physical size of the screen, as well as the technology within, the number of pixels on a screen can vary. Screen resolution is often given in dots per inch (dpi) or pixels per inch (ppi), which is a measurement of the density of dots, or pixels, on a screen (see Figure 13-1). Higher dpi/ppi gives a screen a nicer, polished finish; this is because the increased pixel count corresponds to smaller pixels, which reduces the chance of the human eye's seeing the edge of a color. For example, Apple's Retina display doubles the number of physical pixels on the screen. Because the human eye has trouble distinguishing these smaller pixels, the increased resolution produces cleaner, more vibrant images, which helps users feel immersed in their computing. For developers, however, this increased resolution is more of a headache than a blessing.

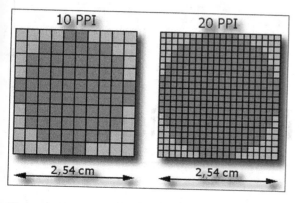

Figure 13-1. Normal vs. high-ppi screens

Typically, when creating a two-dimensional game, a developer will author sprites/images at a specific resolution (for example, 64×64 pixels). This is because there's an expectation that the number of pixels contained in an image will correspond to some physical dimension on the device (or, rather, there's an implicitly expected dpi value that developers are targeting). When a game is being rendered on a HiDPI screen, however, standard resolution bitmap images may look blocky and unpolished, as the number of pixels has increased, but the art content hasn"t. For modern mobile developers, this is a huge problem, considering the massive variety of screen resolutions available today; thus, in order to create the most responsive, smoothest-looking game possible, developers need to come prepared with a few tricks up their sleeves.

It's worth noting that in HTML5, the pixels of a page are not identical to the pixels on the screen. For instance, you may define in Cascading Style Sheets (CSS) that an object is 128 pixels wide, but that has no bearing on its physical dimensions in the real world. On lower-dpi devices, your object will look large; on higher-dpi devices, your object will look small. To address this, the document object model (DOM) has started exposing a window property called devicePixelRatio. This property defines a mapping between CSS pixels and hardware pixels, in terms of a numeric ratio.

For example, if there is a square image that is 100 pixels, and the devicePixelRatio is 2 (for example, -webkit-min-device-pixel-ratio: 2), the device hardware would then have to scale up that image to 200 pixels to take up the same amount of screen real estate. In this case, devicePixelRatio lets us know that two hardware pixels render as one CSS pixel to the screen.

Thankfully, the hardware is doing the heavy lifting for developers, in that images are automatically scaled to various resolutions for the user. Anyone who's worked with photo-editing software, however, can attest that resizing an image is not the best way to preserve clarity and color quality. In fact, algorithms for scaling images are a large and continual topic of research in academia, simply because there's a constant trade-off between image content, time to encode, and perceived image quality output. In an ideal world, a developer would be able to state which type of scaling algorithm the hardware should use for a particular image, but sadly, we"re still far from that. When the device automatically scales the image, bilinear filtering is typically the default algorithm chosen, because of its low performance requirements. For games, however, this is not the best upscaling algorithm to use, as it often results in blurry images that lack crispness. To be fair, there's no single best upscaling filter; game developers may need to experiment with muliple codecs before deciding to move away from bilinear or embracing a different codec for their data set. Table 13-1 shows the most common tablet resolutions available today and their aspect ratios.

Table 13-1. *The Most Common Tablet Resolutions and Their Aspect Ratios*

Name	Resolution	Aspect Ratio
WVGA	800 × 600	1.333
WSVGA	1024 × 576 or 1024 × 600	1.777 or 1.706666
XGA	1024 × 768	1.333
WXGA	1280 × 800 or 1366 × 768	1.6 or 1.7786
WXGA+	1440 × 900	1.6W
SXGA+	1600 × 900	1.777
WUXGA	1920 × 1080 or 1920 × 1200	1.777 or 1.6
QXGA	2048 × 1536	1.333
WQHD	2560 × 1440 or 2560 × 1600	1.777 or 1.6

Getting the Screen Dimensions

Because you're planning to adapt your gameplay mechanics based on screen size, getting the screen dimensions right becomes essential in making your game work correctly. However, you'll soon discover that fetching the size of the window is not identical across all platforms.

Resolutions on the Desktop

Getting screen dimensions on a desktop browser is fairly straightforward. Using window.innerHeight and window. innerWidth will give you the pixel values of the browser window in which the game is located. Fortunately, every modern browser will return the expected value:

```
var canvas = document.getElementById('canvas');
canvas.height = window.innerHeight;
canvas.width = window.innerWidth;
```

Resolutions on Mobile

Mobile display is where fragmentation runs rampant. On a given mobile device, you can be deploying your HTML5 game either in a browser or as an embedded component (also called a webview component) inside a native application (app). Unfortunately, in this environment, you can no longer simply query window.innerWidth, as too many webviews and browsers return conflicting results. For example, some will return NaN (not a number) for window.innerHeight, whereas others won't take orientation into account and will return the physical width. As such, you have to add some additional logic to your code in order to allow for these edge cases. The code that follows sets up the variables that you'd need to determine what the real width and height are of your screen:

```
// sample code for landscape games
//This code snippet is designed for both desktop and mobile use.
var width = window.innerWidth;
var height = window.innerHeight;
var screenRatio;
var realWidth;
var realHeight;
```

Initially, you're just setting some global variables. The width and the height are set to the size of the browser window/device screen. Even though width is set to window.innerWidth, more verification is needed to ensure that the value is correct, for example, checking if you're on a rotated screen. In a game that renders in landscape view, you'd expect the width always to be greater than the height. Thus, checking to see if width is greater than height is a way to confirm that these values are indeed correct:

```
if(width > height)
{
realWidth = width;
realHeight = height;
}
else
{
realWidth = height;
realHeight = width;
}
screenRatio = (realHeight / realWidth);
```

Although this seems a simplistic function, you'd be amazed at how complex the results are across devices. As a test, print out your height, width, and screenRatio from your mobile devices. realWidth and realHeight should be the correct values, even if the wrong dimensions were returned by the window.innerHeight and window.innerWidth calls. You also now have the screenRatio. But wait! There's another issue that must be resolved: some webviews return NaN for window.innerHeight and window.innerWidth. To check if this has happened, screenRatio can be evaluated to see if it's NaN:

```
if(isNaN(screenRatio))
{
if(screen.width > screen.height)
{
realWidth = screen.width;
realHeight = screen.height;
}
else
{
realWidth = screen.height;
realHeight = screen.width;
}
screenRatio = (realHeight / realWidth);
```

Because the only time NaN may be returned for window.innerWidth and window.innerHeight is on an Android device, screen.width and screen.height are an acceptable replacement. Trying to use these calls on a desktop is not recommended, as the browser window can be any size, not just the size of the device screen. screen.width and screen.height have the same problem of sometimes returning incorrect values. Checking to see which has a higher value is still required to determine if the values are correct.

Responsive Canvas

One of the first decisions you'll need to make about your responsive design is what to do, at a high level, with the canvas itself across multiple resolutions and aspect ratios.

Imagine for a moment that you have made a portrait game designed at 768×1,024 pixels. This means that you've created some layout information about where things go in this canvas space, and most likely you have defined the positions of elements in terms of pixels. If you're lucky, your game will be loaded on a device with an identical aspect ratio but a different resolution. That is, you can still be at 4:3, but with double the number of pixels. In this scenario, all your positioning data will be off; your content will be clustered at one corner of the screen, wasting valuable screen real estate.

A slightly worse scenario is that your app may be loaded on a device with a drastically different aspect ratio and dpi. In this case, things won't ever come close to looking right. To solve these problems, you first need to make an executive decision about what to do with your canvas at a high level; thankfully, the solution is simple.

Stretch

The most straightforward way to address responsive design is simply to stretch the canvas to the size of the whole screen, as shown in Figure 13-2. This is probably the easiest solution, but it only works in situations in which the device aspect ratio matches the desired one. The code that follows solves this problem, setting your canvas dimensions to the window dimensions:

```
var canvas = document.getElementById('canvas');
cvs.width = window.innerWidth;
cvs.height = window.innerHeight;
```

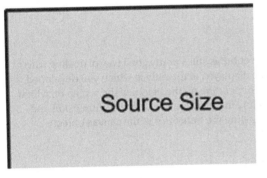

Figure 13-2. *Stretch example*

Float Middle

In reality, stretching the canvas to match the resolution of the device is a bad idea when the aspect ratio doesn't match. In these cases, you have to determine how to position your canvas such that you maintain your desired aspect ratio but can still fit your work properly on the screen.

Because the viewport fits the width of the game to the screen, you can adapt the height of your gameplay to be as tall as the smallest aspect ratio to which you'll be deploying. In other words, if you're deploying to Android, and the smallest height of the screen is 500 pixels (with the viewport on which you'll be running), then that's the maximum height with which the user should be allowed to interact. When the game is playing on a device that has, say, 768 pixels in height, the gameplay will float in the middle, and the background can have more design and ambiance (see Figure 13-3). This is good for puzzle/casual games. You could use this approach for shooting games and platformers, though we don't believe that would be the best solution. In this example, 500 represents the height of the playable portion of the game. The code listed here configures the position of your canvas to float toward the vertical middle of the screen:

```
function floatMiddle() {
var screenTop = (window.innerHeight) / 2 + "px";
document.getElementById('playablePortion').style.top = screenTop;}
```

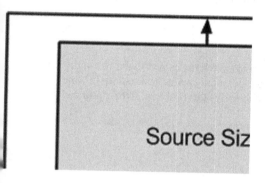

Figure 13-3. *Float middle example*

Fit Inside Screen

Letting the gameplay fit inside the screen is a little obtrusive to the user but is still a pretty good way of dealing with this issue, as shown in Figure 13-4. Basically, the game will always be displayed at the ratio at which you developed it, but black bars will appear on the left and right or top and bottom, depending on the height of the screen on which it's being played. The code that follows accomplishes this by calculating the scale amount for each dimension and determining what the minimum scaled amount should be before applying the transform to the canvas object:

```
var scaleX = canvas.width / window.innerWidth;
var scaleY = canvas.height / window.innerHeight;
var scaleToFit = Math.min(scaleX, scaleY);
stage.style.transformOrigin = "0 0"; //scale from top left
stage.style.transform = "scale(" + scaleToFit + ")";
```

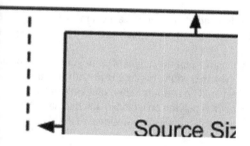

Figure 13-4. *Example of gameplay fitted inside a screen*

An Issue with ReadPixels

The problem with scaling your canvas as a solution to your rendering issues tends to go much deeper than just simple upscaling, however, and extends all the way to how browsers draw the data that eventually end up on-screen to the underlying canvas element. When you draw onto a canvas context, the browser is actually writing to an underlying central processing unit- (CPU-) side memory region called a *backing store*. The backing store is used as a form of double buffering, as you may be drawing to the canvas object while a monitor refresh event occurs. Such an event would present itself in the form of visual glitches to the user. Instead, when the browser draws to the screen, the browser reads the backing store data to paint the previously composed pixels rather than the ones you're drawing at that nanosecond. The device or browser on which your code is running dictates how the backing store is created and maintained, which can have a dramatic impact on memory, performance, and quality.

For instance, when a backing store is created for a canvas on a HiDPI screen (such as Macbook Pro with Retina display), some browsers create the backing store at a scale different from a 1:1 pixel ratio; some browsers scale at 2, whereas others scale at 1.3 or 2.4. It all depends on the device/browser and the arbitrary engineering decisions that created those code paths. The critical point here is that, as you're drawing an image to the canvas, the browser needs to upscale the image to the matching backing store resolution before copying those pixels to their screen destination.

Just as the devicePixelRatio property is used to map hardware pixels to CSS pixels, so, too, a property helps map canvas pixels to backing store pixels: backingStoragePixelData. This property defines the resolution dimensions of the backing store in relation to the canvas. To be clear: devicePixelRatio is the ratio of hardware pixels to CSS pixels, whereas **b**ackingStoragePixelData is the ratio of backing store dimensions to canvas element dimensions.

Unfortunately, all browsers implement the sizing for the backing store independently of each other. This is fine for most games, because they can safely rely on the hardware to upscale the images on their behalf. However, games that use read-back functions, such getImageData(), can run into problems, as the data returned from that function must be scaled down from the backing store size to the canvas size before being returned (for example, a 480×320 canvas on mobile Safari is a 960×640 canvas in the backing store). The result returns downscaled pixels, which often results in visual anomalies. To address this issue, some browsers are adding specific functions to fetch the backing store resolution data directly.

For instance, Safari implements webkitGetImageDataHD(), which will return an image buffer matching the backing store size. To retrieve the correct image data, you have to draw the images to the canvas with dimensions that are divided by the backingStoragePixelData. Once the backing store is created, it's scaled to the right size, thus returning the correct image data. In contrast, Chrome just creates the backing storage at exactly the same size as the canvas. So, what are the trade-offs? With Chrome, you still have to do all the heavy lifting for HiDPI screens if you don't want image blurring. The benefit is that you aren't forced into using more resources, as creating a larger backing store requires a lot more memory. The game's code can be deployed cross-platform and played on Chrome without having to plan specifically for odd backing store creation.

Responsive Layout

Laying out the position of content on your screen is an exceptionally burdensome task. Not only is it prone to massive revisions, between artists, designers, and programmers, but it's also time-consuming and repetitive in cases in which you lack a higher-level development toolchain to handle the layout for you. To complicate things further, you need to do this for each screen resolution.

The most basic developers will simply hand code their offsets into their source code, a technique that works for rapid prototyping but that often falls short once you move beyond that. Savvy developers will embrace a set of files that define the layout per resolution, but, looking at Figure 13-5, you will quickly see that that gets out of control, usually forcing developers to choose a subset of direct resolutions to support and letting the one-offs have visual problems.

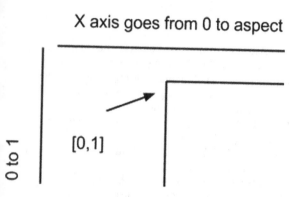

Figure 13-5. *4:3 screen coordinates expressed as absolute and aspectRatio*

A more robust and friendly approach to this problem is to define your layouts not in absolute values, given a specific resolution, but rather in normalized layouts based on aspectRatio. Or, more specifically, instead of defining the position of a screen element as [50, 200], you would define it as [0.001, 0.23].

Basically, for all two-dimensional rendering, you use a normalized coordinate system, in which one corner represents the origin (0, 0), and the opposite corner diagonally represents the extents of the screen, in terms of aspect ratio (1.33, 1.77, and so on).

For example, let's say that you use a normalized coordinate system in which the bottom-left of the screen is (0, 0), the x coordinate increases to the right, and the y coordinate increases upward. The y coordinate of the top of the screen is defined as 1.0. The x coordinate of the right side of the screen is the screen's aspect ratio. Thus, on a 4:3 screen, these are the coordinates of **the** four corners of the screen, as shown in Figure 13-5. In this simple example, this means that y = 0.5 is always the vertical center of the screen,, and that x = aspect/2 is always the horizontal center of the screen, regardless of physical screen size.

For drawing to the canvas, you'll need to adjust your final draw function to convert properly from normalized space to canvas space. For instance, instead of simply calling drawImage with your xy coordinates, you would need to pass in the values modified by the aspect ratio.

The main benefit of this process is that it allows you to reduce the number of quantized layouts that you have to design for your game. Previously, when you were working in pixels as the unit of positioning, you needed a layout definition for almost every combination of screen sizes. (To be fair, using a quantized bucket of layouts would get you close, but you'd have no way of responding to edge cases.) Using a normalized coordinate system, however, lets you define a handful of layouts, each targeting a specific aspect ratio. At worst, you'd need to support one file for each of the unique aspect ratios listed in Table 13-1 for each orientation (portrait or landscape).

Responsive Content

One thing to keep in mind is that even with a normalized coordinate system, you still quickly run into problems regarding the size of the images you're trying to render. The previous technique can properly position them, but if you've authored your sprite to be 64×64 pixels, it may still be incorrect in terms of screen resolution.

In general, anytime your canvas resolution, or dpi, changes, you're going to find a discrepancy with your content. In reality, the previous sections are designed to be simple solutions to a very complex problem. The real problem you're trying to solve for two-dimensional games is how to scale your individual sprites/images to match the proper dimensions and dpi for your target screen.

If you considered a world where resources were free, then you would see that the solution to this problem is to have a version of your two-dimensional content that exactly matches the resolution of the device on which it's being experienced: smartphone, tablet, laptop, desktop, television, watch. The issue with this is that there tends to be an unlimited number of resolutions and form factors on which to experience your content, and drafting pixel-perfect versions of your content can be overly expensive.

From a development-process viewpoint, developers define a handful of specific, explicitly supported resolutions. These may be for a set of trusted devices or a set of resolutions with which the content looks good and doesn't need modification, as illustrated in Figure 13-6. Clients can push their resolutions/dimensions to the server before fetching their image data, allowing clients to get closer to a perfect representation.

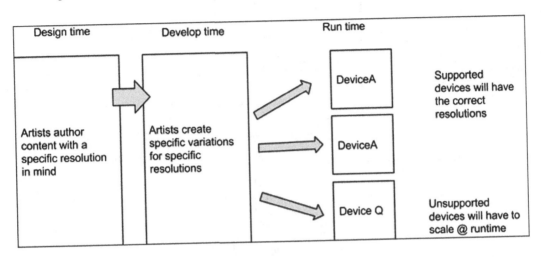

Figure 13-6. *Effect of design and development on supported devices*

Working with a Cloud Computing Resource

Those who are truly daring can go one step further with the help of a cloud computing resource. Rather than simply quantizing resolutions to one of the predefined sets (and coupling the client with one of the adaptive canvas solutions), a cloud computing resource can compute the exact size of the image that you want and return that to the client. These pixel-specific resolution images can then be cached on the server and supplied on-demand to the client as he or she loads your site.

In cases in which a user requests a size that has not yet been computed for the particular resolution, the server can return one of the quantized images and then kick off a cloud computing resource to perform the conversion and cache the result. This allows the second and third users to get the more accurate cached version, while being flexible enough to not crash the first user. Figure 13-7 illustrates the effect of design and development on supported devices when using cloud-computing resources.

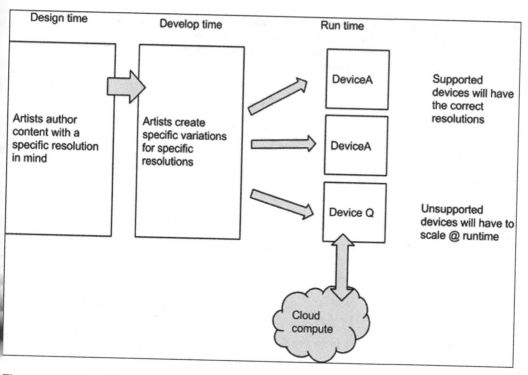

Figure 13-7. *Effect of design and development on supported devices using cloud computing*

The upside of this technique is that you can serve up pixel-perfect images for your games; the downside is the extra overhead involved in doing so.

Conclusion

The truth is that resolution fragmentation is not going away anytime soon; if anything, it is just going to get worse as consumers take advantage of the boom in form factors to experience your content. In the end, when players experience your content, they expect it to work on their device 100 percent of the time with 100 percent of the best gameplay experience possible.

There's no single solution to this problem. Savvy developers will be able to select from the solutions covered in this chapter to fit the needs of their particular games. Most important is that you understand the issues with resolution fragmentation and are continually testing against a host of resolutions in order to give users the best possible outcome.

CHAPTER 14

■ ■ ■

Making a Multiplatform Game

Jon Howard, Executive Product Manager, BBC

Making games is exciting, exhilarating, and hugely fulfilling. Making good games isn't easy. Making great games that work on multiple platforms is . . . what this chapter is about.

From control methods, to interaction design, to maintenance overheads, this chapter looks at many of the issues and opportunities concerning games made for desktop, smartphone, and tablet.

Case Study: Funfair Freak-Out[1]

Scooby Doo Funfair Freak-Out is a game designed and developed for the BBC Television children's website CBBC, the leading kids' web site in the United Kingdom. As a member of the game's development team, it was an honor to work with such cherished and ubiquitous brands as *Scooby-Doo* and CBBC. *Scooby-Doo* is a massive favorite with the large CBBC audience of 6- to 12-year-olds, indeed as it was for their parents—and, for some, their grandparents.

The goal was to make a compelling, fun, and engaging game that could be played and enjoyed on desktop and handheld platforms. The desire was for a game that used the classic *Scooby-Doo* plot devices and that felt like a true interaction with Shaggy, Scooby, Velma, Fred, and Daphne. If we're thinking classic Scooby, then, zoinks, there can be only one setting—a spooky fun fair (see Figure 14-1).

Figure 14-1. Scooby Doo Funfair Freak-Out

---

[1]CBBC, Scooby Doo Fun Fair Freak-Out, www.bbc.co.uk/cbbc/games/scooby-doo-game.

With any game, major decisions need to be made in the investigation phase and then ongoing throughout the project: What is the game? How does the user play it? How deep should the experience be? How will the the project objectives be achieved using the available technologies? This chapter will look at these major building blocks with *Funfair Freak-Out* and consider how they were calculated and resolved in a way that delivers to multiple platforms.

Control Method

The first consideration for any game should be control method. How is a user going to input his or her choices into the game? Anything that is a barrier to easy control is a negative. Does the game have five-point control? Make it three. Need mouse and keyboard? Make it a mouse or keyboard. As the controls become more complicated, the number of engaged users will lessen drastically. Surely, maximizing the number of players is an imperative for most games. This is the primary reason for wanting to make a game that will work on multiple platforms.

Want your game to work on as many devices as possible? Then, you will need to come up with a control method that will work well on keyboard, mouse, touch pad, touch screen, and joypad. This is no easy task. A Venn diagram showing great games that work across all devices (desktop, smartphone, tablet, smart television) will have a very small area overlapped by all.

Of course, it is possible to make a virtual joypad on a touch screen that can implement all the clever interpretation features that can be thrown at the system—auto centering to first touch, analogue style "amount" metrics, velocity change consideration for recentering. Yet, one major factor makes this an ultimately poor experience: the user really just has "pictures under glass."[2]

With a console joypad, ergonomics plays a huge role in giving the user subconscious information about the position of the controls and how they are being engaged. With a keyboard the user has access to discrete controls. These only afford eight directions, but there is constant sensory feedback. With mobiles and tablets the glass interface gives no positive feedback. This is a big problem and probably the main reason it is really hard to name a great smartphone game with joypad like controls.

An option in the application (app) space for mobiles/tablets is the gyroscope. This can be excellent for certain types of games. On the mobile Web, however, access to the gyroscope via HTML5 is problematic; the inability to lock the browser orientation, the specification for `Screen.lockOrientation()`, has yet to be stabilized,[3] meaning that, in practice, it is inadvisable to use the gyroscope. Also, if a goal is to make a game that will really work on desktop, too, then don't expect users to be spinning their laptops around.

Taking all this into consideration, big compromises will need to be made, in game design or in the number of platforms on which the game functions well.

With *Scooby Doo Fun Fair Freak-Out*, we acknowledged the control issues and designed the game to take advantage of them. The school of thought was that the simpler the control method, the better the game experience and the more inclusive the proposition.

The game design focused on how we could get the Scooby gang into a predicament that would allow us to use the very simple controls in a compelling way. We took this to a binary extreme by coming up with a stop-and-go mechanic. Scooby, Shaggy, and the gang are hypnotized at the spooky fun fair.The only commands a player can give are to stop (tap the screen/keyboard/mouse) and to go (release the tap). Everything is then down to the level designs. With big wheels, moving and collapsing platforms, falling crates, zombies, wolf men, ghosts, and *Total Wipeout*-style boxing gloves, timing becomes everything. The scene now set, we have a game that is a platformer, a constant runner, and a puzzler.

Funfair, rollercoaster, and haunted house zones provide the settings. Each zone has ten levels, with a different monster in each and the need to trap the baddie to finish the zone (see Figure 14-2). Once captured, the criminal is unmasked. All great fun and exactly right for the brand.

Brett Victor, "A Brief Rant on the Future of Interaction Design," http://worrydream.com/ABriefRantOnTheFutureOfInteractionDesign, November 2011.

Mozilla Developer Network, "Screen.lockOrientation," https://developer.mozilla.org/en-US/docs/Web/API/Screen. lockOrientation.

Figure 14-2. *Setting a trap*

To make the game, baseline requirements were necessary:

- Parallax scrolling (horizontal and vertical)
- Up to 50 moving items on the screen at any one time
- Large graphics
- A simple physics engine
- Multichannel audio
- Reach as many users as possible

Performance Testing

Before doing any coding on the project, we ran through a process of performance testing on all our target devices as well as some periphery ones. This allowed us to compare our requirements against capabilities across the board in order to get a general feel for device performance as well as investigate the specific requirements for the game.

Other benchmarking systems are available, but we needed specifically to test different methods of representing graphics, and so a simple bespoke test suite was scripted. The suite looked at Canvas, image elements, div elements, CSS3 animation, and background divs and then tested with scaling for each.

■ **Note** The Bugmark Test Suite (see Figure 14-3) has been included with the code for this chapter. Each test is encapsulted, requiring construct, render, and destroy functions. The tests are sequenced, initiated with a number of bugs to render, and timed for a given period. Results are delivered to screen for ease of use.

Run the tests on all the devices you can find to get a sense of performance across the board. There are some very interesting results to note on smart televisions.

Disambiguation: The "bugs" referenced here are the little yellow and orange guys flying around the screen.

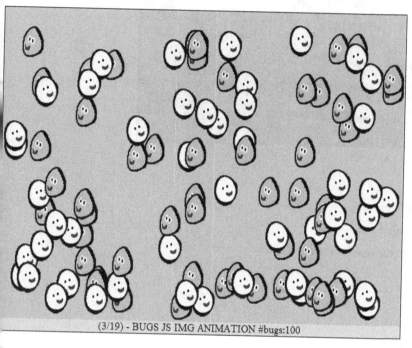

(3/19) - BUGS JS IMG ANIMATION #bugs:100

Figure 14-3. The Bugmark Test Suite

The *Scooby-Doo* game was designed for kids. Young audiences access the Web, through desktop computers, much more than the mobile Web, on smartphone or tablets. There is a much higher-than-average use of older browsers—meaning those that don't implement the canvas element.

Canvas should be the obvious choice for any HTML5 game rendering, but with *Funfair Freak-Out*, potentially up to 20 percent of the audience wouldn't be reached. A difficult decision had to be made.

Benchmarking told us that DOM rendering would fulfill all our requirements within specification and reach 100 percent of our audience. As time goes on, and the old-browser percentage reduces, reasons for not using canvas are dissipating. DOM isn't going away and so will still work, but there isn't a whole lot of HTML5 about it. Web Audio API and other HTML5 components were still used in the project, but when it came to rendering, we felt neater to have a single method.

The compromises of going with DOM:

- No rotation of elements—fine on some browsers, a massive slowdown on others.

- No extensive particle effects—all would have to be prerendered.

- No visual effects via Canvas.

- Not really engaging with HTML5 features for rendering.

So long as simple rules are adhered to, great performance can be achieved with DOM manipulation (see Figure 14-4). Key is that virtually every time the DOM is touched, a redraw is initiated.[4] A tip here is to update only on the condition that a relevant parameter has actually changed.

Figure 14-4. *The big reveal*

Interaction Design

Key to any user experience is how intuitive an interface is as well as how responsive. Many mobile web touch-screen experiences feel a little "laggy." This is likely to be the result of the use of gesture events. For any gesture to be recognized, most browsers need to wait long enough (300ms) to determine if a double tap has been captured.

As a user, when I press a button, my expectation is for an immediate response—300ms can feel like a lifetime and certainly does so in game when timing is critical. Preventing the default action on all gesture/touch events can step around native deficiencies and allow the system to react immediately and under its own volition:

```
event.preventDefault ? event.preventDefault() : event.returnValue = false;
```

I have seen in many other games the use of multiple event listeners on a page, one for each button or interactive ED: engines. My preference is to listen for one key press/mouse interaction/touch per page and then interpret that action.

---

[4]Minimizing the DOM manipulation – (http://swingpants.com/2012/02/08/html5-game-dev-dom-manipulation-its-costly-so-minimise-its-use/)

Physics Engine

In making an HTML5 game, it is vitally important that physics is well represented within the experience.

There are a number of solid-state physics engines available that have been successfully used in a multitude of games. However, when we are talking about working in the mobile Web, there can be major problems. The number of calculations required to deliver constrained, rigid body physics isn't conducive to rendering a game well on a lesser device. The JavaScript game loops need to assign as much of the performance budget as possible to the render cycle; any excessive "juice" being burned by a physics engine could mean constraining your product to use on only the top-end devices and failing to reach as many users as possible.

To mitigate this, in *Funfair Freak-Out* we employed a bespoke physics engine. In the most basic cases, it is possible to implement physics in a couple of lines of code—apply some gravity to an object's velocity, and presto. In this case, there had to be a fair amount of sophistication; we certainly required a system that would allow for collision detection, motors, and moving platforms. What we really needed was to minimize the number of square root calculations required in each game loop. A line intersection model afforded that option.

A simple, classic system would be to use bounding boxes. The drawback here is that the scene then has to be constructed out of blocks, lessening the capability of having organic shapes or slopes and slowing down the level design process.

Line-to-line, rather than box-to-box, intersection gave us the sophistication we were after.

By using a combination of linked lists, bounding boxes, lines, and edges, it is easy to draw scenes that feel organic and natural, with negligible processor overhead.

The base primitive object in the system is the edge, a simple connection between two points. A linked list collection of connected edges can form a line. The line has a bounding box. Now, I can move scene actors around with a first pass of looking at the bounding boxes. If and only if a collision is detected does a test run for line intersection (see Figure 14-5). Doing comparative tests using a single point is dangerous. This could allow an actor to fly through a collision without realizing the possibility of an intersection. But, if I take the velocity of the actor, I can create a bounding box around the start and end points. This will never miss an intersection.

Figure 14-5. Using line intersection rendering

So, the system discovers an intersection. Now, the link list is parsed through, and the edges are calculated for line-to-line intersection. The test is simple and works as follows:

- The whole coordinate system is translated to ensure that the actor's start point is at (0, 0) (see Figures 14-6i and 14-6ii).

- The system is next rotated so that the actor's travel is along the x-axis (see Figure 14-6iii).

- The intersection point is then calculated by determining if the point where y = 0 for the edge is between 0 and the translated actor destination point (see Figure 14-6iv).

- The intersection point is rotated and translated back.

- If there is a result, then you have a contact and deal with it; if not, continue with the game loop.

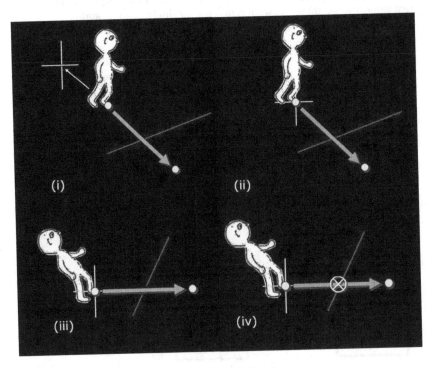

Figure 14-6. *How an intersection point is calculated*

The line intersection physics system has worked very well and is very easy to use when it comes to designing levels. The lines can be drawn onto a scene, delivering an instantly playable sketch of the level.

The system can help performance further with a number of precalculations based on acceleration from the steepness of a slope and friction. These are imparted to connected actors. Every opportunity to take a calculation out of a game loop should be taken. It is important to be a good "processor citizen."

Note A line intersection physics system demo has been included with the code for this chapter. A line of connected edges has been drawn, and a character drops on to it, walking to the edge and back. Pressing a key or touching a screen will stop the character. The artwork is a representation of me by my lovely daughters, Eloisa and Lola. Thanks, kids . . . I think.

Audio

There have been teething troubles with HTML5 and audio. The situation has improved drastically in recent times, with more browsers implementing Web Audio API. On most mobile devices it was the case that sound sprites would need to be used—a single audio file containing all the game sounds. The sprite is constantly played, with the playhead being moved to the relevant time point, enabling playback of the required sound. This works to a degree, but when you have put your all into making a great game, the last thing you want is to settle for single-channel audio.

The logical decision path for which audio method to deliver to a user has to favor multiple-channel audio above all else. *Funfair Freak-Out* implements all three methods, as described in Figure 14-7.

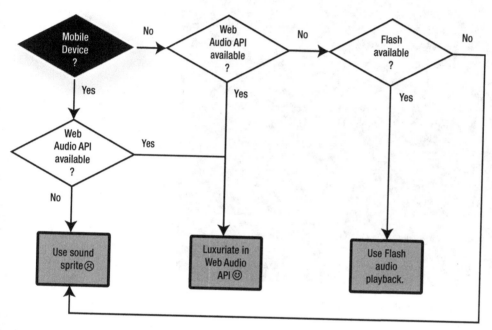

Figure 14-7. *Audio rendering decision tree*

In addition to sound sprites and Web Audio API, a third option is available for desktop: Flash playback. Okay, this sounds like it is going against the grain of open standards, but we are building user-facing products here. The primary concern should be the quality of the final outcome. So, on desktop the ubiquity of Flash and its audio capabilities means that it has to come ahead of sound sprites on the priority list.

Asset Sizes

It is easy to get carried away with adding more and more graphics to a multiplatform HTML5 project. Who is going to argue with a little eye candy? On desktop we are spoiled—the browsers all have a pretty high memory allocation per page. This isn't the case on most mobile devices. Across the many projects that I have seen, problems have begun when the asset set starts to clock in at more than 10MB. The issues range from full browser crashes to graphics disappearing.

There are many hundreds of operating system and device combinations. Even with extensive quality assurance (QA) testing it is difficult to ensure that any multiplatform game will be 100 percent. With the price point of tablets tumbling, so are the specifications. Rather than the memory problems with mobile web–enabled devices easing over time, they are becoming more acute, necessitating stricter controls.

In *Funfair Freak-Out* every effort was made to ensure that the assets would be as small as possible. All the animation cycles were minimized. With the character animations, walk cycles were kept down to 10 or 12 cells on the sprite sheet. This maintained enough frames in a second to feel natural without becoming clunky. The simple color palette of the *Scooby-Doo* animation allowed for the use of the PNG8 format, 8 bit color with indexed transparency. This can typically be less than a third the size of PNG24. For those images that didn't need transparency, the JPEG format was used to great effect.

Two asset sets were made available to the game: high definition (HD) and standard definition (SD). The HD clocked in at 6.75MB, and the SD, at 3.75MB. The appropriate set was delivered, based on screen size and resolution.

All unnecessary transitions (particularly those that added weight) were removed from the game. From screen to screen, elements were reused in differing combinations within each zone. On very few occasions were assets only used once.

For the audio, everything was reduced to mono and 80Kbps (MP3 and OGG). This still sounded great, and the total weight for the MP3 assets was 886KB, with OGG at 777KB.

Certainly, with HTML5 I have come to the conclusion that pushing the boundaries in terms of memory or processor usage should be avoided when trying to reach the greatest audience. There are many other areas in which to experiment, innovate, and deliver quality.

A further issue that is more user-focused relates to data charges when not connected to Wi-Fi. No user wants to discover a massive bill from his or her service provider. Typically, mobile web games are snackable and casual by nature. This is good; it means that the graphical assets can be scaled back. With projects that I am involved in, we set a 5MB budget and afford ourselves a little leeway. Anything above 10MB is regarded as the "danger zone." and we definitely don't want to go anywhere near there.

Interface Design

As device operating systems are upgraded, and updates are applied to browsers, the implicit rules for interface design are changing, and we, as game developers, are continually being required to adapt (we're mainly talking smartphones here). Simplicity and consistency of experience are key, certainly in relation to button placement, input types, and user journeys. With all web games it is important to lead the player to game play as quickly and as obviously as possible. I'm a great believer in the value of a big button on the landing page that says, "Play."

With *Funfair Freak-Out* the character and level selection pages were designed to be "swipeable" via finger or mouse. Supplementary buttons give a choice to those who would rather click or tap through the options. The dual method tested very well with users.

With the browser Google Chrome potentially interfering with play in many games, it is important to design around possible problems. Interface buttons in the bottom corners of a screen will likely interfere with the back and full-screen buttons on iOS devices; too close to the top of the screen, and Chrome could be initiated. These are painful problems that require large exclusion zones around the edge of the screen.

It has been noted in user testing with young children that they will place a device on a table and then lean on the device. Frequently, this will cause the corner of the touch screen to be nudged and input to the device, generated. Ideally, the exclusion zone will deal with the problem areas, but when we are talking about a smartphone, the available real estate is very slight. Heed must be paid to the areas with issues, while hoping that the browser manufacturers don't do further updates to render your expertly crafted interface a relic.

Maintenance

The very first Flash games I wrote back in 1999 still work perfectly today. They have needed no updates, tinkering, or recrafting in any way. The Flash Player took the responsibility of making its content work on each and every browser. Every HTML5 game I have been involved with over the last few years has required a revisit to fix the audio, the rendering, the button placement, and much more. The need for maintenance and QA is a fact of life now. The proprietary "black box" nature of a browser plug-in was fantastic for backward compatibility. In the Wild West of unstable, un-ratified standards, browser manufacturers will deliver interpretations that are anything but standard. It is the nature of competition to deliver features better than your rivals'—"better" frequently meaning "non-standard." For my team, delivering games with complex logic and display rendering systems, we need to assign a large fraction of our budget to a maintenance strand just to keep the games live. Typically, the QA budget rate is from 10 to 20 percent per project, with maintenance being the same again.

So, is there a way to insulate games from changes of standard implementation? Frankly, there is no silver bullet. The problems are coming from multiple areas: crossorigin resource sharing, browser behaviors, audio implementation, memory allocation, page embedding methods—the list goes on. As HTML5 game portfolios get bigger, so does the task of implementing a fix across the whole portfolio. If libraries are shared, then there are possibilities.

We are in a space now in which the interesting JavaScript libraries are still in development, and many haven't even reached release 1.0 yet. This means that backward compatibility can't be guaranteed. Over the next few years, the ecosystem will settle down, and many of the problems will ease. Expectations need to be managed, and budgets, apportioned to acknowledge the current state of play.

Conclusion

Remember, isn't the reason we are working with HTML5 so that we can get our games onto mobile devices? It is very easy to get swept along by all the great advances being made on desktop browsers—the extra performance and Web Graphics Library (WebGL) goodness. Those features and possibilities don't exist as yet in a standard and consistent way across the mobile Web. This doesn't mean, however, that we shouldn't still be excited about the possibilities of what can be achieved. With a mind toward optimization and creative thinking, within the technical constraints, amazing experiences can be produced.

On the desktop, Flash games matured to set a very high standard. This level has been carried on in the app space by some fantastic games. Publishers and clients now seemingly expect this quality from every game build, irrespective of language, technology, or platform. These expectations need to be managed; delivering with quality to multiple platforms is a complicated business.

Scooby Doo Funfair Freak Out was launched in early summer of 2013. It was the most successful game launch ever for CBBC, a portfolio that has seen more than 400 games. Now, a game made with HTML5 and JavaScript has reached the peak! This is undoubtedly due to hitting desktop, smartphone, and tablet at the same time and shows the strength of and potential for multiplatform projects.

■ ■ ■

CHAPTER 15

Developing Better Than Native Games

Florian d'Erfurth, Freelance Game Developer

Back in Chapter 3, we covered the common pitfalls that cause a game to perform poorly, as well as the techniques to address them. Now we will tackle techniques to make your game look and feel just like a native one on mobile.

By applying the techniques learned from high performance JavaScript with the ones that we are about to cover, your game will both perform and look like its native counterparts while being cross-platform. It will be better than native.

Note that you will be able to see all the techniques in action in the demo available in the download pack from www.apress.com along with the source code.

The HTML5 Fullscreen API

The most prominent difference between a native game and a web game is certainly the browser and the system bars all around it. Thankfully, with the fullscreen API you can request a fullscreen status and make the game the center of the player's attention.

Here's how the API looks like for entering fullscreen:

```
canvas.requestFullscreen();
canvas.webkitRequestFullscreen(Element.ALLOW_KEYBOARD_INPUT);
canvas.mozRequestFullScreen();
```

And here's how it looks for exiting fullscreen:

```
document.exitFullscreen();
document.webkitExitFullscreen();
document.mozCancelFullscreen();
```

Yep, that's it. However, you can only enter fullscreen upon user interaction. That is, you must call fullscreen from a touch or click event handler; otherwise it won't work, as shown in Figure 15-1. Figure 15-2 shows it running at full screen.

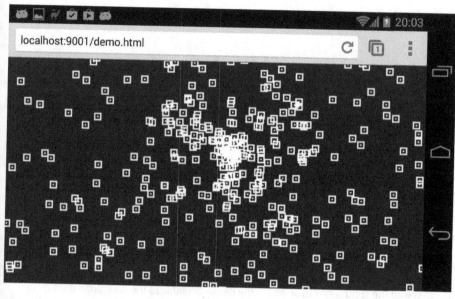

Figure 15-1. Our demo not running fullscreen

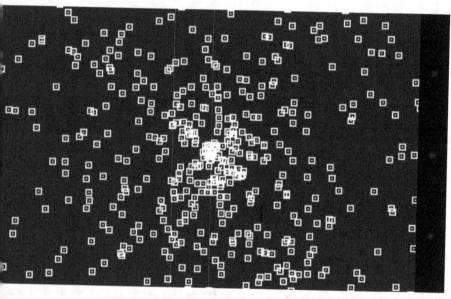

Figure 15-2. Our demo running fullscreen; note the lack of system and address bar

You can see from Figures 15-1 and 15-2 that fullscreen makes a huge difference for the player, who can now enjoy fully immersive experience as opposed to one that just feels like browsing.

Creating a Fullscreen Button

In order for your players to switch to fullscreen you need to provide them with a button. Remember that if you were to call the API programmatically it wouldn't work; you have to call `requestFullscreen` from a touch or click event handler.

Since you should decouple event handling from your game loop (see Chapter 20), you may resort to using a DOM element on top of your game to serve as a fullscreen button as a quick solution. With event handling decoupled from your loop, you cannot call requestFullscreen from the loop when your code detects that an event has happened inside the boundaries of a button. Instead, you can either call requestFullscreen directly from your game's touch or click handler, and in that case you need check the event coordinates against the button area, as shown in Listing 15-1.

Listing 15-1. Calling requestFullscreen directly from your game's touch or click handler

```
onTouch = function(event){
        // retrieve first touch coordinates
        var x = event.touches[0].clientX,
            y = event.touches[0].clientY;

        // isInFullscreenButtonArea detects if the button have been clicked
        if(isInFullscreenButtonArea(x,y)){
                canvas.requestFullscreen();
}
else{ // fullscreen button haven't been touched
        // record event coordinates for later use by our loop
        recordTouch(x, y);
}
};

canvas.addEventListener( 'touchstart', onTouch );
```

You could also create a DOM element such as a **div** with its own event handler to serve as a button, as shown in Listing 15-2.

Listing 15-2. Creating a DOM element with its own event handler to serve as a button

```
onTouch = function(event){
        canvas.requestFullscreen();
};

div.addEventListener( 'touchstart', onTouch );
```

Depending of the structure of your game, one approach might be more convenient to implement than another.

Losing Fullscreen and How to Handle It

On both desktop and mobile you may lose fullscreen state at any time. The user can exit fullscreen himself by hitting a key, by performing a gesture, or by rotating the device; he might also cause fullscreen to exit by switching apps or turning the screen off.

Whether the user exits fullscreen on purpose or accidentally, your game should be able to handle it. The browser fires the fullscreenchange event whenever it enters or exits fullscreen. When your user exits fullscreen, you should give the option to the user to go back fullscreen; you may also choose to pause the game. See the code in Listing 15-3.

Listing 15-3. Giving the user the option to go back fullscreen after exiting it

```
onFullscreenLose = function(){
        showFullscreenButton();
        pauseGame();
};
```

```
document.addEventListener("fullscreenchange", function () {
    if(document.fullscreen == false) onFullscreenLose();
}, false);

document.addEventListener("mozfullscreenchange", function () {
    if(document.mozFullScreen == false) onFullscreenLose();
}, false);

document.addEventListener("webkitfullscreenchange", function () {
    if(document.webkitIsFullScreen == false) onFullscreenLose();
}, false);
```

Going Further

The fullscreen API is still a working draft, and browsers are using prefixed names. I recommend abstracting the fullscreen API using screenfull.js, an awesome cross-browser wrapper for the fullscreen API by Sindre Sorhus. You can get it at https://github.com/sindresorhus/screenfull.js.

Also be aware that the fullscreen API isn't available in all browsers at the time of writing; when it's not available, you can resort to using some hacky techniques like scrolling programmatically to hide the address bar. Check HTML5Rocks for some fresh info on the subject at www.html5rocks.com/en/mobile/fullscreen.

Lowering the Resolution

Your game may very well benefit from lowering its resolution. While CPU power is certainly a bottleneck, fillrate is limited on mobile GPUs (graphics processing units). It is worth noting that fillrate limitations may impact your performance whenever you are using WebGL or Canvas2D since the latter is hardware accelerated and thus uses the GPU.

There is a trend of increased resolution for mobile screens while at the same time GPUs have constraints regarding power consumption and heat production. Not every device with a comfortable resolution will be able to render your game at 60 Hz if you size your canvas at 100% of the screen.

■ **Note** The fillrate is the number of pixels a GPU can render during a second.

When to Lower Resolution

To test if you are fillrate bound on a device, lower the viewport dimensions. If the framerate increases, you are fillrate bound and will benefit from lowering your game resolution.

In the case of a 2D game, you could be fillrate bound because your game is using plenty of transparent layers. You may want to lower the number of transparent sprites before having to resort to lower the resolution. Also, note that if you are using WebGL, fillrate depends on shader complexity, so it's always worth checking if you can simplify your fragment shader, for instance by moving code to your vertex shader.

Fillrate varies widely from one device to another, so it's worth testing your game on as many devices as you can. Listing 15-4 shows some code to compute the frame rate.

Listing 15-4. Computing Frame Rate

```
var t = window.performance.now(),
    frame_count = 0, // increased on each Request Animation Frame (RAF)
                     //so we can compute avg_fps

    avg_fps = 0;      // FPS averaged over many frames

function tick() {
        requestAnimationFrame( tick );

    var n = window.performance.now(),
        raf_delta = n - t,
        current_fps = 1000 / raf_delta;

    t = n;

        // you could compute average fps over many frames
        avg_fps = (avg_fps * frame_count + current_fps) / ++frame_count;

        // you could also add some code to display current_fps in a DOM element
        myElement.innerHTML = current_fps + "FPS";


        // read input, move things, render them
        game.step()
}
```

You could use the average frame rate to trigger resolution lowering (see the next section) but if you choose to do so you should keep in mind the JavaScript engine compilation time discussed previously, since your frame rate will suffer from it if your code hasn't been optimized.

Performance varies widely from device to device, so it might be a good idea to notify the user that his device is not performing well when lowering resolution is not enough.

How to Lower Resolution

To lower the resolution and keep the game area the same size, you will downscale your viewport and canvas sizes, and then upscale the canvas using CSS. As a result, you will compute fewer pixels and the browser will upscale them almost for free. See Listing 15-5 for the code.

Listing 15-5. Lowering the Resolution

```
canvas.width  = width * scaling;
canvas.height = height * scaling;
canvas.style.width = width + 'px';
gl.viewport( 0, 0, width * scaling, height * scaling );
```

Since you're use WebGL and a matrix to transform the vertices, you don't need to do anything else. If you were to use canvas 2D, you would have to scale your sprites and their coordinates to draw them at the right place. In Figure 15-4, you can see that the graphic quality of our demo is severely degraded compared to Figure 15-3. Figure 15-4 exhibits the Bad Way™ of resolution lowering. Next, we'll discuss how to properly downscale your canvas while maintaining graphic quality.

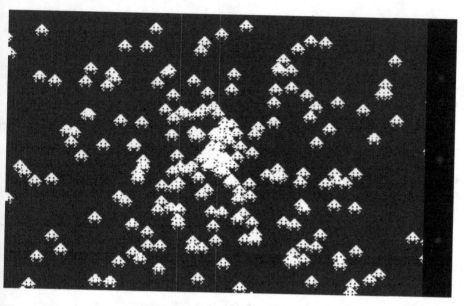

Figure 15-3. *Our demo running at full resolution*

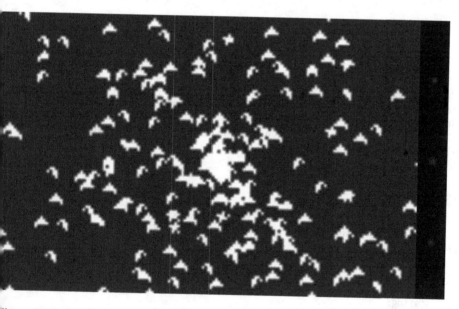

Figure 15-4. *Our demo running at a 4x lower resolution without any optimization*

Keeping Your Sprites Sharp

Blurry sprites look bad. In order for your sprites to keep maximum sharpness, they must be snapped to a pixel grid. See Figure 15-5.

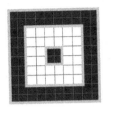 

Figure 15-5. *The left image shows how the particle sprite looks like when snapped to the grid at x:0, y:0. On the right you can see how it looks like at x:0.75, y: 0.75. The green lines represent the outlines of the sprite pixels*

Snapping sprites to the pixel grid is very easy; you just have to round the coordinates before drawing, like this:

```
x = Math.round(x);
y = Math.round(y);
```

If you rescale your sprites and want them to stay sharp, you have to scale them by an integer value; otherwise the sprites pixels won't be aligned to the grid and the results will be interpolated.

Staying Sharp Using Less Pixels

What about lowering the resolution? The most practical case is a "divided by 2" resolution so the pixel grid is twice as large and one pixel now covers the equivalent of four. It also means that you are rendering four times less pixels, and as you've seen before, it may save a lot of work for the GPU. See Figure 15-6.

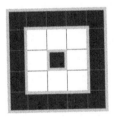 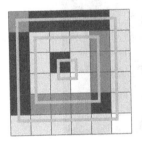

Figure 15-6. *As you can see, snapping is even more important with a lower resolution. Since the grid is larger, interpolated sprites look muddy, and in the case of text using a pixel font, it would probably be illegible*

To snap your sprite to a twice as large grid, you will round odd coordinates to even ones, like so:

```
x = Math.round(x);
if((x & 1) === 1){ x-- } // (x & 1) returns 1 if x is odd
y = Math.round(y);
if((y & 1) === 1){ y-- }
```

Scaling is now much more constrained as you have to scale only by multiple of 2 if you want the sprites pixels to cover an area that can be expressed in round pixels of the new grid. You can see in Figure 15-8 that by snapping our sprites to a grid there is no visible difference compared with Figure 15-7 when halving the resolution.

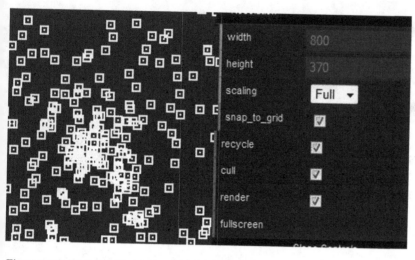

Figure 15-7. *Our demo running at full resolution*

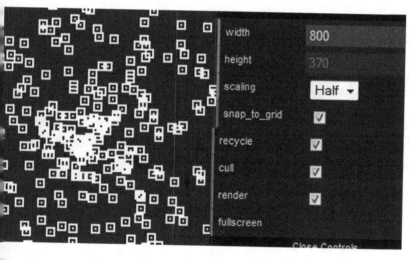

Figure 15-8. *Our demo running at half resolution using grid snapping*

As you can see, keeping your sprites sharp in the case of a lowered resolution is very important and requires some planning at the design stage. Obviously, being able to use the same assets at different resolutions is the cheapest solution but you may also use different spritesheets, each with art adapted to a specific resolution.

Whether you design a low-res spreadsheet or generate one offline, you can benefit from faster load times on less capable devices. A twice as small spritesheet means four times less pixels to send down the wire!

CSS Scaling

When scaling the canvas with CSS to compensate for a lower resolution in order to retain the same size in absolute pixels, the browser is responsible for the upscaling operation. As you probably know from Photoshop, there are different ways to scale an image. Indeed, once upon a time in a CSS3 draft, an "image-rendering" property was made available to hint to the browser about how to scale an image. Unfortunately that property isn't part of the CSS3 final spec and has been moved to CSS4. However, Firefox has implemented it; others, like Chrome, haven't at the time of writing.

```
canvas {
    image-rendering: optimize-contrast;
    image-rendering: -moz-crisp-edges;
    image-rendering: -webkit-optimize-contrast;
}
```

In the figures that follow, image-rendering is set to optimize-contrast, the intended value for pixel art to be scaled properly. Figure 15-9 was done in Firefox; Figure 15-10 was done using Chrome, which does not implement the "image-rendering" property at the time of writing.

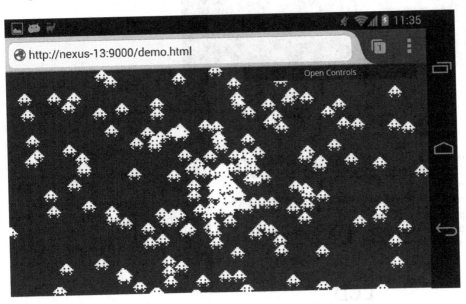

Figure 15-9. *Our demo running in Firefox, where sprites are looking very sharp*

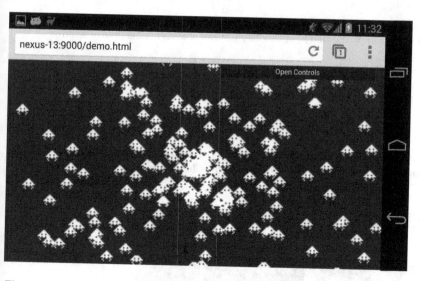

Figure 15-10. *Our demo running in Chrome; note the slight blur and the soft edges*

Motion Blur

Device display panels can affect the sharpness of your sprites when they are moving or animating; LCD pixels take some time to switch from full brightness to black and from black back full brightness again. The result is that your fast-animated sprite can look blurry.

LCD response times vary widely, from 15ms to 35ms on mobile devices. However, OLED panels, a different technology used in some phones, have faster response times. As you can see, display panel responsiveness can have an effect on the look of your sprites. In Figure 15-11, the sprite is moving in a straight line, leaving ghosts behind. Imagine the mess if it was animated or rotating!

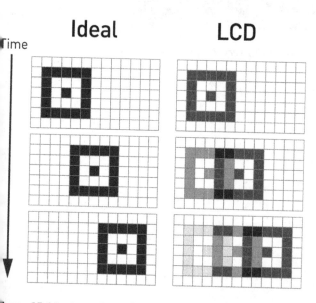

Figure 15-11. *A sequence of images illustrating a sprite moving from left to right*

Unfortunately, there is not much you can do about it in code. However, by taking motion blur into account at the design stage you can mitigate its effects, for instance by avoid high scrolling speed or using sprites with enough contrast so they don't smudge into the background when moving.

Unwanted Behaviors

Unlike native games, ours live in the browser. With this comes pesky gestures like pinch zoom and constrains like the inability to lock the device display to a given orientation.

Disabling Zoom

When playing a game it's very easy to trigger the pinch zoom gesture by accident. To disable zooming, you can use the following line in the <head> of the HTML document:

```
<meta name="viewport" content="width=device-width, initial-scale=1.0, user-scalable=no">
```

Here you declare the viewport, which is the area where your page is being drawn, to be the same width as the device, set zoom or scale to 1.0, and remove the user's ability to zoom your page.

Device Orientation

Your game is probably designed to work in landscape or portrait mode, but not both. Currently a lockOrientation method is suggested in the Screen Orientation API draft. Unfortunately, browsers except for Firefox haven't implemented it, and it is only available there for fullscreen or packaged web apps.

Since you cannot lock orientation, you have to tell the users how they should rotate their devices and prevent them from using the game until their devices are in the right orientation. To do so, you can use window.orientation to determine the current orientation, as shown in Listing 15-6.

Listing 15-6. Using window.orientation

```
checkOrientation = function(){
        if( window.orientation === 90 || window.orientation === -90 ){
            // handle portrait mode
        }
        else if( window.orientation === 0 || window.orientation === 180 ){
            // handle landscape mode
        }
        else{
            // handle not supported device orientation, probably a desktop
        }
};
```

If you want your game to be played in landscape mode, you can pause the game when in portrait and prompt the users to rotate their devices. Obviously you need to know when the orientation changes, so you need to listen for orientationchange, like so:

```
window.addEventListener("orientationchange", function() {
        checkOrientation();
    }, false);
```

Now when the device is in the desired orientation, you have to remove your prompt and let your users resume the game!

Home Screen

Once your game performs well, runs fullscreen, and feels like a native one, the missing piece is a way to launch it like a native game to remove the annoying requirement for the users to have to start the browser and look for your game every time they want to play.

With Safari on iOS and Chrome 32+ on Android, there is a way to declaratively indicate to the browser that your game can run standalone without the need of showing the browser chrome. To do so, you simply add the following meta tags in the <head> of your document:

```
<meta name="apple-mobile-web-app-capable" content="yes">
<meta name="mobile-web-app-capable" content="yes">
```

Now users are able to add a shortcut to their home screen, as shown in Figures 15-12 and 15-13.

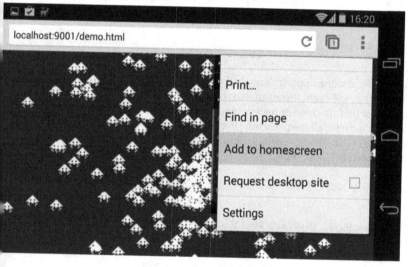

Figure 15-12. Chrome menu with the Add to homescreen item

Figure 15-13. *A shortcut to our demo has been added to the homescreen*

What you have here is a glorified bookmark that will allow users to launch your game directly and without any browser chrome surrounding it. Firefox OS went a different route and does not have a declarative way to achieve the same thing; instead it requires a manifest file. This approach is a little bit more complex and is geared toward publishing on the Firefox Marketplace rather than providing a way to add shortcuts for public-facing web games to users devices.

Icons

You should also specify the icon to be used. iOS and Android do not use the same naming, nor do they recommend the same sizes, as you can see here:

```
<link rel="shortcut icon" sizes="196x196" href="android-hires.png">
<link rel="apple-touch-icon" sizes="76x76" href="ipad.png">
<link rel="apple-touch-icon" sizes="120x120" href="iphone-retina.png">
<link rel="apple-touch-icon" sizes="152x152" href="ipad-retina.png">
```

Android will use the largest shortcut icon available while iOS will pick the apple-touch-icon whose size is recommended for the device.

Detecting Standalone

When a user launches the game using the home screen shortcut, the game will be fullscreen—or more accurately the document will be; in that case you won't need to display a button to switch to fullscreen, as mentioned previously in the "The HTML5 Fullscreen API" section.

While iOS window.navigator.standalone is true when launched from the home screen, in Android there is no such thing, so you will have to guess, using the difference between the window height and the client height. Here's a snippet that works for both Android and iOS:

```
standalone = window.navigator.standalone || ( window.screen.height - window.innerHeight < 40 );
```

At the time of writing, the Android system bar alone is 25px tall and the system bar added to the Chrome navigation bar makes a 73px tall block. In the snippet above, you check that the height difference between the window and the device screen is below 40px, so you have good safety margin in case any of those values change.

Further References

Every OS provides different ways for users to add a web game to their home screen, and these ways are likely to evolve, so be sure to check the links below so you can provide your users with the best experience possible.

Android

A document detailing the home screen apps feature of Chrome for Android:

https://developers.google.com/chrome/mobile/docs/installtohomescreen

iOS

Information from Apple on how to build web applications for Safari:

https://developer.apple.com/library/safari/documentation/AppleApplications/Reference/
SafariWebContent/ConfiguringWebApplications/ConfiguringWebApplications.html

Firefox OS

All about the Open Web App manifest file for Firefox OS:

https://developer.mozilla.org/en-US/Apps/Developing/Manifest

Conclusion

In this chapter you saw how to make a web game feel like a native one by running it fullscreen while maintaining performance and sharpness. You also learned how to allow users to add your game amongst native ones on their home screen.

What is possible is to blur the lines between native and web games; this will continue evolve quickly, and we are likely to see new APIs in each browser whose implementation will differ until some standards emerges. As more exciting new features will be made possible for HTML5 games, you will have to keep an eye on what's new if you wish to stay on top of the game!

CHAPTER 16

Mobile Web Game Techniques with Canvas 2D API

Takuo Kihira, Entrepreneur

When we consider mobile HTML5 games, we usually compare them with native games. One might think that native games are always superior to browser games or that browser games can never touch native games in performance. But check out the top 10 games in the native app market. Often you will find that many of the top-selling games do not use 3D graphics, particle effects, and so on. It seems that we are able to create similar kinds of mobile games in the browser with HTML5.

However, there are two big problems around mobile HTML5 games. One is speed, and the other is compatibility with devices.

Needless to say, HTML5 games execute in the browser. This really means that HTML5 games are working on an emulator or virtual machine, which is called a browser, and of course this is an obvious drawback for performance. Modern browsers are optimized much like a modern virtual machine, but remain much slower than native apps. We have to take pains to create mobile games that perform very well without creating them in native code.

In addition, unfortunately we have to face compatibility issues with various browsers. As you'll see later in this chapter, there are often slight differences, especially between Android legacy browsers, because of their special customizations. For example, it is possible that browser makers customized their browser to make better scores on benchmarks, and they may have achieved it—along with adding lots of small compatibility bugs. Unlike server-side programs, client HTML5 games are recommended to work on not only your own device but also all existing devices and devices that will appear in the future.

After reading the above, you might feel bad about mobile HTML5. However, the advantages of creating mobile HTML5 games exceed the disadvantages. For example, imagine that you are playing a game like SimCity. If you want to let a friend see your town, all you can do is just post a screen shot. Your friends might say, "Cool," but that's all. But, if the game was working on browsers, your friends could see not only the picture, but also the dynamic game screen as soon as they tap your link. The game would be working inside the native Twitter client app without any installation. Native apps could never achieve such a trick.

So how do you create mobile browser games easily for such a wonderful future? You use Canvas!

Why Canvas?

Actually, there are two alternatives to get a native-like expression; one is Canvas, and the other is CSS. Which is the better way to gain speed and avoid compatibility issues? In this chapter, I conclude that Canvas is superior to CSS. Although CSS has a lot of features, its compatibility is catastrophic, especially on Android Legacy Browsers. If you want to support Android, I do not recommend using CSS even if you have a lot of patience. Additionally, it is very difficult to gain speed using CSS when you want to make many sprites move randomly. CSS is not suitable for these types of games.

Compared to CSS, Canvas has few issues. The APIs of Canvas 2D are simple, so there are few differences between devices (although there are still problems.) Additionally, Canvas has the responsibility of all drawing on browsers. This means there is the disadvantage that you have to write tons of code if you want to create animation on your web site, but the advantage is that you can improve your code to detail with techniques and know-how.

On the other hand, CSS has original features such as CSS filters, CSS animations, CSS transforms, and so on. It is good idea to make games using Canvas and CSS together. In addition, the evolution of modern browsers is significant. If the market share of the Chrome browser for Android increases, CSS compatibility and speed will be improved. But as long as you are trying to make good games on mobile HTML5, you must understand the effective ways to create games using Canvas. You'll learn a lot about the Canvas 2D API in this chapter.

The Basis of Canvas

In short, Canvas is a kind of img element with the feature of reading and writing pixel by pixel. You can draw curved lines, text, images, and so on, as you like. Generally you draw the Canvas properly in every frame using JavaScript.

Bitmap Images and Vector Images

The style of managing every pixel in Canvas is known as using bitmap images. Bitmap images are the kind of images you would edit with tools like Photoshop.

The opposite is vector images. These are produced using tools such as Illustrator or Flash. Bitmap images are based on pixels, so when scaled there is a loss of clarity, while vector images can be scaled by any amount without degrading quality because they are based on paths, which are points, line styles, and so on. Vector images are not fit for picture-like complex images.

Although Canvas is bitmap image-based, aiming for drawing pixel by pixel, Canvas contains APIs for both bitmap graphics and vector graphics. So, despite common misunderstanding, you can make animations similar to Flash animations using the Canvas 2D API.

A Bitmap API Example

There are two kinds of Bitmap APIs. One draws images, and the other deals with pixel data. Listings 16-1 and 16-2 provide example code for dealing with bitmap images.

Listing 16-1. DrawImage

```
onload = function() {
  var img = document.createElement("img");
  img.onload = function() {
    var canvas = document.createElement("canvas");
    canvas.width = canvas.height = 300;
    document.body.appendChild(canvas);
    var ctx = canvas.getContext("2d");
    ctx.drawImage(img, 0, 0);
    (function tick() {
      ctx.drawImage(canvas, 0, 0, 300, 300, 10, 10, 280, 280);
      setTimeout(tick, 500);
    })();
  };
  img.src = "lenna.jpg";
};
```

Listing 16-2. Get/PutImageData

```
onload = function() {
  var img = document.createElement("img");
  img.onload = function() {
    var canvas = document.createElement("canvas");
    canvas.width = canvas.height = 300;
    document.body.appendChild(canvas);
    var ctx = canvas.getContext("2d");
    ctx.drawImage(img, 0, 0);

    var imageData = ctx.getImageData(0, 0, 300, 300);
    var data = imageData.data;
    for(var i = 0; i < data.length; i += 4) {
      var c = (data[i] * 0.299 + data[i + 1] * 0.587 + data[i + 2] * 0.114) | 0;
      data[i] = data[i + 1] = data[i + 2] = c;
    }
    ctx.putImageData(imageData, 0, 0);
  };
  img.src = "lenna.jpg";
};
```

In Figure 16-1, you can see the kaleidoscopic image by self-copying a scaled-down image.

Figure 16-1. DrawImage output

In Figure 16-2 you can see the gray-scaled image.

Figure 16-2. ImageData output

In an example, the putImageData and getImagedata API are powerful, but it can be hard to use them in games dynamically because their speed is quite slow. I will show you alternative ways to transform color without these APIs later in this chapter.

Path API Example

The Path API is for drawing many types of shapes, such as lines, circles, and polygons, on a HTML5 canvas. A path is a series of points with drawing instructions between those points. Some helper APIs also exist to draw a rectangle or circle easily. Listing 16-3 shows code that writes a character using Paths (see Figure 16-3).

Listing 16-3. Path Methods

```
onload = function() {
  var canvas = document.createElement("canvas");
  canvas.width = canvas.height = 300;
  document.body.appendChild(canvas);
  var ctx = canvas.getContext("2d");
  ctx.beginPath(); ctx.moveTo(40.35, 18.6);
  ctx.quadraticCurveTo(44.9, 15.6, 44.9, 10.7);
  ctx.quadraticCurveTo(44.9, 5.9, 41.4, 2.95);
  ctx.quadraticCurveTo(37.85, 0, 31.75, 0);
  ctx.lineTo(0, 0); ctx.lineTo(0, 38.55); ctx.lineTo(31.35, 38.55);
  ctx.quadraticCurveTo(46.5, 38.55, 46.45, 28.15);
  ctx.quadraticCurveTo(46.45, 21.75, 40.35, 18.6);
  ctx.moveTo(31.85, 15.65);
  ctx.lineTo(7.55, 15.65); ctx.lineTo(7.55, 6.75); ctx.lineTo(32.1, 6.75);
  ctx.quadraticCurveTo(37.55, 6.75, 37.55, 11.15);
  ctx.quadraticCurveTo(37.55, 13.2, 36.05, 14.45);
  ctx.quadraticCurveTo(34.5, 15.7, 31.85, 15.65);
  ctx.moveTo(31.35, 31.8);
  ctx.lineTo(7.55, 31.8); ctx.lineTo(7.55, 22.45); ctx.lineTo(32, 22.45);
  ctx.quadraticCurveTo(38.9, 22.45, 38.9, 27.35);
  ctx.quadraticCurveTo(38.9, 29.35, 36.9, 30.6);
  ctx.quadraticCurveTo(34.95, 31.8, 31.35, 31.8);
  ctx.fill();
};
```

Figure 16-3. Path methods output

As you can see, the code using a Path might be very complex and hard to maintain. If you want to use a Path inside your game, you should prepare shapes as some data structures and parse data structures dynamically. Later in this chapter, I will show you an effective way to achieve dynamic parsing.

Affine Transformations

Canvas has several other useful transform APIs, such as clipping, drawing text, and an affine transformation. An affine transformation uses parallel and linear translation. Using affine transformations, you can transform shapes and images on a HTML5 canvas. An affine transformation is of special importance when you create Canvas-based games.

You should understand the basics of matrix math if you utilize affine transformations extensively, but there are some helper APIs to make for easier usage: translate, rotate, and scale. You can stack the effects. There are few disadvantages to using transformations; you can use them freely.

Listing 16-4 shows an image that is rotated 30 degree, scaled 1/2, and translated (100px, 100px) in the transformed coordinates (see Figure 16-4). Affine transformations are the only way to transform images like this.

Listing 16-4. Simple Transform

```
onload = function() {
  var img = document.createElement("img");
  img.onload = function() {
    var canvas = document.createElement("canvas");
    canvas.width = canvas.height = 300;
    document.body.appendChild(canvas);
    var ctx = canvas.getContext("2d");
    ctx.rotate(30 * Math.PI / 180);
    ctx.scale(0.5, 0.5);
    ctx.translate(100, 100);
    ctx.drawImage(img, 0, 0);
  };
  img.src = "lenna.jpg";
};
```

Figure 16-4. Simple transform output

Generally, when you scale, rotate, and translate images with the anchor point at (ax, ay), you should transform in the order corresponding to translate, rotate, scale, and translate(-ax, -ay), as shown in Listing 16-5 and Figure 16-5.

Listing 16-5. Transform Example

```
onload = function() {
  var img = document.createElement("img");
  img.onload = function() {
    var canvas = document.createElement("canvas");
    canvas.width = canvas.height = 300;
```

```
    document.body.appendChild(canvas);
    var ctx = canvas.getContext("2d");
    var r = 0;
    (function tick() {
      ctx.save();
      ctx.translate(150 + Math.cos(r) * 100, 150 + Math.sin(r) * 100);
      ctx.rotate(r);
      ctx.scale(0.1, 0.1);
      ctx.translate(-img.width / 2, -img.height / 2);
      ctx.drawImage(img, 0, 0);
      ctx.restore();
      r += 7 * Math.PI / 180;
      setTimeout(tick, 100);
    })();
  };
  img.src = "lenna.jpg";
};
```

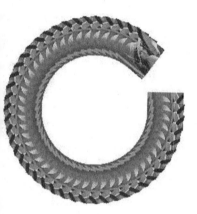

Figure 16-5. Transform example output

When you clear the current transformation, use setTransform(1, 0, 0, 1, 0, 0); or save/restore API.

How to Gain Speed

Unfortunately, mobile devices such as smartphones or tablets are far less performant than a PC. To speed up drawing canvas, you have to struggle with specific optimization techniques. The most effective way is completely different depending on game types, so I will show you some typical techniques for mobile games.

Speeding Up drawImage

Depending on game type, generally the most used API is drawImage. Browser implementations also focus on speeding this API up; for example, modern browsers have GPU support for drawImage. Currently drawImage typically has great performance. Due to its frequency of use, the optimizations of drawImage have led to great impact, which is quite important for almost all games.

drawImage has best performance when it draws an image with the same scale as original image. It is a good idea to avoid scaling because it has a performance impact. If you need to draw an image with scaling, you should consider caching the scaled image with in-memory canvas, which I will describe later in the "In-Memory Canvas" section.

It also has less performance with anti-aliasing, even if the image is the same scale. One might think that performance impact never happens with images of the same scale, but it can happen if you locate the image at a nonintegral floating-point position. JavaScript has only floating-point types describing numbers. There is no integer type inside JavaScript like C, so this happens easily. To fix it, just make the value integer...but never use Math.floor to do this. Math.floor is a built-in function of JavaScript to make numbers integer, but it is much slower than JavaScript implicit converting such as bit operations. Listing 16-6 shows how to make numbers integer.

Listing 16-6. ToInt

```
ctx.drawImage(img, x | 0, y | 0);
```

Some browsers have support to disable anti-aliasing. This is not standardized yet, so please be careful about compatibility of browsers. Listing 16-7 shows how to disable anti-aliasing

Listing 16-7. ImageSmoothingEnable

```
ctx.webkitImageSmoothingEnabled = false;
```

In-Memory Canvas (Offscreen Canvas)

Many games draw the same shapes constantly. You can speed this up a lot if the frequency is expected to be more than once. drawImage takes a Canvas element as the first argument, like img, so you can use the canvas as a cache. The canvas used as a cache is not attached to the DOM; it's just created as an element. We call this kind of canvas "in-memory canvas" or "offscreen canvas." See Listing 16-8 for an example.

Listing 16-8. In-Memory Canvas

```
var cache = document.createElement("canvas");
```

Once you make this canvas and draw shapes used frequently, you just draw the canvas afterwards.

Listing 16-9 shows how to use in-memory canvas. First, prepare the scaled image as cache, and then draw the cache to gain speed. See Figure 16-6 for an example.

Listing 16-9. In-Memory Canvas Example

```
onload = function() {
  var img = document.createElement("img");
  img.onload = function() {
    var canvas = document.createElement("canvas");
    canvas.width = canvas.height = 300;
    document.body.appendChild(canvas);
    var ctx = canvas.getContext("2d");
    ctx.fillRect(0, 0, 300, 300);

    var cache = document.createElement("canvas");
    cache.width = img.width / 10;
    cache.height = img.height / 10;
    cache.getContext("2d").drawImage(img, 0, 0, img.width, img.height, 0, 0, cache.width, cache.height);
```

```
  (function tick() {
    ctx.drawImage(cache, Math.random() * 300 - cache.width / 2, Math.random() * 300 - cache.height / 2);
    setTimeout(tick, 20);
  })();
 };
 img.src = "lenna.jpg";
};
```

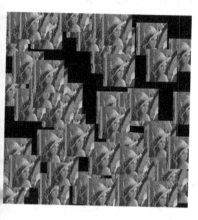

Figure 16-6. In-memory canvas example output

Needless to say, the more caches you create, the more memory you consume. You have to consider the trade-off between speed and memory.

If you are planning to create game engines or middleware, you need to determine which shape is effective for caching. If you cache the shape but it's drawn only once, this is an obvious waste. If you make caches whenever you want, memory issues will be critical soon. You should improve the cache hit ratio by considering which images should be stored and which should not.

Dirty Rect

It makes sense to redraw every frame if your target devices have the capability to achieve it, but unfortunately most current devices have trouble with performance. To reduce redrawing, it is a good idea to reuse existing drawn data on Canvas. You can restrict the area of drawing frame by frame to gain speed. This method is called Dirty Rect, and it improves the performance significantly in some kinds of games.

Dirty Rect is simple; you register whenever you have a dirty region that needs to be drawn. The region is represented as a rectangle. There are two dirty region types. One is the region that a disappearing object occupied, and the other is one that a newly appearing object is occupying. Considering moving objects, the object disappears from the previous position and appears in the current position (Figure 16-7).

Figure 16-7. Dirty Rect

There are two major implementations of Dirty Rect with the Canvas API (Figure 16-8). One is registering all dirty regions as clipping regions using `clip()` method, and drawing all shapes inside the clipping area. The other is clipping only one big rectangle as a clipping region, which includes all dirty regions, and drawing all the shapes inside.

 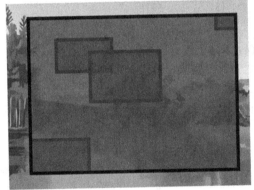

Figure 16-8. Two types of Dirty Rect

The former fits when there are few moving objects, and the latter fits when there are lots of moving objects. You should choose the best method for your game after considering their pros and cons.

If your game needs to redraw full screen every frame because you have to register the entire screen as dirty region, you can avoid the Dirty Rect method. But in this case, it is good idea to have a flag to determine whether to draw or not. The flag will help to prevent consuming battery power. I will discuss this in detail later in the "Battery Problems" section.

Color Transformation

When a character is damaged in a game, you might want to make the character red as an effect. You can achieve this with pixel-by-pixel processing using get/putImageData, which I showed earlier in the "Bitmap API Example" section, but it takes a lot time. So you need a faster way to transform color.

The solution is the globalCompositeOperation property. This property is useful to filter images. You can specify how to draw shapes over existing images by using this property. You can see the effect of each of the operators in Listing 16-10.

Listing 16-10. Global Composite Operations

```
onload = function() {
  var operations = ["source-over", "source-atop", "source-in", "source-out",
          "destination-over", "destination-atop", "destination-in", "destination-out",
          "lighter", "copy", "xor", "darker"];
  for(var i = 0; i < operations.length; i++) {
    var div = document.createElement("div");
    div.innerHTML = ":" + operations[i];
    document.body.appendChild(div);
    var canvas = document.createElement("canvas");
    canvas.width = canvas.height = 75;
    div.insertBefore(canvas, div.firstChild);
    var ctx = canvas.getContext("2d");

    ctx.fillStyle = "#03f";
    ctx.fillRect(5, 5, 50, 50);
    ctx.beginPath();
    ctx.fillStyle = "#f50";
    ctx.arc(45, 45, 25, 0, Math.PI * 2, false);
    ctx.globalCompositeOperation = operations[i];
    ctx.fill();
    ctx.globalCompositeOperation = "source-over";
    ctx.strokeRect(0, 0, 75, 75);
  }
};
```

Figure 16-9 shows the results of using the globalCompositeOperation property.

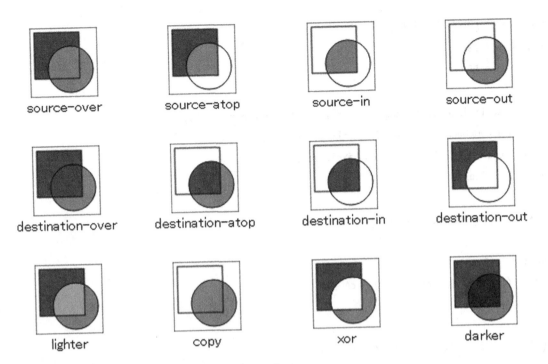

Figure 16-9. The results of global composite operations

Please keep in mind that the "darker" operator is non-standard, but almost all modern mobile browsers, including Chrome, Android Legacy Browser, and MobileSafari support this operator. There are some effects that are unable to show without the darker operator.

If you are interested in the browser implementation of each operator, see Table 16-1.

Table 16-1. Global Composite Operators

Operator	FA	FB
source-over	1	1-aA
destination-over	1-aB	1
source-in	aB	0
destination-in	0	aA
source-out	1-aB	0
destination-out	0	1-aA
source-atop	aB	1-aA
destination-atop	1-aB	aA
Xor	1-aB	1-aA
Copy	1	0
Lighter	1	1

Figure 16-10 shows the meaning of FA and FB.

```
cO = cA * FA + cB * FB
aO = aA * FA + ab * FB
```

where

- cX is the pre-multiplied color component of pixel X, in the range [0, 1]
- aX is the alpha component of pixel X, in the range [0, 1]
- A and B are the source and destination pixels respectively
- O is the output pixel.

darker has special implementation;

Chrome:

```
aO = 1 - (1-aA) * (1-aB)
cO = Math.min( (1-aA) * cB + cA, (1-aB) * cA + cB)
```

Safari:

```
aO = aA + aB
CO = 1 - ( (1-cA) * aA + (1-cB) * aB) / aO
```

Figure 16-10. Formula of global composite operations

Color Transformation Using Alpha

The easiest method of color transformation is to use alpha transparency. This method is not only easy but very fast, so you can use this aggressively.

The code in Listing 16-11 draws a transparent image with color transformation using the "source-atop" operator. Browsers avoid drawing the transparent pixels, and draw an alpha-blended green color on existing pixels. As a result, the image shows a green face (Figure 16-11). You can use this effect for damaging effects in your game.

Listing 16-11. Color Transform with Alpha

```
onload = function() {
  var img = document.createElement("img");
  img.onload = function() {
    var canvas = document.createElement("canvas");
    canvas.width = img.width;
    canvas.height = img.height;
    document.body.appendChild(canvas);
    var ctx = canvas.getContext("2d");
    ctx.drawImage(img, 0, 0);

    ctx.globalCompositeOperation = "source-atop";
    ctx.fillStyle = "rgba(0, 255, 0, 0.6)";
    ctx.fillRect(0, 0, canvas.width, canvas.height);
  };
  img.src = "http://www.w3.org/html/logo/downloads/HTML5_Logo_512.png";
```

Figure 16-11. Color transform with alpha output

Separate RGB Channels

If you want to adjust color transformations in detail, you can separate and merge RGB channels using globalCompositeOperation operators. This is effective for game engines.

The code in Listing 16-12 separates each channel using the darker operator (Figure 16-12). You can modify each image precisely with alpha-blending. After finishing modifications, the code merges all channels using the lighter operator. As I said, darker is a non-standard operator but almost all mobile browsers support it.

Listing 16-12. Separate RGB Channels

```
onload = function() {
  var img = document.createElement("img");
  img.onload = function() {
    var canvas = document.createElement("canvas");
    canvas.width = img.width;
    canvas.height = img.height;
    document.body.appendChild(canvas);
    var ctx = canvas.getContext("2d");
    ctx.drawImage(img, 0, 0);

    ctx.globalCompositeOperation = "source-atop";
    ctx.fillStyle = "rgba(0, 255, 0, 0.6)";
    ctx.fillRect(0, 0, canvas.width, canvas.height);
  };
  img.src = "http://www.w3.org/html/logo/downloads/HTML5_Logo_512.png";
};
```

Figure 16-12. Separate RGB channels output

This method is slow because it invokes drawImage seven times, but it's much faster than put/getImageData. If you want more speed, it's good idea to cache each channel. With cached channels, you can make a fading colors animation.

Optimization on Drawing Paths

Some games use Paths a lot. When you are planning to support vector images on your game engine, it's especially important to draw Paths fast.

If your target browsers support the Path object (such as on iOS7), you may use it aggressively. With the Path object, you can reuse the shape of a drawing. But please note that currently quite a few browsers support the Path object, so it's better to check that your target browsers are supporting the Path object before using it.

It is common to build Paths from outside data sources like JSON. In this case, you don't need to parse and build draw functions every time you need them. With new Function, you can reduce the overhead drastically.

Listing 16-13 generates the drawing code in Listing 16-14.

Listing 16-13. Generating JavaScript Codes

```
onload = function() {
  var canvas = document.createElement("canvas");
  canvas.width = canvas.height = 300;
  document.body.appendChild(canvas);
  var ctx = canvas.getContext("2d");

  var svg = ("M 51.35 38.55 L 30.35 0 L 21 0 L 0 38.55 L 8.3 38.55" +
          " L 12.7 30.3 L 38.65 30.3 L 43.05 38.55 L 51.35 38.55" +
          " M 34.9 23.5 L 16.5 23.5 L 25.7 6.45 L 34.9 23.5").split(" ");
```

```
  var body = "ctx.beginPath();";
  for(var i = 0; i < svg.length; i+=3) {
    var pos = svg[i + 1] + "," + svg[i + 2];
    if(svg[i] == "M") { body += "ctx.moveTo(" + pos + ");"; }
    if(svg[i] == "L") { body += "ctx.lineTo(" + pos + ");"; }
  }
  var func = new Function("ctx", body + "ctx.fill();");
  func(ctx);
};
```

Listing 16-14. The Generated Codes

```
ctx.beginPath();ctx.moveTo(51.35,38.55);ctx.lineTo(30.35,0);ctx.lineTo(21,0);
ctx.lineTo(0,38.55);ctx.lineTo(8.3,38.55);ctx.lineTo(12.7,30.3);ctx.lineTo(38.65,30.3);
ctx.lineTo(43.05,38.55);ctx.lineTo(51.35,38.55);ctx.moveTo(34.9,23.5);ctx.lineTo(16.5,23.5);
ctx.lineTo(25.7,6.45);ctx.lineTo(34.9,23.5);ctx.fill();
```

After generating drawing codes as a function, just use this function. No more parsing is needed. To adjust position or scaling, you just use an affine transformation.

Use GPU Effectively

In the old days, browsers drew Canvas with software rendering using the CPU, not GPU. But almost all current modern browsers support GPU rendering, increasing the importance of techniques that utilize the GPU.

When you need to draw with the GPU, you have to transfer the image data from CPU to GPU. You don't need to transfer every time because your browser tries to cache the image data inside the GPU. You need to transfer image data if you want to draw an image not existing in the GPU cache.

Optimizations for using the GPU are very effective when you use drawImage a lot. drawImage is very fast as is, with significant advantages when internally utilizing the GPU cache. It is a very good idea to design to use the GPU cache effectively.

However, there is no obvious way to use the cache precisely; it depends on the implementation of browsers. So you need to struggle to put the image in the cache area preferably. The basic strategy is to use a small number of images. Sometimes it is also effective to avoid large images because the browser may need to clear and overwrite the existing GPU cache area.

In addition, please keep in mind that browsers never use the cache when you indicate Canvas at the first argument of drawImage. If you want to use the GPU cache with canvas such as in-memory canvas, you can convert the Canvas element to img element. See Listing 16-15.

Listing 16-15. Convert from Canvas to Img

```
var src = canvas.toDataURL();
var img = document.createElement("img");
img.src = src;
```

It needs initial costs to convert from canvas to img, but after that you can push the image to the GPU cache. This is an especially effective technique for game engines.

Keeping Canvas Applications Stable

It is very hard to keep canvas applications stable. As I mentioned, compatibility issues are critical. Additionally, mobile devices don't have a large amount of memory. And finally, despite PC browsers having no power limits, for mobile devices you have to take care regarding battery usage.

If you want to create a technical one-time demo, this section is not so important. But if you are planning to create games, which many users play for a long time, it's important to support several devices, avoid crashing browsers, and prevent excessive battery consumption. I will show you techniques to work around these issues in this section.

Browser Compatibility

There are less compatibility issues on Canvas than CSS. Nevertheless we have to struggle to support a range of browsers on existing devices. It is especially tough to support Android legacy browsers; it will annoy you very much.

As mentioned earlier, Android makers customize their browser excessively, so you may face many kinds of problems around compatibility issues. For example, the simple code in Listing 16-16 won't work well on several devices.

Listing 16-16. A Famous Troublesome Code

```
ctx.clearRect(0, 0, w, h);
```

If you face compatibility issues, you should throw away any preconceived notion that such simple code must work well, and be completely suspicious about browser implementations.

To find troublesome code, it's reasonable to comment out several lines or blocks of code from the entire code to locate the problem via bisecting. Next, try to make the smallest problem code, which can reproduce the same issue. Finally, you will find the workaround to avoid the problem. The workaround for Listing 16-16 is shown in Listing 16-17.

Listing 16-17. Workaround

```
ctx.clearRect(0, 0, w + 1, h + 1);
```

To find out the real problem, it's good idea to try to think like a browser writer. Imagine what kind of processing goes on inside the browser that may cause the problem. To get the fastest result, consider how you would implement the browser. It's the easiest way to fix the issue: you make a hypothesis about implementation, and validate it time after time.

Sometimes the GPU causes the compatibility bugs. There is no option to disable GPU rendering, but you can disable it by just setting the target canvas width or height to more than 2048px. It turns off GPU rendering, and turns on CPU rendering. If you find a bug in GPU rendering, you can avoid it by preparing a large canvas for particular devices.

Again, you'll need to struggle a great deal to support all Android devices. Therefore, it's sometimes a good idea to give up supporting devices whose market share is insignificant.

Memory Problems

It's important not to consume too much memory, because mobile devices have very limited amounts of RAM. If you use memory over the limit, the browser will crash, will freeze, and will skip drawing in the browser. When you face those kinds of problems, you should investigate memory usage.

You must also confirm that garbage collection successfully collected the unused canvases, especially when you use In-Memory Canvas. Some mobile browsers seem not to collect canvas elements at all, so if you find this kind of problem, you need to prepare a large In-Memory Canvas and reuse it again and again.

You also need to be aware of memory leaks. Every image and canvas consumes lot of memory, so you should release the reference to them properly. You can check the memory leak with your PC using the Heap Snapshot feature in Chrome Dev Tools.

You should control garbage collection itself. It takes about 10ms for one minor garbage collection (GC), so it is critical for 60fps games. Sometimes a major GC can stop the world for a second or more, which kills the fun of games like action games. To control GC, you need to allocate all the memory including Canvasses and arrays on initialization, and never allocate any more during the game.

Battery Problems

It's ideal if you can prevent excessively consuming the battery. Mobile game users are very sensitive to games consuming a lot of battery. They'll avoid playing games eventually if they feel the game is battery hungry. It's important to design games not to consume too much power.

Generally speaking, the consumption of battery correlates with CPU utilization. So one good solution is to keep CPU utilization low if you can. Unfortunately, usually mobile CPUs have little margin. If you have any available CPU, you might want to increase frames per second. However, you should consider an option to drop framerate to save battery for particular scenes, such as a main menu.

The GPU can also consume a lot of battery. For example, the code in Listing 16-18 consumes battery rapidly, even though the CPU is not working much at all.

Listing 16-18. Consuming Battery

```
(function draw() {
  setTimeout(draw, 16);
  ctx.fillRect(0, 0, ctx.canvas.width, ctx.canvas.height);
})();
```

By reducing drawing, the Dirty Rect method I mentioned earlier helps with battery management. You don't need to adopt the entire Dirty Rect method. It can be effective to simply skip frames properly when you don't need to redraw.

Profiling on the Real Devices

I described many techniques around mobile HTML5; however, the most important is to profile correctly on a real device. You should gather the real time profiling data of drawing codes from not a PC but from mobile devices, and improve your game based on the real data.

If you are developing on Android, you may use Android Debug Bridge or Chrome Remote debugging. If you are developing on iOS, you may use Inspector. Modern browsers support remote debug features so you can check the status of a mobile device on your PC in real time. By doing this investigation you can choose the best method to resolve current problems.

As you see from the information provided in this chapter, making mobile HTML5 games is like exploring minefields. However, I believe that the benefits of mobile browser games are quite significant. I hope you agree with me, and you create lots of fine mobile browser games.

■ ■ ■

CHAPTER 17

Faster Map Rendering

Colt "MainRoach" McAnlis, Developer Advocate, Google

Any two-dimensional game is going to, at some point, have a separation between semistatic background content and dynamically animated foreground content. The background content can become a burden to the rendering pipeline, as it can easily consume megabytes of data as well as a hefty chunk of your rendering pipeline. In this chapter, I'm going to discuss a few strategies for overcoming this burden, providing trade-offs where your game may need them.

The MAP Object

You generally need somewhere to store your map data once you load them, and you start by declaring a map class that will contain all the information you're looking for. I'm going to get ahead of myself here and describe a few of the data types you'll need:

```
//from TILEDmap.js

function TILEDmap(){
    this.currMapData= null;    //copy of the tile information for this map
    this.tileSets= new Array(); // a list of the tile sets (ie textures) used for this map
    this.viewRect= { //the view-rect defines the part of the map that's currently visible to the user.
      "x": 0,
      "y": 0,
      "w": 1000,
      "h": 1000
    };
    this.numXTiles= 100;   //number of x and y tiles  on the map
    this.numYTiles= 100;
    this.tileSize= {    //the size of a given tile, in pixels
      "x": 64,
      "y": 64
    };
    this.pixelSize= { //size of the entire map, in terms of pixels
      "x": this.numXTiles * this.tileSize.x,
      "y": this.numYTiles * this.tileSize.y
    };
```

```
    this.imgLoadCount=0;      //we may be loading many loose images, as such keep a count of how many
have been loaded
    this.fullyLoaded=false; //don't start rendering until everything is loaded

//.....important functions go here


}
var gMap = new TILEDmap();
```

Note that it's important to create a global gMap object here, as you'll need to reference it from a few callbacks as well as code inside this file.

Fetch the Data from the Server

Your map data have to come from somewhere, and chances are that you'll need to save your content in JavaScript Object Notation (JSON) and upload it to your web server to be loaded into your game. If you're unfamiliar with the process of grabbing blobs of data from a URL, you can use the handy application programming interface (API) XMLHttpRequest (XHR) to do just that. XHR has many uses, features, and settings that are beyond the scope of this chapter; here, you need it simply to fetch your text-based map data file.

One thing worth noting about this *load* function is that the response function will call a parse operation on the JSON, and this is where the real magic happens:

```
//from TILEDmap.js

//--------------------------
  this.load= function ()
  {
    var xhr = new XMLHttpRequest();

    //this is a hard-coded URL to where the map file is sitting
    xhr.open("GET", "./data/map.json", true);

    //note that the data is standard text, so you need to set the mime type accordingly
    xhr.overrideMimeType('text/plain; charset=x-user-defined');

    //here we define what happens when the data-fetch attempts to complete; this callback will be executed
    xhr.onreadystatechange = function()
    {
      //did we successfully get the data?
      if (xhr.readyState != 4 || xhr.responseText =="")
        return;

      //go ahead and pass the fetched content to the parsing system
      gMap.parseMapJSON(xhr.response);

    };

    //execute the XHR
    xhr.send();

};
```

I'm going to cover parsing the map data in a moment, but first I'd like to point out that, in this chapter, I will be introducing a couple different ways to render your map. As such, the source code will require a bit of fragmentation in order to show off these principles. For instance, each technique has a separate type of draw function, so you allow the map object simply to call the global override the onDrawMap function to handle the technique-specific details. Note that here, however, you don't let the map draw until it has been entirely loaded into memory. This is important, because otherwise, you may end up rendering partially loaded information, which may not be visually pleasing to your users:

```
//from TILEDmap.js

//---------------------------
  this.draw= function (ctx)
  { //
        if(!this.fullyLoaded) return;

  onDrawMap(ctx); //offload the actual rendering of this map to some external function
  };
```

Loading a Tiled Map

Most maps come from a pregenerated artist tool. Usually, some plucky artist gets to sit down (alongside a designer) and map out the visuals for a game. In this case, you'll find that the Tiled editor is a great tool to use to generate maps, and, lucky for us, it outputs to a JSON format. I'll skip over how to create a map using the Tiled editor and point you to the relevant documentation on this topic. For the sake of this tutorial, I'm going to work with an existing tiled map from the Girls Raised in Tennessee Science (GRITS) Collaborative Project (see Figure 17-1).

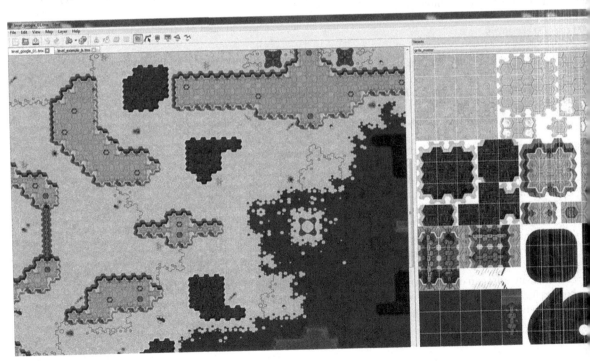

Figure 17-1. *The Tiled editor*

Before I dive into the "gritty" details, you should know that there's lots of great content that Tiled dumps out on our behalf. Here's the overall layout of the file, highlighting the things to care about:

- Height, width, orientation, tile height, tile width, and version
- Properties dictionary (name-value pairs)
- Layers array
  - Data (array of integers specifying which tile to draw)
  - Layer name
  - Width, height, visibility, opacity
  - Layer type (tile layer or object layer)
- Tilesets array
  - Image (grits_master.png)
  - firstgid (this is very important—it lets you know what tile you're referencing in the data).
  - img width, img height, margin, spacing, tile width, tile height

Parsing the Map Data

Parsing the map data is quite simple: once you've received the JSON data, you have to convert them to a JavaScript object, using the JSON.parse method. For the sake of ease, you cache some of the values' directions so that you can fetch them later without an indirection:

```
//from TILEDmap.js

this.parseMapJSON=function(mapJSON)
{
   //go ahead and parse the JSON data using the internal parser
   //this will return an object that we can iterate through.
      this.currMapData = JSON.parse( mapJSON );

   //simply cache all the values from the map for ease-of-use
      var map = this.currMapData;
    this.numXTiles = map.width;
    this.numYTiles = map.height;
    this.tileSize.x = map.tilewidth;
    this.tileSize.y = map.tileheight;
    this.pixelSize.x = this.numXTiles * this.tileSize.x;
    this.pixelSize.y = this.numYTiles * this.tileSize.y;
```

In Tiled, an artist can drop in a group of images and start placing tiles from any of the images on the map as he or she sees fit. During the loading of your tiled data, you must also load the atlases that were used to create the map, listed inside the .JSON file (see Figure 17-2).

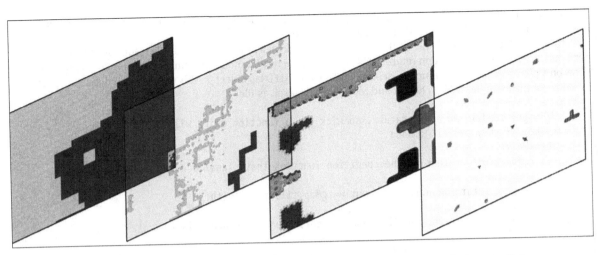

Figure 17-2. *An exploded view of the layers of a map (left to right): base layer, accents on the base, walls layer, additional accents*

One of the more important aspects of loading these images is that the loading process is *asynchronous*, meaning that it will occur without blocking the execution flow of your application. As such, you can run into a strange situation, in which your code starts executing the main loop before you have all your content loaded. To address this, you create an imgLoadCount variable for the map object, which is incremented as each image finalizes its load operation:

```
//from TILEDmap.js

//load our tilesets if we are a client.
    var gMap = this;
    gMap.imgLoadCount = 0; //reset our image loading counter
    for (var i = 0; i < map.tilesets.length; i++)
    {
            //load each image and store a handle to it
        var img = new Image();
        img.onload = new function()
                {gMap.imgLoadCount++;}; //once the image is loaded, increase a global counter

            //NOTE that the TILED data puts some gnarly relative path data into the file
            //let's get rid of that, since our directory structure in the shipping product is not the same
            //as in the editor layout.
        img.src = "../data/" + map.tilesets[i].image.replace(/^.*[\\\/]/, '');

            //store this data in a way that makes it easy to access later:
        var ts = {
          "firstgid": map.tilesets[i].firstgid,
          "image": img,
          "imageheight": map.tilesets[i].imageheight,
          "imagewidth": map.tilesets[i].imagewidth,
          "name": map.tilesets[i].name,
          "numXTiles": Math.floor(map.tilesets[i].imagewidth / this.tileSize.x),
          "numYTiles": Math.floor(map.tilesets[i].imageheight / this.tileSize.y)
        };
        this.tileSets.push(ts);
```

Because the `img.onload` function callbacks occur async style, you need to create a method that polls the state of `gMap.imgLoadCount` to determine if all the images are loaded.

The `checkWait` function is a nice little helper that will kick off a timer to check for the results of a function periodically. Once the test function returns TRUE, it will call the result function. Again, in your simple example, you allow onMapDataLoaded to be a function defined outside the TILEDMap object. In this way, you can define the postload function for the examples in this chapter and reuse the TILEDMap.js file:

```
//images load in an async nature, so kick off a function which will poll
//to see if they are all loaded
checkWait(
        function() //this is the condition function that's called every instance
        {
                return gMap.imgLoadCount == gMap.tileSets.length;
        },
        function () //this is the function called once the above is true
         {
                onMapDataLoaded();
        });


    }
};//end of map object
```

For your simple example, once all the images are loaded, you allow yourself to say that the map is "loaded," and rendering logic can start working:

```
//0-forward.html

//these functions are specific to this approach
    function onMapDataLoaded()
    {
        gMap.fullyLoaded = true;
    }
```

Rendering Tiled Data

Once you understand the layout of a Tiled file, you can quickly see how the rendering process occurs. The file consists of a set of *layers* that are stacked on top of each other. (The first layer in the array is the lowest, or first to be drawn, and subsequent layers replace the pixels drawn by previous layers.) Each layer contains a list of "tiles" that occupy it, in which the tile points to the index of the texture used to render it.

With this in mind, rendering the map is pretty straightforward. You walk through each layer, and each tile in that layer, and draw the specified sprite on the screen. Generally, the most complex piece of logic that you have to deal with here is to determine where the tile should reside in world-space, given that you only have an index to its location in the layer data.

Understanding the Data Format to Render

The Tiled editor expects you to load into it a series of texture atlases to use for adding texture information to your map. In addition, Tiled also expects the tiles for a map to be homogenous in size across atlases, such that you can index a specific tile in a specific atlas simply by having the (x, y) coordinate of the tile in tilespace. To distinguish between two atlases, Tiled will define a range of IDs for the tiles that belong to the atlases. In this way, every tile in your map will have a unique ID that you can quickly reference; even better, you can determine which atlas each tile came from.

Table 17-1. *An Example GID-to-Range Table for Textures Used in a Map: the Number of Tiles a Texture Defines Is Related to Its Dimensions, Which Determine what Ranges Are Described*

Texture Name	firstgid	ID Range
No tile here	0	0
base_tiles.jpg	1	1–127
ground_accents.png	128	128–255
ground_foliage.png	256	256–1023
static_objects.png	1024	1024–2047

Rendering the entire tiled map becomes somewhat straightforward if you keep the following in mind:

- Walk through each layer.

- Walk through each tile on that layer.

- If the tile value is nonzero, do the following tasks:

  - Walk through all the atlases, and find out which atlas the index belongs to.

  - Draw the tile on the screen.

Let's do that again, but in code form. First, let's talk about how, given an ID from a tile, you can determine what atlas it's from and what its pixel coordinates are in that atlas:

```
//--------------------------
this.getTilePacket= function (tileIndex) {
  //this is the packet we'll return after fetching
  var pkt = {
    "img": null,
    "px": 0,
    "py": 0
  };

  //walk through the tile-sets and determine what 'bucket' this index is landing in
  //TILED defines this by providing a 'firstgid' object which defines where this tile's indexes start
  var i = 0;
  for (i = this.tileSets.length - 1; i >= 0; i--)
  {
    if (this.tileSets[i].firstgid <= tileIndex)
      break; //FOUND it!
  }

  //copy the information from this tileset
  pkt.img = this.tileSets[i].image;
  //we need to define what the 'local' index is, that is, what the index is in the atlas image for this tile
  //we do this by subtracting the global id for this tileset, which gives us a relative number.
  var localIdx = tileIndex - this.tileSets[i].firstgid;
  var lTileX = Math.floor(localIdx % this.tileSets[i].numXTiles);
  var lTileY = Math.floor(localIdx / this.tileSets[i].numXTiles);
  pkt.px = (lTileX * this.tileSize.x);
  pkt.py = (lTileY * this.tileSize.y);
```

```
    //return!
    return pkt;
  };
```

For the sake of argument, here is a version of rendering, called forward rendering, which could be considered "brute force." Effectively, you're going to walk to each layer and then walk through all the tiles in that layer and draw the tile on its canvas:

```
function onDrawMap(ctx)
  {
    //we walk through all the layers
    for (var layerIdx = 0; layerIdx < gMap.currMapData.layers.length; layerIdx++)
      {
        //is this a tile layer, or an object layer?
        if (gMap.currMapData.layers[layerIdx].type != "tilelayer") continue;

        var dat = gMap.currMapData.layers[layerIdx].data;

        //find what the tileIndexOffset is for gMap layer
        for (var tileIDX = 0; tileIDX < dat.length; tileIDX++)
          {
            var tID = dat[tileIDX];
            //if the value is 0, then there's no tile defined for this slot, skip it!
            if (tID == 0)
              continue;

            var tPKT = gMap.getTilePacket(tID);

            var worldX = Math.floor(tileIDX % gMap.numXTiles) * gMap.tileSize.x;
            var worldY = Math.floor(tileIDX / gMap.numXTiles) * gMap.tileSize.y;

            // Nine arguments: the element, source (x,y) coordinates, source width and
            // height (for cropping), destination (x,y) coordinates, and destination width
            // and height (resize).
            ctx.drawImage(tPKT.img, tPKT.px, tPKT.py, gMap.tileSize.x, gMap.tileSize.y, worldX,
worldY, gMap.tileSize.x, gMap.tileSize.y);

          }
      }
  }
```

Coordinate Spaces and View-Rect

With the current code, you run into the issue of coordinate spaces. The canvas has coordinates, (0, width) and (0, height). These are not equal to the coordinates of the map, (0, map width) (a.k.a. world-space coordinates). As such, you end up drawing only the part of the map whose coordinates are identical to the canvas coordinates. This, of course, is less than the desired output, as you want the ability to render whatever part of the map your player happens to occupy.

For this, I introduce the concept of a *view-rect*. The view-rect is a rectangle that defines what part of the map, in world coordinates, is currently visible in canvas coordinates. To put it differently, you use the view-rect to map world-space to view-space:

```
//.......
            var tPKT = gMap.getTilePacket(tID);

            //test if gMap tile is within our world bounds
            var worldX = Math.floor(tileIDX % gMap.numXTiles) * gMap.tileSize.x;
            var worldY = Math.floor(tileIDX / gMap.numXTiles) * gMap.tileSize.y;
            if ((worldX + gMap.tileSize.x) < gMap.viewRect.x || (worldY + gMap.tileSize.y) < gMap.
viewRect.y || worldX > gMap.viewRect.x + gMap.viewRect.w || worldY > gMap.viewRect.y + gMap.
viewRect.h) continue;

            //adjust all the visible tiles to draw at canvas origin.
            worldX -= gMap.viewRect.x;
            worldY -= gMap.viewRect.y;

            // Nine arguments: the element, source (x,y) coordinates, source width and
            // height (for cropping), destination (x,y) coordinates, and destination width
            // and height (resize).
            ctx.drawImage(tPKT.img, tPKT.px, tPKT.py, gMap.tileSize.x, gMap.tileSize.y, worldX,
worldY, gMap.tileSize.x, gMap.tileSize.y);

//.......
```

An added benefit of the view-rect is that it allows you to do visibility culling on your tiles, such that you render only the tiles that are visible to the user rather than drawing every tile in the map, regardless of whether it's on-screen or not.

To use the view-rect properly, you instruct the update function of your simple example to modify the view-rect, based on the position of the player in the world:

```
coregame.js
function draw(){
//....other drawing functions here
            //make sure the player is at the center of the screen
            gMap.viewRect.x = (pPos.x - ( canvas_width / 2 ) );
            gMap.viewRect.y = (pPos.y - ( canvas_height / 2 ));
            gMap.viewRect.w = canvas_width;
            gMap.viewRect.h = canvas_height;
```

Fast Canvas Rendering with Precaching

One of the big problems with the forward rendering method for two-dimensional maps is that it easily becomes a performance bottleneck once the number of layers, tiles, and overlapping tiles increases. Each draw call can have subsequent overhead associated with it, and if you're not careful, you can end up redrawing massive portions of your screen, thus wasting cycles on pixels that will never be visible to the user.

For instance, if each tile area on the screen had four or five image tiles placed on it, your draw count per frame will, in effect, have quadrupled with the new map (see Figure 17-3).

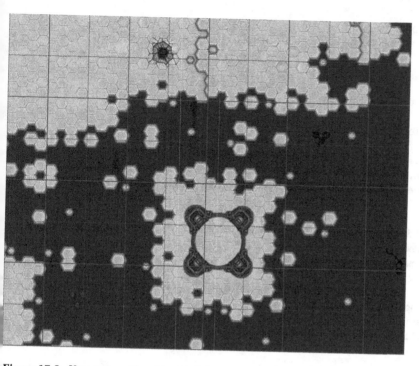

Figure 17-3. *Your map with a 64 × 64 tile boundary grid overlaid on it*

The obvious solution here is to reduce the number of draws per frame. One of the main ways of fixing this problem involves taking the raw map-rendering data and using the concept of offscreen canvas rendering to reduce the number of draw calls.

This process works by dividing the entire map into 1,024 × 1,024 sections and prerendering each section into a larger texture (see Figure 17-4). At render time, you can draw the pregenerated textures instead of each individual tile. Thus, rather than incurring the overhead of thousands of draw calls per tile, you simply have to do eight or so draws per frame for all the static map data.

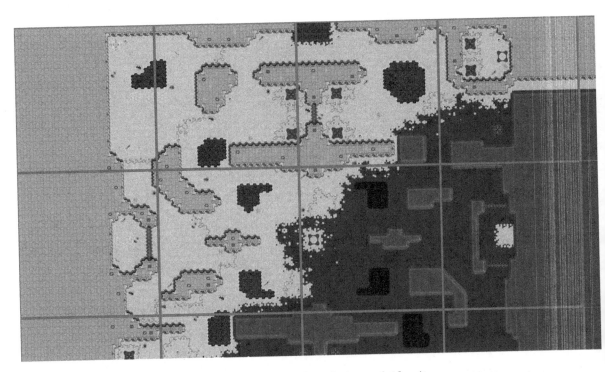

Figure 17-4. *Your map with the 1,024 × 1,024 canvas tile boundaries overlaid on it*

The result is a trade-off between memory and draw-call performance. Yes, you are churning up more memory for the canvases (each canvas tile is approximately 4MB), but you reduce the draw call to 1–6 per frame (down from approximately 400), which shows a great performance improvement.

Creating a CanvasTile

To perform offscreen canvas rendering requires use of an *offscreen canvas*. To help with this process, I have created a new concept, which I'm calling canvasTile. This will represent a canvas object that you render into and use later. In effect, a canvas tile will represent some subsection of the real estate of the map and allow you to prerender the environment into its texture object for later use:

```
function CanvasTile(){
    this.x=0; //world x,y, width and height of this tile
    this.y=0;
    this.w=100;
    this.h=100;
    this.cvsHdl=null; //a handle to the canvas to draw into
    this.ctx=null; //the 2d context for said canvas
```

```
//----------------------------
this.create=function(width,height)
{

    this.x = -1;
    this.y = -1;
    this.w = width;
    this.h = height;
    //create a brand new canvas object, which is NOT attached to the dop
    //this will make the canvas 'offscreen' in that we can render into it, use it, but it
    //will not be visible to the end user directly
    var can2 = document.createElement('canvas');
    can2.width = width;
    can2.height = height;
    this.cvsHdl = can2;
    this.ctx = can2.getContext('2d');

};
```

In the forward-rendering model, you needed to add viewport culling to reduce the number of draw calls per frame. Although you now have fewer objects to draw, you must still do viewport culling in order to reduce the number of pixel-processing operations that occur unnecessarily. As such, your canvasTile class contains an isVisible function:

```
function CanvasTile(){
//......................
  //----------------------------
    this.isVisible=function()
    {
      var r2 = gMap.viewRect;
      var r1 = this;
      return gMap.intersectRect(  {top:r1.y,
                          left:r1.x,
                          bottom:r1.y+r1.h,
                          right:r1.x+r1.w},
                          {top:r2.y,
                          left:r2.x,
                          bottom:r2.y+r2.h,
                          right:r2.x+r2.w});

    };
```

The goal of this technique is to be able to prerender the entire map into separate canvasTiles and then render only the visible ones during the main loop. As such, you have to create a container to hold all the canvasTiles, such that the map can fill and iterate on them:

```
Map.canvasTileSize={"x":1024,"y":1024};
Map.canvasTileArray=[];
```

Filling the Cache

Once the map data have been parsed, and the images have been loaded, you can continue filling your cache:

```
function onMapDataLoaded()
    {
        preDrawCache();

    }
```

Now that you have the basic object, you must create a two-dimensional array of canvasTiles that covers the world-space map correctly. To do this, you divide the size of the map (on each axis) by the size of each canvasTile (which is tunable) to get the number of canvasTiles along that axis. You store these in an array for retrieval later.

Most important, once you create the array, you call fillCanvasTile, which will do all the work of filling in the canvas with the proper tile data:

```
function preDrawCache()
    {
        //determine the number of canvases across, and down for the given map
        //dividing the overall pixel size of the map by the size of your canvas tiles does this
        var xCanvasCount = 1 + Math.floor(gMap.pixelSize.x / gMap.canvasTileSize.x);
        var yCanvasCount = 1 + Math.floor(gMap.pixelSize.y / gMap.canvasTileSize.y);
        var numSubCanv = xCanvasCount*yCanvasCount;

        //now for each 'cache tile' go through, create it, and fill it with graphics information
        for(var yC = 0; yC <yCanvasCount; yC ++)
        {
          for(var xC = 0; xC <xCanvasCount; xC ++)
          {
            var k = new CanvasTile();
            k.create(gMap.canvasTileSize.x,gMap.canvasTileSize.y);
            k.x = xC * gMap.canvasTileSize.x;
            k.y = yC * gMap.canvasTileSize.y;
            gMap.canvasTileArray.push(k);

            //draw this region of the map into this canvas
            fillCanvasTile(k);
          }
        }

        //once we've filled the cache, we're loaded!
        gMap.fullyLoaded = true;
    };
```

To fill the canvasTile object, you need to modify your rendering function from the last article. Before, you were taking into account the entire view-rect when rendering. Now, you can extend this concept by culling against the suggested canvasTile bounds rather than the view-rect itself. This lets you easily reuse your existing code to fill your new canvasTiles:

```
function fillCanvasTile(ctile)
 {

    var ctx = ctile.ctx;
    //clear the tile itself
    ctx.fillRect(0,0,ctile.w, ctile.h);

    //create a mini-view-rect for this tile, which represents its bounds in world-space
    var vRect={ top:ctile.y,
            left:ctile.x,
            bottom:ctile.y+ctile.h,
            right:ctile.x+ctile.w};

      //most of this logic is the same
      for (var layerIdx = 0; layerIdx < gMap.currMapData.layers.length; layerIdx++)
      {
        if (gMap.currMapData.layers[layerIdx].type != "tilelayer") continue;

        var dat = gMap.currMapData.layers[layerIdx].data;
        //find what the tileIndexOffset is for gMap layer
        for (var tileIDX = 0; tileIDX < dat.length; tileIDX++) {
        var tID = dat[tileIDX];
        if (tID == 0) continue;

        var tPKT = gMap.getTilePacket(tID);

        //test if gMap tile is within our world bounds
        var worldX = Math.floor(tileIDX % gMap.numXTiles) * gMap.tileSize.x;
        var worldY = Math.floor(tileIDX / gMap.numXTiles) * gMap.tileSize.y;

        //figure out if the cache-tile rectangle intersects with the given smaller tile
        var visible= intersectRect( vRect,
                    {top:worldY,left:worldX,bottom:worldY + gMap.tileSize.y,right:worldX +
gMap.tileSize.x});
            if(!visible)
              continue;

        // Nine arguments: the element, source (x,y) coordinates, source width and
        // height (for cropping), destination (x,y) coordinates, and destination width
        // and height (resize).

        ctx.drawImage(tPKT.img,
                tPKT.px, tPKT.py,
                gMap.tileSize.x, gMap.tileSize.y,
                worldX - vRect.left,
                worldY - vRect.top,
                gMap.tileSize.x, gMap.tileSize.y);

      }
    }
}
```

Draw!

The creation and filling of canvasTiles occur at initialization time for your app. Later on, in order to render, you simply need to determine if a given canvasTile is visible to the view-rect, using box-box intersection code (see Chapter 16). If it is, draw it as though it were any other tile:

```
function onDrawMap(ctx)
    {
        //aabb test to see if our view-rect intersects with this canvas.
        for(var q =0; q < gMap.canvasTileArray.length; q++)
        {
            var r1 = gMap.canvasTileArray[q];

            if(r1.isVisible())
                ctx.drawImage(r1.cvsHdl, r1.x-gMap.viewRect.x,r1.y-gMap.viewRect.y);
        }
    }
```

Results

With caching, the performance improvements can be drastic. Frame rate on lower-end machines can shoot through the roof, although this comes at the cost of large memory overhead.

For a large map, your canvas will incur approximately 4MB per 1,024×1,024 tile. For example, a map of 6,400×6,400 pixels would yield a 7×7 array of tiles, landing you at 196MB of data; 196MB, however, is huge, unyielding, and maybe too uncompromising, especially if the map sizes increase. It would be great to mix the performance of Tiled caching with lower memory restrictions.

Because the preallocation takes up so much memory, it keeps you from being able to distribute specific large map sizes to players with machines that cannot handle the memory requirements. If you're working with a strong, memory-full device, then, by all means, this technique works great, but for more restricted devices, you may need an alternate solution.

Using a Free List of Canvases

So, let's review.

The forward-rendering path is great on memory, because it uses only the loaded texture atlases and draws from them each frame. Performance suffers here, however, owing to the recomputation of large portions of the screen with each frame, wasting precious central processing unit (CPU) cycles.

Conversely, the caching path is great on performance, drastically reducing the number of draws per frame. However, this technique is horrible on memory, taking up a large portion of your the available space on your application (app).

This situation requires a middle-of-the-road compromise between memory and performance. The goal is to have some notion of cached tile content, but maybe not the entire map, all the time.

To achieve this, you create a relatively small array of canvasTile objects (the size of the pool is up to the developer or, more specifically, the constraints of the device on which you're working. You use these canvases as a pool for the visible screen. As a section of the screen becomes visible, you try to cache the map into a tile and use the tile for as many frames as possible.

Once you run out of free tiles to use, you evict the oldest tile (that is, the tile that was filled the longest time ago), replacing it with the new content.

This technique lands midway between the two previous techniques for two reasons:

1. The technique will place an upper limit on the amount of memory needed for your canvasTiles; regardless of the map size, you will only ever eat up the same data.

2. The technique requires some additional processing overhead, as each canvasTile will need to be filled in as it moves in and out of the view-rect.

As any hard-core computer scientist will tell you, the most important thing about a caching system is how the objects are evicted and retained within it. Simple caching systems, such as Least Recently Used (LRU), will keep a counter on an object, and once the cache is filled, will use the oldest object, repurposing it to be filled with the new information.

AGE AND COST CONSIDERATIONS

You should take into account age and cost when deciding which cache textures to reuse. *Cost* represents the work value associated with refilling an object with information. In your example some tiles may be more expensive to regenerate than others. As such, evicting the high-cost objects from the cache can represent a worst-performance burden, as opposed to evicting younger textures, which may be faster to repopulate. This trade-off is important for any type of texture-caching system.

Shameless plug: you can read more on this topic in my essay "Efficient Cache Replacement Using Age and Cost Metrics," in *Game Programming Gems 7* (Cengage Learning, 2008).

A New CanvasTile

Because users can run around your map quite randomly (especially in the case of teleporter fights), the oldest canvasTile (that is, the tile that was created the longest time ago) is not a good enough metric. The oldest tile may be the one currently visible on screen, which is a less-than-ideal choice for eviction. As such, you need a way to determine the oldest unseen tile. For our purposes, you allow a canvasTile to chart how old it is, relative to not being visible in the viewport:

```
function CanvasTile(){
        this.x=0;
        this.y=0;
        this.w=100;
        this.h=100;
        this.cvsHdl=null;
        this.ctx=null;
        this.isFree=true; //is this tile being used currently?
        this.numFramesNoVisible=0; //how many frames has this NOT been visible?
```

You add an update function to each canvasTile, which will check how long it has been visible to the user. Once a threshold is reached, you consider this tile to be evicted from the cache and available for use in the future:

```
/-----------------------------
    this.update=function()
    {
        //if this tile is free, then there's no logic to be done here
        if(this.isFree) return;
```

```
//if i'm not visible, age me, and see if we can free me from the cache
if(!this.isVisible())
{
  this.numFramesNoVisible++;

  if(this.numFramesNoVisible > 100)    //promote to freed
  {
    this.isFree=true;
    this.x = -1;
    this.y = -1;
  }
}
};
```

Because you're caching your tiles, you need to generate a pool of them once all the content has been loaded. You can create the objects themselves, but you do not fill them in at load time; you wait until you have validation from the viewport to start the cycles.

You'll also notice in the code that follows that the size of the tiles has been changed. In the previous example, you used large, 1,024×1,024 textures, as they represented a good compromise between allocation and draws per frame. (Depending on hardware restrictions, ideally you'd precache the entire static background into one large texture, but that may cause additional memory pressure.) In the case of using a free list, you can get away with a smaller tile size, as you'll be reusing them often:

```
gMap.canvasTileSize={"x":256,"y":256};
function onMapDataLoaded()
  {
    //preallocate a small pool of canvases to use
    numCanvases=30;
    for(var i =0; i < gMap.numCanvases; i++)
    {
      var k = new CanvasTile();
      k.create(gMap.canvasTileSize.x,gMap.canvasTileSize.y);
      gMap.canvasTileArray.push(k);
    }

    gMap.fullyLoaded = true;

}
```

When the viewport tests visibility against the world, it needs to determine if the targeted section of the map has been cached by the tiling system. If so, you have to use the canvasTile to render. If the section has not been cached, you must find a valid texture from the cache to use. You do this in two steps:

1. Cycle the canvases to see if any of them are free for use; these textures are easy to grab and quick to track down.

2. If the cache is full (that is, all the textures have been allocated), then you need to go through it and decide which is the oldest and repurpose that texture for your new needs.

```
//-----------------------------
fetchFreeCanvas:function()
{
        //do we have a free canvas?
        for(var i =0; i < this.canvasTileArray.length; i++)
        {
                if(this.canvasTileArray[i].isFree)
                {
                        this.canvasTileArray[i].isFree = false;
                        return this.canvasTileArray[i];
                }
        }

        //no free canvas yet, find one of the used canvases..
        //pick the one with the highest age
        var oldest = 0;
        var winner = null;
        for(var i =0; i < this.canvasTileArray.length; i++)
        {
                if(this.canvasTileArray[i].isFree) continue;
                if(this.canvasTileArray[i].numFramesNoVisible > oldest)
                {
                        oldest = this.canvasTileArray[i].numFramesNoVisible;
                        winner = this.canvasTileArray[i];
                }
        }

        winner.isFree = false;
        return winner;
},
```

Drawing the Map

To draw your map, you first need to update all your canvasTiles in order to make any necessary adjustments to their ages and potentially allow them to free themselves from the cache. It is important to do this step first, because you're about to start walking the map and reusing tiles where you can get your hands on them:

```
function onDrawMap(ctx)
{
    //do an update of our canvas arrays
or(var i =0; i < gMap.canvasTileArray.length; i++)
 gMap.canvasTileArray[i].update();
```

The real chaos of this function comes from knowing which tiles have been cached and which haven't. In effect, you must segment the map and determine which of the larger segmented areas have active residency in your cache. Once you know your canvasTile coordinates, you can walk through the cache and try to find a tile that has already been filled with that data. If you find one, you can continue on and use it during rendering. If you don't find a canvasTile that contains information, then you need to go through the cache and populate it with the map information:

```
//determine what canvasTilings would be visible here, expand our view rect to smooth tiling artifacts..
var xTileMin = Math.floor((gMap.viewRect.x) / gMap.canvasTileSize.x);
var xTileMax = Math.floor((gMap.viewRect.x+gMap.viewRect.w) / gMap.canvasTileSize.x);
```

```
var yTileMin = Math.floor((gMap.viewRect.y) / gMap.canvasTileSize.y);
var yTileMax = Math.floor((gMap.viewRect.y+gMap.viewRect.h) / gMap.canvasTileSize.y);

if(xTileMin <0) xTileMin=0;
if(yTileMin <0) yTileMin=0;
var visibles=[];
for(var yC = yTileMin; yC <=yTileMax; yC ++)
{
  for(var xC = xTileMin; xC <=xTileMax; xC ++)
  {
    var rk = {
        x:xC * gMap.canvasTileSize.x,
        y:yC * gMap.canvasTileSize.y,
        w:gMap.canvasTileSize.x,
        h:gMap.canvasTileSize.y
        };

    var found = false;
    for(var i =0; i < gMap.canvasTileArray.length; i++)
    {
      if(gMap.canvasTileArray[i].doesMatchRect(rk.x,rk.y,rk.w,rk.h))
      {
        found = true;
        visibles.push(gMap.canvasTileArray[i]);
      }
    }

    if(found) continue;

    var cv = fetchFreeCanvas();
    cv.x = rk.x;
    cv.y = rk.y;
    fillCanvasTile(cv);
    visibles.push(cv);
  }
}
```

At this point, rendering is straightforward; you simply walk through the visible tiles and draw them on the screen. All the heavy lifting has been done already, so you're mostly good to go:

```
var r2 = gMap.viewRect;
//aabb test to see if our view-rect intersects with this canvas.
for(var q =0; q < visibles.length; q++)
{
  var r1 = visibles[q];
  var visible= intersectRect(  {top:r1.y,left:r1.x,bottom:r1.y+r1.h,right:r2.x+r2.w},
                    {top:r2.y,left:r2.x,bottom:r2.y+r2.h,right:r2.x+r2.w});

  if(visible)
    ctx.drawImage(r1.cvsHdl, r1.x-gMap.viewRect.x,r1.y-gMap.viewRect.y);
}

}
```

Results

Caching is an effective bridge between preallocation and memory constraints. In general, though, the technique can create some hitching in your frame rate. Effectively, the cost of caching a tile is mitigated over the number of frames in which it's reused, so you may get spikes of batches of draw calls when a frame is first visible and has to be filled.

Conclusion

In this chapter, I've discussed how to address performance issues that result from the rendering of static map content. Reducing the number of draws per frame is ideal for every situation as a means of keeping frame rate consistent. Nevertheless, one must be mindful of the memory issues involved with precaching too much information. As with most techniques, the best solution is to profile your application across many devices and determine what the right configuration is for your end user's experience.

■ ■ ■

CHAPTER 18

HTML5 Games in C++ with Emscripten

Chad Austin, Senior Technical Director, IMVU

If you had told me ten years ago that I'd someday compile real-time, 3D C++ games into JavaScript so I could run them in web browsers, I would have thought you were crazy. Since then, software has shifted from retail stores and optical discs to online app stores and web applications. Internet users have become increasingly security-conscious, and JavaScript engines have gotten faster by orders of magnitude.

The Web is the ultimate platform. It is secure: applications have no direct access to the local machine. It is seamless: users merely have to click a link to experience your game or web site. It is royalty-free: if you can host a web page, you can distribute a web app. It is capable: with the advent of HTML5 and WebGL, web applications have access to an increasing set of functionality, such as gamepads, full screen display, and local storage. And now, the web is fast too: with the advent of technologies like Mozilla's asm.js and Google's Portable Native Client, web applications can approach native performance.

Compiling code to JavaScript is not new. Google's GWT compiles Java into JavaScript. Haxe is a game development language that targets many platforms, including JavaScript. JSIL compiles .NET programs into JavaScript. Mandreel makes it easy to port C, C++, and Objective C games to a variety of platforms, including Windows Phone and JavaScript.

More recently, an open source C++-to-JavaScript compiler called Emscripten has gained prominence and momentum. In the past, I've argued passionately that compiling C++ to JavaScript was a bad idea and that defining a portable bytecode was a better direction for the Web. However, the future is created by the people who invent it. Alon Zakai, with a vision in his head and persistence in his actions, created Emscripten as an open source project. Eventually Mozilla hired him and gave him funding to continue full-time development on Emscripten. Emscripten has since been proven viable and even Epic's Unreal Engine 3 has been ported to HTML5 with it. While I would have loved to have seen Google's Native Client technology gain adoption, I now believe that compiling C++ to JavaScript has strong survival genes: Emscripten-generated code runs on all recent browsers, including Internet Explorer 10, and Native Client is a far more complicated piece of technology.

In this chapter, I will describe how Emscripten works, why it's fast, what's possible, and then I will demonstrate what it's like to port an existing C++ game to the browser. Being new, Emscripten is rough around the edges, but I will cover the common problems you may run into and how to address them.

What is Emscripten?

Emscripten relies heavily on LLVM, a set of open source compiler tools. The LLVM project provides both Clang, a compiler from C++ to platform-independent LLVM instructions (known as LLVM IR), and a set of platform-independent optimization passes and tools. The LLVM project is hosted at http://llvm.org/. With the help of

LLVM, Emscripten translates C or C++ into JavaScript so it can run directly from web browsers. You can think of Emscripten as the sum of three components:

- A compiler from LLVM IR into a subset of JavaScript.

- A set of convenience tools that make it easy to use LLVM and Clang to compile C++ into JavaScript.

- A standard set of libraries and APIs, like libc, libc++, SDL, OpenGL, and zlib, to ease porting efforts.

Before we dive any deeper, I can hear you exclaim "But isn't JavaScript much slower than native code? Why would I want to compile my fast native code into slow JavaScript? How could my game's performance possibly be acceptable?"

We will dig into how compiling C++ to JavaScript has acceptable performance in more detail later, but let's look at some numbers first. In 2011, C++ compiled to JavaScript ran at less than 10% of the speed of the equivalent native code—a 10x slowdown or more, depending on the code. That's pretty terrible, but times have changed.

Table 18-1 shows the results from a software skeletal animation benchmark I ran in 2011, comparing vertex transform rate between a scalar floating point native implementation and the equivalent Emscripten-compiled program.

***Table 18-1.** Native vs. Emscripten Performance in 2011*

	Vertices/sec	Slowdown
Native gcc 4.2	63355501	1
Emscripten	5184815	12.2

Since then, JavaScript engines have learned to recognize and optimize the particular style of code generated by Emscripten and other C++-to-JavaScript compilers. Table 18-2 is the same benchmark run today, this time having Emscripten generate the asm.js subset of JavaScript.

***Table 18-2.** Native vs. Emscripten Performance in 2014*

	Vertices/sec	Slowdown
Native gcc 4.2	61215975	1
Firefox 27 asm.js	32282000	1.90
Chrome 32 asm.js	24036000	2.55

The absolute numbers differ from 2011's as the benchmark was run on a different machine, so focus on the relative slowdown. With Emscripten compiler and JavaScript engine improvements, C++ compiled to JavaScript can run at 40-50% of native speed, a huge improvement from the 2011 numbers.

Emscripten-generated JavaScript, run in a browser, will likely never match native code performance, as the Web is expected to be secure, and security sandboxes generally impose some overhead. However, it's conceivable that, in time, C++ code compiled into JavaScript for the browser could run with a mere 5-15% overhead relative to native, given that Google's Native Client code performs within 5% of native. There is a fair amount of room for browser optimization technology to improve. You can track cross-browser asm.js benchmarks at http://arewefastyet.com/.

How Emscripten Works

Under the hood, Emscripten compiles C++ into JavaScript in two main phases. First, Emscripten invokes LLVM's Clang to compile your C and C++ source code into LLVM IR, which is a representation of a program somewhere between source code and compiled object code. Afterwards, Emscripten translates the LLVM IR into optimized JavaScript (see Figure 18-1).

Figure 18-1. *The Emscripten compiler workflow*

Let's walk through the steps one by one.

Clang

Clang is an open source C and C++ compiler. It translates your source code into LLVM IR, which is basically a typed, hardware-independent assembly language (see Figure 18-2). LLVM IR defines functions, and its typed local variables roughly correspond to CPU registers. For example, consider a C function named lerp to linearly interpolate two floating point numbers, as shown in Listing 18-1.

Figure 18-2. *The Clang stage*

Listing 18-1. lerp in C

```
float lerp(float a, float b, float t) {
    return (1 - t) * a + t * b;
}
```

The same lerp function would be represented in LLVM IR as shown in Listing 18-2.

Listing 18-2. lerp in LLVM IR

```
define internal hidden float @_lerp(float %a, float %b, float %t) nounwind readnone inlinehint ssp
    %1 = fsub float 1.000000e+00, %t
    %2 = fmul float %1, %a
    %3 = fmul float %t, %b
    %4 = fadd float %2, %3
    ret float %4
}
```

The LLVM IR captures the semantic meaning of the C code, but gives it a consistent structure so that Emscripten can translate it into JavaScript.

Emscripten

After Clang converts C or C++ source code into LLVM IR, Emscripten takes over (see Figure 18-3). Emscripten translates the LLVM IR into JavaScript operations. It leverages the fact that the JavaScript language has operators and expressions that match C semantics for signed and unsigned 32-bit integer math.

Figure 18-3. *The Emscripten stage*

The aforementioned lerp function would get compiled and optimized into the JavaScript shown in Listing 18-3.

Listing 18-3. lerp Translated to JavaScript

```
function _lerp(a, b, t) {
  return(1 - t) * a + t * b
}
```

As you can see, for functions that operate only on arguments, the original C and resulting JavaScript often look similar. However, the vast majority of C and C++ functions involve some kind of memory access. To illustrate how Emscripten implements pointers and memory access, let's compare C and JavaScript implementations of strlen;. The standard C strlen function, when translated to JavaScript, dereferences pointers by indexing into the HEAP8 array (Listings 18-4 and 18-5).

Listing 18-4. strlen in C

```
size_t strlen(const char *str) {
    const char *s = str;
    while (*s) ++s;
    return s - str;
}
```

Listing 18-5. strlen in JavaScript

```
function _strlen(str) {
  for(var s = str;0 != (HEAP8[s] | 0);) {
    s = s + 1 | 0
  }
  return s - str | 0
```

Note that these examples are simple C functions to illustrate basic code generation concepts. As C++ can be considered syntax sugar on top of C semantics, all the same principles apply to compiled C++ code.

In Listing 18-5, you can see that char* pointer dereferences are converted to HEAP8 array access. The next section shows how memory access works in general.

Memory Representation

To understand JavaScript strlen, you must know how Emscripten represents memory. The Typed Array specification, used in WebGL, HTML5 Canvas, and XMLHttpRequest Level 2, introduces a mechanism by which JavaScript can read from and write to contiguous blocks of binary data. An ArrayBuffer stores a sequence of contiguous bytes which can be accessed and interpreted through ArrayBufferView objects. For example, the Int8Array object exposes the ArrayBuffer as if it were signed 8-bit integers and Float32Array exposes the same memory as if it were IEEE 32-bit floats.

Emscripten's memory space is a single JavaScript ArrayBuffer accessed through one of each of ArrayBufferView type. For example, HEAP8, used in _strlen above, is an Int8Array through which signed 8-bit integer values are read from and written to the program's memory. Pointers, such as the variables str and s above, are simply numeric indices into the heap. Emscripten has ArrayBufferViews for 32-bit and 64-bit floats, as well as the full range of 8-, 16-, and 32-bit integers, both signed and unsigned.

Arithmetic

In JavaScript, all numbers are 64-bit IEEE floats. Using floating point numbers to represent pointers into the heap would be silly and slow, so to inform JavaScript optimizers that these variables can be made into integers, Emscripten sprinkles | 0 throughout the function. The x | 0 expression coerces the number x into a signed integer, allowing JavaScript engines to optimize, say, c = c + 1 | 0, into a fast, native increment instruction.

Through clever type analysis, JavaScript engines can even notice when it's possible to reduce 64-bit precision floating point operations to 32-bit precision floating point operations without changing the semantics of the code.

You are beginning to discover why Emscripten-generated JavaScript is fast. It uses a compact ArrayBuffer for memory, so the garbage collector doesn't have to do anything. Variables are always numbers, not objects, which means there are no dynamic method calls or hash table lookups. Clever use of JavaScript's |, >>, and >>> operators indicate the code has integer semantics. All of this means that just-in-time optimizers can translate JavaScript directly into fast machine code.

These high-performance JavaScript conventions have been codified in a standard called asm.js.

What is asm.js?

asm.js is a subset of JavaScript: that is, it adds no new semantics to the existing JavaScript language. All asm.js code has identical behavior in browsers that do not specifically support it, though it runs much faster in browsers that recognize and optimize asm.js constructs.

The asm.js subset of JavaScript is restricted enough that it can be treated as a low-level compile target. It only exposes operations that can be directly translated into native machine instructions. Traditional JavaScript engines optimize code dynamically during execution with so-called just-in-time (JIT) compilation. asm.js, on the other hand, can be recognized, compiled, and optimized ahead-of-time (AOT), resulting in consistent, predictable, high performance, which is especially important for games.

asm.js sparked controversy in the web and game development communities. Is JavaScript the right way to specify what is effectively a virtual machine bytecode? Does asm.js break the "View Source" nature of the open web? Can native code performance really be achieved with this approach?

However, to us game developers, those discussions are somewhat academic. asm.js is real and it works well in practice, so if you want your game on the secure, cross-browser, open platform of the Web, targeting asm.js is a great option. You can read more about asm.js at http://asmjs.org/.

The Emscripten Toolchain

Emscripten consists of three parts: the compiler from LLVM to JavaScript, a set of library implementations that make it convenient to port existing codebases, and helpful tools and scripts for managing the entire compile process.

One of those tools, emcc, behaves much like gcc and can be dropped into most existing build systems. (For C++, em++ is the Emscripten replacement of g++.) Rather than producing native object files, emcc and em++ produce LLVM IR files. When linking, instead of generating a native executable, the final executable target is either an HTML page or a single JavaScript file, depending on whether the program stands alone or will be integrated into an existing web application.

Thus, compiling a simple Hello World program with Emscripten is as simple as Listing 18-6.

Listing 18-6. Compiling Hello World with emcc

```
$ cat helloworld.c
#include <stdio.h>
int main() {
    printf("Hello world!\n");
}
$ emcc -o helloworld.html helloworld.c
```

emcc and em++ offer dozens of Emscripten-specific options, including custom optimizations and output format adjustments. They are not in scope for this chapter, but it's worth reading through emcc --help.

Graphics Support

C++ programs in Emscripten have access to the entire range of browser capabilities by making direct calls to JavaScript with *embind*, which we explore in the "Audio Support" section below. Most programs, however, would take advantage of Emscripten's convenient access to WebGL for 3D graphics or HTML5 Canvas for 2D graphics.

WebGL

Emscripten exposes WebGL to programs through one of two OpenGL modes: OpenGL ES 2 and OpenGL Legacy Emulation. By default, your code only has access to the OpenGL ES 2 functions, which are translated almost directly to WebGL calls, as WebGL is based on the OpenGL ES 2 specification. However, if your code uses legacy fixed function calls, you can enable the LEGACY_GL_EMULATION option which attempts to translate those calls into WebGL calls with some degree of accuracy.

For very basic OpenGL applications, LEGACY_GL_EMULATION will likely come close to the original OpenGL semantics, but for anything more complicated than a few textures and vertex buffers, the LEGACY_GL_EMULATION mode is likely inadequate. At the time of this writing, there is talk of replacing LEGACY_GL_EMULATION with maintained and supported OpenGL emulation layer such as Regal (https://github.com/p3/regal), but I recommend limiting your games to the OpenGL ES 2 subset and not using an OpenGL emulation layer. Plus, if your game targets OpenGL ES 2, it can run natively on mobile platforms too!

Canvas

For games that only use 2D graphics, WebGL is not necessary. 2D games can render with the HTML5 Canvas API either through SDL or embind to access the 2D canvas context directly. To see an example of how to use embind, see the audio example in Listing 18-7.

Audio Support

For audio, Emscripten provides implementations of both SDL_audio and OpenAL. If you need more direct access to the browser's JavaScript audio APIs, there are several ways to access JavaScript from C++. One of them is embind, a Boost.Python-like interface to JavaScript objects. embind is included with Emscripten, but requires the `--bind` option passed to emcc. To illustrate how embind can be used to access browser APIs, the program in Listing 18-7 plays a two-second tone by using embind to directly manipulate Web Audio API JavaScript objects.

Listing 18-7. Accessing the Web Audio API from C++ with embind

```cpp
#include <emscripten/bind.h>
#include <emscripten/val.h>
#include <math.h>

using namespace emscripten;

const double PI = atan(1) * 4;

int main() {
    val AudioContext = val::global("AudioContext");
    if (!AudioContext.as<bool>()) {
        AudioContext = val::global("webkitAudioContext");
    }
    val context = AudioContext.new_();

    int duration = 2;
    int sampleRate = 44100;

    int numberOfFrames = duration * sampleRate;

    val buffer = context.call<val>("createBuffer", 1, numberOfFrames, sampleRate);
    val data = buffer.call<val>("getChannelData", 0);

    for (int i = 0; i < numberOfFrames; ++i) {
        data.set(i, val(sin(440.0 * PI * i / sampleRate)));
    }

    auto source = context.call<val>("createBufferSource");
    source.set("buffer", buffer);
    source.call<void>("connect", context["destination"]);
    source.call<void>("start", 0);
}
```

There are a handful of constructs in this snippet worth calling out. The `val::global` function, given a string, returns the global JavaScript value with that name. `val` is a C++ type defined by embind that represents a handle to a JavaScript value.

Given a `val`, properties can be set with `val::set` and JavaScript methods can be called with `val::call<ReturnValue>(arguments...)`.

In short, the code in Listing 18-7 is a C++ transliteration of the JavaScript in Listing 18-8.

Listing 18-8. Accessing the Web Audio API from JavaScript

```
function main() {
    var audioContext = window.AudioContext;
    if (!audioContext) {
        audioContext = window.webkitAudioContext;
    }
    var context = new audioContext();

    var duration = 2;
    var sampleRate = 44100;

    var numberOfFrames = duration * sampleRate;

    var buffer = context.createBuffer(1, numberOfFrames, sampleRate);
    var data = buffer.getChannelData(0);

    for (var i = 0; i < numberOfFrames; ++i) {
        data[i] = Math.sin(441.0 * Math.PI * i / sampleRate);
    }

    var source = context.createBufferSource();
    source.buffer = buffer;
    source.connect(context.destination);
    source.start(0);
}
```

With embind, anything you might write in JavaScript can be transliterated to C++, and thus the browser's capabilities are exposed to your game.

▪ **Note** When compiling the program in Listing 18-8, make sure to use the `--bind` emcc option to enable embind support.

Input Events

Emscripten provides three ways to access user input events: SDL input, glut, and direct access to browser events. If your application is built on SDL (www.libsdl.org/), using the SDL input events is an obvious choice. If all you need is quick access to an OpenGL context and keyboard and mouse events, glut, the OpenGL Utility Toolkit, is also available. Emscripten includes the open source FreeGLUT (http://freeglut.sourceforge.net/) implementation.

Finally, if your game benefits from direct access to browser events, use embind to connect your C++ code to JavaScript event callbacks such as `canvas.onmousemove`.

Performance

Current benchmarks show that Emscripten-compiled asm.js code is about a factor of two slower than the equivalent native code. This is possible because most native machine operations have direct analogues in JavaScript semantics. Remember that asm.js is restricted to JavaScript expressions that can be efficiently translated to machine code. Memory loads and stores are represented by `ArrayBuffer` reads and writes. Integer addition is represented by `((x|0)+(y|0))|0`. Unsigned integer comparison is represented by `((x>>>0) < (y>>>0))`. 32-bit integer multiplication is represented by `Math.imul(x, y)`.

`Math.imul` is an interesting case, actually. Previous and current JavaScript specifications, ECMAScript 3 and ECMAScript 5, don't have an expression that directly corresponds to C's 32-bit integer multiplication. The function in Listing 18-9 implements C-like multiplication in JavaScript.

Listing 18-9. 32-bit Integer Multiplication Fallback

```
// courtesy of https://developer.mozilla.org/en-US/docs/Web/JavaScript/Reference/Global_Objects/
Math/imul
function imul(a, b) {
  var ah  = (a >>> 16) & 0xffff;
  var al = a & 0xffff;
  var bh  = (b >>> 16) & 0xffff;
  var bl = b & 0xffff;
  // the shift by 0 fixes the sign on the high part
  // the final |0 converts the unsigned value into a signed value
  return ((al * bl) + (((ah * bl + al * bh) << 16) >>> 0)|0);
}
```

`Math.imul` will be introduced in ECMAScript 6 (and is already available in Firefox and Chrome!) so that asm. js can efficiently translate it into a native multiply instruction. In addition, there are upcoming JavaScript proposals to expose other native instruction capabilities such as SIMD vector processing and 32-bit floating arithmetic. (All numbers in JavaScript are IEEE 64-bit floats.) Beyond instruction-level performance, as of ECMAScript 5, JavaScript has no access to shared-memory threads, though WebWorkers provide support for message-passing concurrency.

In short, the Web is a bit less capable than native platforms, but it's certainly powerful enough to run a wide range of games, especially since the gap between desktop PCs and mobile phones is much larger than the gap between native code and asm.js. Moreover, we can expect improvements to performance over time. Emscripten, being a new compiler, still has room for improvement in its code generation. At the time of this writing, Alon Zakai is rewriting the compiler as a proper LLVM backend rather than a set of programs that parse LLVM IR directly. Emscripten as an LLVM backend is expected to enable further LLVM optimizations.

Concurrently with improvements to the Emscripten compiler itself, browsers are optimizing for asm.js. In November 2013, Google and Opera announced that their browsers have faster asm.js code generation (http://www.unrealengine.com/en/news/epic_citadel_cleared_for_chrome_and_opera_browsers/). I predict that the performance of asm.js will continue to improve. It's unrealistic to assume that the restricted, secure asm.js will equal native code performance, but if it reaches 80% to 90% of the performance of native code, then asm.js will be sufficiently fast that we can treat it like any other first-class target.

Debugging

Sadly, if you're used to IDEs with wonderful debuggers like Visual Studio or even simpler tools like WinDbg or gdb, Emscripten is a step backwards. There are no Emscripten debuggers, though you can invoke emcc with the -g flag and use your web browser's JavaScript debugger. With -g, emcc tries hard to preserve function and variable names, so it's not terribly painful to figure out what's happening at runtime from within a JavaScript debugger. Unfortunately, all current JavaScript debuggers are painfully slow given the large JavaScript files that Emscripten produces.

Thus, most of the time, it's easiest to fall back on traditional `printf` debugging.

However, there is one trick that comes in handy. Much like Win32's `DebugBreak()` function or x86's `__asm int 3`, in Emscripten, you can cause the debugger to break on a line of code with `asm("debugger");`. In Emscripten, `asm()` allows insertion of arbitrary JavaScript into the generated code, and the JavaScript debugger statement causes the debugger to kick in when that code is reached. I recommend inserting `asm("debugger");` into your assertion and fatal error functions, as shown in Listing 18-10.

Listing 18-10. Breaking into the Debugger on Fatal Errors

```
void fatal_error(const char* message) {
    fprintf(stderr, "fatal error: %s\n", message);
#ifdef __EMSCRIPTEN__
    asm("debugger");
#elif defined(WIN32)
    DebugBreak();
#endif
    abort();
}
```

Since debugging Emscripten-generated code is not pleasant, I recommend maintaining a native Windows, Mac, or Linux build of your game and using that for active development. That way, you'll know that any problems that occur in the Emscripten build are Emscripten-related.

A Game Port

Now that we've covered Emscripten from a high level, let's take an existing game and port it to the Web. Alas, I can't share any proprietary engine code, but there are a few open source 3D games that will provide an example of the kind of problems you might face when bringing a C++ game to the Web with Emscripten.

Choosing a Game

For this demonstration, I chose to port the game AstroMenace. It's simple, 3D, has few dependencies, and sufficiently rich that it provides a good example of what's possible on the Web. As you'll see, a game that didn't depend on the OpenGL fixed function pipeline would have been much easier, so when you port your game or engine to Emscripten/WebGL, it helps to have a pure OpenGL ES 2.0 renderer.

Getting Emscripten

To port a game to Emscripten, you need two things: the game's source code and the latest Emscripten. As a point of detail, I am assuming you are using Linux or Mac OS X. The Emscripten compiler runs on Windows but it's a little easier from the Linux or Mac command lines.

Note Many Emscripten tools are written in Python, and per PEP 0394 (www.python.org/dev/peps/pep-0394/), the Emscripten tools attempt to run the python2 command by default. On most Linux distributions, python2 is a symlink to whatever version of Python 2 is installed, but on Mac you may have to create this symlink yourself with sudo ln -s usr/bin/python /usr/bin/python2.

At the time of this writing, the best way to get Emscripten is to download the Emscripten SDK from ttp://emscripten.org. However, you may want to maintain your own local fork of the Emscripten git repository, in case you need to modify anything during the porting effort. My local modifications for the purposes of the AstroMenace game port are available at https://github.com/chadaustin/emscripten.

You can follow the development process, in its unfiltered fits and starts, at my git repository at ttps://github.com/chadaustin/AstroMenaceEmscripten/.

Building the Game

After grabbing the source code, my first attempt was to write an `emscripten-build` shell script that uses Emscripten's `emcc` and `em++` commands to compile the source into HTML. Listing 18-11 shows the initial build command.

Listing 18-11. Initial Emscripten Build Attempt

```
em++ -Wall -o AstroMenace.html $(find AstroMenaceSource -iname '*.cpp')
```

As you can see, `em++` is used similarly to `g++`. `-Wall` enables all warnings, and the remainder of the command says to compile all C++ source files into the `AstroMenace.html` program, which can then be loaded in a web browser.

The script in Listing 18-11 at least got me to the point where I could start using compile and link errors to drive the rest of the port. Well, almost. Because Emscripten is compiling C++ to JavaScript, unlike a traditional platform, it's perfectly okay to reference symbols that aren't defined. Emscripten assumes that undefined functions refer to external JavaScript implementations. Sometimes having C++ directly call external JavaScript functions is a valid and useful technique. However, for a self-contained program, like a game written entirely in C++, you generally want an undefined function to fail the build. Passing `-s ERROR_ON_UNDEFINED_SYMBOLS=1` to `emcc` or `em++` will fail the build until all referenced symbols are defined.

Third-Party Dependencies and a Real Build System

The first round of undefined symbol errors, shown in Listing 18-12, were related to libogg and libvorbis, which were easy enough to integrate. I invoked `emcc` to produce an LLVM IR file from the libogg and libvorbis .c files, which was then added to the source list for AstroMenace.html. libogg and libvorbis can be downloaded from `www.xiph.org/downloads/`.

Listing 18-12. Undefined libogg and libvorbis Symbols

```
Error: unresolved symbol: ov_read
Error: unresolved symbol: ov_open_callbacks
Error: unresolved symbol: ov_info
Error: unresolved symbol: ov_pcm_total
Error: unresolved symbol: ov_clear
Error: unresolved symbol: ov_comment
Error: unresolved symbol: ov_pcm_seek
```

Next came freealut, which integrated much like libogg and libvorbis. The freealut source code is checked into Emscripten itself, so I just used that.

At this point I realized that using a shell script to compile AstroMenace was becoming 1) slow, as it caused a full rebuild each time, and 2) annoying, as I had to specify long lists of source files, so I switched the build system over to SCons, a Python-based build system. SCons is available at `www.scons.org/`. Emscripten does not require SCons: Make or any other build system is also suitable.

FreeType (an open source TrueType font renderer) was the hardest dependency because I had to be precise about specifically which FreeType source files to include in the build system. If you include every .c file, you will include multiple implementations of the same functions and see duplicate symbol definition errors. FreeType is also included in the Emscripten tree.

Progress! The code finally compiles and links. However, loading `AstroMenace.html` in a browser gave JavaScript errors.

Loading Game Content

Loading `AstroMenace.html` caused the browser to show the JavaScript error in Listing 18-13.

Listing 18-13. First Load Error in Browser

```
abort() at Error
    at stackTrace (AstroMenace.html:993:15)
    at abort (AstroMenace.html:510736:25)
    at __Z10FileDetectPKc [FileDetect(char*)] (AstroMenace.html:61135:121)
    at __Z8vw_fopenPKc [vw_fopen(char*)] (AstroMenace.html:61172:12)
    at __ZN12cXMLDocument4LoadEPKc [cXMLDocument::Load(char*)] AstroMenace.html:62962:13)
    at __Z16LoadXMLSetupFileb [LoadXMLSetupFile(bool)] (AstroMenace.html:275626:13)
    at Object._main (AstroMenace.html:87596:15)
    at Object.callMain (AstroMenace.html:510655:30)
    at doRun (AstroMenace.html:510695:25)
    at AstroMenace.html:510705:19
```

As you can see, the stack trace is fairly readable, making it possible to figure out the approximate location of the error. After stepping through the code in the Chrome developer tools JavaScript debugger, I noticed that a variable representing a function pointer from the `SDL_RWops` struct was completely bogus.

Further exploration uncovered that Emscripten's current `SDL_RWFromFile` implementation does not match the header: it returns an opaque integer ID when the SDL API expects that the result of `SDL_RWFromFile` is a struct containing function pointers. Thus, attempting to dereference the pointer returned by `SDL_RWFromFile` returned data from bogus memory, so the function pointer was invalid, tripping an invalid virtual call assertion.

To work around this problem, I removed the SDL filesystem support from Emscripten's SDL and replaced it with `SDL_rwops.c` from the SDL 1.2 source code itself. Note that, should you take an approach like this, you will need to satisfy the terms of SDL's LGPL license in some way. Under the LGPL, the end user must be able to substitute their own implementation of any LGPL code, such as SDL, and since Emscripten does not have stable support for dynamic linking, you may struggle to satisfy the LGPL. In this case, because I'm porting an open source game anyway, there are no problems.

There are plans to replace Emscripten's SDL 1.2 and 1.3 implementations with SDL 2.0, which is licensed under the permissive zlib license. SDL 2.0 would resolve all of these problems.

Finally I reached a point where the compiled `AstroMenace.html` produced errors about a missing game data pack, as shown in Listing 18-14.

Listing 18-14. Missing Game Assets

```
Can't find the file /home/emscripten/.astromenace/amconfig.xml AstroMenace.html:61
XML file not found: /home/emscripten/.astromenace/amconfig.xml AstroMenace.html:61
Can't open XML file for write /home/emscripten/.astromenace/amconfig.xml AstroMenace.html:61
*** Can't find VFS file /bin/gamedata.vfs AstroMenace.html:61 ***
*** gamedata.vfs file not found or corrupted. AstroMenace.html:61 ***
```

`gamedata.vfs` is a compiled "packfile" of art, generated from source art assets by the game itself when run with special flag. Since the game isn't running in Emscripten, I needed a pre-built `gamedata.vfs`. I could have built and compiled the game on a native platform to produce `gamedata.vfs`, but I found it easier to download a precompiled binary from the AstroMenace web site and use its `gamedata.vfs` file.

Linking a data file into an Emscripten program is accomplished with emcc's `--preload-file` option. Specifically, I checked `gamedata.vfs` into `AstroMenace/bin` and added the build option `--preload-file bin@/bin` so the generated code has access to `/bin/gamedata.vfs`.

When using --preload-file, Emscripten-compiled code uses XMLHttpRequest to download the embedded filesystem image in advance of launching the game, but XMLHttpRequest doesn't work with file:// URLs. Thus, a real HTTP server is needed to test the game. Python provides a simple HTTP server.

```
python -m SimpleHTTPServer
```

Since gamedata.vfs is over 100MB and Emscripten by default allocates 16 MiB for the application's entire memory space, I also needed to increase the total memory size to 200 MiB with the emcc option -s TOTAL_MEMORY=209715200. I picked 200 MiB because 100 MiB is used for the game assets, and I surmised that 100 MiB was sufficient for all runtime allocations. If I turned out to be incorrect, the program would have told me with an out-of-memory error.

Getting the Game to Run

As web pages are single-threaded and event-based, it's bad behavior for JavaScript to wait by spinning in a loop. Thus, the default Emscripten implementation of the SDL_Delay function crashes if you call it on the main Emscripten thread, so I removed it from Emscripten and replaced it with a function that does nothing. Instead, I could have also simply removed all calls to SDL_Delay from AstroMenace's loading code. I will discuss the main loop in more depth later in this chapter.

Now all the data files load but the application crashes with the disappointing OpenGL error shown in Listing 18-15.

Listing 18-15. Emscripten Legacy Emulation OpenGL Error

```
WebGL: getParameter: parameter: invalid enum value 0x821b @
http://localhost:8000/build/AstroMenace.js:5798
WebGL: getParameter: parameter: invalid enum value 0x821c @
http://localhost:8000/build/AstroMenace.js:5798
WebGL: getParameter: parameter: invalid enum value 0xd31 @
http://localhost:8000/build/AstroMenace.js:5798
WebGL: hint: invalid hint @ http://localhost:8000/build/AstroMenace.js:5954
WebGL: texImage2D: format does not match internalformat @
http://localhost:8000/build/AstroMenace.js:9603
uncaught exception: glMaterialfv: TODO
```

Emscripten's OpenGL legacy emulation layer does not currently implement glMaterialfv or glLightfv. Instead, it throws an error with the message "TODO" whenever they are called. Thus, it's time to pull in a real OpenGL emulation layer: Regal. The Regal project is available at https://github.com/p3/regal.

Integrating with OpenGL, Attempt #1: Regal

I ran into several gaps in Emscripten's legacy GL emulation support. First, glLightfv and glMaterialfv simply throw an exception when called. Second, AstroMenace targets OpenGL 2.1 and GLSL 1.20, so its shaders start with #version 120. Since WebGL is based on OpenGL ES 2.0 and GLSL 1.00, its shaders must be marked with #version 100.

Rather than deal with all of this myself, I decided to try integrating Regal, a legacy OpenGL emulation on top of OpenGL ES 2. I turned off the -s LEGACY_GL_EMULATION option, and instead included Regal's source code from within the build system. Then I spent several fruitless evenings attempting to get Regal to run. I ran into issues with illegal asm.js function pointer casts, null GL function pointers, infinite loops, and too many JavaScript local variables being generated when calling into the compiled Regal code. I was not able to clearly determine why Regal didn't work, but I hope that in the near future the Emscripten implementation of LEGACY_GL_EMULATION is swapped out for something like Regal. I did port a very simple OpenGL demo (https://github.com/chadaustin/nehe-emscripten) to Emscripten and Regal and got it to work with some help from Emscripten's community, so Regal is probably viable after applying some elbow grease.

In practice, any game that runs on Android or iOS would have an OpenGL ES 2 rendering pipeline and thus would not require any kind of OpenGL legacy emulation layer.

Integrating with OpenGL, Attempt #2: Simplifying the AstroMenace Renderer

For the purposes of this demonstration, I opted for something easier than getting Regal to work reliably. I disabled lighting and materials in the application and switched back to LEGACY_GL_EMULATION. To verify that my changes to AstroMenace's source code weren't breaking the game itself, I spun up a native development environment (specifically, an Ubuntu VM) so I could begin modifying and testing the original game code. After each change, I verified that the game still compiled and ran. After removing support for shadow maps, MSAA, occlusion queries, anisotropic filtering, texture compression, and various other fancier rendering capabilities, I finally had an Emscripten-compiled game that actually rendered 3D. The 3D output was obviously glitchy, with corrupted vertex buffers, largely due to the incomplete and buggy Emscripten legacy GL emulation layer. However, as I mentioned before, if a game's rendering code is limited to the OpenGL ES 2 subset, porting it to Emscripten and WebGL will be dramatically easier.

The Main Loop

Finally, it's worth discussing one significant change needed when most games are brought to Emscripten: the browser is an event-based platform. JavaScript runs with a single execution thread in the context of a web page. That means that, while JavaScript is running, the browser cannot update the page nor display anything to the screen. Many browsers can't even process user input while JavaScript is running. This causes some problems when trying to integrate traditional game loops with a web page. A traditional game's main loop is structured as shown in Listing 18-16.

Listing 18-16. Traditional Game Main Loop

```
while (running) {
    process_input();
    simulate_world();
    render_graphics();
    wait_for_next_frame();
}
```

On a web page, while such a loop is running, the browser cannot handle user input events or graphics updates. Thus, the browser will assume your script is hung and ask the user to kill it. Instead of waiting for the next frame in a blocking game loop, you must instead ask Emscripten to call your game when it's time for the next frame, as shown in Listing 18-17.

Listing 18-17. Emscripten Game Main Loop

```
void main_loop();
int main() {
    // initialization code
    // ...
    // at game startup, usually at the end of main()
    emscripten_set_main_loop(main_loop, 60, false);
```

```
void main_loop() {
    process_input();
    simulate_world();
    render_graphics();
}
```

Note that, in Listing 18-17, the game loop is handled by the browser, allowing it to update the display and response to input events. The loop body, however, is implemented by the game in the main_loop() function, giving your game control over its simulation and rendering.

The Emscripten Platform

So far we've discussed Emscripten's compiler, how to access the browser's graphics, sound, and input APIs, and how to port a C++ game to the Web with Emscripten. Now let's talk about releasing the same game on multiple platforms.

As with any multiplatform development strategy, simply consider Emscripten as just another platform, like iOS, Android, or Windows. Your engine will need some Emscripten-specific platform components, such as input device detection and configuration, the ability to invoke HTML5's full screen and pointer lock APIs, and any other browser-specific APIs. The web's capabilities come from the browser through JavaScript, but they need to be accessed through Emscripten.

At the time of this writing, Emscripten is not a complete product; rather, it's more of a functional proof of concept. You will likely run into gaps in the platform, though they are being addressed over time. Various platform components may be missing, incomplete, unspecified, or subject to change. For example, even though Emscripten has built-in support for much of SDL and OpenGL fixed-function, I had to stub out or implement the functions in Listing 18-18 when porting AstroMenace.

Listing 18-18. Unimplemented Emscripten Functions Used by AstroMenace

```
glPushAttrib
glPopAttrib
gluErrorString
glLightf
glMaterialfv
glLightfv
SDL_GetWMInfo
SDL_GetGammaRamp
gluBuild2DMipmaps
alIsSource
alSourceRewind
SDL_WaitEvent
```

Don't be intimidated, however! The rate at which Emscripten is improving is impressive. Over the period in which I have been using Emscripten, many of its bugs and limitations have been fixed.

If you discover a gap in the platform capabilities, you can either implement said gap in Emscripten itself or implement a stub in your own code. Of course, make sure you file a bug against Emscripten itself! The Emscripten community is helpful and responsive, so perhaps it will be fixed before you notice.

Predicting the Future

Compiling C++ to high-performance JavaScript is cutting edge. We can't predict exactly how the next decade will play out, but since Emscripten and asm.js are very new, it's easy to imagine significant performance and code generation improvements. However, the biggest room for improvement comes from new and richer web browser APIs. As of now, WebGL exposes the least common denominator of graphics APIs: OpenGL ES 2. When a version of WebGL that exposes OpenGL ES 3 is available, games can take advantage of increased graphical fidelity and capabilities.

When WebCL (a JavaScript API for GPU computing via OpenCL) is widespread, games can offload arbitrary computation to the GPU. WebCL could also make it possible to access any idle CPU cores and vector units, making better use of overall system resources.

I'm not sure that Emscripten itself will remain the dominant toolchain for compiling to JavaScript, but, if not, something else will take its place. Compiling to JavaScript isn't going away anytime soon. The fact that you can run your compiled code in all browsers, even if they don't specially optimize for asm.js, is too powerful.

If you have a C++ game and you want your players to download and play it securely, with no friction, in a web browser, give Emscripten a chance.

■ ■ ■

CHAPTER 19

Introduction to TypeScript: Building a Rogue-like Engine

Jesse Freeman, Developer Evangelist, Amazon

What Is TypeScript?

TypeScript (http://typescript.org) is a typed superset of JavaScript that compiles to plain JavaScript. TypeScript is cross-platform, runs on any browser, and is open source. Microsoft created it, and it's hands down one of the best languages for building HTML5 games. One of the great things about TypeScript, apart from adding typing to JavaScript, is that it allows you to start using some of the cool features of ECMAScript 6 (ES6) now, even though it may be years away from being finalized. This means that you can put to good use classes and other higher-level constructs that you find in languages such as C# and Java; moreover, TypeScript is incredibly similar to ActionScript 2 and 3. The final key advantage of TypeScript is that it outputs human readable JavaScript, plus you can use existing JavaScript libraries or inject the code directly into your TypeScript classes and start taking advantage of typing provided by the compiler.

To help you better understand why TypeScript is so great, I have designed a rogue-like engine for you to build in this chapter. Rogue engines are one of my favorite things to tinker with because their simplicity lends itself to some creative ways to manipulate and visualize tile-based levels. In the example, I will walk you through setting up TypeScript, explain some of the more complex concepts of the language, and show off how—with the help of typing—you can achieve polymorphism at scale, which is traditionally difficult to do in JavaScript alone. But first, let's go through an overview of the language itself.

Language Overview

You will find that, out of the gate, TypeScript is incredibly similar to JavaScript. This is good because, when it comes to picking up TypeScript, the learning curve is rather low. If you have a background in ActionScript, Java, or C#, you will easily understand the more advanced language features quickly. If not, you will learn a lot from this chapter. At its core, TypeScript is all about typing. There are three primitive types that you need to know:

```
var name: string = "Jesse Freeman";
```

As you can see, you simply use the string type for any strings.

```
var age: number = 34;
```

Here, numbers are typed as numbers. Because this is still JavaScript, at the end of the day, you don't have int, float, or double, as you would find in other typed languages.

```
var likesGames: boolean = true;
```

And, you can see that you can easily type booleans, as you would expect to use the Boolean type.

Another advantage of the compiler is type inference. This allows you to declare variables without having to type them explicitly. So, the previous code could also be done like this:

```
var name = "Jesse Freeman";
var age = 34;
var likesGames = true;
```

So long as the compiler can fully qualify what the type will be, it will automatically figure it out for you. Now, arrays and objects can also be typed:

```
var myArray = any[];
```

As you can see, the any type is being used to define a generic array. This means that the compiler will ignore mixing and matching of types inside of the array. You could easily type it to something specific, such as string or number, if you knew that the contents of the array would always be the same.

```
var myArray:string[] = ["Jesse", "Freeman"];
```

TypeScript also supports classes. This is very important, because, although classes are not a native part of JavaScript, every developer has his or her own way of making them. This could be problematic when you work in larger teams or when you want to keep your code consistent across developers.

Let's take a look at a simple class:

```
class Player {
        name: string;
        age: number;
        likesGames:boolean;
        constructor(name: string, age: number, likesGames:boolean) {
                this.name = name;
                this.age = age;
                this.likesGames = likesGames;
        }
}
```

To create a new player, you would use the new constructor:

```
var player = new Player("Jesse Freeman", 34, true);
```

Likewise, the JavaScript that is generated for this class looks like this:

```
var Player = (function () {
    function Player(name, age, likesGames) {
        this.name = name;
        this.age = age;
        this.likesGames = likesGames;
    }
    return Player;
})();
```

Clearly, it's very easy to read. The TypeScript compiler is highly optimized to generate human-readable JavaScript, unlike some other JavaScript compilers you may have seen. This means that, if you decide to stop using TypeScript, you can simply take the generated JavaScript and just use that. That is a huge advantage over similar JavaScript compilers.

There is a lot more to TypeScript than what was covered here. Let's save that for the rest of the chapter and have you start making a rogue game engine right away.

Setting Up TypeScript

There are two ways to set up TypeScript: the first is through Visual Studio, as a plug-in, and the second is through Node.js. I am going to focus on the latter, as it's cross-platform, and you can do some really interesting automation with Node and Grunt. If you are unfamiliar with either of these two technologies, I highly recommend your checking out Chapter 23, which covers them.

To get started, you will need to open the command line. On a Mac, use Terminal. For Windows, I use Git Bash, which is part of Git's installer. You must install Grunt globally on your computer before you begin. You can do that by typing the following code snippet at the command prompt:

```
>npm install -g grunt-cli
```

Now, you will want to create a directory and navigate to it. This new directory, which I have called RogueTS, is going to be where you do all your work. You will create a package.json file by typing this at the command prompt:

```
> npm init
```

Next, you have to answer a few questions about the project. Figure 19-1 shows you how I configured mine.

```
● ● ○                RogueTS — node — 84×16

About to write to /Users/jessefreeman/Dropbox/Dev/TypeScript/RogueTS/package.json:

{
  "name": "RogueTS",
  "version": "1.0.0",
  "description": "A TypeScript Roguelike Engine.",
  "main": "index.html",
  "scripts": {
    "test": "echo \"Error: no test specified\" && exit 1"
  },
  "author": "Jesse Freeman",
  "license": "MIT"
}

Is this ok? (yes) ▊
```

Figure 19-1. *Once you have filled out all the questions, npm will generate a package.json file for you*

From here, you must install all the modules that are required to run TypeScript as well as to automate your project. (I will go through this quickly, so, again, if you have never used Grunt before, see Chapter 23 for more details.) Type the following code at the command prompt:

```
npm install typescript --save-dev
```

This will install the TypeScript compiler into your project directory, as illustrated in Figure 19-2.

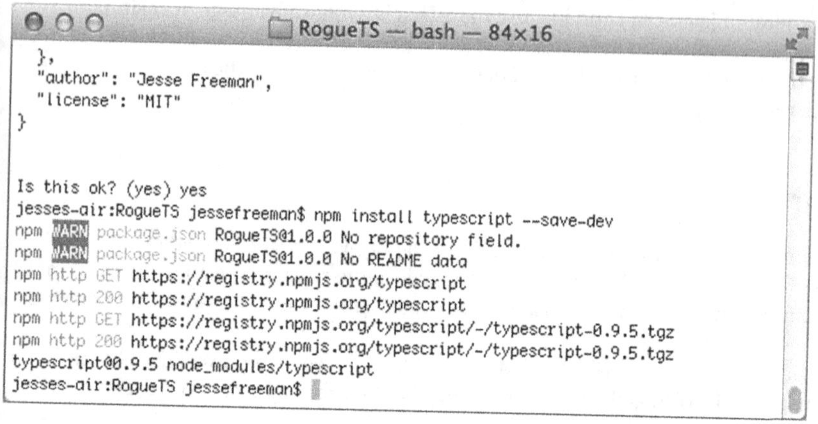

```
O O O                    🗀 RogueTS — bash — 84×16
    },
    "author": "Jesse Freeman",
    "license": "MIT"
}


Is this ok? (yes) yes
jesses-air:RogueTS jessefreeman$ npm install typescript --save-dev
npm WARN package.json RogueTS@1.0.0 No repository field.
npm WARN package.json RogueTS@1.0.0 No README data
npm http GET https://registry.npmjs.org/typescript
npm http 200 https://registry.npmjs.org/typescript
npm http GET https://registry.npmjs.org/typescript/-/typescript-0.9.5.tgz
npm http 200 https://registry.npmjs.org/typescript/-/typescript-0.9.5.tgz
typescript@0.9.5 node_modules/typescript
jesses-air:RogueTS jessefreeman$ ▊
```

Figure 19-2. Here, you can see that npm was used to install the Typescript compiler, and it has been downloaded and installed correctly

Next, you will want to run through the following commands, one at a time, and let each of them install before moving on to the next plug-in:

```
npm install grunt-typescript --save-dev
npm install grunt-contrib-watch --save-dev
npm install grunt-contrib-connect --save-dev
npm install grunt-open --save-dev
```

Now, if you take a look at the package.json file in your project, you should see all your modules installed under the developerDependencies JavaScript Object Notation (JSON) object, as follows:

```
"devDependencies": {
        "typescript": "~0.9.1-1",
        "grunt": "~0.4.1",
        "grunt-typescript": "~0.2.4",
        "grunt-contrib-watch": "~0.5.3",
        "grunt-contrib-connect": "~0.5.0",
        "grunt-open": "~0.2.2"
```

Note that you may have different version numbers, as npm installs the latest one.

Next, you need to create a GruntFile.js in your project. Open it, and let's import your modules:

```
module.exports = function (grunt) {
    grunt.loadNpmTasks('grunt-typescript');
    grunt.loadNpmTasks('grunt-contrib-watch');
    grunt.loadNpmTasks('grunt-contrib-connect');
    grunt.loadNpmTasks('grunt-open');
```

Now, you can start configuring your Grunt tasks. After the last bit of code with your `grunt.loadNpmTask` call, add the following code inside the module's function statement:

```
grunt.initConfig({
    pkg: grunt.file.readJSON('package.json'),
});
```

Note that there is a trailing comma after the `package.json`. You are going to continue adding each task object to this JSON file. Start by putting the next task object after the comma, on a new line:

```
connect: {
    server: {
        options: {
            port: 8080,
            base: './deploy'
        }
    }
},
```

Connect is a task that will create a server locally in the directory in which you run it. This will be helpful when it comes to testing your project. Add the next task:

```
typescript: {
    base: {
        src: ['src/**/*.ts'],
        dest: 'deploy/js/game.js',
        options: {
            module: 'amd',
            target: 'es5'
        }
    }
},
```

This task will help you run the TypeScript compiler on your code. As you can see, you are setting the source to a src folder, which you will create later on, and the output will be a single game.js file in your deploy directory. Also, as far as options go, you set your module output type to amd. Because you are going to be combining all your TypeScript modules into a single file, you won't have to worry about loading them via a module manager, as with `Require.js`. Also, you are going to set your target to ECMAScript 5 (ES5), which allows you to take advantage of TypeScript's more advanced features, such as getters and setters. HTML5 games require the canvas tag to run, so you don't really need to worry about supporting ECMAScript 3 (ES3), as canvas doesn't work on those older browsers. Next, add the final two tasks:

```
watch: {
    files: 'src/**/*.ts',
    tasks: ['typescript']
},
open: {
    dev: {
        path: 'http://localhost:8080/index.html'
    }
}
```

Watch lets you have Grunt monitor a directory for changes. Here, you can see that you are setting up Grunt to check for any changes to .ts (TypeScript) files and call the typescript task, which will run the compiler on the files in the src directory. This will allow you to generate your game.js file automatically anytime you click the Save button in a .ts file. The last task simply enables you to open the browser and load your game for testing.

To make all this work, you need to add one final thing to the end of your GruntFile, right after the closing]); for your task objects:

```
grunt.registerTask('default', ['typescript', 'connect', 'open', 'watch']);
```

This will register the default task for Grunt as follows: compile your TypeScript files, start the server, open the http://localhost:8080 URL in your default browser, and then watch the src directory for any changes to your .ts files. Although this may seem like a lot of work, you will quickly get used to this kind of setup for TypeScript, and it's incredibly similar to how you would automate your normal JavaScript development (instead of having the TypeScript compiler combine JavaScript files, you would use a task called *concat*). The last thing you need to do is set up your project directory, as shown in Figure 19-3.

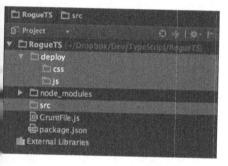

Figure 19-3. *Note that I have added a deploy directory with a css and a js folder as well as a src directory to the project*

You will want to set up a few files to get started. Create an index.html file in your deploy folder with the following content:

```
<!DOCTYPE html>
<html lang="en" xmlns="http://www.w3.org/1999/xhtml">
<head>
    <meta charset="utf-8" />
    <title>RogueTS</title>
    <link rel="stylesheet" href="css/game.css" type="text/css" />
    <script src="js/game.js"></script>
</head>
<body>
        <h1>RogueTS Test</h1>
    <canvas id="display" width="800" height="480" />
</body>
</html>
```

Now, you will need to make a `game.css` file in your css folder:

```css
body
{
    margin: 0px;
    padding: 0px;
    background-color: black;
}
```

Finally, you make your `main.ts` file, which will go in your src folder. Simply put in it the following content:

```
console.log("Hello TypeScript");
```

You should now have a project that looks like Figure 19-4.

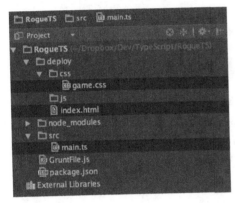

Figure 19-4. *You should now have an index.html, a game.css, and a main.js file*

If you go back to the command line and run the following code at the root of your game's project directory, it should start the build script:

```
> grunt
```

Assuming that everything worked correctly, you will see your game's index page in the browser, along with your trace to the console window, as displayed in Figure 19-5.

Figure 19-5. *The browser should automatically open with your new game's index page; open your browser's console to see the log message*

And there you have it! TypeScript is fully configured, and you have an automated workflow for compiling and testing your game's code. Now, let's dig into the language and build out your game.

Creating Your Game Class

In your src folder, you will want to start setting up the location where your rogue game's code will live. You are going to make all your game code live inside its own module, called *rogue*. Modules are a great way to help encapsulate the scope of your code so that it doen't sit in the global scope or conflict with other JavaScript code, which you may have running on the page. To help you better organize this, you will need to create a rogue folder inside src and a game.ts file, as demonstrated in Figure 19-6.

Figure 19-6. *You will be keeping all your rogue game .ts files in their own folder inside your src directory*

Next, put the following content inside the folder:

```
module rogue {
    export class Game {
        constructor (public display: HTMLCanvasElement) {
            console.log("display", display);
        }
    }
```

This is the basic structure for setting up your modules and classes. As you can see, you define the module at the top as rogue and then include your class. You can have several classes in a single module file or break them up over different files. I personally tend to keep classes that are part of the same module in one file. I also take advantage of the keyword "export," which tells the compiler to make the class publically accessible. Although you can have private and public classes in TypeScript, it doesn't necessarily translate 100 percent to JavaScript, as everything is public. Using the keyword "export" is a good way to let the compiler validate those classes that allow access to themselves outside their package, and it's helpful when you are building more complex projects with TypeScript. As you continue to stub out the rest of the game, you will get a better sense of what this means.

Another thing to point out about this class is that you are using a shorthand notation to set up your display property automatically in the constructor. Normally, you would define the public display on the class itself, above the constructor, but in TypeScript, you can save some time by simply defining an argument in your constructor as private or public, which will automatically set it as a property of your class. This is incredibly helpful. Also, note that you are typing the display property to HTMLCanvasElement. TypeScript is well aware of the native HTML element types, and each has its own unique type. This will allow you to have the compiler validate that you are using the correct application programming interfaces (APIs) on the element. You can also define your own constants, but I will not get into that for this project. Simply note that doing so is helpful for avoiding typos when accessing anything; this is one of the great advantages of using a typed language.

If you click the Save button and go back to the command prompt, you should see it compile and give you the okay that the file is done, as shown in Figure 19-7.

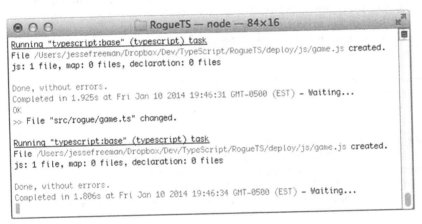

Figure 19-7. *As you can see at the bottom of the command prompt, the typescript task has run, and it compiled without any errors*

Check the deploy/js folder, and open the game.js file. You should see something like the one displayed in Figure 19-8.

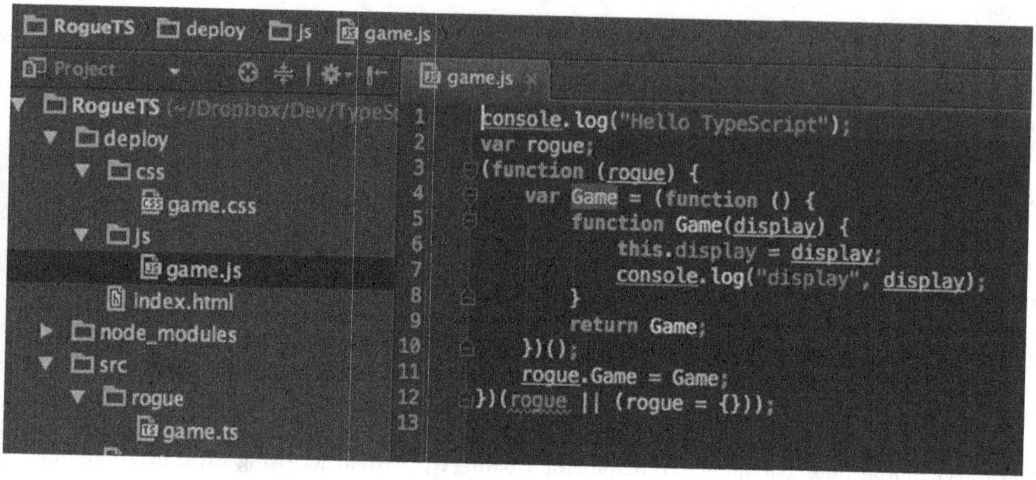

Figure 19-8. *Your first generated JavaScript file from TypeScript*

You now have your module and class compiled into JavaScript. Note again that this JavaScript is fully readable. If you ever find yourself no longer wanting to use TypeScript, you can simply take all the JavaScript files out and use them without TypeScript or even tell the compiler to generate each TypeScript file separately.

Next, let's get this connected in your `main.ts` file. Replace "Hello TypeScript" with the following code:

```
window.onload = () => {
    var canvas = <HTMLCanvasElement>document.getElementById('display');
    var rogueTS = new rogue.Game(canvas);
};
```

You may recognize that you are setting up an onload call to get the canvas and create your RogueTS game. What may look strange is how you actually set up this callback. The arrow notation => is how TypeScript binds a callback to a generic method. The biggest advantage of this in TypeScript, which you will see later in the chapter, when you set up your game loop (see the section "Drawing to Canvas"), is that the compiler will actually fix scoping in this generic function for you. To pass the scope back to a generic method, you may have had, at some point, to do a scope hack similar to this one:

```
var that = this;
```

TypeScript alleviates the need for this completely when you take advantage of the arrow notation. You will continue to use this notation as you build out your game, so don't worry; you will get more hands-on time with it.

Note that you get a reference to the canvas via a normal `document.getElementById` call. What may look strange is the addition of `<HTMLCanvasElement>` before it. This is called *casting*. Basically, because TypeScript sits on top of JavaScript, which is an untyped language, when you make JavaScript calls, you will always get back a generic object. You will have to type cast these objects to allow TypeScript to do its type checking correctly. You may also notice that you don't set an explicit type to your canvas variable. The compiler is smart enough to infer the type of var by the casting type. This can save you some time by not having to worry too much about adding types to each variable you define locally in a method or function.

You also create a new reference to your game. If you have ever used the new constructor in any language, including JavaScript, this should look very familiar to you. As you can see, you need to include the module name, plus the class, so you call `rogue.Game` and pass in a reference to the canvas. If you go back to the page in your browser and refresh, you should see the `canvas` element being traced out to the console, as shown in Figure 19-9.

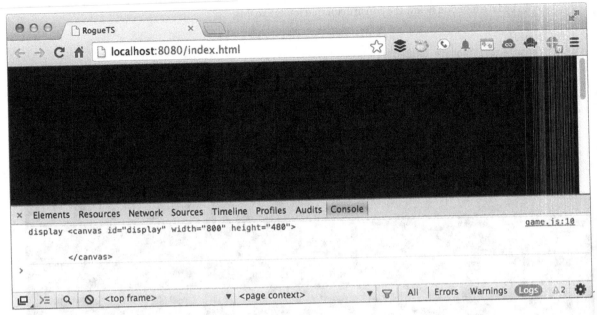

Figure 19-9. *By logging the value of the display to the console, you can see that the value has been correctly set*

Now, you are ready to move on to something a little more exciting: drawing to the canvas.

Drawing to Canvas

If you have ever worked with the canvas, which I assume you have, as you made it this far in the book, you will find that everything is the same in TypeScript. Just think of TypeScript as JavaScript with some extra features, and typing, of course, which you can choose to use or ignore. That is perhaps the best thing about TypeScript: you can revert to writing normal JavaScript at any point, and the compiler will simply ignore TypeScript. If you want the added protection of compiler checking, just add types, and you are good to go.

Before you start rendering to the canvas, you are going to need to set up a basic game loop. In your game.ts file, remove your console log, and add the following code in its place:

```
// Create and start the game loop
var gameloop = () => {this.update(); requestAnimationFrame(gameloop);}
gameloop();
```

Here, you are simply setting up an anonymous function, called gameloop. Inside it, you will notice that you are calling an update method (which you will set up next). Then, you use requestAnimationFrame, which requires a callback method to in turn call gameloop. This establishes a continuous loop that you can use to poll for input and render graphics to your canvas. One thing to note is that your game is going to be turn based, so you don't do much in the way of monitoring frames per second (FPS)or adjusting for slowdown between frames to calculate the time between each loop. Let's assume that your game runs its render and that everything works fine in a single frame, so in a real game, you may want to make adjustments with a little more logic. Finally, you call the gameloop function, which starts the loop.

Create an update function below the constructor that looks like this:

```
update():void{
        console.log("update called");
}
```

Now, you should be able to save the file, make sure that it compiles, and refresh the page. In the console, you will see that update being called in time with the browser's requestAnimationFrame, as demonstrated in Figure 19-10.

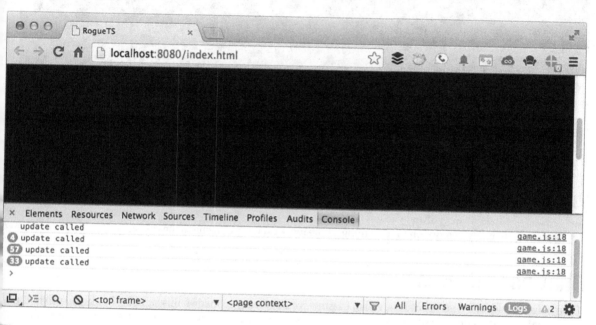

Figure 19-10. *As you can see, update is being called a lot, as the loop is going to continue to run without interruption*

Let's also add a draw method call to your update function and to the method itself. Replace "update called" console.log with this:

```
if (this.invalid) {
        this.draw();
```

Next, create the new method:

```
draw():void{
        console.log("draw called");
        this.invalid = false;
```

Finally, you have to add a property to your class, right above the constructor called invalid, as follows:

```
invalid: boolean = true;
```

This is a neat technique that is common in rendering engines that only need to redraw themselves when changes happen to the display. In this case, you want to render only once and not render when nothing is happening on the screen. Rogue is turn based, so taking advantage of the invalid flag is a great way to control manually when something renders to the screen. Run the example in the browser, and you should see that console.log gets called only once (see Figure 19-11).

Figure 19-11. Now, your draw call happens only once

Also, make sure to set invalid to true by default so that the first time update gets called, draw does as well. After a draw happens, it sets the invalid flag back to false and turns off the renderer. It's important to note that update is still being called, but that is okay. You always want to be calculacting what the next frame should be doing, such as accepting user input, calculating artificial intelligence (AI), or performing other processor-intensive tasks, while there is no need to update the display. Now, all you have to do is to create your map and a way to render it.

To start, above the game.ts constructor, add the following property:

```
tiles: any[];
```

Then, before the render loop, create the following simple, two-dimensional array:

```
this.tiles = [["#","#","#","#","#","#","#","#","#"],
             ["#"," "," "," ","#"," "," "," ","#"],
             ["#"," "," "," "," "," "," "," ","#"],
             ["#"," "," "," ","#"," "," "," ","#"],
             ["#","#","#","#","#","#","#","#","#"]
             ]
```

You can probably discern the structure of the map by looking at the array, but it's basically two rooms connected by a hallway. In your game, you will use "#" to represent walls and " " to represent the floor, where the player can walk. Now, let's switch gears and create your basic renderer. To get started, create a new file, called renderer.ts, in the rogue folder within src. From here, you are going to want to set up your basic module structure:

```
module rogue.renderer {
}
```

Next, you define a common API for your renderer to use, taking advantage of an interface, which is part of the TypeScript language. Interfaces allow you to define all the public methods on a class, and you can use the interface to type to instead of the class that inherits it. If you have never worked with interfaces before, it should make a little more sense as you get started building it out. Here is your IMapRenderer interface, which should go inside your rogue.renderer module:

```
export interface IMapRenderer {
    draw(tiles: any[]):void;
    drawTile(column: number, row: number, currentTile: string): void;
    clearMap(): void;
}
```

As you can see, you have three public-facing APIs: draw, drawTile, and clearMap. These will represent the basic calls that you can make on the map class once you create it. You will also notice that the draw call accepts an array of tiles, but it has been left generic by using the any[] array type. This allows you to extend your map later if you decide to use numbers instead of strings to represent the tile values. This is useful if you want to map each tile to a sprite ID, for example. Now, you are ready to set up the basic code in your game.ts file to render the map. Go back to that file, and add the following property to the top of the class, just below the invalidate property:

```
renderer: renderer.IMapRenderer;
```

You are going to create a renderer, and its type is IMapRenderer, which is the interface you just created. This is an important part of object-oriented programming called *polymorphism* (from the Greek *polys*, "many," and *morphe*, "form"), meaning "the provision of a single interface to entities of different types." This is what will enable you to grow your application and let each of your classes be completely decoupled from the concrete implementation of the class, instead relying on its interfaces or public methods. As you set up your renderer, the game engine doesn't have to know anything about the actual class that is in charge of drawing a map; it just requires that whatever you set the renderer to do is able to call draw, drawTile, and clearMap. To help illustrate this, let's add the following code to your draw method and replace the "draw called" console.log:

```
his.renderer.draw(this.tiles);
```

Now, your game is ready to draw the tiles that you defined. If you try to run this, however, it will fail, because an interface doesn't include the logic to execute anything. To do that, you will need to create a class that implements your new interface.

Before moving on, there is one more important thing I should mention regarding interface type. You may have noticed that you can simply type to it by referring to it as renderer.IMapRenderer instead of by its full module name, rogue.renderer.IMapRenderer. This is because the renderer module is inside the rogue module. Just because they are in different files doesn't mean that they have their own individual scope. Therefore, when a class is inside a module, the class doesn't need to use the fully qualified module path name; you can drop the module name to which the class belongs and access the class itself. You will see more of this later on, but in some cases, you will have to use fully qualified module paths. I will do my best to explain these differences.

Next, go back into your `renderer.ts` file, and add the following class under your interface:

```
export class CanvasMapRenderer implements IMapRenderer{
}
```

When you click the Save button, you should see errors similar to those shown in Figure 19-12.

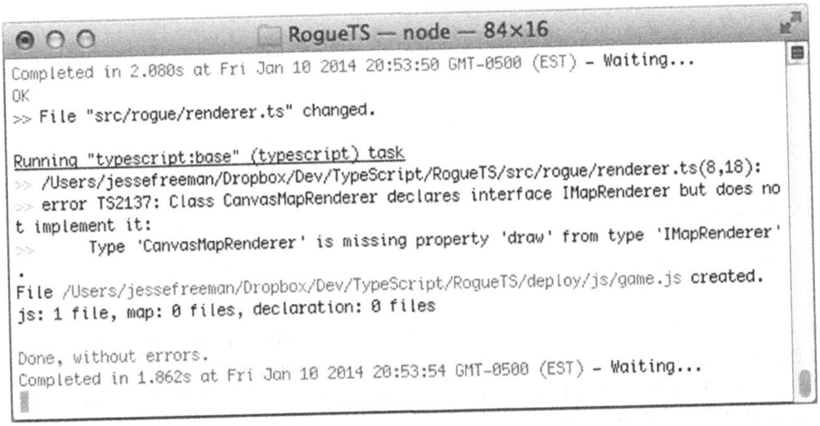

```
●●●                    RogueTS — node — 84×16
Completed in 2.080s at Fri Jan 10 2014 20:53:50 GMT-0500 (EST) - Waiting...
OK
>> File "src/rogue/renderer.ts" changed.

Running "typescript:base" (typescript) task
>> /Users/jessefreeman/Dropbox/Dev/TypeScript/RogueTS/src/rogue/renderer.ts(8,18):
>> error TS2137: Class CanvasMapRenderer declares interface IMapRenderer but does no
t implement it:
>>      Type 'CanvasMapRenderer' is missing property 'draw' from type 'IMapRenderer'
.
File /Users/jessefreeman/Dropbox/Dev/TypeScript/RogueTS/deploy/js/game.js created.
js: 1 file, map: 0 files, declaration: 0 files

Done, without errors.
Completed in 1.862s at Fri Jan 10 2014 20:53:54 GMT-0500 (EST) - Waiting...
```

Figure 19-12. As you can see, an error informs you that your class is not implementing your interface

The compiler is telling you that, even though you implemented the interface in your class, you still didn't add the actual methods defined in it. An interface is like a contract that guarantees the rest of the code that anything implementing it will always have the public methods it defines. Let's make the compiler happy before moving on and adding the actual render logic. Create these three methods on your CanvasMapRenderer:

```
public draw(tiles: any[]):void{
}
public drawTile(column: number, row: number, currentTile: string): void {
}
public clearMap(): void {
}
```

Now, if you go back to your `game.ts` file, you can assign this new class to the renderer property that you added before. Add the following code to your game's constructor, just above your game loop:

```
this.renderer = new renderer.CanvasMapRenderer();
```

Click the Save button, and look at the console. You should now see that the compiler is satisfied, and you can begin adding logic to your renderer. Go back into the `renderer.ts` file, and add the following constructor to your CanvasMapRenderer:

```
constructor (private canvas: HTMLCanvasElement, private tileRect: geom.Rectangle) {
    this.target = this.canvas.getContext("2d");
}
```

You also must add the following property above it:

```
target: CanvasRenderingContext2D;
```

What this means is that your CanvasMapRenderer needs a reference to the canvas in your HTML file as well as the dimensions of the tiles. You now create a new class, called Rectangle, which will be one of two geometry classes required in your game engine. Create a new file, called geom.ts, in your rogue folder inside src, and put in it the following content:

```
module rogue.geom {

    export class Point{
        constructor(public x:number = 0, public y:number = 0){}
        clone():Point{
            return new Point(this.x, this.y);
        }
    }
}
```

As you can see, you have a new package, called *geom*, and a class called Point. Point is a very simple class: it affords you an easy way to type against an x, y coordinate in your game. Now, whenever you want to represent a position, such as the player's x, y values, you can create a new point and access its public x, y properties. Next, you need to create your Rectangle. Following your Point class, add this:

```
export class Rectangle extends Point{
    constructor(x:number, y:number, public width: number = 0, public height:number = 0){
        super(x,y);
    }
}
```

This may be new to you if you have never worked with inheritance before in a language. Just as the CanvasMapRenderer implemented your IMapRenderer interface, so, too, one class can actually inherit logic from another class. To do this, you use the keyword "extends" when defining the class. From here, you can not only set up your own additional logic, but also pass values up to the parent class from which it extends. In this case, Rectangle needs to store the x, y width and height values for your game. It would be silly just to retype your properties for x and y, so you have Rectangle build onto the Point class, take its constructor's x, y values, and pass them up to the "super" class, which in this case is Point. Super is what you use to access a parent method. Because your Point class automatically creates an x, y property with its value defaulting to 0, you just pass those up to the super class and add the width and height arguments to the constructor. This allows you to do some very cool things as you get deeper into inheritance. TypeScript also supports method overriding and overloading.

Now that you have your Rectangle class, it's time to go back into your renderer and add the rest of the logic. Add the following content in the CanvasMapRenderer draw method:

```
this.clearMap();
var row: number;
var column: number;
var total: number = tiles.length;
var rowWidth: number = tiles[0].length;
var currentTile: string;
```

Here, you are going to clear the map, which you will add later on, and then set up some local variables to represent the values that you will need as you loop through the tiles in the array to draw them. It's always good practice, and it helps with performance, to precalculate and predefine variables used in for loops, especially the nested for loop you are about to write. Now, add the following loops to your draw method:

```
for (row = 0; row < total; row++) {
    for (column = 0; column < rowWidth; column++) {
        currentTile = tiles[row][column];
        this.drawTile(column, row, currentTile);
    }
}
```

As you can see, you are simply looping through the rows, and, at each row, you loop through the column to get the tile. This will in essence render out each tile in the grid. You can access any tile from your two-dimensional array by calling tiles[row][column]. As you run through the loop, you get a reference to your tile, which is either "#" or " ", to represent walls or floors. Then, you pass the column, row, and tile values over to your drawTile method. Let's add the following code to that now:

```
//Change tileRect's x,y position
this.tileRect.x = column * this.tileRect.width;
this.tileRect.y = row * this.tileRect.height;
//Draw tile to the canvas
this.target.fillStyle = this.tileColor(currentTile);
this.target.fillRect(this.tileRect.x, this.tileRect.y, this.tileRect.width, this.tileRect.height);
//Draw outline around tile
this.target.strokeStyle = "black";
this.target.strokeRect(this.tileRect.x, this.tileRect.y, this.tileRect.width, this.tileRect.height);
```

This should be very standard stuff if you have ever worked with the canvas before. The target is your two-dimensional context, which you defined at the top of the class, and you are simply modifying the tileRect, which represents the size of your map's tile to update its x, y position according to where you want to render it next. You use fillRect and strokeRect with the x, y width and height values of your tileRect to render your map.

You may have noticed the method in there called tileColor. This will represent your lookup table for determining what color to use on each tile, based on its type. Let's add the following method to the end of the CanvasMapRenderer:

```
private tileColor(value: string): string {
    switch (value) {
        case " ":
            return "#ffffff";
            break;
        case "@":
            return "#ff0000";
            break;
        default:
            return "#333333";
    }
}
```

In this private method, you have a simple switch statement that returns a color value based on the tile type. As you can see, you are adding one special tile type, "@", which is going to be your player. The last thing you need to do is add the code to clear your canvas, so add the following code to your empty clearMap method:

```
this.canvas.width = this.canvas.width;
```

This is a neat trick that clears a canvas quickly by simply setting its width to itself. There is no need to mess with adding a method to repaint the canvas with a solid color, unless you want to change the background to something other than black.

At this point, you should have everything that is required to see your map. You just have to make one minor correction to your renderer setup in the game.ts file. Replace

```
this.renderer = new renderer.CanvasMapRenderer();
```

with

```
this.renderer = new renderer.CanvasMapRenderer(this.display, new geom.Rectangle(0, 0, 20, 20));
```

Save your changes, make sure that everything passes the compiler, and refresh your web page. You should see something similar to the rendering displayed in Figure 19-13.

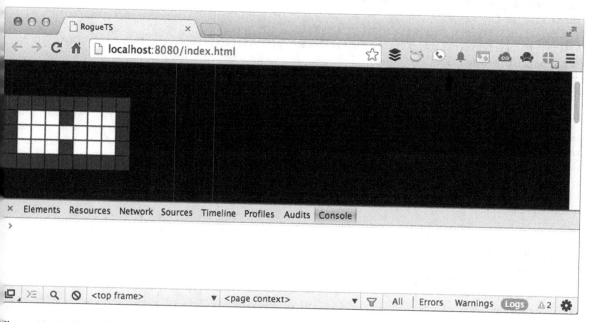

Figure 19-13. *You will now see your game's map being rendered to the screen*

And that is how you get your map rendering. Before moving on, let's talk a little more about extending classes and why it's important. You may have noticed that your renderer was called CanvasMapRenderer and not just MapRenderer. That was intentional. Rogue is traditionally a text-based game. You could easily have created a text renderer, called TextMapRenderer, that simply modified it to display each tile as its value and not bothered with canvas at all. All you would need to do is implement the IMapRenderer interface and change out your draw, drawTile, and clearMap methods to manipulate text on the page instead. This is where the true power of TypeScript lies. You can take advantage of interfaces to help abstract your code base in ways that encourage extensibility, composition, and inheritance as it grows. This is critical when you are working in larger teams and need to make sure that you have structure and balance in your code base, an inherent problem with JavaScript, as each developer may have his or her own ways of implementing classes or have problems reading other developers' code.

Handling Movement

You now have the basic engine up and running for creating a map and displaying tiles. Let's add a player to the map and deal with registering input from the user as well as basic collision detection. But, before you do that, you are going to need to abstract your map a little more to make it easier to work with. Right now, it's simply a multidimensional array. Let's create a map class and expose some APIs to access the underlying data. You will do this by making a new file, called map.ts, with the following content:

```
module rogue.map {
    export interface IMap{
        getWidth(): number;
        getHeight(): number;
        getTiles(): any[];
        getTileType(point: geom.Point): string;
    }
}
```

Again, you will see that you start with a simple interface to define your map's public properties: getWidth, getHeight, getTiles, and getTileType. Let's build out the map below your interface:

```
export class TileMap implements IMap {

    constructor (private tiles: any[]) {}

    public getTileType(point: geom.Point): string {
        return this.tiles[point.y][point.x];
    }

    public getWidth(): number {
        return this.tiles[0].length;
    }

    public getHeight(): number {
        return this.tiles.length;
    }

    public getTileID(row: number, column: number): number {
        return row * this.getWidth() + column;
    }

    public getTiles(): any[] {
        return this.tiles;
    }
}
```

Nothing here should be too surprising. You accept an array of tiles, and each method lets you access the tile data without directly manipulating it. This is critical when it comes to encapsulation. You always want to make sure that the data are protected when you try to access them. If you remember back to your Point class, you may have noticed that you have a clone method on it. This allows you to get a copy of the data so that they stay protected inside your class, and you don't accidently corrupt them. Although you don't have any safeguards here in the map class, you definitely don't want to be directly accessing the array itself, and this class enables you to safeguard your engine from changes in the map data structure. What if you decide that you need to use a new file format for the map data instead of a two-dimensional array? Perhaps something that is easier to serialize and deserialize, such as JSON, for saving state in your game? You can safely change that, and the rest of your game will never know, so long as you return the expected values in getTileID and getTiles. A JSON map class can simply return the tile data as an array so that your renderer doesn't break, and you can continue to grow and expand your game's code base.

Now go back to your game.ts file and implement the map. Add the following property to your class:

```
map: map.IMap;
```

And, below the map data, add the following code to instantiate the map class with the tile data:

```
this.map = new rogue.map.TileMap(this.tiles);
```

Next, you will modify the draw call to look like this:

```
this.renderer.draw(this.map.getTiles());
```

Note how you are asking the map for its tiles instead of passing in the array directly. Again, this is your encapsulation, which lets you extend and modify your map over time to better fit your needs. The renderer doesn't care so long as it gets a single two-dimensional array to render out. Before adding the player, run the game in the browser, and check that there are no compiler errors. The game should look the same as before (see Figure 19-14).

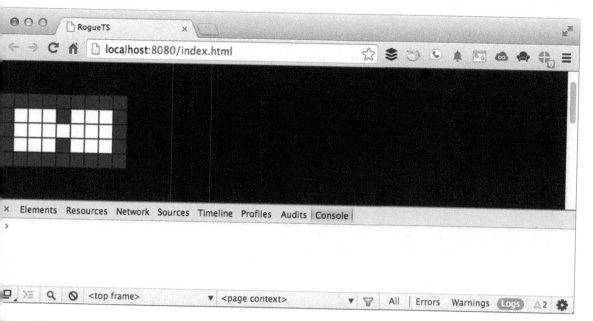

Figure 19-14. *Everything should look the same, with no compiler errors*

So, with a cleaned-up map, you are able to create a placeholder position for the player. To do this, add the following property to your game class:

```
playerPosition: geom.Point;
```

You will set that up following the map in your constructor:

```
this.playerPosition = new geom.Point(1,1);
```

This will put the player in the upper-left corner of your map, in an open tile. To draw the player, simply add the following line of code after rendering the map in your draw call, then reset the invalidate property:

```
this.renderer.drawTile(this.playerPosition.x, this.playerPosition.y, "@");
```

If you save, check the compiler, and refresh your browser. You will see that you now have a red square representing your player, as illustrated in Figure 19-15.

Figure 19-15. *You should now see the red square, which is the player*

By exposing the internal method of the renderer for drawing a single tile, you can use it to place additional tiles on top of the map. You can render out the entire map and then do another pass to render out the player, monsters, treasure chests, and decoration. You may be thinking, "Why not do this all in a single pass?" The reason is that you want these graphics to sit on top of the map. Right now, you don't notice the difference, as they are all squares of the same size. However, if your player were a sprite and had transparency, you would want it to appear on top of the floor; through optimization techniques, you could cut down on the additional draw calls by simply rendering out only what's in the player's immediate field of vision. Now, let's make this player move.

You will need to create a new class, called input.ts, in your rogue folder. As before, add to it the following code:

```
module rogue.input {
}
```

This time, though, instead of an interface, you are going to create something called an *enum* (enumerator). Enums allow you to store name-value pairs in easy-to-reference lookup tables. Here is your first enum:

```
export enum Keyboard {
            LEFT=37,
            UP=38,
            RIGHT=39,
            DOWN=40,
};
```

If you have ever worked with keyboard events, you know that you must reference their values. As you can see, you store each key value in this enum so that you can reference, for instance, the left key as Keyboard.LEFT. This is a lot better than referencing it directly, by its value of 37. Then, you will need a second lookup table of points that represent the directions in which the player can move. Unfortunately, enums can only contain numbers, and you will want your reference object to have points. Luckily, you can still create something very similar to an enum, but as a generic object, like so:

```
export var Directions = {
    UP: new geom.Point(0, -1),
    DOWN: new geom.Point(0, 1),
    RIGHT: new geom.Point(1, 0),
    LEFT: new geom.Point(-1, 0)
}
```

Here, you are setting up points to represent directions in which the player will move. Figure 19-16 provides a handy reference to what this actually looks like on a grid:

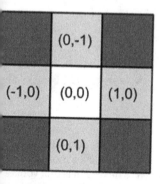

Figure 19-16. *As you can see, you simply do math on the x, y position in order to move the player up, down, left, or right*

You will use these direction points to help with collision detection later on in this section. For now, you need to start setting up your Input class and working with JavaScript's input events in TypeScript. Create the following class:

```typescript
export class Input {
}
```

From here, you set up the basic constructor and add a listener for the keyboard events within it:

```typescript
constructor (){
    window.addEventListener("keyup", event => this.keyup(event) , false);
}
```

Again, you can see that the TypeScript arrow notation is being used to define the event callback. You add the listener and then bind the returned event to your keyup method, which you will create next:

```typescript
keyup( event: Event ):void {
        event.stopPropagation();
        event.preventDefault();
        var keyCode = event["keyCode"];

        switch (keyCode){
                case Keyboard.UP:
                        this.newDirection = Directions.UP;
                        break;
                case Keyboard.RIGHT:
                        this.newDirection = Directions.RIGHT;
                        break;
                case Keyboard.DOWN:
                        this.newDirection = Directions.DOWN;
                        break;
                case Keyboard.LEFT:
                        this.newDirection = Directions.LEFT;
                        break;
        }
}
```

There is a lot in this method, but it's pretty straightforward stuff. You stop the event from propagating and then do a switch on the event keyCode. Because you typed the event to Event, you can attempt to access its properties directly, just like you do in JavaScript. There is one problem, however: TypeScript's compiler doesn't recognize keyCode as part of the event type. To get around this, you access the property in array notation, which bypasses the compiler's type-checking system and lets you still access the property on the object and not get an error. This is a neat trick if you run into type issues and don't have the time or the know-how to fix them. The rest of the switch statement assigns the direction point to a property called newDirection. Add this to your class, above the constructor:

```typescript
newDirection: geom.Point;
```

Finally, you just need to create your clear method, which will allow you to reset the Input class on each frame by adding the following code to the end of the class:

```typescript
clear():void {
    this.newDirection = null;
}
```

Before moving on, note that you didn't add an Input interface to help cut down on the amount of code you have here. This interface could easily be added, allowing you to support a mouse, touch screen, or joystick down the road. You can simply create a common interface for input in your game and classes for each type and then, at runtime, swap them out, based on the user's device or preferred input. Always think of how to take advantage of TypeScript's language, such as interfaces and support for typing, which you may not be used to in traditional JavaScript development.

At this point, you can begin to integrate this interface into your game class. Switch back to the game.ts file, and add the following property to your game class:

```
input: input.Input;
```

Now, you need to add the following code to your constructor, before the map data:

```
this.input = new input.Input();
```

In your update method, you want to check if the newDirection property was set. Add this before you test for the invalid flag and draw call:

```
if (this.input.newDirection) {
    this.move(this.input.newDirection);
    this.input.clear();
}
```

As you can see, the Input class is polled for its newDirection. From here, you make a call to a move method and pass in the value. Then, you clear the input for the next frame so that the player needs to press and release the arrow key in order to move. Add the following method to your game class:

```
move(newDirection:geom.Point): void {

    var tmpPoint: geom.Point = this.playerPosition.clone();
    tmpPoint.x += newDirection.x;
    tmpPoint.y += newDirection.y;

    var tile: string = this.map.getTileType(tmpPoint);
    switch (tile) {
        case " ":
            this.playerPosition = tmpPoint;
            this.invalid = true;
            break;
    }
}
```

This will represent the core of your collision detection. It's actually really simple. You clone the player's current position and then add the newDirection x, y values to it. From here, you can preview the next tile the player is going to enter by getting it from the map via its getTileType method. This is another reason it was important to abstract the tile array data inside the map class and expose an easier way to access individual tiles. Once you have the next tile, you simply see if it's empty via a switch. If so, you set the current player's position to the temporary point and invalidate the display. The game loop will automatically update the display on the next frame. Run the game, and you should be able to move around now, as illustrated in Figure 19-17.

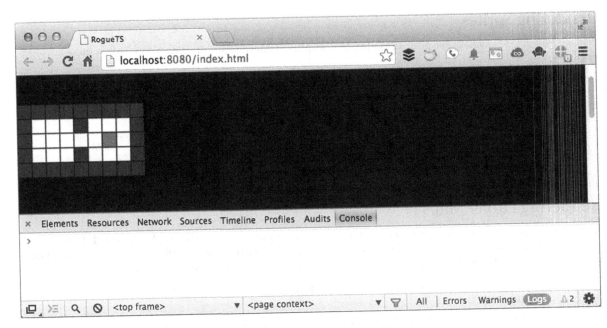

Figure 19-17. Here, you can see that you can now move the player around the map

Extending Your Engine

At this point, you have a fully functional engine for a rogue-like game written in TypeScript. There are several places to which you may want to extend the functionality of this engine. Following are some of the top things you might do next to explore further how TypeScript works.

Adding Enemies and Treasure

It's relatively easy to add additional items to the game. Because the basic foundation is there, you need only follow these steps:

1. Add a method to the map class that allows you to find empty tiles easily.

2. Build a helper class to populate the dungeon with items and monsters.

3. Move the player position into the map populater class, and have it store the ID, tile type, and point for each object in the map.

4. Add new colors, based on each item; also, perhaps use an "m" for monster (or "m1," "m2," and so on for different types of monsters) and an "x" for treasure chests.

5. Modify the render's `tileColor` to display each new tile type with its own unique color.

6. In your game's render code, simply loop through the array of game objects stored in the populator manager, and have them draw to the map, just as you did with the player originally.

7. In your move code, you can add more values to the switch statement to call methods that handle picking up treasure or attacking monsters.

Rendering Sprites

You can extend the CanvasMapRenderer to use images, or sprites, instead of just drawing colors. Follow these easy steps:

1. Create a preloader to handle loading in images before the game runs.

2. Extend the CanvasMapRenderer with a new SpriteMapRenderer.

3. Override the drawTile method with a way to look up sprites and paint them to the canvas.

4. Replace the reference to the old CanvasMapRenderer with the new SpriteMapRenderer; everything should work just the same, but with new images instead of colored boxes.

Rendering Larger Maps

Right now, the map renderer simply draws every tile you give it. It doesn't even follow the player around. This could be really bad for performance and gameplay. If you want to have much larger maps, create a MapSelection class that can capture a range of tiles from the map and better manage how you render it. Here is what that would look like:

1. Create a MapSelection class that wraps the map class and that can access and manipulate the tile data.

2. Add new methods onto the map class to make it easier to select tiles from rows by range, for example, getting five tiles around a center point, which would represent the player.

3. Update the selection class's center point, based on the player's position as it moves through the levels.

4. Use the MapSelection tiles instead of all the tiles from the map when you call the renderer.

As you can see, this engine is easily extensible, and you have set up enough of the foundation to allow you to continue to build on top of it and make the game your own. Rogue games are great engines to build when you are starting out making games in a new language. Hopefully, you now have greater insight into how TypeScript can be a very useful addition to any traditional JavaScript game's architecture. Even if you write the core of the engine in TypeScript and implement it in JavaScript, you still have the additional help that a compiler offers: checking over your code and making sure that you don't make easy-to-overlook mistakes.

CHAPTER 20

Implementing a Main Loop in Dart

John McCutchan, Software Engineer, Google

At the heart of your favorite games is the game loop. At the core of the game loop is control over the game clock. In each frame the game does some or all of the following: updates the game state, triggers timers, processes user inputs, renders graphics, and plays audio. Each of these operations must be synchronized using a virtual clock controlled by the game loop. This chapter explains how to implement a deterministic and efficient main loop for any type of game designed from the ground up to run in the browser.

This chapter uses the Dart programming language (www.dartlang.org/) for reference code but the focus of this chapter is not on Dart. Dart should be familiar to programmers coming from languages like Java or C#, and the code does not make use of any of Dart's higher-level features. All DOM calls can be easily mapped to their JavaScript equivalents.

Implementing a main loop must be done with respect to the browser's execution model. The Dart program cannot execute endlessly; it must yield control back to the browser every frame. User inputs are delivered via asynchronous event callbacks and the rendering is synchronized with the browser by performing rendering in the *frame* callback.

User inputs are delivered as discrete events through callbacks registered with the browser. The browser delivers a different input event per device type. For example, there are four separate event sources for key down, key up, mouse button down, and mouse button up. The main loop should record all user inputs into a single stream of input events between frames, allowing input code to process all inputs in one location. Processing complex user inputs like chords or sequences will be covered as well.

When you finish this chapter you will be able to build a robust, reusable, main loop upon which you can build games.

Sample Code

The source code included with this chapter is written in Dart. *Dart* is an object-oriented programming language that can run in any browser by being compiled to JavaScript or run in a version of Chromium that includes the Dart virtual machine (VM). Even though the source code is written in Dart, the focus of this chapter is on the main loop for games, and the concepts, design, and algorithms discussed in this chapter do not depend on Dart functionality.

Dart

Dart is an object-oriented programming language designed to be familiar to programmers coming from object-oriented languages like Java or C#. The Dart language is stricter than JavaScript and, in turn, programs written in Dart can run significantly faster than programs written in JavaScript. An example of Dart is shown in Listing 20-1.

Listing 20-1. An Example of Dart

```dart
main() {                          // This is where the app starts executing.
  print(new Fibonacci(10));       // Print a new object's value.
}

class Fibonacci {                 // Define a class.
  int original, fibo;             // Declare variables with (optional) types.
  String toString() => '$fibo';   // Define a method using shorthand syntax.

  Fibonacci(int value) :          // Define a constructor with list initializer.
    original = value, fibo = fib(value) {
  }

  static int fib(int n) {         // Define a class method.
    if (n < 2) {                  // Control flow and expressions.
      return n;
    } else {
      return fib(n-1) + fib(n-2); // Arithmetic operators.
    }
  }
}
// Want terser code? Write a one-line function instead:
// fib(n) => n < 2 ? n : (fib(n - 1) + fib(n - 2));
```

Dart provides a familiar but modern syntax. Contrary to JavaScript, Dart has first-class support for classes and allows for (optional) type annotations, which are used only during development to catch programmer errors early.

game_loop

The sample code provided in this chapter is part of the game_loop package available via Dart's package management tool, pub. If you decide to write your next game in Dart, you can use the code directly. However, if you decide to use a different language, it should be trivial to port the code from Dart to your language of choice.

The easiest way to get game_loop is to add it as a dependency in your project's pubspec.yaml. You can always find the source code for the latest version of game_loop in its GitHub repository at http://github.com/johnmccutchan/game_loop.

nterfacing with the Browser

Before discussing main loops in detail, it is important to understand that the browser is in control of the main loop. The browser places constraints on the main loop because it is in control of when the loop executes and provides the inputs (time, render signal, and user input) needed to make progress. An example of the browser controlling the main loop is requestAnimationFrame, which dictates when the main loop must render the game into the page or compositing. This is the display synchronization point. You request to receive this event by registering a frame callback with requestAnimationFrame. The next time your game should draw itself to the screen, the frame callback will be executed. It is important to understand that the browser tells you when to render, not the other way around. This example demonstrates how, in general, the browser is in control of the main loop.

Inputs

This section covers the inputs that your main loop will receive from the browser. This includes user input as well as the display synchronization event and time.

Time

A monotonically increasing count of the number of milliseconds since the page was loaded is passed as a parameter to the callback registered with `window.requestAnimationFrame`. You can query this time source on demand with `window.performance.now`. Relying on different sources of time can lead to hard-to-track-down bugs. Be sure to only use the time parameter passed into `window.requestAnimationFrame` and the time values read from `window.performance.now`.

Display Sync

This is the game's heartbeat. It doesn't matter how your game is rendered (2D canvas, WebGL, or just plain DOM); render updates must be performed inside the frame callback registered with `window.requestAnimationFrame`. By relying on `requestAnimationFrame` to initiate rendering, your game will be in synchronization with the display's v-blank and with the browser's internal rendering system. Expect `requestAnimationFrame` to be called every 16.6 ms (60 FPS) in ideal circumstances, but, when system load is high or the user is looking at another tab, the rate will be throttled down. Your main loop must execute correctly with any time gap between successive frame callback calls.

User Input

In the browser, user input is received via many different event streams. Each event stream is dedicated to a certain type of event. Examples include

- TouchStart
- TouchEnd
- TouchCancel
- TouchMove
- KeyDown
- KeyUp
- MouseMove
- MouseDown
- MouseUp
- MouseWheel

All of the above streams deliver events independently. Developing a system that unifies all of the different event sources with the game logic update loop is essential to a good main loop.

Outputs

This section covers the outputs from your main loop. This includes unseen internal game states as well as audio and video output.

Game State

Game state is not (directly) displayed to the player. It is used to drive the output that the player sees displayed on the screen and hears through the speakers. The main loop controls when and at what rate the game state is updated, thus it is considered an output of the main loop.

Display

The main loop is told when to display the game via requestAnimationFrame. The entire game view should be rendered whenever requested by the browser.

Audio

Unlike rendering, audio can be scheduled to play in the future by the developer. Inside the frame callback, audio will be scheduled for playback.

Designing a successful main loop requires understanding and working with the browser, which activates the main loop with timers, rendering requests, and user input events.

Your First Main Loop and What's Wrong with It

The code snippet in Listing 20-2 is an example of the typical main loop that many programmers start with. It rests on top of requestAnimationFrame and updates game state and then renders the game before registering for the next display synchronization signal.

Listing 20-2. Typical main Loop

```
var lastTime;  // null.
void frame(num time) {
  if (lastTime == null) {
    // Determine an origin in time.
    lastTime = time;
    // Skip this frame.
    window.requestAnimationFrame(frame);
    return;
  }
  // Compute delta time.
  var dt = time - lastTime;
  lastTime = time;
  // Update game.
  update(time, dt);
  // Render game.
  render(time, dt);
  // Register for next display signal.
  window.requestAnimationFrame(frame);
```

```dart
main(List<String> args) {
  // Setup game.
  ...
  // Startup main loop.
  window.requestAnimationFrame(frame);
}
```

At first glance, the above main loop is quite reasonable, but it has subtle and important flaws. The largest bug is that it does not have a fixed time step, which means the game logic will run non-deterministically. Non-deterministic game logic can have real impacts on gameplay. For example, a user on a fast machine may be able to complete the game but a user on a slower machine may not be able to make a jump or might get stuck in a wall because the time step used to update the game world changes each frame.

Quest for Determinism

A good main loop provides a deterministic framework that the game-specific logic can be built on. This section explains how to build a robust main loop that incorporates all input sources and updates the game deterministically.

Fixed Time Step

The first step is to lock the time delta used to update your game state. This means no matter how much time has elapsed between frame callbacks, the game state is updated as if a fixed amount of time has elapsed, like so:

```dart
// Update game.
const fixedDt = 16.0;  // milliseconds
update(gameTime, fixedDt);
gameTime += fixedDt;
```

The above code snippet is sufficient to get deterministic game update behavior but suffers from another problem: it leaks time. Consider the case when 18 milliseconds elapses between frame callbacks but you only move the game forward by 16 milliseconds. You've lost 2 milliseconds. Not much time, but the game will lose around 3.6 seconds per minute. It adds up.

Accumulating Time

The fix for leaking time is straightforward. Extra time must be accumulated across frames and fed back in, like so:

```dart
// Compute delta time.
var dt = time - lastTime;
lastTime = time;
accumulatedDt += dt;
const fixedDt = 16.0;  // milliseconds
while (accumulatedDt >= fixedDt) {
  // Update game.
  update(gameTime, fixedDt);
  accumulatedDt -= fixedDt;
  gameTime += fixedDt;
}
```

The wall clock time delta is accumulated each frame, and when the accumulated time delta is greater than or equal to the fixed time step, it calls the game update function with a fixed time step. With the above code, the main loop doesn't leak time and provides a deterministic update step. It can suffer from a problem on slow machines: the update method takes longer to execute than the fixed time step. When this happens, the accumulated time delta grows unbounded and the application spends more and more time inside the update loop.

Falling Behind

On slow machines, it's possible that the wall clock time required to update the game state is greater than the fixed time step. When this happens, the game clock falls behind the wall clock. There are a few ways of handling falling behind. If the game can support it, scale back on some of the computation so that the game update requires less time than the fixed time step. If the game cannot be simplified, you may want to indicate to the player that their machine may be too slow to enjoy the game. Regardless, you must guard against the accumulated time delta growing too large because it can happen even on fast machines: when a user switches away from the tab for a few minutes and comes back, suddenly you have a couple minutes of game updates to process.

A better solution is the following code:

```
// Compute delta time.
var dt = time - lastTime;
lastTime = time;
accumulatedDt += dt;
const fixedDt = 16.0;   // milliseconds
if (accumulatedDt > 2.0 * fixedDt) {
  // Lose time.
  accumulatedDt = 2.0 * fixedDt;
}
while (accumulatedDt >= fixedDt) {
  // Update game.
  update(gameTime, fixedDt);
  accumulatedDt -= fixedDt;
  gameTime += fixedDt;
}
```

This code will drop as much time as is necessary to keep the accumulated delta time below a threshold. In this code, that threshold is twice the fixed game step update time.

Seeing into the Future

There is one last issue to consider and that is the remaining accumulated time. If there is any remaining time and you render without taking it into consideration, you are displaying the state of the game that is already out of date. How you can work around this will be covered in the section below on rendering with interpolation.

User Input

The browser delivers each input event with a separate callback invocation. The callback invocations transition execution from C++ code in the browser to your script code and then back. As quickly as possible the script code should add the input event to a queue of events and exit. Processing the queued input events is done in the frame callback synchronized with the game state update.

Detecting and classifying user input is done on the queue of input events and is game-specific. For example, a first person shooter game needs to know if the W, A, S, or D keys are down and how much the mouse has moved since the last frame. The main loop is only responsible for providing the buffer of input events to the game.

Timers

The internal game clock (gameTime) is managed by the main loop. Any in-game timers, such as the timer tracking the door that stays unlocked for two seconds after the player steps from a pressure plate, must be kept in sync with the game clock. If the in-game timers used a different clock than the game update, the timers would not fire when expected. You can solve this by moving the timer time forward inside the main loop, like so:

```
// Compute delta time.
var dt = time - lastTime;
lastTime = time;
accumulatedDt += dt;
const fixedDt = 16.0;  // milliseconds
if (accumulatedDt > 2.0 * fixedDt) {
  // Lose time.
  accumulatedDt = 2.0 * fixedDt;
}
while (accumulatedDt >= fixedDt) {
  // fire timers.
  fireTimers(gameTime, fixedDt);
  // Update game.
  update(gameTime, fixedDt);
  accumulatedDt -= fixedDt;
  gameTime += fixedDt;
}
```

Include support for both periodic (repeating) and single shot timers as well as support for cancelling timers.

Rendering

The final task of the main loop is to trigger rendering of the game. Rendering is always done in the frame callback, which is synchronized with the browser's own rendering pipeline.

On Demand

Rendering is done on demand and initiated when the browser invokes the frame callback registered with window. requestAnimationFrame. After updating the game timers and state, the game is rendered. When the browser tab holding the game is not focused, the rate at which the frame callback is executed drops, possibly to 0.

Interpolation

Consider what happens when the render frame callback is fired but the accumulated time is not enough to trigger a game logic update. The render is supposed to use the current state, but the game state is from the past (see Figure 20-1 It is possible to compensate for this by projecting the game object's display transformation from the last game update to the current time. This can be done either through interpolation or extrapolation.

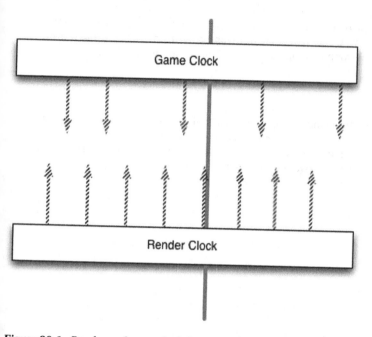

Figure 20-1. *Render and game clock (arrows represent renders/updates, and the line is the current time)*

Interpolation requires that the game keep the two most recent game states, and the renderer interpolates between the two states. This is done in code as follows:

```
renderTransform(frame, x) = transform(state[1]) * (x) + transform(state[0]) * (1.0 - x);
```

The render transform is interpolated between the transform at state[1] and the transform at state[0], resulting in a smooth motion even if a render occurs between game state updates.

Extrapolation can be used by factoring in object velocity:

```
renderTransform(frame, x) = transform(state) + integrate(velocity(state), x);
```

The extrapolated transformation may end up being wrong. For example, the object may disappear from the scene before it gets to the extrapolated position. Extrapolation has the added benefit of only requiring a single snapshot of the game state.

Whether the renderer uses stale, interpolated, or extrapolated object transforms depends on the game and rendering engine. Generally a game looks better, because animations will be smoother, if it compensates for the discrepancy between the game clock and the renderer clock.

User Input Processing

User input processing is game-specific, but the main loop can provide generalized input type support for mapping from raw input events to game input events, along with chord (multiple simultaneous buttons down or up) detection and sequence (a specific sequence of input events) detection.

Digital Input

Digital inputs are either on or off. Keys, mouse buttons, digital gamepad buttons are either up or down. Digital inputs have the following properties:

- Digital input id (key code, button id, and so on)

- Last time pressed

- Last time released

Detecting if a digital button is up or down can be implemented by the following code:

```
bool get down => lastTimePressed >= lastTimeReleased;
bool get up => lastTimeReleased < lastTimePressed;
```

Analog Input

Analog inputs have a value inside a limited range (e.g., -1.0 to 1.0 or 0.0 to 1.0). Analog sticks and buttons on gamepads are examples of analog inputs. Analog inputs have the following properties:

- Analog input id (key code, button id, and so on)

- Last time updated

- Value

Users of analog inputs may want to consider applying a dead zone filter to the value. Dead zone filters cancel small movements in the analog value by mapping the value back to 0.0. This helps the input feel less twitchy.

Positional Input

Positional inputs are positions in a 2D coordinate system. Mouse cursor and finger positions are examples of positional inputs. Positional inputs have the following properties:

- Positional input id (mouse id, touch id)

- X position

- Y position

- Delta x position

- Delta y position

- Time

In each frame there may be many positional input values for a specific device. A first person shooter may accumulate the delta x and delta y position values for the entire frame and use the aggregate to adjust the view angle of the player. A touch-based game may move a kinematic object through the scene based on the input values.

Game-Specific Code

Mapping from raw input values to game-specific input values allows game controller code to be reconfigured by the player. The player can decide which button or combination of buttons is used for the jump action (see Figure 20-2). Game-specific inputs are modeled using the same three generalized input types mentioned above, but the state of these virtual inputs have values set by game-specific code.

Figure 20-2. *The player decides which button or combination of buttons is used for the jump action*

Chords

Chords are another virtualized input type. A chord is active when multiple event states occur simultaneously, such as when the analog stick is held up and the A button is pressed (see Figure 20-3). A chord may or may not be triggerable when other buttons are pressed. Chords can be detected by tracking the state of the individual inputs involved in the chord over time and checking if the chord is active after each input event.

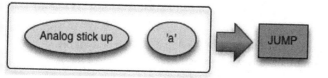

Figure 20-3. *The analog stick is held up and the A button is pressed*

Sequences

Sequences are active when multiple event states occur in a specific order and within a certain amount of time. A famous example is the Konami code: UP, UP, DOWN, DOWN, LEFT, RIGHT, LEFT, RIGHT, A, B, A, B, START. A directed graph state machine can model sequences. The sequence starts off in the READY state, and as each input event is processed, the sequence can move forward to the next state or back to the READY state if an invalid input is encountered (see Figure 20-4).

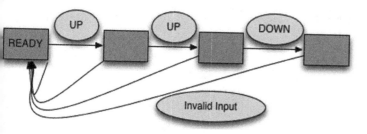

Figure 20-4. *A sequence starts off in the READY state, processes each input event, and can move forward to the next state or back to the READY state*

Conclusion

This chapter has covered the design and implementation of a deterministic main loop that was designed to run in a browser. If you are a Dart programmer, you can use this library today by adding the game_loop package as a dependency in your pubspec.yaml. If you are still using JavaScript, keep in mind the following when implementing your own main loop:

- Your main loop is driven by your *frame* callback registered with requestAnimationFrame.

- Your game update function needs a stable time delta: your frame callback must track how much time has elapsed and call the update function when enough time has elapsed.

- Watch out for leaking time and unbounded time accumulation.

- Game timers should be built into the main loop so they are kept in sync with the game time.

- User input from the browser should be buffered and available to be processed in the game update function.

- Render time may be ahead of game time. Use extrapolation or interpolation to get smooth graphics.

- Abstract inputs into digital (down or up), analog (-1.0 to 1.0), and positional (touch and mouse cursor).

By building on a solid main loop you can easily add support for detecting chorded inputs and sequence inputs.

■ ■ ■

Saving Bandwidth and Memory with WebGL and Crunch

Brandon Jones, Software Engineer, Google

When it comes to optimization, both real-time 3D applications and web pages happen to share a common target: images. Images, whether they take the form of textures or <img> tags, often make up the majority of the visual information on your screen at any given time. The metrics for optimization differ based on the medium, however. 3D apps, such as games, need images that can be loaded quickly, drawn fast, and take up as little memory as possible by taking advantage of hardware-supported texture compression formats. Web pages, on the other hand, are primarily concerned with the bandwidth required to download the images to your device, skewing heavily towards small, lossy formats like JPG. In other words, 3D apps are concerned about the size of the image in video memory and web apps are concerned about the size of the file on the server.

WebGL sits at the intersection between these two worlds and, unfortunately, it's not always easy to satisfy the demands of both. This chapter will examine the Crunch compression format as a way to achieve both low memory usage and small file size, making it the best of both worlds!

The Goal

In this chapter, you will be constructing a library that can be used to load compressed textures, both from DDS and CRN files. In order to demonstrate the library, I've created a simple WebGL image gallery that demonstrates loading and displaying the file types discussed, illustrated in Figure 21-1.

Figure 21-1. *Simple WebGL image gallery*

The gallery application isn't very complex, but it's designed to stress a couple of aspects of the texture-loading library in order to compare various approaches:

- It continuously downloads new images. This stresses the amount of bandwidth used, and it favors image files that are as small as possible.

- Textures are constantly being swapped in and out of memory, so the app favors textures whose video memory footprint is as small as possible.

Although this particular example is fairly contrived, the requirements are not unheard of for real-world applications. For example, the virtualized texturing techniques used in id Software's Rage (http://rage.com), on both game consoles and iOS, rely on a constantly-updated texture pool and well-compressed images on disk to display a large world in which every surface is uniquely textured. While most WebGL apps won't require that level of complexity, there are very few apps that wouldn't benefit from faster load times and less memory usage.

Browser-Supported Images

Before diving into the details of texture compression, let's first review the formats that browsers support natively. This may be old news to many developers, but it's still interesting to look at the numbers involved. Since we're looking at reducing load times, we'll focus our attention on the file sizes produced by each format, taking into account the capabilities and limitations of each.

For the gallery application, I took several pictures at various locations around the Google campus in Mountain View, as seen in Figure 21-2. The images were then saved in the various browser-supported formats using GIMP's default export settings for each. Each image is 1024×1024 pixels with no opacity information. I've picked three of them to use for the comparison.

Figure 21-2. *Photos taken at various locations around Google's Mountain View campus*

Look at Table 21-1. Which two formats can you quickly take out of the running?

Table 21-1. *Files Sizes of Various Browser-supported Formats*

	BMP	GIF	PNG	JPEG	WEBP
Slide_10	3072 KB	422 KB	1601 KB	378 KB	152 KB
Slide_13	3072 KB	666 KB	1986 KB	531 KB	243 KB
Slide_15	3072 KB	428 KB	1369 KB	303 KB	79 KB

BMP

Every browser supports BMPs, but they're almost never used, and Table 21-1 demonstrates why. BMPs are raw, uncompressed RGB data. As such, they make for pretty huge image files. If you need lossless data, PNGs are always smaller and support an alpha channel, so there's no good reason to use BMP.

GIF

GIFs are an odd historical artifact that refuses to die. Sporting unimpressive compression and palletized color, their only upside (animation) is not one that WebGL can use effectively. Don't even bother with them for 3D content.

The rest of the image formats have pros and cons, and which one you use depends on your needs.

PNG

PNGs have several things going for them. First of all, they're lossless, which is very important for certain types of texture information like normals. They can also store an alpha channel, which is obviously necessary for transparent textures, but it can also be used to store extra data channels like specular information if transparency is needed. This makes PNGs very versatile and, as such, they tend to be the default choice for many WebGL applications. You can see from Table 21-1, however, that the resulting images can still be fairly large, which is something that needs to be weighed against the technical benefits. If you do find that you need to use PNGs I recommend looking at tools like http://pngcrush.com to reduce their size.

JPEG

JPEG is the defacto image format of the Internet. It is popular because it produces images that are pretty tiny compared to the other formats. That small footprint comes at the cost of precision, however, since JPEG is a lossy format. As such, it tends to work well for photo-like images (such as our sample textures), but it can make a mess of textures that require more precision, such as normal maps. JPEG also lacks an alpha channel, which makes it inappropriate for anything that needs transparency. Still, if your texture can deal with the format restrictions, JPEG is clearly the winner on the file size front.

WEBP

WebP is the most interesting file format you probably can't use. On paper, it looks like the perfect format: it supports both lossless and lossy compression, alpha channels, and typically provides better compression than even the mighty JPEG! The singular downside is browser support: as of this writing, only Chrome and Opera support the format. (Firefox has expressed interest in the format, but it does not support it at this time.) Depending on your target audience, however, this may still be a viable option. If you are building a Chrome App, for example (https://developer.chrome.com/apps/), WebP would easily be the best format to use. You can find out more about this up-and-coming format at http://webp.org.

For the gallery application, you don't need transparency and you're not concerned about artifacts caused by lossy compression. Thus you'll use JPEGs as your default to take advantage of the small file size.

Memory Use

If the only thing that you had to worry about was bandwidth, the choice would be easy. You would go with PNG for lossless or transparent textures, JPEG when you can afford to be lossy, or WEBP if your projects scope allows it. Done! As mentioned earlier, however, bandwidth only covers half of the optimization story. The other half is how much memory the image takes up in video memory.

The problem is that your GPU doesn't know how to decode a JPEG. Nor should it! Decoding an image format like a JPEG is relatively slow, and your rendering speed would plummet if your GPU had to parse every frame of the file. As a result, when you use any of the native browser image formats as the source of a WebGL texture, they are uploaded to GPU memory fully decoded and uncompressed. This means that while your 1024×1024 JPEG may only take up 250KB on your disk, it expands to a whopping 3MB in your GPU's memory! (1024 * 1024 * 24 bits-per-pixel = 3MB) In other words, no matter what image format you use, when it reaches your video card, every image is the size of a BMP. At those sizes, you can fill up your video memory pretty quickly.

There's also a secondary problem related to the large image size: the image can take a long time to upload. The exact time varies by browser and hardware, but on my reasonably beefy 15" Retina MacBook uploading a 1024×1024 JPEG to the GPU via texImage2D using Chrome usually takes somewhere between 11 and 18ms, during which time the rest of the JavaScript is blocked. You can see this for yourself by running the gallery application and opening up the browser's JavaScript console. For the purposes of this demonstration, each texture upload is timed and output to the development console, so you should see output like this:

```
pload Texture: 16.233ms webgl-util.js:54
pload Texture: 17.495ms webgl-util.js:54
pload Texture: 14.923ms webgl-util.js:54
pload Texture: 11.640ms webgl-util.js:54
pload Texture: 11.645ms webgl-util.js:54
pload Texture: 14.235ms webgl-util.js:54
pload Texture: 15.599ms webgl-util.js:54
pload Texture: 11.946ms webgl-util.js:54
```

This is problematic for real-time 3D applications, which typically strive to render at 60 frames per second. This means that each frame must complete within about 16ms. If a single texture takes 18ms to upload, it means that you've completely missed one frame update and have eaten into the next one just to put one texture on your graphics card! Even an upload time of 11 or 12ms is bad, however, because it only leave 4ms to 5ms to render the rest of your scene. That's plenty for a simple scene like our gallery, but it's not nearly enough for even moderately complex 3D scenes.

Compressed Textures

The solution is to use *compressed textures*, a staple of 3D games for many years. Unlike compressed image formats like JPEG or PNG, which examine the entire file and then compress based on large features and common patterns, compressed textures use fixed-rate compression schemes that operate on small blocks of pixels. The GPU is optimized to decompress those blocks on the fly during rendering. This allows the texture to remain compressed in memory, taking up a fraction of the memory that it otherwise would have. The compression is lossy, which typically makes compressed textures inappropriate for data textures like normal maps, but they usually work well for diffuse information (much like JPEGs).

There are multiple compressed texture formats, each with different compression characteristics and hardware support. One of the most common ones is S3 Texture Compression (S3TC), which is more commonly known as DXT due to its inclusion in Direct X from version 6 forward. At this point, DXT compressed textures are supported by almost any PC you can purchase, and are also available on many mobile devices.

Using compressed textures on phones or tablets is still somewhat tricky because each device tends to have a preferred compression format that is usually owned by the device's GPU manufacturer. For example, all iOS devices support Imagination's PVRTC format, but none of them support DXT. Since iOS devices don't support WebGL as of this writing, however, and DXT is one of the more common formats, we'll focus on it for the purposes of this article. Just be aware that if you're targeting mobile, you'll first need to check for support and have fallback textures encoded in a different format to ensure that your app runs correctly.

There are five DXT variants, each with different properties, of which WebGL supports three via the WEBGL_compressed_texture_s3tc extension (`http://www.khronos.org/registry/webgl/extensions/WEBGL_compressed_texture_s3tc`):

- *DXT1* is the smallest variant, sporting a 6:1 compression ratio. (For every 6 bytes of uncompressed data, DXT1 only requires 1 byte.) That shrinks your 1024×1024 images from 3MB to 512KB! The downside is that DXT1 doesn't support alpha channels but, depending on the texture, that may or may not be a problem.

- *DXT3* has a compression ratio of 4:1, and it supports 4 bits of alpha data per pixel. This makes DXT3 best suited for images that have sharp alpha transitions.

- *DXT5* also has a 4:1 compression ratio, but it handles smooth alpha transitions better than DXT3.

Loading DDS Files

DXT compressed textures are often read from DDS files, which is a container format developed by Microsoft. The format is fairly simple and well documented, consisting of little more than a header followed by the texture data. Because the browser doesn't support it natively, however, it requires you to parse the file manually in JavaScript. Fortunately this isn't very difficult! Let's walk through building a simple DDS parser library. There's a fair bit of code involved, but taken piece by piece there's nothing too complicated here. I'll refer to this library as dxt_util.js. You can find the completed version in the source code for this chapter.

First off, you'll need to define some utility functions, so look at Listing 21-1.

Listing 21-1. DDS Parsing Utility Functions

```
// Builds a numeric code for a given fourCC string
function fourCCToInt32(value) {
  return value.charCodeAt(0) +
    (value.charCodeAt(1) << 8) +
    (value.charCodeAt(2) << 16) +
    (value.charCodeAt(3) << 24);
}


// Turns a fourCC numeric code into a string
function int32ToFourCC(value) {
  return String.fromCharCode(
    value & 0xff,
    (value >> 8) & 0xff,
    (value >> 16) & 0xff,
    (value >> 24) & 0xff
  );
}


// Calcualates the size of a DXT texture level in bytes
function dxtLevelSize(width, height, bytesPerBlock) {
  return ((width + 3) >> 2) * ((height + 3) >> 2) * bytesPerBlock;
}
```

Now let's define some constants, as shown in Listing 21-2.

Listing 21-2. DDS Constants

```
// DXT formats, from:
// http://www.khronos.org/registry/webgl/extensions/WEBGL_compressed_texture_s3tc/
var COMPRESSED_RGB_S3TC_DXT1_EXT  = 0x83F0;
var COMPRESSED_RGBA_S3TC_DXT1_EXT = 0x83F1;
var COMPRESSED_RGBA_S3TC_DXT3_EXT = 0x83F2;
var COMPRESSED_RGBA_S3TC_DXT5_EXT = 0x83F3;

// DXT values and structures referenced from:
// http://msdn.microsoft.com/en-us/library/bb943991.aspx/
var DDS_MAGIC = 0x20534444;
var DDSD_MIPMAPCOUNT = 0x20000;
var DDPF_FOURCC = 0x4;

var DDS_HEADER_LENGTH = 31; // The header length in 32bit ints.

// Offsets into the header array.
var DDS_HEADER_MAGIC = 0;

var DDS_HEADER_SIZE = 1;
var DDS_HEADER_FLAGS = 2;
var DDS_HEADER_HEIGHT = 3;
var DDS_HEADER_WIDTH = 4;

var DDS_HEADER_MIPMAPCOUNT = 7;
```

```
var DDS_HEADER_PF_FLAGS = 20;
var DDS_HEADER_PF_FOURCC = 21;

// FourCC format identifiers.
var FOURCC_DXT1 = fourCCToInt32("DXT1");
var FOURCC_DXT3 = fourCCToInt32("DXT3");
var FOURCC_DXT5 = fourCCToInt32("DXT5");
```

Next, you'll add the function that actually parses the DDS file and extracts the necessary information from it. This function will take an array buffer containing the file contents (which I'll cover how to get in a moment) and two callbacks, one which is called when the file is parsed correctly and one that's called in the case of an error. The parsed callback will accept six arguments: the raw DXT texture data as a TypedArray, the width and height of the highest texture level, the number of levels the DXT data contains, the internal format of the data (one of the COMPRESSED_* codes defined in Listing 21-2), and finally, the number of bytes per block for this format, to make size calculations easier. If that sounds like a lot of information, don't stress! The DDS file provides all of that information for you!

Listing 21-3. Parsing a DDS File

```
// Parse a DDS file and provide information about the raw DXT data it contains to the given
callback.
function parseDDS(arrayBuffer, callback, errorCallback) {
  // Callbacks must be provided.
  if (!callback || !errorCallback) { return; }

  // Get a view of the arrayBuffer that represents the DDS header.
  var header = new Int32Array(arrayBuffer, 0, DDS_HEADER_LENGTH);

  // Do some sanity checks to make sure this is a valid DDS file.
  if(header[DDS_HEADER_MAGIC] != DDS_MAGIC) {
    errorCallback("Invalid magic number in DDS header");
    return 0;
  }

  if(!header[DDS_HEADER_PF_FLAGS] & DDPF_FOURCC) {
    errorCallback("Unsupported format, must contain a FourCC code");
    return 0;
  }

  // Determine what type of compressed data the file contains.
  var fourCC = header[DDS_HEADER_PF_FOURCC];
  var bytesPerBlock, internalFormat;
  switch(fourCC) {
    case FOURCC_DXT1:
      bytesPerBlock = 8;
      internalFormat = COMPRESSED_RGB_S3TC_DXT1_EXT;
      break;

    case FOURCC_DXT3:
      bytesPerBlock = 16;
      internalFormat = COMPRESSED_RGBA_S3TC_DXT3_EXT;
      break;
```

```
      case FOURCC_DXT5:
        bytesPerBlock = 16;
        internalFormat = COMPRESSED_RGBA_S3TC_DXT5_EXT;
        break;

      default:
        errorCallback("Unsupported FourCC code: " + int32ToFourCC(fourCC));
        return;
  }

  // Determine how many mipmap levels the file contains.
  var levels = 1;
  if(header[DDS_HEADER_FLAGS] & DDSD_MIPMAPCOUNT) {
    levels = Math.max(1, header[DDS_HEADER_MIPMAPCOUNT]);
  }

  // Gather other basic metrics and a view of the raw the DXT data.
  var width = header[DDS_HEADER_WIDTH];
  var height = header[DDS_HEADER_HEIGHT];
  var dataOffset = header[DDS_HEADER_SIZE] + 4;
  var dxtData = new Uint8Array(arrayBuffer, dataOffset);

  // Pass the DXT information to the callback for uploading.
  callback(dxtData, width, height, levels, internalFormat, bytesPerBlock);
}
```

Now that you have a function to read data out of a DXT file, let's work on actually allowing users to load one. To make the process as user-friendly as possible, you'll define a class called DXTLoader that provides the interface for loading these textures. In order to use DXT textures, you have to first query for the WEBGL_compressed_texture_s3tc extension. You do that in the loader classes constructor, and users can check to make sure the extension is supported by calling the supportsDXT method on the class instance (see Listing 21-4).

Listing 21-4. DXTLoader Constructor and SupportsType Method

```
// This class is our public interface.
var DXTLoader = function(gl) {
  this.gl = gl;

  // Load the S3TC (DXT) extension, if it's available
  this.ext = null;
  var vendorPrefixes = ["", "WEBKIT_", "MOZ_"];
  for(i in vendorPrefixes) {
    this.ext = gl.getExtension(vendorPrefixes[i] + "WEBGL_compressed_texture_s3tc");
    if (this.ext) { break; }
  }
}


// Check to see if compressed textures are supported by this browser/device.
DXTLoader.prototype.supportsDXT = function() {
  return !!this.ext;
```

Next you'll add a function to take the DXT data provided by parseDDS and upload it to the GPU, as shown in Listing 21-5.

Listing 21-5. _uploadDXT Method

```
// Uploads the compressed DXT data to the GPU.
DXTLoader.prototype._uploadDXT = function(dxtData, width, height, levels, internalFormat,
bytesPerBlock, texture, callback) {
  var gl = this.gl;
  gl.bindTexture(gl.TEXTURE_2D, texture);

  var offset = 0;

  // Loop through each mip level of DXT data provided and upload it to the given texture.
  for (var i = 0; i < levels; ++i) {
    // Determine how big this level of DXT data is in bytes.
    var levelSize = dxtLevelSize(width, height, bytesPerBlock);
    // Get a view of the bytes for this level of DXT data.
    var dxtLevel = new Uint8Array(dxtData.buffer, dxtData.byteOffset + offset, levelSize);
    // Upload!
    gl.compressedTexImage2D(gl.TEXTURE_2D, i, internalFormat, width, height, 0, dxtLevel);
    // The next mip level will be half the height and width of this one.
    width = width >> 1;
    height = height >> 1;
    // Advance the offset into the DXT data past the current mip level's data.
    offset += levelSize;
  }

  // We can't use gl.generateMipmaps with compressed textures, so only use
  // mipmapped filtering if the DXT data contained mip levels.
  if (levels > 1) {
    gl.texParameteri(gl.TEXTURE_2D, gl.TEXTURE_MAG_FILTER, gl.LINEAR);
    gl.texParameteri(gl.TEXTURE_2D, gl.TEXTURE_MIN_FILTER, gl.LINEAR_MIPMAP_NEAREST);
  } else {
    gl.texParameteri(gl.TEXTURE_2D, gl.TEXTURE_MAG_FILTER, gl.LINEAR);
    gl.texParameteri(gl.TEXTURE_2D, gl.TEXTURE_MIN_FILTER, gl.LINEAR);
  }

  // Notify the user that the texture is ready.
  if (callback) { callback(texture, null); }
}
```

In the case that something fails, you don't want to leave the user with an unrenderable texture or a texture with old data in it, so you'll also define a function to clear the texture to a 1x1 opaque black pixel in the case of an error (see Listing 21-6).

Listing 21-6. _clearOnError Method

```
// When an error occurs set the texture to a 1x1 black pixel
// This prevents WebGL errors from attempting to use unrenderable textures
// and clears out stale data if we're re-using a texture.
DXTLoader.prototype._clearOnError = function(error, texture, callback) {
  console.error(error);
```

CHAPTER 21 ■ SAVING BANDWIDTH AND MEMORY WITH WEBGL AND CRUNCH

```
  var gl = this.gl;
  gl.bindTexture(gl.TEXTURE_2D, texture);
  gl.texImage2D(gl.TEXTURE_2D, 0, gl.RGB, 1, 1, 0, gl.RGB, gl.UNSIGNED_BYTE, new Uint8Array([0, 0, 0]));
  gl.texParameteri(gl.TEXTURE_2D, gl.TEXTURE_MAG_FILTER, gl.NEAREST);
  gl.texParameteri(gl.TEXTURE_2D, gl.TEXTURE_MIN_FILTER, gl.NEAREST);

  // Notify the user that an error occurred and the texture is ready.
  if (callback) { callback(texture, error); }
}
```

Finally, tying it all together, you define the function that users of this library will actually call to load a texture: loadDDS. This function queries the texture from the server, parses the returned bytes, and sends the parsed results to either our upload or error functions.

The code to load a DDS file from the server is a relatively simply AJAX request, with the biggest difference being that you request the responseType be an Array Buffer, which makes it faster and easier for you to parse (and is what the parseDDS function already expects), as shown in Listing 21-7.

Listing 21-7. loadDDS Method

```
// Loads a DDS file into the given texture.
// If no texture is provided one is created and returned.
DXTLoader.prototype.loadDDS = function(src, texture, callback) {
  var self = this;
  if(!texture) {
    texture = this.gl.createTexture();
  }

  // Load the file via XHR.
  var xhr = new XMLHttpRequest();
  xhr.addEventListener('load', function (ev) {
    if (xhr.status == 200) {
      // If the file loaded successfully parse it.
      parseDDS(xhr.response, function(dxtData, width, height, levels, internalFormat, bytesPerBlock) {
        // Upload the parsed DXT data to the texture.
        self._uploadDXT(dxtData, width, height, levels, internalFormat, bytesPerBlock, texture,
callback);
      }, function(error) {
        self._clearOnError(error, texture, callback);
      });
    } else {
      self._clearOnError(xhr.statusText, texture, callback);
    }
  }, false);
  xhr.open('GET', src, true);
  xhr.responseType = 'arraybuffer';
  xhr.send(null);

  return texture;
```

This function takes in a source URL (src) and optionally an existing texture handle and a callback that will be called when the texture is finished loading. If not, the existing texture is provided. You create one here and return it as a convenience for the user. The basic code to load a DDS texture then looks like this:

```
var dxtLoader = new DXTLoader(gl);
var dxtTexture = dxtLoader.loadDDS(imageUrl);
```

And that's it! You can now use this compressed texture like you would any other, but it takes up 1/4th to 1/6th the space of the alternative. When all is said and done, the code to load a DDS file into a WebGL texture is about 130 lines, which isn't bad at all. It should be noted, however, that this code only targets DDS files that WebGL can support. Some of the more advanced DDS features, like cubemap support, have been ignored for the sake of simplicity.

To see DDS loading in action, open up the gallery application again and select "DDS" from the format drop-down menu in the upper-left corner. You shouldn't notice any difference in the images being shown but, on the back end, it will begin loading the textures from DDS files rather than JPEGs. Also, if you open the JavaScript console, it will show the amount of time it takes to upload the DXT data using the compressedTexImage2D call. (The time it takes to parse the file should be negligible.) You should notice a stark difference from the upload times for the JPEGs! While the uncompressed image data takes 11ms to 18ms to upload, the compressed data loads in well under a millisecond, usually only taking 0.15ms to 0.2ms with Chrome!

The unfortunate part is that since these formats use fixed rate compression, they are pretty much guaranteed to be noticeably larger than that of their JPEG counterparts. Table 21-2 shows the new compressed sizes of the images shown previously in Table 21-1.

Table 21-2. *Comparison of DDS and JPEG Image File Sizes*

	DDS (DXT1)	JPEG
Slide_10	683 KB	378 KB
Slide_13	683 KB	531 KB
Slide_15	683 KB	303 KB

You can see that, in some cases, the JPEGs are half the size of the DXT files! Compressed formats like DXT are great for saving video memory, but at the cost of extra bandwidth. Luckily for you, however, there's a newer format that provides the best of both worlds!

Crunch

The Crunch texture format (https://code.google.com/p/crunch/) was developed in 2009 by Rich Geldreich. It is essentially another level of compression on top of the fixed-rate DXT compression format. Because of this it yields file sizes that are as good as, and often better than, JPEG! See Table 21-3.

Table 21-3. *Comparison of Crunch (CRN) File Sizes with DDS and JPEG*

	CRN (DXT1)	DDS (DXT1)	JPEG
Slide_10	189 KB	683 KB	378 KB
Slide_13	221 KB	683 KB	531 KB
Slide_15	186 KB	683 KB	303 KB

These three sample images show significantly smaller file sizes than JPEG— something that's true of every image in your gallery application. That's not always the case with every image, and is highly dependent on image content. Nonetheless, you can generally count on CRN files being seriously small. Even better, since you can also store DXT3/5 formats with CRN as well, it allows you to save transparent textures that are almost always far smaller than their PNG counterparts. Unfortunately, since DXT compression is inherently lossy, PNGs are still your best bet if you need lossless textures.

The downloads on the Crunch site provide Windows command-line tools that make it very easy to convert images of various formats into CRN files. (Mac and Linux users can build the compression tools from source.) Converting a JPEG file, for instance, is as easy as the following:

```
crunch.exe /DXT1 -file input_image.jpg
```

This code snippet creates an `input_image.crn` file in the current directory. You can also convert larger sets of image files by using wildcard characters. There are a lot of options to control how the conversion process proceeds, and you can find out more about the various flags available by running `crunch.exe` without any arguments. There's enough flexibility here that the compression process should feel right at home as part of your build process or art pipeline.

Using CRN files in a 3D application is a two-step process. The file is first run through a decompressor, which very quickly transcodes from the Crunch format into a buffer of DXT texture data. This is then uploaded to the GPU as a normal compressed DXT texture. The Crunch source code includes a lightweight C++ header file that handles all of the decompression. Since you're using WebGL, however, you've got to do the transcoding in JavaScript.

The truth be told, it would be entirely possible to write a Crunch decoding routine in JavaScript by hand, but it wouldn't be anywhere near as simple as the DDS reader shown earlier. Not only that, but after writing the initial decoder, you would have to update it manually any time the Crunch C++ library is updated with new features or bug fixes. That's hardly an attractive idea to someone that just wants smaller texture files.

Emscripten

Fortunately, you have Emscripten at your disposal. While the tool has already been covered in Chapter 18, I'll briefly review it again in case you skipped that chapter. Emscripten, written by Alon Zakai, is a C++-to-JavaScript cross-compiler. Within certain limitations, it can take many C++ files or projects and produce JavaScript that can run on most browsers. The resulting script resembles assembly code and isn't typically human readable, but the benefit of not needing to re-code entire projects by hand makes that a small price to pay. Furthermore, Emscripten's outputs conform to the `asm.js` spec, which means that the resulting code can be further optimized by some browsers, such as Firefox, and it can achieve performance that is within 2X of native code.

The self-contained nature of Crunch's decoder (a single `.h` file) makes it very easy to compile with Emscripten. The only additional thing required on your part is a small C++ wrapper to indicate those functions you need to be able to access. Evan Parker, who created a proof-of-concept Crunch loader with Emscripten in 2012, originally did this work, and the code in Listing 21-8 is a minor modification of his original work. This source is also available at `crunch_js/crunch_lib.cpp` in the chapter's source code.

Listing 21-8. Emscripten/Javascript Interface

```
#define PLATFORM_NACL // This disables use of 64 bit integers, among other things.

#include <stddef.h>    // For NULL, size_t
#include <cstring>     // for malloc etc

#include "crn_decomp.h"
```

```
extern "C" {
  unsigned int crn_get_width(void *src, unsigned int src_size);
  unsigned int crn_get_height(void *src, unsigned int src_size);
  unsigned int crn_get_levels(void *src, unsigned int src_size);
  unsigned int crn_get_dxt_format(void *src, unsigned int src_size);
  unsigned int crn_get_bytes_per_block(void *src, unsigned int src_size);
  unsigned int crn_get_uncompressed_size(void *p, unsigned int size, unsigned int level);
  void crn_decompress(void *src, unsigned int src_size, void *dst, unsigned int dst_size,
unsigned int firstLevel, unsigned int levelCount);
}

unsigned int crn_get_width(void *src, unsigned int src_size) {
  crnd::crn_texture_info tex_info;
  crnd::crnd_get_texture_info(static_cast<crn_uint8*>(src), src_size, &tex_info);
  return tex_info.m_width;
}

unsigned int crn_get_height(void *src, unsigned int src_size) {
  crnd::crn_texture_info tex_info;
  crnd::crnd_get_texture_info(static_cast<crn_uint8*>(src), src_size, &tex_info);
  return tex_info.m_height;
}

unsigned int crn_get_levels(void *src, unsigned int src_size) {
  crnd::crn_texture_info tex_info;
  crnd::crnd_get_texture_info(static_cast<crn_uint8*>(src), src_size, &tex_info);
  return tex_info.m_levels;
}

unsigned int crn_get_dxt_format(void *src, unsigned int src_size) {
  crnd::crn_texture_info tex_info;
  crnd::crnd_get_texture_info(static_cast<crn_uint8*>(src), src_size, &tex_info);
  return tex_info.m_format;
}

unsigned int crn_get_bytes_per_block(void *src, unsigned int src_size) {
  crnd::crn_texture_info tex_info;
  crnd::crnd_get_texture_info(static_cast<crn_uint8*>(src), src_size, &tex_info);
  return crnd::crnd_get_bytes_per_dxt_block(tex_info.m_format);
}

unsigned int crn_get_uncompressed_size(void *src, unsigned int src_size, unsigned int level) {
  crnd::crn_texture_info tex_info;
  crnd::crnd_get_texture_info(static_cast<crn_uint8*>(src), src_size, &tex_info);
  const crn_uint32 width = tex_info.m_width >> level;
  const crn_uint32 height = tex_info.m_height >> level;
  const crn_uint32 blocks_x = (width + 3) >> 2;
  const crn_uint32 blocks_y = (height + 3) >> 2;
  const crn_uint32 row_pitch = blocks_x * crnd::crnd_get_bytes_per_dxt_block(tex_info.m_format);
  const crn_uint32 total_face_size = row_pitch * blocks_y;
  return total_face_size;
}
```

```cpp
void crn_decompress(void *src, unsigned int src_size, void *dst, unsigned int dst_size, unsigned int
firstLevel, unsigned int levelCount) {
  crnd::crn_texture_info tex_info;
  crnd::crnd_get_texture_info(static_cast<crn_uint8*>(src), src_size, &tex_info);

  crn_uint32 width = tex_info.m_width >> firstLevel;
  crn_uint32 height = tex_info.m_height >> firstLevel;
  crn_uint32 bytes_per_block = crnd::crnd_get_bytes_per_dxt_block(tex_info.m_format);

  void *pDecomp_images[1];
  pDecomp_images[0] = dst;

  crnd::crnd_unpack_context pContext =
      crnd::crnd_unpack_begin(static_cast<crn_uint8*>(src), src_size);

  for (int i = firstLevel; i < firstLevel + levelCount; ++i) {
    crn_uint32 blocks_x = (width + 3) >> 2;
    crn_uint32 blocks_y = (height + 3) >> 2;
    crn_uint32 row_pitch = blocks_x * bytes_per_block;
    crn_uint32 total_level_size = row_pitch * blocks_y;

    crnd::crnd_unpack_level(pContext, pDecomp_images, total_level_size, row_pitch, i);
    pDecomp_images[0] = (char*)pDecomp_images[0] + total_level_size;

    width = width >> 1;
    height = height >> 1;
  }

  crnd::crnd_unpack_end(pContext);
}
```

If you're primarily a JavaScript developer, this C++ code can look pretty dense and difficult to read, but it's mostly fairly mechanical data transformation to ensure that you have entry points that JavaScript can communicate with once the library has been compiled with Emscripten. Don't worry if it doesn't make much sense to you, just use the crunch_lib.cpp file provided with the book source. What you're really concerned about is getting the compiled JavaScript code.

To compile this shim using Emscripten, you'll first need to install the Emscripten SDK (https://developer. mozilla.org/en-US/docs/Emscripten/Download_and_install) and the Crunch source code (https://code. google.com/p/crunch/), then copy the crunch_js folder from this chapter's source into the Crunch source folder. Finally, open the crunch_js folder and run the command line shown in Listing 21-9.

Listing 21-9. Emscripten Compile Command Line

```
emcc -O3 crunch_lib.cpp -I../inc -s EXPORTED_FUNCTIONS="['_malloc', '_free', '_crn_get_width', '_
crn_get_height', '_crn_get_levels', '_crn_get_dxt_format', '_crn_get_bytes_per_block',
'_crn_get_uncompressed_size', '_crn_decompress']" -o crunch_lib.js
```

This will output a file called crunch_lib.js, which contains the JavaScript result of the compile. Don't bother trying to read it; it's been optimized using the closure compiler into a blob of characters that's not at all human readable. (If you want a slightly less obfuscated version, remove the -O3 flag.) Don't worry, though, all you need to know is that the functions that were listed in the EXPORTED_FUNCTIONS array can now be called on the Module object when you load that code file.

Now let's go back to the DXTLoader library you were working on earlier and add Crunch support! You'll need to load the contents of the newly built crunch_lib.js somehow. You can do this by including the file in your HTML headers like any normal JavaScript, but you can make life a little easier for users of your library by embedding it in the file itself.

At the top of the dxt_utils.js file add a function named LoadCrunchDecoder which returns a variable named Module, like so:

```
function LoadCrunchDecoder() {
  // Emscripten compiled code goes here.
  return Module;
}
```

Then copy the entire contents of crunch_lib.js into this function. You're putting it inside a function for two reasons. One is that it prevents any variables that Emscripten may create from accidentally polluting the global scope and two is so that you can decide when you want to initialize the crunch reader, which will come in handy in just a moment.

Next, just like with the DDS loading code you'll need a few constants defined to assist in the Crunch loading. Add the code in Listing 21-10, just below the DDS constants you defined earlier.

Listing 21-10. Crunch Constants

```
// Taken from crnlib.h
var CRN_FORMAT = {
  cCRNFmtInvalid: -1,

  cCRNFmtDXT1: 0,
  // cCRNFmtDXT3 is not currently supported when writing to CRN - only DDS.
  cCRNFmtDXT3: 1,
  cCRNFmtDXT5: 2

  // Crunch supports more formats than this, but we can't use them here.
};

// Mapping of Crunch formats to DXT formats.
var DXT_FORMAT_MAP = {};
DXT_FORMAT_MAP[CRN_FORMAT.cCRNFmtDXT1] = COMPRESSED_RGB_S3TC_DXT1_EXT;
DXT_FORMAT_MAP[CRN_FORMAT.cCRNFmtDXT3] = COMPRESSED_RGBA_S3TC_DXT3_EXT;
DXT_FORMAT_MAP[CRN_FORMAT.cCRNFmtDXT5] = COMPRESSED_RGBA_S3TC_DXT5_EXT;
```

Next, you're going to add the code that calls into the Emscripten-compiled code to decode a Crunch file. This is probably the most complicated part of the entire library, so get ready! First off, in order to decompress the crunch files you will need a buffer of data to decode the DXT information into. That can be somewhat large and a bit expensive to create, so you only want to do it once if you can help it. Similarly, you want to be able to load the Emscripten modules only once and only when needed. In order to accomplish this, you're going to use some functional scoping tricks to create some "private" variables, as shown in Listing 21-11.

Listing 21-11. decompressCRN function, Part 1

```
// Parse a crunch file and decompress the contained texture into raw DXT data, which is then passed
to the callback.
var decompressCRN = (function() {
  // Variables which are cached between calls to the function, hidden here with some function
scoping tricks.
```

```
  var dst = null;
  var dxtData = null;
  var cachedDstSize = 0;

  // The emscripten module.
  var Module = null;

  // Copy an array of bytes into or out of the emscripten heap.
  function arrayBufferCopy(src, dst, dstByteOffset, numBytes) {
    var i;
    var dst32Offset = dstByteOffset / 4;
    var tail = (numBytes % 4);
    var src32 = new Uint32Array(src.buffer, 0, (numBytes - tail) / 4);
    var dst32 = new Uint32Array(dst.buffer);
    for (i = 0; i < src32.length; i++) {
      dst32[dst32Offset + i] = src32[i];
    }
    for (i = numBytes - tail; i < numBytes; i++) {
      dst[dstByteOffset + i] = src[i];
    }
  }

  return // Decompression function (we'll fill this in in a moment.)
})();
```

What's happening here is that you're creating an anonymous function (and with it a new variable scope), creating your "private" variables and a utility function within that scope, and returning the actual decompression function. You then immediately call the anonymous function and assign its return value to decompressCRN, which will be what you call to decompress the texture.

The actual decompression function looks like the code in Listing 21-12. (It gets inserted at the return statement in the code from Listing 21-11.)

Listing 21-12. decompressCRN function, Part 2

```
// This is the actual function that is executed when you call decompressCRN.
return function(arrayBuffer, callback, errorCallback) {
  // Callbacks must be provided.
  if (!callback || !errorCallback) { return; }

  // If the emscripten module has not been loaded yet do so now.
  // Executes the massive code blob at the top of the file.
  if (!Module) {
    Module = LoadCrunchDecoder();
  }

  // Copy the contents of the arrayBuffer into emscriptens heap.
  var srcSize = arrayBuffer.byteLength;
  var bytes = new Uint8Array(arrayBuffer);
  var src = Module._malloc(srcSize);
  arrayBufferCopy(bytes, Module.HEAPU8, src, srcSize);
```

```
// Determine what type of compressed data the file contains.
var format = Module._crn_get_dxt_format(src, srcSize);
if (!DXT_FORMAT_MAP[format]) {
  errorCallback("Unsupported image format");
  return;
}

// Gather basic metrics about the DXT data.
var levels = Module._crn_get_levels(src, srcSize);
var width = Module._crn_get_width(src, srcSize);
var height = Module._crn_get_height(src, srcSize);
var bytesPerBlock = Module._crn_get_bytes_per_block(src, srcSize);

// Determine the size of the decoded DXT data.
var dstSize = 0;
var i;
for (i = 0; i < levels; ++i) {
  dstSize += dxtLevelSize(width >> i, height >> i, bytesPerBlock);
}

// Allocate enough space on the emscripten heap to hold the decoded DXT data
// or reuse the existing allocation if a previous call to this function has
// already acquired a large enough buffer.
if(cachedDstSize < dstSize) {
  if(dst) { Module._free(dst); }
  dst = Module._malloc(dstSize);
  dxtData = new Uint8Array(Module.HEAPU8.buffer, dst, dstSize);
  cachedDstSize = dstSize;
}

// Decompress the DXT data from the Crunch file into the allocated space.
Module._crn_decompress(src, srcSize, dst, dstSize, 0, levels);

// Release the crunch file data from the emscripten heap.
Module._free(src);

// Pass the DXT information to the callback for uploading.
callback(dxtData, width, height, levels, DXT_FORMAT_MAP[format], bytesPerBlock);
};
```

Here's what's happening. First off, if this is the first time you're calling this function, you load the Emscripten module by calling LoadCrunchDecoder. That way none of that potentially expensive code is executed at all unless you actually need it. (See, I told you that putting it in a function would come in handy!)

Next, you copy the bytes of the Crunch data you've been given into Emscripten's virtual "heap." In Emscripten compiled code, the C++ heap is represented by a large, pre-allocated TypedArray, which is accessed with Module.HEAPU8 in the code in Listing 21-12. (As the name suggests, this is a Uint8Array view of the heap buffer.) Under this setup, memory allocations are simply reserved ranges of the array and pointers are integer offsets into the array (which is pretty close to how native memory management works anyway). This means that anytime you want Emscripten to operate on any data, you have to copy it into that heap manually. You're using a simple helper function here (arrayBufferCopy) to handle the copy.

Once the data has been copied into the heap, you use a "pointer" to it (an integer offset into the heap typed array) to call several functions to query information about the DXT data the Crunch file contains, such as the width and height, number of mip levels, etc. Once you have all that, you calculate how large the decompressed DXT will be. You use this to "malloc" the appropriate amount of space on the Emscripten heap to receive the decoded data.

Finally, you get to call the all-important _crn_decompress function, which does all the heavy lifting of decompressing the bytes of the Crunch file into the plain old DXT information the GPU needs! Once that's done, you free up the memory that you allocated to copy the Crunch data into and then call the provided callback, giving it the newly decoded DXT data and all the necessary numbers to go with it. Note that you didn't actually need to copy the decoded data out of the Emscripten heap, but instead you just created a view of the heap data at the appropriate offset and size. This is because the Emscripten heap is already a TypedArray, which is what compressedTexImage2D requires anyway. As such, as long as you don't allow anything to overwrite the Emscripten data before you've uploaded the texture, you can simply give compressedTexImage2D the view. Less copying equals faster code, so this is definitely a win!

So now that you can decode the Crunch data, let's tie it all together by adding another method to the DXTLoader class (see Listing 21-13).

Listing 21-13. loadCRN Method

```
// Loads a CRN (Crunch) file into the given texture.
// If no texture is provided one is created and returned.
DXTLoader.prototype.loadCRN = function(src, texture, callback) {
  var self = this;
  if(!texture) {
    texture = this.gl.createTexture();
  }

  // Load the file via XHR.
  var xhr = new XMLHttpRequest();
  xhr.addEventListener('load', function (ev) {
    if (xhr.status == 200) {
      // If the file loaded successfully parse and decompress it.
      decompressCRN(xhr.response, function(dxtData, width, height, levels, internalFormat,
bytesPerBlock) {
        // Upload the parsed and decompressed DXT data to the texture.
        self._uploadDXT(dxtData, width, height, levels, internalFormat, bytesPerBlock, texture,
callback);
      }, function(error) {
        self._clearOnError(error, texture, callback);
      });
    } else {
      self._clearOnError(xhr.statusText, texture, callback);
    }
  }, false);
  xhr.open('GET', src, true);
  xhr.responseType = 'arraybuffer';
  xhr.send(null);

  return texture;
```

This is practically identical to the loadDDS function, so there's not much to say about it. The only real difference is that you're calling decompressCRN on the xhr.response instead of parseDDS!

So now you can load, decompress, and upload a Crunch texture! Let's see how well it works. First, open up the gallery application again, and select "CRN" from the format select. This will start loading images from Crunch compressed files rather than JPEGs. As with the other formats, you output the time spent uploading to the console, and you should see that the upload times match the DDS files closely (after all, it's almost the same data.) You're also logging the amount of time spent decompressing the file from the Crunch format to the DXT data, and unfortunately that number isn't as pretty. On my machine, decompressing typically takes 8ms to 13ms for each 1024×1024 texture. That puts us back in the same timeframe as uploading the JPEG, and it is a big step back from the parsing and upload times of the DDS files. Nevertheless, there's one crucial difference: since the majority of the time is now spent in JavaScript that's not interacting with WebGL, you can move much of the processing into a Web Worker.

Workers

Web Workers are a limited form of parallel processing for JavaScript, similar to using multiple threads but with more safety mechanisms built in. The biggest limitation of workers is that they have no DOM access, nor can they access anything derived from the DOM. This means that no WebGL interaction can occur within a worker. The best you can do is to process everything into a form where it's ready to be passed directly into WebGL when it's passed back to the main thread.

Getting the code to use Web Workers isn't as difficult as you may think. The first step is to move the Crunch constants, the LoadCrunchDecoder function, and the decompressCRN function into a new file, which you'll call crunch-worker.js. Then add the code in Listing 21-14 to the bottom of the file.

Listing 21-14. crunch-worker.js Message Handling

```
// Worker message handler
onmessage = function(msg) {
  // Calls to the worker contain a URL to load and the associated pending texture ID.
  var src = msg.data.src;
  var id = msg.data.id;

  // Notifies the main thread that DXT data is ready.
  function uploadCallback(dxtData, width, height, levels, internalFormat, bytesPerBlock) {
    postMessage({
      id: id,
      dxtData: dxtData,
      width: width,
      height: height,
      levels: levels,
      internalFormat: internalFormat,
      bytesPerBlock: bytesPerBlock
    });
  }

  // Notifies the main thread that an error has occured.
  function errorCallback(error) {
    postMessage({
      id: id,
      error: error
    });
  }
```

```
// Load the file via XHR
var xhr = new XMLHttpRequest();
xhr.addEventListener('load', function (ev) {
  if (xhr.status == 200) {
    // If the file loaded successfully parse and decompress it.
    decompressCRN(xhr.response, uploadCallback, errorCallback);
  } else {
    errorCallback(xhr.statusText);
  }
}, false);
xhr.open('GET', "../" + src, true);
xhr.responseType = 'arraybuffer';
xhr.send(null);
};
```

To communicate with the worker "thread," you will send it messages, which is this case will be a simple JSON object containing a URL to load and a unique ID to identify which texture is being loaded. onmessage is the function that will handle those messages as you send them. You may notice that the code shown here is very similar to that of the previously defined loadCRN function. In fact, it is mostly the same—the big difference being that once the decompression is complete, or if an error occurs, you call postMessage with the results rather than making any WebGL calls. This is because workers cannot access any part of the DOM, and since WebGL is tightly bound to the canvas tag it means WebGL cannot be used in a worker either. Instead you need to pass the decompressed data back to the main script, which is what postMessage does.

That's it for the worker file, so now let's go back to dxt-util.js to add the code to create the worker and communicate with it. First off, since the texture decompression will now be asynchronous and handled in a different thread, you need a way to track textures between the time you request it be loaded and the time the worker sends it back. For this purpose you'll define a very simple CrunchPendingTexture class, as shown in Listing 21-15.

Listing 21-15. CrunchPendingTexture Class

```
var nextPendingTextureId = 0;
var CrunchPendingTexture = function(texture, callback) {
  this.id = nextPendingTextureId++;
  this.texture = texture;
  this.callback = callback;
```

As you can see, each CrunchPendingTexture is given a unique ID which will be passed to the worker and back, and holds the texture that is being loaded and the callback the library user specified should be called when the loading was completed.

Next, you'll update the DXTLoader constructor function, as shown in Listing 21-16.

Listing 21-16. Worker-enabled DXTLoader Constructor

```
var DXTLoader = function(gl) {
  this.gl = gl;

  // Load the S3TC extension, if it's available
  this.ext = null;
  var vendorPrefixes = ["", "WEBKIT_", "MOZ_"];
  for(i in vendorPrefixes) {
```

```
  this.ext = gl.getExtension(vendorPrefixes[i] + "WEBGL_compressed_texture_s3tc");
  if (this.ext) { break; }
}

// When using a worker process we must keep track of the pending texture
// loads so that we can correctly correlate the DXT data to the desired
// texture when the worker completes.
this.pendingTextures = {};

// Reload this file as a worker.
this.worker = new Worker("crunch-worker.js");

var self = this;
// The worker's message handler.
this.worker.onmessage = function(msg) {
  // Find the pending texture associated with the data we just received
  // from the worker.
  var id = msg.data.id;
  var pt = self.pendingTextures[id];
  if (!pt) { return; }

  // Remove the pending texture from the waiting list.
  delete self.pendingTextures[id];

  // If the worker indicated an error has occured handle it now.
  if (msg.data.error) {
    self._clearOnError(msg.data.error, pt.texture, pt.callback);
    return;
  }

  // Upload the DXT data returned by the worker.
  self._uploadDXT(
      new Uint8Array(msg.data.dxtData),
      msg.data.width,
      msg.data.height,
      msg.data.levels,
      msg.data.internalFormat,
      msg.data.bytesPerBlock,
      pt.texture,
      pt.callback);
  };
}
```

The first few line have stayed the same, but the remainder is the other half of the worker communication. First, you define a dictionary to store pending textures in, then you create the worker object, giving it the name of the script to load. Then you define the worker's onmessage handler, which is what gets called any time the worker calls postMessage. The code it contains is pretty simple: look up which texture was loaded with the ID that was passed back and then either call _clearOnError if the worker gave you an error message or _uploadDXT if you got back valid data.

Finally, you need to replace the logic of loadCRN. This function actually gets significantly simpler now that the AJAX request and decode is being handled in the worker. Instead all the new loadCRN needs to do is track a new CrunchPendingTexture and send the message to the worker to begin loading the Crunch file (see Listing 21-17).

Listing 21-17. Worker-enabled loadCRN Method

```
DXTLoader.prototype.loadCRN = function(src, texture, callback) {
  if(!texture) {
    texture = this.gl.createTexture();
  }

  // If we're using a worker to handle the decoding create a pending texture
  // and put it on the waiting list.
  var pending = new CrunchPendingTexture(texture, callback);
  this.pendingTextures[pending.id] = pending;
  // Then tell the worker to load the CRN file.
  this.worker.postMessage({id: pending.id, src: src});

  return texture;
}
```

And just like that, you've worker-ized your loading! Now all the heavy-duty decompression happens in the worker while the WebGL calls remain on the main thread where they belong.

To see this in action, open up the gallery application once more, select the "CRN" format, and then choose "Decompress in a Worker" from the new select that appears. The decompression times will no longer appear in the console, but they should be roughly the same as what you were seeing earlier when the decompression was taking place in the main thread. The difference now is that the decompression can happen in parallel to the main thread, which only needs to handle the quick upload.

Now you are able to load your tiny crunched textures, decompress them asynchronously, and upload them to the GPU as compressed DXTs. You've achieved your goal of minimizing bandwidth and video memory, not blocking your rendering pipeline as much, and used some cool new web technologies to do it! Hooray!

This approach isn't without a downside, however. In order to send the decoded DXT data over the worker thread, the data must be copied. This creates "trash" for the garbage collector to clean up, and it can lead to longer or more frequent garbage collects. Typically, you could avoid this copy by using a Transferable Object, which allows you to give ownership of an object like an `ArrayBuffer` over to another worker or to the main thread without copying. That's not an option in your case, however, because you can only transfer buffers, not views. To do that would require you to transfer the entire Emscripten "heap" to the main thread and back again. That's not only overkill but it would also prevent other Crunch textures from being decoded until you returned the buffer to the worker. In the end, the copy and subsequent garbage collection is an unfortunate but necessary side effect of using Emscripten.

Notes on dxt-util.js

The version of dxt-util.js that is included with the source code for this chapter performs all of the same logic that you walked through, but has a couple of differences that make it easier to use as a drop-in library for any project. First off, the library puts everything in a DXTUtil "namespace," which lessens the chance of collisions with other libraries and protects the variables you declare within that scope from outside modification, which is a fairly common and prudent thing for JavaScript libraries to do. This means that you actually create an instance of the loader class by calling

```
var loader = new DXTUtil.Loader(gl, true);
```

The second argument given there is a Boolean to indicate whether or not Crunch files should be decoded in a Worker. Given the benefits described in this chapter, most of the time you'll want this set to true, but it's convenient for demonstrations like the Gallery app to be able to toggle it off and on.

Another convenience is that there's no separate worker file. The worker logic has been packaged into `dxt-util.js` itself and the file loads itself again as the worker script. This means you only have one file to deploy. The code is distributed under a BSD license, so feel free to use it in any project you wish!

Conclusion

WebGL applications must be sensitive to both download times and GPU memory use, metrics that often conflict with one another. By using Crunch you can create texture files as small or smaller than the equivalent JPEGs while also using a fraction of the video memory. Emscripten allows you to make use of the existing C++ decoding library without needing to rewrite it by hand in JavaScript, which reduces both development time and maintenance. Finally, by performing the texture decode in a Web Worker, you can avoid blocking the main thread for everything but the texture upload, which is far faster than uploading an uncompressed image of the same size.

CHAPTER 22

■ ■ ■

Creating a Two-Dimensional Map Editor

Ivan Popelyshev, Game Developer, bombermine.com

This chapter expands on the techniques covered in Chapter 6. You will get the most from this chapter if you have worked through that one first.

To address issues with your map and layer format, you must first approach the problem from an asset-creation standpoint. In this chapter, I will introduce you to the basics of creating a map editor, using the *autotiles* feature6.

The basic features of a graphic editor are

1. zoom, scroll

2. save/load image

3. palette

4. brush

The graphics editor allows you to compare the appearance of a map with and without autotiling. The graphics editor can be used in production for editing maps created by users, and you can create a game based on its architecture

Figure 22-1 shows how the map editor will look at the end of this chapter. Figure 22-2 shows how it will look after running the final application code in Chapter 6.

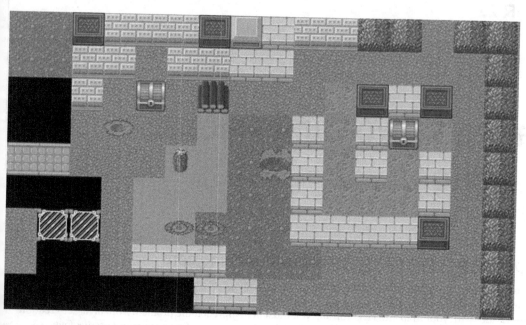

Figure 22-1. *Autotiles off*

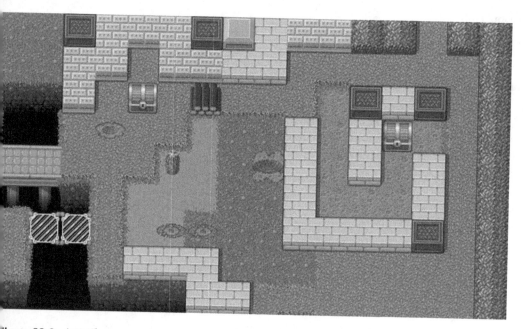

Figure 22-2. *Autotiles on*

List of Tiles

Different tiles can exhibit different behaviors and render differently in the game, and you need one class for each tile type. A basic implementation has only a constructor and no custom methods for rendering or behavior. Each tile can be found either by name or by ID. Tile.id is an autogenerated, 0-based integer that will be used in map serialization. Specific types of tiles are described in Chapter 6.

You will use the extendTile function to implement inheritance, as is the case in object-oriented programming. This function will help you spawn different types of tiles, and each can have a specific rendering algorithm or logic to determine which sprite you need to draw:

```
function extendTile(Type, obj) {
        var newClass = function Tile(name, obj) {
                this.name = name;
                if (obj) for (var key in obj)
                        if (obj.hasOwnProperty(key))
                                this[key] = obj[key];
        }
        var proto = new Type();
        for (var key in obj)
                if (obj.hasOwnProperty(key))
                        proto[key] = obj[key];
        newClass.prototype = proto;
        return newClass;
}
```

Now, you use extendTile to generate basic tiles. This example is for a dual-layered structure made up of SurfaceTile and ObjectTile; object tiles are placed on top of the surface tiles:

```
var Tile = extendTile(function() {}, {})
var SurfaceTile = extendTile(Tile, {type: 0, layer: 0})
var ObjectTile = extendTile(Tile, {type: 1, layer: 1})
```

The TileList is going to be used for tile storage. You can add new tiles, get them by name or JD, and add new properties to already created tiles, using the apply method:

```
var TileList = function() {
        this.byId = []
        this.byName = {}
}

TileList.prototype = {
        defaultSurface : null, defaultObject: null,
        add : function(tile) {
                // if tile exists, dont add it
                if (this.byName[tile.name]) return
                tile.id = this.byId.length;
                this.byId.push(tile);
                return this.byName[tile.name] = tile;
        },
```

```
    get : function(id) { return this.byId[id] || this.byName[id] || null; },
    apply : function(names, obj) {
            for (var i=0;i<names.length;i++) {
                    var t = this.byName[names[i]]
                    for (var key in obj) if (obj.hasOwnProperty(key)) t[key] = obj[key];
            }
    },
    addMany : function(Type, names, obj) {
            for (var i=0;i<names.length;i++)
                    this.add(new Type(names[i], obj))
    }
}}
```

List of Sprites

Let the side of a square tile be $32 = 2^5$ pixels. Before the editor starts, you need to load all necessary sprites; otherwise, the first attempt to paint the window will fail:

```
var TILE_SIZE = 32, TILE_SIZE_BITS = 5;
```

The format of objects added to SpriteList is as follows:

```
function Sprite(name, source, x, y) {
        this.name = name; this.source = source;this.x = x;this.y = y;
}
Sprite.prototype = {}

var SpriteList = function() {
        this.byId = []
        this.byName = {}
```

Later, you will use sprite collections for generating tiles, depending on the tile types, and you will generate the proper sprite names, depending on the type and name of each tile (see the section "Basic Tileset Configuration"). addSpriteSheet makes a list of sprites from a graphic file and a list of sprite names:

```
SpriteList.prototype = {
        loaded: 0, total: 0,
        onComplete: null,
        add: function(sprite) {
                sprite.id = this.byId.length
                this.byId.push(sprite);
                this.byName[sprite.name] = sprite;
        },
```

The next function loads sprite file names and a corresponding two-dimensional array of names; to skip a row, use "". This function is used later, in the default configuration (see the section "Basic Tileset Configuration"). You arrange all the tile images into a number of files. Each file contains a grid with 32 × 32 cells that hold a number of images. For each file with images, you will call that function. The function OnComplete will be called after all images are loaded:

```
addSpriteSheet: function(filename, names) {
        var self = this;
        var img = new Image();
        img.onload = function() {
                self.loaded++;
                if (self.loaded == self.total && self.onComplete) //Are all images loaded?
                        self.onComplete();
        }
        this.total++;
        img.src = filename;
                // Parsing 2-dimension array of names and generating sprites objects
        for (var i=0; i<names.length; i++)
                for (var j=0;j<names[i].length;j++) {
                        var name = names[i][j];
                        if (name != "") {
                                this.add(new Sprite(name, img, j*TILE_SIZE, i*TILE_SIZE));
                        }
                }
        }
}
```

Basic Tileset Configuration

Why bother to creating tiles and sprites separately? Most tile editors use integers to enumerate the tiles and store a maplike array of integers. In real life, however, sad things happen. One moment your artist friend makes you a pretty tileset (see Figure 22-3), and the next, she completely reorders the tiles while adding new ones (see Figure 22-4). This is why you must create a configuration that allows for easy migration. Also, people who make modifications to your game will be grateful if you implement it in this manner.

Figure 22-3. Pretty tileset

Figure 22-4. *Tileset version 2; unexpected changes*

You need a separate object to describe the concrete game configuration—the lists of sprites and tiles and the correspondence between them. Depending on the game, each tile can be rendered in a unique way and can have a unique behavior. Moreover, one game can have a number of configurations, basic and modified. Each configuration has init and afterInit methods. Each modification will add some new way of rendering; in a real game, it can add a new behavior, too. This approach is especially useful for modifying the game, and the game's fans will appreciate it.

Figure 22-3 displays an 8 × 3 tileset. *Grass, gravel, sand,* and *dirt* appear beneath all other tiles on the canvas. Let's assign them the SurfaceTile type. *Brick, wall, bush, block,* and *metal* are solids. They will have shadows. There are versions of brick, bush, and wall that appear without the bottom wall; you will use it when there is a solid tile underneath them. *Abyss* is transparent and doesn't have a sprite. Deep_default and deep_bridge are versions of abyss that appear only if there is something on top of that tile. All other tiles have the type ObjectTile, and to make less code in configuration, they can be described as "all sprites that were not used." By default, the map will be filled with grass.

In a basic configuration, however, none of this matters. You have two types: ObjectTile and SurfaceTile. You are creating five surface tiles, and each sprite that is not used will create an ObjectTile in the addUseless method (see the section "Binding Sprites to Tiles"). The abyss tile will have a unique way of rendering in one of the modifications, so you create it only if it was not created in the init method of other configurations.

ObjectTile and SurfaceTile are still almost empty, but functionality is added to them later in rendering and in other steps:

```
var BasicConfig = {
init: function(game) {
        var tiles = game.tiles, sprites = game.sprites
        tiles.defaultObject = tiles.add(new ObjectTile("nothing"));
        tiles.addMany(SurfaceTile, ["grass", "gravel", "sand", "dirt"]);
        tiles.defaultSurface = tiles.get("grass")
        sprites.addSpriteSheet("img/tiles.png", [
                ["grass",        "gravel",        "sand",        "dirt",        "hole1",        "hole2",
"hole3",  "hole4" ],
                ["deep_default", "deep_bridge", "forcefield", "bridge_h", "bridge_v",  "chest",
"lumber", "cactus"],
                ["brick-plain",  "brick",        "wall-plain",  "wall",        "bush-plain","bush",
"block",  "metal" ]
        ]);
        sprites.addSpriteSheet("img/horses.png", [ ["horse1", "horse2", "horse3"] ])
```

As mentioned earlier, afterInit is used for adding new behaviors and modding (modifying). Define abyss if the other mods didn't do it in their init function:

```
afterInit: function(game) {
        var tiles = game.tiles, sprites = game.sprites
        //abyss can be created in a mod!
        tiles.add(new SurfaceTile("abyss"));
        tiles.bind(sprites);
} }
```

Binding Sprites to Tiles

After you configure sprites and tiles, you need to bind all sprites to tiles with the same name and create tiles for sprites that were not used. Because some types of tiles can bind multiple sprites, you will add the bind method in Tile class and override it later.

All sprites that are not used in the configuration will be added as object tiles by the addUseless method:

```
Tile.prototype.bind = function(sprites) {
        this.sprite = sprites.get(this.name);
        if (sprites.hasOwnProperty(this.name)) {
                var sprite = tile.sprite = sprites.get(this.name);
                sprite.timesUsed++;
        }
}
```

Every time you bind a sprite to a tile, timesUsed will be increased. In the end, sprites that are not used will create an ObjectTile for themselves:

```
Sprite.prototype.timesUsed = 0;
SpriteList.prototype.get = function(name) {
        if (this.byName.hasOwnProperty(name)) {
                var sprite = this.byName[name];
                sprite.timesUsed++;
                return sprite;
        }
}
```

In this example, you use this mechanism to generate object sprites. You assume that all unused object sprites can be put on top of the surface layer; in practice, this is reasonable only when you have several surface objects and many other ones:

```
TileList.prototype.addUseless = function(TileType, sprites) {
        var list = sprites.byName;
        var names = [];
        for (var key in list)
                if (list.hasOwnProperty(key) && list[key].timesUsed == 0)
                        names.push(list[key].name);
        this.addMany(TileType, names);
        for (var i=0;i<names.length;i++) {
                this.byName[names[i]].sprite = list[names[i]];
        }
}
```

```
TileList.prototype.bind = function(sprites) {
        var list = this.byId;
        for (var i=0;i<list.length;i++)
                list[i].bind(sprites);
}
```

Map Field and Its Serialization to JSON

Your map field has two layers: surface and objects. Actually, there is no specific reason for the two-layer limit; it's just the case on which we're working in this chapter, based on the author's experience with dynamic multiplayer worlds. As discussed previously, the code can be expanded as you like without too much effort.

Sometimes, dynamic tile indexes prevent the hacking of a multiplayer game. If the order of the tiles in the list is always random, a hacker would have to track all those dynamic IDs.

Serialization is the difficult part here, because between saving the map and loading it after application restart, the configuration can change, and that changes all tile indexes. This is not a problem if you store the names of the tiles that you were using for specific indexes. Later, you can load and save the map from localStorage. Note that you can't add functions to objects that will be saved, because you are going to use JavaScript Object Notation (JSON) format:

```
function createTwoDimArray(dim1, dim2, def) {
        var res = [];
        for (var j=0;j<dim1; j++) {
                var a = [];
                for (var i=0;i<dim2; i++)
                        a.push(def);
                res.push(a);
        }
        return res;
}
```

MapField is a basic object for rendering the entire field, based on simple two-dimensional arrays and created for each type of tile (surface and object):

```
function MapField(tiles, cols, rows) {
        this.tiles = tiles;
        this.cols = cols;
        this.rows = rows;
        this.surface = createTwoDimArray(rows, cols, tiles.defaultSurface);
        this.objects = createTwoDimArray(rows, cols, tiles.defaultObject);
}

MapField.prototype = {
        rows: 0,
        cols: 0,
        checkBounds: function(col, row) {
                return col>=0 && col < this.cols && row>=0 && row < this.rows;
        },
        getSurface: function(col, row) {
                return this.checkBounds(col, row) && this.surface[row][col] || this.tiles.defaultSurface
        },
```

```
getObject: function(col, row) {
        return this.checkBounds(col, row) && this.objects[row][col] || this.tiles.defaultObject
},
setSurface: function(col, row, value) {
        this.checkBounds(col, row) && (this.surface[row][col]=value)
},
setObject: function(col, row, value) {
        this.checkBounds(col, row) && (this.objects[row][col]=value)
},
```

Load and save methods can be used to exploit client-side data storage, for instance, localStorage:

```
load: function(data) { //load previously saved data
        var rows = this.rows = data.rows;
        var cols = this.cols = data.cols;
        var list = [];
        for (var i=0;i<data.tiles.length;i++)
                list.push(this.tiles.byName[data.tiles[i]])
        this.surface = [];
        this.objects = [];
        for (var i=0;i<rows;i++) {
                this.surface.push([]);
                for (var j=0;j<cols;j++)
                        this.surface[i].push(list[data.surface[i][j]] ||
this.tiles.defaultSurface)
                this.objects.push([]);
                for (var j=0;j<cols;j++)
                        this.objects[i].push(list[data.objects[i][j]] ||
this.tiles.defaultObject)
        }
},
save: function() {
        data = { tiles:[], surface: [], objects: [] }
        var rows = data.rows = this.rows
        var cols = data.cols = this.cols
        var list = this.tiles.byId
        for (var i=0;i<list.length;i++)
                data.tiles.push(list[i].name)
        for (var i=0;i<rows;i++) {
                data.surface.push([]);
                for (var j=0;j<cols;j++)
                        data.surface[i].push(this.surface[i][j].id)
                data.objects.push([]);
                for (var j=0;j<cols;j++)
                        data.objects[i].push(this.objects[i][j].id)
        }
        return data
    }
}
```

Camera

To render a world, you need a *camera*, which contains the transformation information from display coordinates to world coordinates. Coordinates describe a *transform* on a map (*centerX*, *centerY*) that corresponds to the center of the screen and a *scale*. The clientRect function constructs a rectangle on the map that corresponds to the display rectangle: (*rect.x*, *rect.y*) to (0, 0), (*rect.x* + *rect.w*, *rect.y* + *rect.h*) to (*displayWidth*, *displayHeight*). The following code implements the camera and clientRect functions:

```
function Rect(x, y, w, h) {
        this.x = x
        this.y = y
        this.w = w
        this.h = h
}

Rect.prototype = {
        contains: function(x, y) {
                return this.x <= x && x < this.x + this.w && this.y <= y && y < this.y + this.h
        }
}

var Camera = function(map, canvas) {
        this.canvas = canvas; this.map = map
        this.centerX = this.mapWidth() >> 1
        this.centerY = this.mapHeight()>> 1
}

Camera.prototype = {
        mapWidth: function() { return this.map.cols * TILE_SIZE },
        mapHeight: function() { return this.map.rows * TILE_SIZE },
        displayWidth: function() { return this.canvas.width },
        displayHeight: function() { return this.canvas.height },
        context: function() { return this.canvas.getContext("2d") },
        centerX: 0,
        centerY: 0,
        scale: 1,
        map: null,
        canvas: null,
        clientRect: function() {
                var dw = this.displayWidth(), dh = this.displayHeight();
                var dw2 = dw >> 1, dh2 = dh >> 1
                // (0, 0) in display corresponds to (rect.x, rect.y)
                // (displayWidth, displayHeight) to (rect.x+rect.w, rect.y+r.h)
                return new Rect(this.centerX - dw2*this.scale, this.centerY - dh2*this.scale,
 w*this.scale, dh*this.scale);
        },
        moveBy: function(dx, dy) {
                //move center by display coordinates
                this.centerX = Math.min(Math.max(this.centerX - dx * this.scale, 0), this.mapWidth());
                this.centerY = Math.min(Math.max(this.centerY - dy * this.scale, 0), this.mapHeight());
        },
```

```
        point: function(x, y) {
                //from display to world coordinates
                x -= this.displayWidth()>>1;
                y -= this.displayHeight()>>1;
                x *= this.scale
                y *= this.scale
                x += this.centerX;
                y += this.centerY;
                return {x:x, y:y}
        },
        round: function() {
                this.centerX = Math.round(this.centerX);
                this.centerY = Math.round(this.centerY);
        }
}
```

Renderer

After all that logic, at last you can draw something. The renderer object's drawing is shaped not only by the camera; the renderer also stores something in cache to make the rendering process faster. Nevertheless, you will not use caching in this baseline implementation. If you like, you can set up two canvases, and one renderer will work with two cameras. The renderer calculates the rectangle of tiles on the map that needs to be drawn and processes every tile twice during the cycle.

The process of drawing autotiles can be described by two methods: *auto* determines the magic number, which depends on the neighboring cells, and *render* takes that magic number and renders the tile. If the rendering process starts to slow down the application, magic numbers can be stored in cache and recalculated whenever the tile is changed. For C/C++ applications the time required to calculate the magic number is comparable to the actual rendering time. Both methods depend on a tile, so let's add them as functions to Tile and override this later:

```
var Renderer = function(map, sprites) {
        this.map = map
        this.tiles = map.tiles
        this.sprites = sprites
}

Renderer.prototype = {
        //renderer is different from camera, cause render can store cache on some info, not
dependent on a camera
        render: function(camera) {
                var displayWidth = camera.displayWidth()
                var displayHeight = camera.displayHeight()

                //get view rect on map
                var r = camera.clientRect();
                var map = this.map

                var context = this.context = camera.context()
                context.fillStyle = "black"
                context.fillRect(0, 0, displayWidth, displayHeight);
```

```
        // scale && translate Standard operations
        context.save()
        context.scale(1.0/camera.scale, 1.0/camera.scale);
        context.translate(-r.x, -r.y);

        //clipping rect for tiles We want to make visible only those tiles which are on screen
        var minI = r.x >> TILE_SIZE_BITS, maxI = (r.x+r.w) >> TILE_SIZE_BITS;
        var minJ = r.y >> TILE_SIZE_BITS, maxJ = (r.y+r.h) >> TILE_SIZE_BITS;
        minI = Math.max(minI, 0); maxI = Math.min(maxI, map.cols-1);
        minJ = Math.max(minJ, 0); maxJ = Math.min(maxJ, map.rows-1);

        //for each visible tile
        for (var j=minJ; j<=maxJ; j++)
              for (var i=minI; i<=maxI; i++) {
                    //draw surface, if tile has sprite
                    var tile = map.getSurface(i, j)
                    var autotile = tile.auto(map, i, j)
                    tile.render(this, autotile, i*TILE_SIZE, j*TILE_SIZE)

                    tile = map.getObject(i, j)
                    autotile = tile.auto(map, i, j)
                    tile.render(this, autotile, i*TILE_SIZE, j*TILE_SIZE)
              }
        context.restore();
    }
}

Tile.prototype.render = function(renderer, autotile, x, y) {
        var sprite = this.sprite
        if (!sprite) return
        renderer.context.drawImage(sprite.source, sprite.x, sprite.y, TILE_SIZE, TILE_SIZE, x, y,
TILE_SIZE, TILE_SIZE);
}

Tile.prototype.auto = function(map, i, j) {
```

Figure 22-5 shows how it will look if you create all the described objects and connect a camera to the canvas.

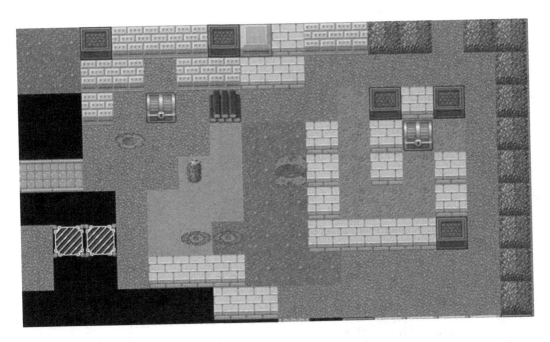

Figure 22-5. *Autotiles off*

Editor

Editor is a special class that contains methods for all editor tools. There are two tools: the *brush* places a selected tile on the map, and the *cursor* scrolls the map and picks objects. In this demo, cursor picking is not used, but you can override this if action is required. There is also a special case: if you use brush with a surface tile, the object is removed from the cell.

Recall your coding a serialization algorithm for MapField (see the section "Map Field and Its Serialization to JSON"). Now, it's time to use the map. The load and save functions store the map in localStorage. For each site, the domain browser stores a series of key-value objects. Your map is stored under the key mapData:

```
function Editor(map) { this.map = map; this.tiles = map.tiles }

Editor.prototype = {
      selected: null,
      modified: false,
      brushAt: function(point) {
            var x = point.x >> TILE_SIZE_BITS, y = point.y >> TILE_SIZE_BITS;
            var tile = this.selected
            if (tile) {
                  if (tile.layer == 0) {
                        //if tile is surface, delete the object and place the tile
                        this.map.setSurface(x, y, tile)
                        this.map.setObject(x, y, this.tiles.defaultObject)
                  }
```

```
                    else
                            this.map.setObject(x, y, tile)
                        this.modified = true
                }
        },
        cursorAt: function(point) {
//no action. Reserved for the game.
        },
```

You need to use localStoage in order not to lose your work each time the page is updated. Of coure, you can also provide a back end here:

```
        load: function() {
                if (localStorage['mapdata']) {
                        this.map.load(JSON.parse(localStorage['mapdata']));
                        this.modified = false
                }
        },
        save: function() {
                if (this.modified) {
                        localStorage['mapdata'] = JSON.stringify(this.map.save());
                        this.modified = false
                }
        }
}
```

Builder Window

Now, it's time to implement a window that will allow you to select a tile from a palette for a brush (see Figure 22-6). Let's call the corresponding class BuilderWnd.

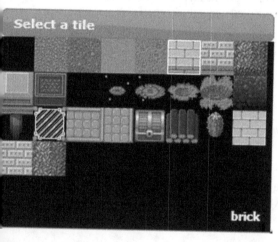

Figure 22-6. *Builder window*

The number of columns in the grid is calculated using the formula `Math.floor(canvas.width / TILE_SIZE)`. That way, if someone resizes the canvas, the number of columns will change automatically.

There are several ways to divide and take the integer part in JavaScript. `Math.floor(X / Y)` does it; X/Y | 0 works, too, but when Y is a power of 2, it's better to use right bit shift. It works because any bitwise operation removes the fractional part of a number. Similarly, you can use left bit shift if you need to remove the fractional part and multiply by a power of 2, using one operator.

The rendering algorithm draws a corresponding sprite for each tile in the tileset, in the same order. The tile number ID has the coordinates `col = id % cols`, `row = Math.floor (id / cols)` in the grid. Each column and row has a side `TILE_SIZE`.

Mouse events are the real problem. `event.pageX` and `event.pageY` contain absolute coordinates, and so to determine the canvas coordinates, you have to subtract offsets of each parent in the document object model (DOM):

```
function BuilderWnd(editor, sprites, canvas) {
        this.editor = editor; this.tiles = editor.tiles; this.sprites = sprites; this.canvas = canvas;
        this.initMouseEvents(canvas); this.redraw();
}


BuilderWnd.prototype = {
        click: function(x, y) {
                var index = (y >> TILE_SIZE_BITS) * this.cols + (x >> TILE_SIZE_BITS)
                this.editor.selected = index >= 0 && index < this.tiles.byId.length?
this.tiles.byId[index]: null
        },
        initMouseEvents: function(canvas) {
                var self = this;
                $(canvas).mousedown(function(e) {
                        var x = e.pageX;
                        var y = e.pageY;
                        var t = e.target;
                        while (t != document.body) {
                                x -= t.offsetLeft;
                                y -= t.offsetTop;
                                t = t.parentNode;
                        }
                        self.click(x, y);
                        self.redraw();
                        e.preventDefault();
                        e.stopPropagation();
                });
        },
        redraw: function() {
                var canvas = this.canvas

                canvas.width = canvas.parentNode.clientWidth;
                canvas.height = canvas.parentNode.clientHeight;
                this.cols = canvas.width >> TILE_SIZE_BITS
                this.rows = canvas.height >> TILE_SIZE_BITS
```

```
            var context = canvas.getContext("2d")
            context.fillStyle = "black"
            context.fillRect(0, 0, canvas.width, canvas.height)
            var tiles = this.tiles
            for (var i=0;i<tiles.byId.length; i++) {
                    var x = (i%this.cols) * TILE_SIZE
                    var y = (i/this.cols|0) * TILE_SIZE
                    var sprite = tiles.byId[i].sprite
                    if (sprite)
                            context.drawImage(sprite.source, sprite.x, sprite.y, TILE_SIZE,
TILE_SIZE, x, y, TILE_SIZE, TILE_SIZE)
            }
            var name = "undefined";
            if (this.editor.selected) {
                    var sel = this.editor.selected
                    name = sel.name

                    var x = (sel.id%this.cols) * TILE_SIZE
                    var y = (sel.id/this.cols|0) * TILE_SIZE
                    //stroke width 1.0 => line center must be X.5
                    context.strokeStyle = "white"
                    context.lineWidth = 1.0
                    context.strokeRect(x + 0.5, y + 0.5, TILE_SIZE-1, TILE_SIZE-1)
            }

            context.fillStyle = "white";
            context.textAlign = "right";
            context.font = "bold 11px Tahoma, Arial";
            context.fillText(name, canvas.width - 10, canvas.height - 10);
    }
}
```

Main Window

You're almost there! You can't edit a big map if it can be scrolled. You have to take care of the press and release events of mouse buttons to separate map scrolling (drag) from selecting an object (to be used later). This is the same problem as with coordinates in the previous window. However, this time the canvas will have only one parent—there is no need of cycles.

To separate scrolling from picking, use this strategy: while the mouse cursor is no more than 5 pixels from the place where the button was pressed, it's picking. In the case of a window resize, you resize the canvas, too:

```
function MainWnd(renderer, camera, editor) {
        this.renderer = renderer;
        this.camera = camera;
        this.canvas = camera.canvas;
        this.map = camera.map;
        this.editor = editor;

        this.initMouseEvents(this.canvas)
        this.initResize(this.canvas)
```

```
MainWnd.prototype = {
        tool: 0,
        redraw: function() {
                this.renderer.render(this.camera);
        },
        initMouseEvents: function(canvas) {
                var pressed = false, drag = false;
                var startX = 0, startY = 0;
                var camera = this.camera, editor = this.editor
                var self = this;

                function doDrag(x, y) {
                        if (!drag && (Math.abs(x-startX)>=5 || Math.abs(y-startY)>=5)) {
                                //more than 5 pixels mouse move => drag the map!
                                drag = true;
                        }
                        if (drag) {
                                var dx = x - startX, dy = y - startY;
                                startX = x;          startY = y;
                                camera.moveBy(dx, dy);
                        }
                        return drag;
                }

                function mouseDown(mx, my) {
                        pressed = true; drag = false;
                        startX = mx; startY = my;
                        if (this.tool == 1)
                                editor.brushAt(camera.point(mx, my));
                        self.redraw();
                }
                function mouseMove(mx, my) {
                        if (!pressed) return;
                        //move mouse with pressed key => drag map or draw with pencil
                        if (self.tool == 0) {
                                doDrag(mx, my);
                        } else if (self.tool == 1) {
                                editor.brushAt(camera.point(mx, my));
                        }
                        self.redraw();
                }
                function mouseUp(mx, my) {
                        if (!pressed) return;
                        pressed = false;
                        if (self.tool == 0) {
                                //if map is not dragged, then click at object
                                if (!doDrag(mx, my))
                                        editor.cursorAt(camera.point(mx, my));
                        } else if (self.tool == 1) {
                                editor.brushAt(camera.point(mx, my));
                        }
```

```
                            editor.save();
                            self.redraw();

                            //after map drag with zoom != 1.0, camera coordinates can be not integers,
lets fix it!
                            camera.round();
                        }

                    $(canvas).mousedown(function(e){
                            mouseDown(e.pageX - e.target.offsetLeft, e.pageY - e.target.offsetTop);
                    });
                    $(canvas).mousemove(function(e){
                            mouseMove(e.pageX - e.target.offsetLeft, e.pageY - e.target.offsetTop);
                    });
                    $(canvas).mouseup(function(e){
                            mouseUp(e.pageX - e.target.offsetLeft, e.pageY - e.target.offsetTop);
                    });
            },

        initResize: function(canvas) {
                var self = this;
                var resize = function() {
                        canvas.width = window.innerWidth-20;
                        canvas.height = window.innerHeight-20;
                        self.redraw();
                }
                $(window).resize(resize);
                resize();
        }
}
```

index.html with jQuery UI

Now, let's make this look like a serious enterprise application. Go to the jQuery user interface library (jQuery UI) web site (http://jqueryui.com), and download latest version. Make sure that you include the *dialog* widget. (*Start* is the author's preferred theme.) Also, don't forget about jQuery itself. This pretty line creates all the stuff you implemented: window.app = new App([BasicConfig]);. There are three placeholders in the code below: one for modifications, one for configurations, and one for active configurations. Every autotile algorithm will be added as a modification. The result is shown in Figure 22-7.

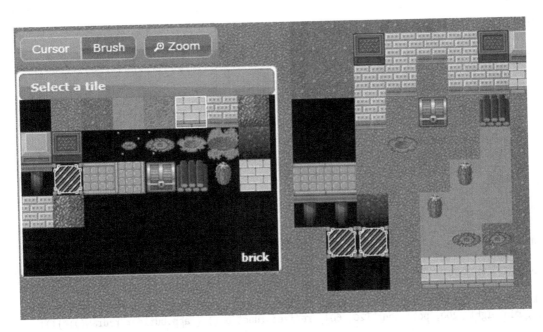

Figure 22-7. *Map editor, autotiles off*

```
<html>
<head>
    <meta http-equiv="Content-Type" content="text/html; charset=UTF-8"/>
    <meta name="viewport" content="width=device-width, initial-scale=1, maximum-scale=1, user-scalable=0"/>
        <link href="css/start/jquery-ui-1.10.3.custom.css" rel="stylesheet">
        <script src="lib/jquery-1.10.2.min.js"></script>
        <script src="lib/jquery-ui-1.10.3.custom.min.js"></script>
        <!-- GAME -->
        <script src="core/tilelist.js"></script>
        <script src="core/tileeventlist.js"></script>
        <script src="core/map.js"></script>
        <script src="core/sprite.js"></script>
        <script src="core/editor.js"></script>
        <script src="core/renderer.js"></script>
        <script src="core/binder.js"></script>
        <!-- PLACEHOLDER FOR MODS -->
        <!-- PLACEHOLDER FOR CONFIGS -->
        <!-- UI -->
        <script src="core/builder.js"></script>
        <script src="core/main.js"></script>
        <!-- Application -->
        <script src="core/app.js"></script>
        <script>
$(function() {
        initUI();
        window.app = new App([BasicConfig /* PLACEHOLDER FOR ACTIVE CONFIGS */ ]);
});
```

```javascript
function initUI() {
        $( "#action-zoom" ).button({
          icons: {
                primary: "ui-icon-zoomin"
          }
        }).click(function(){
                if (app.camera.scale == 1.0)
                        app.camera.scale = 1.5;
                else app.camera.scale = 1.0;
                app.redraw();
                return false;
        });

        $( "#tool-cursor" ).click(function() {
                app.main.tool = 0;return false;
        }).next().next().click(function() {
                app.main.tool = 1;return false;
        }).parent().buttonset();

        $("#builder-dialog").dialog({dialogClass: "build_dialog", width:320, height:300,
minWidth:240, minHeight: 200, position: [20, 60], resize: function() { app.builder.redraw(); }});
}
</script>
<style>
  #toolbar { padding: 4px; display: inline-block;position: absolute; left: 20px; top: 20px; }
  body {
                font-family: "Trebuchet MS", "Helvetica", "Arial",  "Verdana", "sans-serif";
                font-size: 62.5%;
        }
  #builder { }
  .build_dialog .ui-dialog-content { padding: 0; overflow: hidden }
  .build_dialog .ui-dialog-titlebar-close { display:none }
</style>
</head>
<body>
<canvas id="screen" border="0"></canvas>
<div id="toolbar" class="ui-widget-header ui-corner-all">
  <span id="tool">
    <input type="radio" id="tool-cursor" name="tool" checked="checked" /><label
for="tool-cursor">Cursor</label>
    <input type="radio" id="tool-brush" name="tool" /><label for="tool-brush">Brush</label>
  </span>
  <button id="action-zoom">Zoom</button>
/div>

div id="builder-dialog" title="Select a tile">
  <canvas id="builder"></canvas>
/div>
/body>

/html>
```

Conclusion

In this chapter, you created a two-dimensional map editor from scratch for tile-based map fields. This application is not far from actual game production. You have made a lot of progress, and now you know how to generate maps consisting of several layers (though you used two layers only), attach sprites, and make a correspondence between object types and sprites. You have learned a simple way of organizing a camera. The final result is a miniapplication for map editing, which you can use for enriching your games.

Here are some suggestions on how to make this editor of real value in your game application:

- Separate the map into chunks, render them separately, and cache chunks that were not changed in the offscreen buffer.

- Unload chunks that are too far from the camera-view rectangle. That way, the editor will work with big maps.

- Load chunks by network. Multiplayer sandbox game—yay!

- Add a touch events handler.

- Add game logic, for example, redstone logic, from Minecraft. To do this, you will need a new layer that can store data for tiles containing advanced logic. For redstone, it should be power level; for switches, you will need on/off enumeration.

- Add entities and simple physics for colliding with solid tiles—RPG Maker, yay!

- Create hexagonal autotiles.

- Euclidean space is boring—use hyperspace to create a hyperrogue game!

- Go in three dimensions, and make a voxel-based game.

- Make an 80286 computer with redstone.

- Using your knowledge from Chapter 6, make an HTML5 massively multiplayer online (MMO) game.

- Deploy your application on a cloud server (for example, Heroku).

- Conquer the world with your multiplayer sandbox of awesomeness!

- And . . . may the Force be with you!

■ ■ ■

CHAPTER 23

Automating Your Workflow with Node.js and Grunt

Jesse Freeman, Developer Evangelist, Amazon

Insanity: doing the same thing over and over again and expecting different results.

—Albert Einstein

As developers, we tend to do a lot of repetitive tasks. We are constantly compiling code, packaging it, and deploying it to different places. As the project scales, the complexity of these processes continues to grow. If there is one constant among humans, it's that we are not great at doing repetitive tasks, especially complex ones. Sure, we can do one single task over and over again, but anything more complicated, and the system quickly breaks down. This isn't anything new; Henry Ford realized it when he took advantage of the assembly line to lower the cost of making cars. We can do the same thing for our own code by taking advantage of automation.

Automating Your Workflow

If you come from working with other programming languages, such as Java or ActionScript, the idea of automation may not be alien to you. When compiled, these languages rely on Java, and, as such, it is easy to integrate them into build-script languages, which are built on the same languages, such as Ant, Maven, and even Scala. As JavaScript developers, we can take advantage of Node.js to handle the running of all our automation scripts. Node.js is incredibly powerful, and, when paired with a build system, such as Grunt, , we can attain results similar to those other languages.

Right now you may be thinking, "How can a build script help me with my game?" JavaScript isn't compiled like Java, and, in order to package it, you simply upload it to the server. However, if you have tried to support multiple platforms before, or looked for ways to compress and optimize your code, you know that there is more involved than just sending your code up to a server via file transfer protocol (FTP) to get it running. Let's take a look at some of the unique advantages to automating your workflow, which will be the focus of this chapter.

Optimize and package your game: Games are the biggest abusers of resources when running. Games usually have thousands of lines of code, hundreds of assets, and lots of additional files that need to be loaded at runtime. You can minimize and compress your game's code to shrink its size and combine the requested files to cut down on load time.

Deploy to multiple platforms: HTML5 games live in more than one place nowadays. You may want to publish the game to your server, submit it to a Web store, or put it in a wrapper to run natively.

Create a reproducible build process: If you are working as part of a large team, or even on your own, you will want to make sure that you can quickly set up and run the game's code at the same time whenever you set up a project from scratch or share it with another developer.

As you can see, there is a lot that you can take advantage of with automated build scripts, but it's not easy work. It requires you to sit down and map out your process and how to optimize that process. In this chapter, I will walk you through the basics of how I create my own build scripts and give you suggestions on how to apply these solutions to your own project. To get started, you will need to download and install Node.js.

Installing Node.js

One of the reasons I picked Node.js to build my automation solution was because of how easy it is to install locally. When most people hear "Node," they think "server side." Little do they know that Node.js features a powerful command-line integration with an operating system (OS) that can be run locally. Moreover, Node.js runs on Windows, MacIntosh, and Linux, making it ideal for any developer's coding platform of choice. To get started, you will need the correct installer for your OS. You can get it from the official Node.js web site (http://nodejs.org). As you can see in Figure 23-1, you simply click the Downloads button, and the site will automatically detect your OS.

Figure 23-1. *You can get the latest build of Node.js at* http://nodejs.org

Once the installer has downloaded, run through the installer wizard, leaving the default settings, as shown in Figure 23-2.

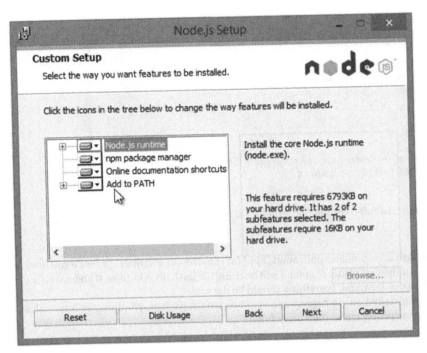

Figure 23-2. Make sure to install all the default features so that Node.js works properly for your build script project

There is one important thing to note if you are on Windows. I am not a big fan of the command prompt on Windows, because I come from a Linux background. That being said, I have had great success with Git Bash, which comes installed with Git. You can get them both from http://git-scm.com. If you want to use a Bash command line for Node.js on Windows, it is critical that you install Git Bash before Node.js.

Once you start the installation process, there are two things that you will want to make sure to configure. The first is Windows Explorer integration, which you will enable with the Git Bash Here option, as demonstrated in Figure 23-3.

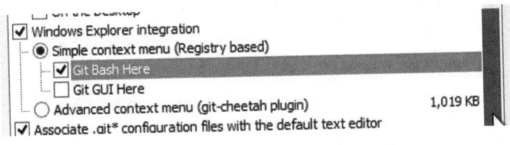

Figure 23-3. Make sure to add the Git Bash Here option when installing Git Bash

This allows you to right-click any folder and open Git Bash in that directory. This saves you a bit of time, as opposed to trying to find it via the command line. Next, you must adjust the PATH environment by selecting the Use Git Bash only option, as shown in Figure 23-4.

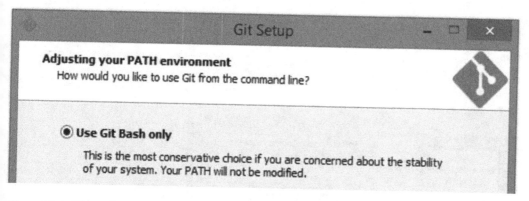

Figure 23-4. *This will make Git Bash the default command prompt for Git and the other command-line tools that you will be using in this chapter*

This option will ensure that Git Bash is your main application (app) for running Git and Node.js (once you have it installed) from the command line. For the rest of this chapter, I will be using Git Bash on Windows. If you are on a Mac, because it uses Bash by default in the Terminal, everything should be the same.

By now, you should have Node.js installed on your computer. Simply open Git Bash on Windows, or Terminal on Mac; enter the following command at the prompt; and then press Enter:

```
>npm
```

You should see something similar to the screen shown in Figure 23-5.

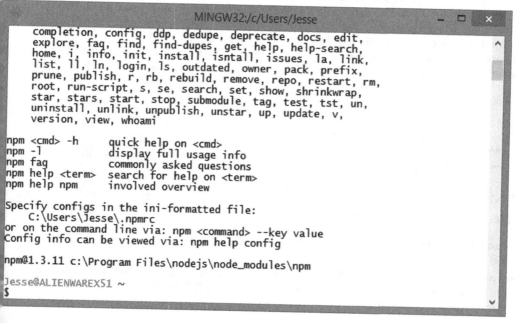

igure 23-5. *If you don't pass npm any commands, it will print out the instructions*

Here, you are just testing that Node Package Manager (npm) is working and correctly installed. If you don't see instructions to run npm, you may need to restart your computer or try reinstalling Node.

Command-Line Primer

I could have brought this up at the beginning, but I didn't want to scare you off. If you haven't noticed by now, you will be using the command line a lot for running your build script. Some people are terribly afraid of the command line, so I thought I would just cover the basics here. The first thing to keep in mind is that nothing bad will happen, so long as you take your time and are careful about what you enter at the prompt. The command line is an incredibly powerful tool, and, as a Web developer, you should become very familiar with it, especially as you go deeper into code automation and working with servers. For reference, Table 23-1 contains a few of the most common Bash commands that you will be using plus descriptions of how they work:

Table 23-1. *Common Bash Commands and Examples*

Action	Command	Description
Print working directory	> pwd	This will show you your current path on the file system.
List contents of directory	> ls	This will let you see everything inside the current directory you are in.
Change directory	> cd /path/to/new/folder	This will let you navigate into a new folder.
Go back	> cd ../	This navigates back one directory.
Make new folder	> mkdir FOLDER_NAME	This allows you to make new folders on the file system.
Delete	> rm FILE_TO_DELETE	This allows you to delete and file a folder on the system.
Delete all files	> rm -rf FOLDER_TO_DELETE	If you are trying to delete a directory with multiple files and folders inside it, you will need to force it to perform the delete recursively.
Clear console	> clear	This command will clear the console window.
Stop running command	Ctrl+C	Some commands that you run will require input or will continuously run and need to be stopped manually.

There are lots of great resources on the Web that cover how the command line works. It's important to note that these are Bash commands, so if you are not using Git Bash on Windows, and instead favor the default command line, some of these will be different.

To get your feet wet, let's create a new folder for your test project. In the command line, you will use the following commands to create a new directory, move into it, and then make sure that you are in the right place:

```
> mkdir NodeSampleProject
> cd NodeSampleProject
> pwd
```

You can see these commands being run in Figure 23-6.

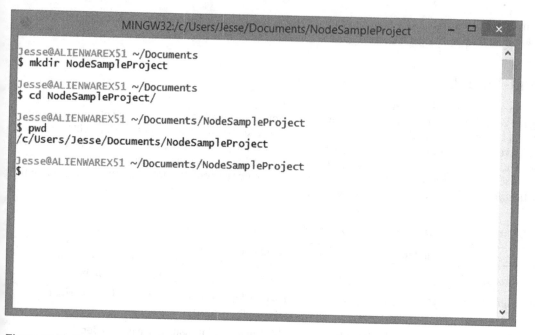

Figure 23-6. *Here, you can see that you have created a new directory, navigated into it via the cd command, and printed the working directory to make sure that you are in the right place*

Introduction to npm

Now that I have covered installing Node.js and how to use the command line, you are ready to look at npm, which is at the core of Node. npm allows you to add new features and functionality to your vanilla installation of Node.js. On its own, Node doesn't do much outside of allowing you to run it via the command line. There are literally hundreds of packages that you can download from http://npmjs.org that can be added to Node to make it more powerful. It is really easy to install new packages. You simply use the following command:

```
npm install PACKAGE_NAME
```

Over the rest of this chapter, I will discuss different types of packages that you will need to install to create more powerful build scripts. The biggest advantage that npm affords is its ability to help you manage your package dependencies. By tracking which packages you install in your project, it becomes easier to share this list with other team memebers or reinstall a specific version when setting up a project from scratch. To do this, you will have to create a package JavaScript Object Notation (JSON) file for your own project. At this point, you should be inside the new folder that you created in the previous section. Run the following command to activate npm's project setup wizard:

```
npm init
```

You should see the screen displayed in Figure 23-7.

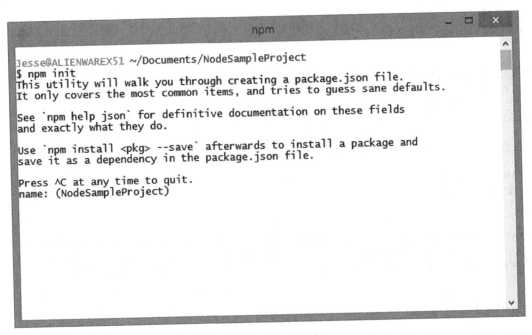

Figure 23-7. *Entering "npm init" will begin the process of creating the package.json file*

As you can see, the wizard will automatically create the package JSON for your project. Simply answer the questions the wizard asks. To start, you must give the package JSON a name. Once this is done, the wizard will ask you to confirm all your values, as illustrated in Figure 23-8.

```
name: (NodeSampleProject) NodeSampleProject
version: (0.0.0) 1.0.0
description: A sample nodejs project
entry point: (index.js) index.html
test command:
git repository:
keywords:
author: Jesse Freeman
license: (BSD-2-Clause)
About to write to c:\Users\Jesse\Documents\NodeSampleProject\package.json:

{
  "name": "NodeSampleProject",
  "version": "1.0.0",
  "description": "A sample nodejs project",
  "main": "index.html",
  "scripts": {
    "test": "echo \"Error: no test specified\" && exit 1"
  },
  "author": "Jesse Freeman",
  "license": "BSD-2-Clause"
}

Is this ok? (yes)
```

Figure 23-8. *Answer all the questions, and you will see a sample of the package.json file before you save it*

Now, if you look in your directory, you will see a package.json file. Open it with your text/code editor of choice, and it should have the following structure:

```
{
  "name": "NodeSampleProject",
  "version": "1.0.0",
  "description": "A sample nodejs project",
  "main": "index.html",
  "scripts": {
    "test": "echo \"Error: no test specified\" && exit 1"
  },
  "author": "Jesse Freeman",
  "license": "BSD-2-Clause"
}
```

Over time, as you add new packages to your project and continue to flesh out your build script, this file will automatically populate with anything you install via npm. You will come back to this file later on, when you start adding more Node modules to your project. For now, let's focus on installing the first package, which is Grunt.

Installing Grunt

Grunt is a JavaScript task runner. This means that you can define a set of tasks, similar to macros in other programs, that can run in order and be strung together to build more complex operations, which will become your final build script. To get started, you will need to install Grunt's command-line tools globally on your computer, which will allow Grunt to work in any project you create moving forward. To do this, enter the following command at the prompt:

```
> npm install -g grunt-cli
```

As the tools install, you should see the downloaded output, as shown in Figure 23-9.

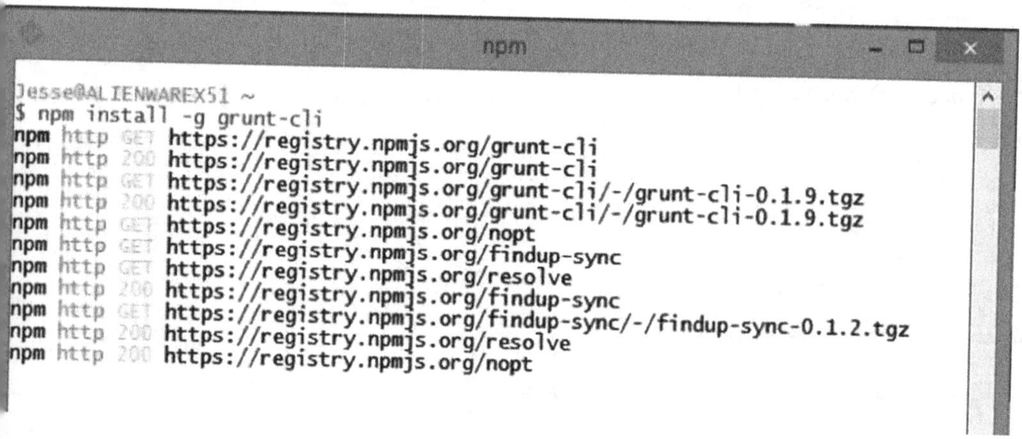

Figure 23-9. As each part of the package is downloaded, it will be displayed at the command prompt

Basically, npm is downloading and installing everything required to run Grunt on the command line.

Tip One thing to note is the –g you used in your command for installing Grunt. This flag indicates that it will be installed globally.

In the next section, you will install your packages locally to the project. Grunt is the only one you want to be able to access in any project on which you're working.

Creating a Grunt File

At this point, you are ready to create your build script. Grunt requires a case-specific file named GruntFile.js ×in the root of your project. Let's create that in your code editor of choice, and I will go over how each part of the script works plus how you can add onto it.

Once you have created your GruntFile.js, open it, and add to it the following code:

```
module.exports = function (grunt) {
    grunt.initConfig({
        pkg: grunt.file.readJSON('package.json')
    });
}
```

This is the basic template for your script. There is not much you can do, so let's set up a basic server and have it display an index page with "Hello World" on it. Create an index.html file in your project. Next, you will want to install a simple Node server module, called *connect*. Grunt has its own standard library of modules, called *tasks*. You can see a full listing of these at http://gruntjs.com/plugins. You can install them throughnpm. Switch back to the command line, and enter this:

```
> npm install grunt-contrib-connect --save-dev
```

There are a few things to point out here. Recall how you used npm to install Grunt on the command line. Here, though, you will notice that you are not using the global flag –g and instead add --save-dev. This is a special flag that tells npm not only that you are going to install this module locally, but also that you want to save a reference to it in your project.json file. This is very important, as it will allow you to manage module dependency as your project grows. Let's open the project.json file and take a look at what was added there. You should now see the following code toward the bottom of the file:

```
"devDependencies": {
    "grunt-contrib-connect": "~0.3.0",
}
```

Keep in mind that you may be using a different version from what I show here, as the plug-ins are constantly being updated by their authors. Pretty cool, right? Anything you install with --save-dev will automatically be added to your dev dependencies in your project.json file. Now, when you distribute your project, or if ever have to set it up again from scratch, npm will simply read these dependencies and install them for you. We'll talk about how that works later in this section. For now, you will need to set up the connect module in your GruntFile. Switch back to the GruntFile.js, and add the following code just above the grunt.initConfig line:

```
grunt.loadNpmTasks('grunt-contrib-connect');
```

This is how you load tasks into Grunt. The module you just installed into your script will now be imported. To configure the module, you will need to make a new task. Add the following code below the line with pkg: grunt. file.readJSON. Make sure that you add a comma to that line first, because you are adding the code to an existing JSON object. The code should look like this:

```
pkg: grunt.file.readJSON('package.json'),
        connect: {
            server: {
                options: {
                    port: 8080,
                    base: './',
                    keepalive: true
                }
            }
        }
```

As you can see, the connect task has its own configuration object. You name the configuration after the task name, and, in this case, you call it connect. Connect accepts several configuration objects. For this example, you are simply going to register a port number and base it on where the root of the server should host. Here, this will be inside the current directory. Also, for this example, you need to set the keepalive property to true. Connect will only run so long as Grunt is running, so without this, the build script would execute, and the server would be shut down.

Now, at the end of the line of code, just before the closing curly brace, add the following code:

```
grunt.registerTask('default', ['connect']);
```

To run a task, you have to set a task name. Here, you are using default and an array to list the tasks to run, and you are only calling connect. Default is the main task that this script will run, and, as you can probably guess, it will run whenever you call the script. You can create all kinds of tasks with their own unique names. Later on, I'll show you some ways to configure and run them. Before you can run this script, you need to create an index.html page for the server to load. Add the following code to the document:

```
<!DOCTYPE html>
<html>
  <meta charset="utf-8" />
  <head>
    <title>Grunt Demo Project</title>
  </head>
  <body>
    <h1>Hello World</h1>
  </body>
</html>
```

Now that you have a file to load, go back to the command line, and enter the following command:

```
grunt
```

This is how you run the build script. The code will automatically call the default task. You should see the server start up at the command prompt, as shown in Figure 23-10.

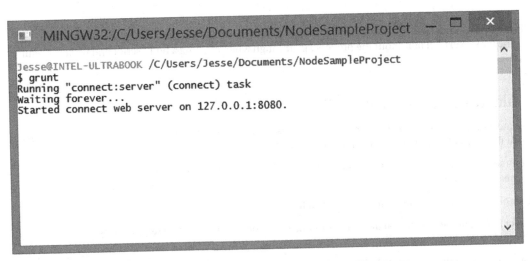

Figure 23-10. *Here, you can see that connect is starting the web server at 127.0.0.1 and port 8080; your specific Internet protocol (IP) address may be slightly different*

This tells you that you have a server running at localhost on port 8080. Open your browser, and enter `http://localhost:8080`. You should now see your Hello World page, as illustrated in Figure 23-11.

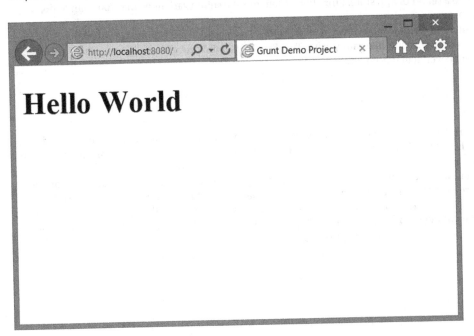

Figure 23-11. *You should now see the Hello World page when you go to* `http://localhost:8080`

As you can see, it's incredibly easy to sett up a server and host a file with Grunteasy. If you have ever had to instal and configure Apache, you will appreciate how simple this is. Of course, the server is really basic. It's not running PHP or anything else, but merely hosting the page. For most HTML5 games, this is all you need to do your local testing. Now, let's stop the server. Go back to the command prompt, and press Ctrl+C. This will end the server.

At this point, you have seen the basic steps for creating a build script with Grunt. You find the task module you want to install with npm, import it into your GruntFile, create a configuration object for it, and then add it to your task or make a new one for it. Next, I'll talk about the process I go through when creating a build script and what is useful for HTML5 games.

What Should Your Build Script Do?

Sometimes, the most difficult part of creating a build script is just figuring out what you need it to do without trying to boil the ocean. At the heart of all my HTML5 game build scripts are the following tasks:

1. Copy source code to a tmp folder so that I don't make changes to the original source code or mess anything up.

2. Combine all JavaScript into a single JavaScript file.

3. Inject JSON and other external data into my combined code to cut down on unnecessary external connections and additonal load times.

4. Uglify and minimize to a single JavaScript file.

5. Delete any unnecessary files.

6. Perform builds for each platform to which I want to deploy the game.

As you can see, there isn't a lot here. Each step is critical to the end result, which is packaging the game and getting it ready to publish to a server or app store. From here, there may be subtle variations that you want to do, based on the framework that you are using.

To see how this sort of build script works with an actual project, I suggest you see Chapter 19 . This chapter walks you through how to build a simple, rogue-like game, using TypeScript. Its build process is fully automated, taking advantage of all the content covered in this chapter.

Conclusion

Creating build scripts, or any kind of automated workflow, takes a good deal of work. It's not difficult work, mind you, just a lot of planning and thought on how to build out a robust automation plan as well as how to scale up or down to fit your ever-changing needs.

Over time, you will start to understand better how to break apart your scripts to make them more modular and reusable across all your projects. Creating build scripts is an art form all its own and an integral part of any serious developer's workflow. The time saved on packaging and deploying games alone is worth the up-front investment in making the build script. I wouldn't work on a single HTML5 game without some form of build script, even if it only compressed the JavaScript and minified it before uploading.

CHAPTER 24

Building a Game with the Cocos2d-html5 Library

Shun Lin, Founder, Cocos2d-html5

HTML5 games are becoming more and more important in the mobile gaming industry. There are already many casual and social games available in HTML5. Compared to native games, HTML5 games support real-time updating, click-to-play without the need for installations, and efficient development cycles.

Cocos2d-html5 was created for HTML5 game development, focusing on mobile web games and hybrid games via Cocos2d JavaScript Binding (JSB). The Cocos2d JSB is a wrapper code that sits between native code and JavaScript. It enables HTML5 developers who don't have experience in C++ and mobile app development to make games with Cocos2d-html5 and then deploy them as native mobile apps.

In this section, I will introduce the core concepts of Cocos2d-html5 and set up a working demo to demonstrate how easy it can be to build a game. The game can run on desktop browsers or mobile browsers, and it can also run as a native app with native performance without any change to the game code.

What Is Cocos2d?

The original Cocos2d is a game framework written in Python, and it inspired the creation of Cocos2d-iPhone, Cocos2d-x, and Cocos2d-html5, which has rocked the mobile gaming industry with over a 25 percent adoption rate by game developers. Some of the reasons why Cocos2d is so appealing are the flow control via scenes, a plethora of transitions, fast and easy sprites, actions that allow you to animate everything easily, tiled maps, menus, and OpenGL support.

Why Was Cocos2d Created?

Before Cocos2d was created, the process of creating a 2D game was not easy, as developers had to build all of the components they needed for game development. The original Cocos2d developers decided to build a lighter and faster framework for game development without reinventing the wheel. Cocos2d makes many of the core concepts of a 2D game clearer and easier.

What Makes Cocos2d the Best Choice for Your 2D Game Development?

A large number of games in the Apple App Store and Google Play are made with Cocos2d, including many best sellers. There are over 400,000 Cocos2d developers around the world. Cocos2d is probably the de facto game engine in China for mobile games, and it has been taught in a course at the South China University of Technology (SCUT).

The API of Cocos2d is clearly defined, and it is easy to learn and use. All of the APIs in the Cocos2d family share the same root and style. If you know the core concepts, you can easily switch to another Cocos2d-like framework.

Another reason behind its popularity is the active Cocos2d community. The community is an amazing place for tutorials and articles about Cocos2d, and people in the community are willing to share their experience with you. A dedicated, full-time team maintains Cocos2d and releases a new version every six weeks. ChuKong, one of the gaming industry giants in China, financially backs Cocos2d.

Moreover, there are abundant tools for Cocos2d game development, such as CocoStudio, Particle Designer, Spine, Animation Editor, Font Editor, TileMap Editor, TexturePacker, Physics Editor, and so on. Most of them are free or open source.

Finally, Cocos2d-x and Cocos2d-html5 support cross-platform development, so you can deploy games to the most popular platforms without code modification.

What Sets Cocos2d Apart from Other Similar Frameworks?

Compared to other game frameworks, Cocos2d-x is superior because it is open source, free-of-charge, user-friendly, and provides multi-platform support. Cocos2d makes 2D game programming easier and faster. It clarifies the key components of 2D game programming with an easy-to-learn, easy-to-use API, which makes it an outstanding framework compared to others. If you google "Cocos2d," you will find that the community is very large, active, and developer-friendly. These key points set Cocos2d apart from other similar frameworks.

What Is Cocos2d-html5?

Cocos2d-html5 is an open-source 2D web game framework, released under a generous MIT License (http://en.wikipedia.org/wiki/MIT_License). It is the HTML5 version of Cocos2d-x. The focus of Cocos2d-html5 development is bridging Cocos2d between browsers and native applications. On top of the framework provided by Cocos2d-html5, one can write games in JavaScript and have the game run on browsers that support HTML5. The API is completely compatible with that of Cocos2d-x JSB. Thus Cocos2d-html5 games can run using Cocos2d JSB on Cocos2d-x without or with very little modification.

Why Was Cocos2d-html5 Created?

Although Cocos2d-x is a cross-platform game framework, it is not accessible to browsers. Cocos2d-html5 was created to embrace HTML5, allowing applications and games created with it to run natively in browsers. It brings an easy-to-learn, easy-to-use API style to the HTML5 gaming world.

What Are the Main Differences in Cocos2d and Cocos2d-html5?

Cocos2d is designed for desktop and mobile platforms, while Cocos2d-html5 is designed for HTML5-ready browsers and web apps. Moreover, Cocos2d-html5 supports desktop and mobile platforms via the Cocos2d JSB, and it brings with it the hybrid app online updating feature.

It is becoming more and more feasible to develop and debug games on browsers. Browsers, such as Chrome, provide you with many useful debugging and profiling tools. After finishing your game on the Web, you can quickly port it to iOS or Android via Cocos2d JSB.

Extending the Power of Cocos2d-html5 with Cocos2d JavaScript Binding

You can now use Cocos2d-html5 to write games running on HTML5-compatible browsers. With the power of the Cocos2d JSB, you can use the same code base to run on a PC, mobile device, or even embedded systems. If you want to know more about JavaScript Binding and the corresponding generators, check out this link: https://github.com/Cocos2d/bindings-generator.

Understanding Cocos2d

In the Cocos2d world, everything is a node, and the world is mainly constructed from three types of nodes:

- A scene node
- Some layer nodes
- Lots of sprite nodes

Only one scene can be running at a time, which includes one or more layers, and layers that contain sprite nodes that are actually displaying something, such as an image, a character, an explosion, and so forth.

Basic Concepts of Cocos2d

Before creating the first scene of your game, you should be familiar with the basic concepts of Cocos2d. If you are already familiar with these concepts, you can skip to next section.

Now, let's go over a few things about the framework and its basic concepts.

Director

The cc.Director is a shared (singleton) object that takes care of navigating between scenes. It is an important component for controlling the flow of the game. It knows which scene is currently active and allows you to change scenes by replacing the current scene or pushing a new one onto the scene stack. When you push a new scene onto the stack, cc.Director pauses the previous scene but keeps it in memory. Later, when you pop the top scene from the stack, the paused scene resumes from its last state. cc.Director is also responsible for initializing the scheduler, action manager, and touch dispatcher.

Scene

A *scene* (implemented with the cc.Scene object) is more or less an independent piece of the app workflow. (Some people call them "screens" or "stages.") Your app can have many scenes, but only one of them can be active at a given time.

For example, you could have a game with the following scenes: Intro, Menu, Level 1, Level 2, Winning Scene, Losing Scene, and High Scores. You can think of each one of these scenes as a separate application that can be connected to other scenes with a small amount of "glue" code. For example, the Intro scene might go to the Menu scene when it finishes, and the scene for Level 1 might lead to the scene for Level 2 (if the player wins) or to the Losing scene (if the player loses). An example of how scenes might flow in a game is shown in Figure 24-1.

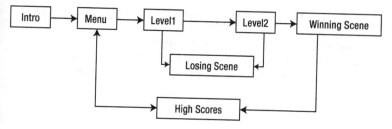

Figure 24-1. *Example game flow*

A Cocos2d cc.Scene is composed of one or more cc.Node objects, added as children to the scene. Subclasses of cc.Node, such as cc.Layer and cc.Sprite, give the scene its appearance and behavior. Typically, you implement your screens as subclasses of cc.Layer and add them to a blank instance of cc.Scene. Afterwards, you implement your other graphics and game objects as cc.Node and add them as children to the cc.Layer you created.

Because scenes are a subclass of cc.Node, they can be transformed manually or programatically by using cc.Action. See *Actions* at http://cocos2d-x.org/wiki/Actions for more information.

There is also a family of cc.Scene classes called *transitions*, implemented with the cc.TransitionScene class. These allow you to create special transition effects when switching from one scene to another, such as fading, and sliding in from the side.

Layer

A cc.Layer is a cc.Node, and it is often used as a container for displayable elements. Layers know how to draw themselves and may be semi-transparent, allowing players to see other layers behind them. cc.Layer is very useful in defining your game's appearance and behavior, so expect to spend a considerable amount of your programming time coding cc.Layer subclasses. A series of Cocos2d layers in a regular menu scene are shown in Figure 24-2.

A regular menu scene

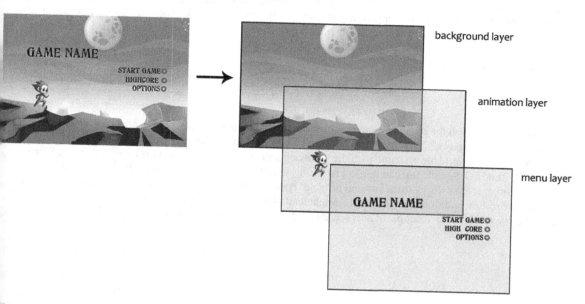

igure 24-2. *Cocos2d layers*

The cc.Layer is where you define touch event handlers. By implementing a method to handle one of the touch events (cc.TouchBegan, cc.TouchMoved, cc.TouchEnded, or cc.TouchCancelled), a cc.Layer can react to the player's interaction. These touch events are propagated to all of the layers within a scene, from front to back, until the claimed layers catch the event and accept it.

While complex applications will require you to define custom cc.Layer subclasses, Cocos2d provides several predefined layers. Some examples include cc.Menu (a simple menu layer), cc.ColorLayer (a layer that draws a solid color), and cc.LayerMultiplex (a layer that lets you multiplex its children, activating one while disabling the others).

Layers may contain any cc.Node as a child, including cc.Sprite, cc.Label, and even other cc.Layer objects. Because layers are a subclass of cc.Node, they can be transformed manually or programatically by using cc.Action.

Sprite

A Cocos2d cc.Sprite is similar to sprites that you find in other game engines. It is a 2D image that can be moved, rotated, scaled, animated, or subjected to other transformations. Sprites (implemented using the cc.Sprite class) can have other sprites as children. When a parent is transformed, all of its children are transformed as well. Because sprites are a subclass of cc.Node, they can be transformed manually or programatically by using cc.Action.

Coordinate System

Cocos2d-html5 uses the same coordinate system as OpenGL, which is also called "the right-handed Cartesian coordinate system." It is popular in the gaming industry; however, it is different from traditional top-left coordinate systems used in web page designs. The Cocos2d coordinate system is illustrated in Figure 24-3.

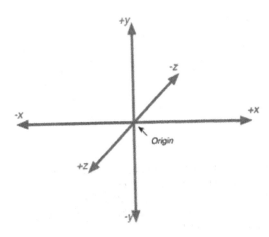

Figure 24-3. *Cocos2d coordinate system*

For a 2D game,

- The x-axis starts at the left side of the screen and increases to the right.

- The y-axis starts at the bottom of the screen and increases upwards.

The origin (x = 0, y = 0) is at the bottom-left corner of screen. It is the first quadrant of the right-handed Cartesian coordinate system.

The anchor point is used for both positioning and rotating of an object. The anchor point coordinate is a relative coordinate. For example, the anchor point in position (0, 0), which is always defined in Cocos2d shorthand as cc.p(0, 0), corresponds to the farthest bottom-left part of that object, while cc.p(0.5, 0.5) corresponds to the center of the object. When setting the position of the object, the object is positioned such that the anchor point will be at the coordinates specified in the setPosition() call. For example, Figure 24-4 shows the result of a blue circle sprite positioned with the code shown in Listing 24-1. Similarly, when rotating the object, it is rotated about the anchor point.

Figure 24-4. *Anchor point*

Listing 24-1. Sprite has an anchorPoint of cc.p(0, 0) and a Position of cc.p(0,0)

```
// create sprite
var sprite = cc.Sprite.create ( "bluecircle.png" ) ;
sprite.setAnchorPoint ( cc.p( 0 , 0 ) ) ; // Anchor Point
sprite.setPosition ( cc.p( 0 , 0 ) ) ;
this.addChild ( sprite ) ;
```

Action

Actions are like orders given to any cc.Node object. These actions usually modify some of the object's attributes, such as position, rotation, scale, and so forth. If these attributes are modified over a period of time, they are cc.IntervalAction actions; otherwise, they are cc.InstantAction actions. For example, the cc.MoveBy action modifies the position property during a certain time period, so it is a subclass of cc.IntervalAction. In another example, the following code snippet moves a sprite 50 pixels to the right and 10 pixels to the top over a period of 2 seconds:

```
sprite.runAction(cc.MoveBy.create(2, cc.p(50, 10)));
```

Animation

In Cocos2d, animations are bound to animated actions. You can use a sequence of images to create an animation. After the animation is created, you can use the code shown in Listing 24-2 to play the animation on a sprite.

Listing 24-2. Move a Sprite 50 Pixels to the Right and 10 Pixels to the Top over a Period of 2 Seconds

```
var animation = cc.Animation.create ( ) ;
for ( var i = 1 ; i < 15 ; i ++ ) {
    var frameName = "res/Images/grossini_dance_" + ( ( i < 10 ) ? ( "0" + i ) : i ) + ".png" ;
    animation.addSpriteFrameWithFile ( frameName ) ;
}
animation.setDelayPerUnit ( 2.8 / 14 ) ;
animation.setRestoreOriginalFrame ( true ) ;
var action = cc.Animate.create ( animation ) ;
sprite.runAction ( cc.Sequence.create ( action, action.reverse ( ) ) ) ;
```

Scheduler

The *Scheduler* is responsible for triggering the scheduled callbacks. There are two different types of callbacks (selectors) in Cocos2d:

- *Update Selector*: The update selector will be called on every frame. You can customize its priority: the lower the value, the earlier it is called.

- *Custom Selector*: A custom selector will be called on every frame, or with a customized interval of time.

Custom selectors should be avoided whenever possible. Update selectors are faster and consume less memory.

Touch Event

Cocos2d supports two different ways of handling touch events, which are described in CCTouchDelegateProtocol.js. There is the TargetedTouchDelegate event and the StandardTouchDelegate event.
TargetedTouchDelegate offers two benefits:

- You don't have to deal with an event set, as the dispatcher does the job of splitting them. You get exactly one cc.Touch per call.

- You can claim a cc.Touch by returning true in onTouchBegan. Updates of claimed touches are sent only to the delegate(s) that claimed them. So if you get a move/ended/cancelled update, you can be certain that it's your touch. This frees you up from having to do numbers checks when using multi-touch.

StandardTouchDelegate also has two benefits:

- Splitting an event set is something that you must do. You can get each cc.Touch from the event set.

- You don't need to state true or false in cc.TouchesBegan. All of your touch callbacks will be called when you touch the screen.

The difference between TargetedTouchDelegate and StandardTouchDelegate is as follows:

- TargetedTouchDelegate processes touch events one by one, while StandardTouchDelegate processes touch events in an event set. Thus when you need to process a multi-touch, you should choose StandardTouchDelegate.

- TargetedTouchDelegate has a higher priority to get a touch event than StandardTouchDelegate.

- TargetedTouchDelegate supports priority: the lower the value of the priority, the earlier it is to get the event. StandardTouchDelegate doesn't support priority.

- TargetedTouchDelegeate can swallow touch events and prevent dispatching it to a low-priority one. You can set your priority and swallowsTouches parameters when you register your touch delegate with cc.registerTargetedDelegate(priority, swallowsTouches, delegate).

Introduction to the Directory Structure

The latest Cocos2d-html5 release package at the time of this writing (v2.2.2) contains the engine core module, extension modules, external libraries, samples, and templates. It doesn't contain the Cocos2d JSB files, and you have to download the corresponding Cocosd-x package when you want to publish Cocos2d JSB applications.

The Cocos2d-x team is working on a Cocos2d-js project that includes both the Cocos2d-html5 and Cocos2d JSB. The Cocos2d-js v3.0 alpha will be released in March 2014. For more information about Cocos2d-js, visit https://github.com/cocos2d/cocos2d-js.

The directory structure is illustrated in Figure 24-5. It contains eight folders and four files.

Figure 24-5. Directory structure

- The /root/template/ directory is used for creating new Cocos2d-html5 projects. All of your game resources, such as images, sounds, background music, and configuration files, should go in the /root/template/res folder. Your game source code files should go into /root/template/src.

- The /root/Cocos2d/ directory hosts the engine's core module, audio module, and other modules, and the /root/extension/ directory hosts some useful modules, such as EditBox, CocosBuilder Reader, and CocoStudio Reader, and so on. These two directories contain expanded files, while /root/lib/ has a compressed file containing these two directories together.

- The /root/external directory hosts physics engines, such as box2d and chipmunk.

- The /root/HelloHTML5World/ directory contains a simple "Hello World" demo.

- The /root/license/ directory includes all of the license files in this project and, as mentioned previously, the license of Cocos2d-html5 is from MIT, and it is the freest open source license.

- Within the Samples directory, you can find the usage of all classes in Tests. It also includes sample games. All of the tests and games can be run on JSB. This is where you should start.

- The /root/tools/ directory includes the JS Doc tool and closure compiler. The /root/template/build.xml directory is the configuration file for the closure compiler, and you can package your game into a single file in advanced mode via ANT. You simply need to add your game's JS files and then type ant in the console in the directory of /root/template/ directory.

- The AUTHORS.txt contains the core developer and contributor information.

- The CHANGELOG.txt contains the change information for all versions.

- The index.html is the entry file of the engine samples and demos.

- The README.mdown contains an introduction to Cocos2d-html5.

Introduction to the Tiled Editor

There are various tools in the Cocos2d community that can help you to develop your game professionally and efficiently. In this chapter, you will use the Tiled Editor to build the game map for the live demo, so that's the only tool I'll be discussing here. Information regarding other tools is available on the Cocos2d web site.

The Tiled Editor is a tool that allows for the easy creation of map layouts. It is versatile enough to allow you to specific more abstract things, such as collision areas, enemy spawn positions, or power-up positions. It saves all of this data in a convenient, standardized TMX format.

What is TMX?

The TMX (Tile Map XML) map format used by the Tiled Editor is a flexible way to describe a tile-based map. It can describe maps with any tile size, number of layers, and number of tile sets, while also allowing custom properties to be set on most elements. Besides tile layers, it can also contain groups of objects that can be placed freely.

Why Tiled Editor?

The reason I use the Tiled Editor is because it allows you to focus on more important things in your game when you have a standardized system and a powerful, flexible tool already in place. With the Tiled Editor, you'll be able to take a few tile sets, create your levels, and then be on your way.

In addition, with the Tiled Editor's help, all of the map layout information is stored in the TMX file. This is powerful because it allows you to send the TMX file to a player, and then instantly have the layout available without having to re-download the client (assuming that the TMX map uses textures that are already on the player's computer

Getting Started on Built-in Examples

Installing Cocos2d-html5 is as easy as extracting it and running the index.html file. It can be downloaded from the official Cocos2d-x web site at Cocos2d-x.org/download (see Figure 24-6). Just save the downloaded .zip file; you will extract the code on a web server default path later.

Cocos2d-x

Written in C++ and OpenGL ES 1.1/2.0, runs on iOS, Android, BlackBerry, Bada, Marmalade, Windows, Windows Phone, Linux and more.

Download v2.2.2

Cocos2d-html5

Written in javascript, based on HTML5 technology. This branch focuses on mobile browsers and hybrid apps of mobile.

Download v2.2.2

Figure 24-6. *Cocos2d-x download page*

Cocos2d-html5 releases a new version every six weeks. v2.2.2 was the latest version in use at the time of this writing, so this book will use version v2.2.2.

Next, you are going to install a web server. You have several options here:

- *XAMPP*: Windows, Macintosh, and Linux
- *WAMP*: Windows
- *MAMP*: Macintosh

Follow these steps to install the web server.

1. Download one version of your platform.
2. Follow the default instructions to install it.
3. Specify the installation directory.
4. Copy the extracted Cocos2d-html5 files to the root directory.
5. Open your browser, and input "localhost" in the address bar.

Review the Built-in Examples

When you have downloaded and installed the web server successfully, it is highly recommended that you go through the built-in examples. They cover over 95 percent of the features of Cocos2d-html5, and they are also the most valuable learning resource that you can obtain at present.

When you start your web server and enter `localhost` in your browser's address bar, you will see the screen shown in Figure 24-7.

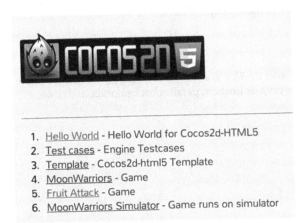

1. Hello World - Hello World for Cocos2d-HTML5
2. Test cases - Engine Testcases
3. Template - Cocos2d-html5 Template
4. MoonWarriors - Game
5. Fruit Attack - Game
6. MoonWarriors Simulator - Game runs on simulator

Figure 24-7. *Cocos2d-html5 index page*

As you can see, there are many demos and sample games. If you are new to Cocos2d-html5, you may want to give the MoonWarriors demo a try first.

Review the Tests

Figure 24-8 shows what happens when you open the link named Test cases. It will show you all of the built-in tests that come with Cocos2d-html5.

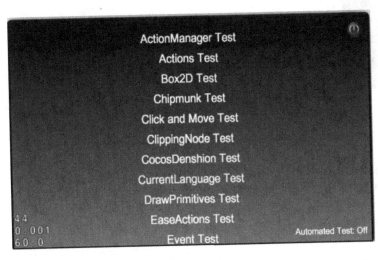

ActionManager Test

Actions Test

Box2D Test

Chipmunk Test

Click and Move Test

ClippingNode Test

CocosDenshion Test

CurrentLanguage Test

DrawPrimitives Test

EaseActions Test

Event Test

Automated Test: Off

Figure 24-8. *Cocos2d-html5 tests*

The tests are the best learning resources available. If you make changes to the source file, you will see the result immediately. It is a much faster way to learn and obtain the features that you need for your game than by trying to create everything from scratch by yourself.

Taking a Look at the Sample Games

There are two types of full game samples built-in with Cocos2d-html5. All of the source code is completely free and open to you. The following sections provide a short introduction to these sample games.

MoonWarriors

The first game listed on the index page is MoonWarriors (see Figure 24-9). It is a vertical shooting game. In this sample game, many useful game techniques are applied, including tile-map, animation, parallax backgrounds, and so on. You can dive into the source code for more information.

Figure 24-9. *MoonWarriors opening screen*

Fruit Attack

This is a matching game. You can swap the position of a nearby fruit, and if there are three or more of the same type of fruits in a vertical or horizontal direction, you have a match and the same fruits will be cleared (see Figure 24-10).

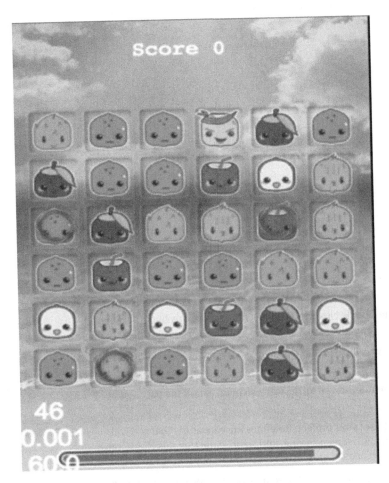

Figure 24-10. Fruit Attack game screen

Setting Up Your First "Hello World" Project

When creating new game project, I suggest that you create your project based on the template folder. To simplify matters, copy the template folder and rename the root folder to where you extracted the Cocos2d-html5 archive. The template includes five files and two directories, as shown in Figure 24-11.

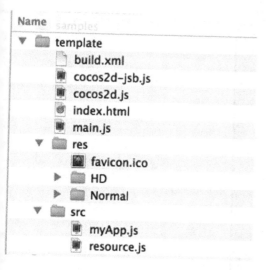

Figure 24-11. *Cocos2d template structure*

- The build.xml file is used for the Google closure compiler. You can use this file to package all of your game and engine files into a single file.

- The Cocos2d-jsb.js file is the entry file for the JSB project.

- The Cocos2d.js file is the entry file of index.html. It defines project configuration, such as render mode, debug mode, frame rate, and so forth. You also need to add the user's game JavaScript files list to the file.

- The index.html file is the entry file of your project. It defines the canvas div that you will use in your game, viewport setting, full screen setting, and so on. Note that this HTML page references only one JavaScript file (Cocos2d.js).

- The main.js file initializes the game setting, sets different resolution resources for the search path, initializes the multi-resolution adaption, and launches the game.

- The res directory contains all of your resources, including images, sounds, background music, and configuration files. You can put different resolution resources in different subdirectories and set the corresponding path in main.js.

- The src directory includes all of the JavaScript files used in the game. The resource.js file defines all of the resources used in the game. In addition, you can separate your resources into different groups and preload them on demand.

Building the Tower Defence Game

In this section, you will start to create a tower defence game step by step based on Cocos2d-html5. I will also cover deploying the game to the web server and packaging all JavaScript files into a obfuscated single file for security.

Overview

Before coding, take a look at the overview of the game and then dive into its component details to learn its features.

The tower Defence gameplay is very simple and straightforward. The sample game will only require three scenes: main menu, game play, and game over. The main menu scene and game over scene are quite simple, while the game play scene has many layers to contain different elements, as shown in Figure 24-12.

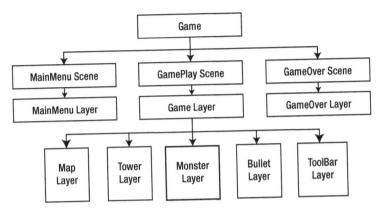

Figure 24-12. *The scenes and layers of the tower defence project*

The Tower Defence Gameplay Scene

The game play scene contains a game layer and five sublayers: the Map layer, Tower layer, Monster layer, Bullet layer, and Toolbar layer. All of the layers will be introduced later.

The game play scene contains most of game logic in the game. There is a predefined path where all enemies walk. There are two gun towers on the path to defeat the enemies. The attack range of the tower is limited to a circle, and you can adjust the position of towers. There are two types of towers and three types of enemies. If your score is greater than 2,000, you win. You lose if one monster passes through the gate.

The key to winning is to reposition the towers in the right place or add the right monsters in the menu to help you to get a high score quickly.

Designing the Required Game Components

In order to make the tower defence game, you'll design the following components:

1. A main menu for the game, a game play scene, and a game over scene.

2. The map has a predefined path. The path can be modified easily. In your game sample, you will use tiled maps to edit the path.

3. There are two types of towers. The towers are gun towers and support repositioning. You must implement drag-and-drop functionality for the towers, and it should be easy to modify their properties.

4. There are different types of enemies with various running speeds and hit points. You'll use the CardinalSplineTo action to make the enemies follow the path.

5. There is collision detection mechanism between the enemy and bullets fired from the tower. In this example, you'll use QuadTree to implement collision detection. QuadTree is a tree data structure in which each internal node has exactly four children.

6. Setting up the conditions for winning or losing a game.

A Step-by-Step Process for Making the Tower Defence Game

Now let's create the game step by step. The name of your project is HalloweenDefence. You can refer to the repository on github: `https://github.com/linshun/HalloweenDefence`. The directory structure is shown in Figure 24-13.

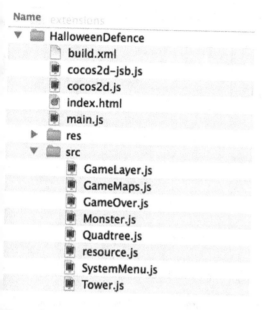

Figure 24-13. *Directory structure of HalloweenDefence*

You can deploy the existing project to a web server, and then play it in a browse.

Creating the Tower Defence Project

As mentioned earlier, you can copy the template folder and then paste and rename it. You will create the game based on the template.

After the game folder is created, open up the `index.html` file and set the gameCanvas to 480×318 pixels. This is the design resolution of the game, which I will discuss later. You also need to set `screen-orientation` to landscape mode.

Cocos2d-html5 supports the features of multi-resolution adaptation, and all of your game's coordinates are based on the design resolution, no matter the size of your browser's window. It is easy for you to enable the multi-resolution adaptation feature. Listing 24-3 provides the code to do so.

Listing 24-3. The `applicationDidFinishLaunching` Function Enables the Multi-resolution Adaptation Feature in `main.js`.

```
applicationDidFinishLaunching : function ( ) {

    // initialize director
    var director = cc.Director.getInstance();

    // Set full screen mode to SHOW_ALL mode.
    cc.EGLView.getInstance().setDesignResolutionSize(480, 318,
        cc.RESOLUTION_POLICY.SHOW_ALL);
```

```
// Resize the game canvas when browser size changed
cc.EGLView.getInstance().resizeWithBrowserSize(true);

// turn on display FPS
director.setDisplayStats(this.config['showFPS']);

// set FPS. the default value is 1.0/60 if you don't call this
director.setAnimationInterval(1.0 / this.config['frameRate']);

//load resources
cc.LoaderScene.preload(g_resources, function () {
    director.replaceScene(new this.startScene());
}, this);

return true;
}
```

The first half of the code in Listing 24-3 initializes the `director`, and it enables the multi-resolution adaptation feature of the engine and the auto resize event. It is enabled by default on the template. The `setSearchPaths` feature code should be removed, and you need to delete the HD and Normal folder under the `res` directory. Then copy all of the resources to the `res` directory.

There are five modes of multi-resolution adaptation.

1. `EXACT_FIT`: The entire application is visible in the specified area without trying to preserve the original aspect ratio.

2. `NO_BORDER`: The entire application fills the specified area without distortion, but possibly with some cropping, while maintaining the original aspect ratio of the application.

3. `SHOW_ALL`: The entire application is visible in the specified area without distortion while maintaining the original aspect ratio of the application. Borders can appear on two sides of the application.

4. `FIXED_HEIGHT`: The application takes the height of the design resolution and modifies the width of the internal canvas so that it fits the aspect ratio of the browser's window.

5. `FIXED_WIDTH`: The application takes the width of the design resolution and modifies the height of the internal canvas so that it fits the aspect ratio of the browser's window.

In this game, you'll choose the `SHOW_ALL` mode. For more details about cocos2d multi-resolution adaptation, visit http://www.cocos2d-x.org/wiki/Multi_resolution_support.

The rest of the code turns on the statistics display, sets the frame rate, and preloads the resources.

After defining the game display, it is recommended that you configure your project setting in Cocos2d.js (see Listing 24-4).

Listing 24-4. Project Setting Configuration in Cocos2d.js

```
( function ( ) {
    var d = document ;
    var c = {
        COCOS2D_DEBUG : 2 , //0 to turn debug off, 1 for basic debug, and 2 for full debug
        box2d : false ,
        chipmunk : false ,
        showFPS : true ,
        loadExtension : false ,
        frameRate : 60 ,
```

```
        renderMode : 1 ,       //Choose of RenderMode: 0(default), 1(Canvas only), 2(WebGL only)
        tag : 'gameCanvas' , //the dom element to run Cocos2d on
        engineDir : '../Cocos2d/' ,
        //SingleEngineFile:'../../lib/Cocos2d-html5-v2.2.2.min.js',
        appFiles : [
                'src/GameLayer.js' ,
                'src/GameMaps.js' ,
                "src/Monster.js" ,
                "src/Tower.js" ,
                'src/resource.js',
                "src/QuadTree.js",
                'src/SystemMenu.js',
                "src/GameOver.js"
                ]
        } ;
} ) ( ) ;
```

When you create your own JavaScript files for the game, remember to add them into the appFiles array. Similarly, you have to define all of your resources in resources.js and then preload them (see Listings 24-5A and 24-5B). Remember to add resources.js and other new JavaScript files into the appFiles array.

Listing 24-5A. Adding Background Tile Maps to the Resources Preloading Array in resources.js

```
var s_DtMapsTmx = "res/DtMaps.tmx" ;
var s_DtMapsImage = "res/DtMaps.png" ;
var g_resources = [
    //image
    { src : s_DtMapsImage } ,
    //tmx
    { src : s_DtMapsTmx }
] ;
```

Listing 24-5B. applicationDidFinishLaunching Function Preloads Resources in main.js

```
applicationDidFinishLaunching : function ( ) {

    //load resources
    cc. LoaderScene.preload ( g_resources , function ( ) {
        director. replaceScene ( new this.startScene ( ) ) ;
    } , this ) ;

    return true ;
```

The g_resouces will be preloaded when the engine executes the applicationDidFinishLaunching() function in ain.js.

After preloading, the engine will call this.startScene() to launch the game. this.startScene is an operator nd member of the class cocos2dApp. It will set the start scene SytemMenuScene to this.startScene in the ctor() nction, which is your game main menu. Next, take a look at launching code on the last line of the main.js file. he game will be launched after executing this code.

```
ar myApp = new cocos2dApp(SystemMenuScene);
```

Creating Main Menu Scene for the Game

The main menu scene will display the title of the game, the game theme, and a start button that allows you to begin the game (see Figure 24-14).

Figure 24-14. *HalloweenDefence main menu*

It is very easy to create the game. It is built on one layer that contains two sprites and a menu item. Now let's create a SystemMenu.js file and add it to appFiles array. Then, let's extend a SystemMenuLayer from cc.Layer and then add sprites and menu items to it. The code for doing this is provided in Listing 24-6.

Listing 24-6. Defining SystemMenuLayer Class in SystemMenu.js

```
var SystemMenuLayer = cc.Layer.extend ( {          //extend a SystemMenuLayer from standard cc.Layer
    init : function ( ) {
        this._super ( ) ;
        var winSize = cc.Director.getInstance( ).getWinSize ( ) ;

        // init background
        var background = cc.Sprite.create ( s_StartBG ) ;
        background.setPosition ( winSize. width / 2, winSize.height / 2 ) ;   //set the position to
screen center
        this.addChild ( background , 0 ) ;         // add the background image to the layer

        // init title
        var title = cc.Sprite.create ( s_HalloweenDefence ) ;
        title.setPosition ( winSize.width / 2, winSize.height * 3 / 4 ) ;
        this.addChild ( title , 1 ) ;

        // add start button
        // create the menu item with normal image and selected image, and set the callback function.
        var StartItem = cc.MenuItemImage.create (
        s_Start ,
```

41

```
        s_StartSelected ,
            function ( ) {
                // when clicked, launch the game play scene.
                cc.Director.getInstance( ).replaceScene( new GameScene ( ) ) ;
            } , this ) ;
        StartItem.setAnchorPoint ( cc.p( 0.5, 0.5 ) ) ;

        var menu = cc.Menu.create ( StartItem ) ;   // create the menu with the start menu item
        menu.setPosition( cc.p( 0 , 0 ) ) ;
        this.addChild ( menu , 1 ) ;
        StartItem.setPosition ( winSize.width / 2, winSize.height / 2 - 20 ) ;
    }
} ) ;
```

Now the game main menu layer is ready, and you can connect it to the main menu, as shown in Listing 24-7.

Listing 24-7. Connecting the SystemMenuLayer to SytemMenuScene in SystemMenu.js

```
var SystemMenuScene = cc.Scene.extend ( {
    onEnter : function ( ) {
        this._super ( ) ;
        var layer = new SystemMenuLayer ( ) ;
        layer.init ( ) ;
        this.addChild ( layer ) ;
    }
} ) ;
```

Once the scene is created, an onEnter() function should be defined. It defines the SystemMenuLayer as its child. You can also define SystemMenuLayer in the ctor() function instead of the onEnter() function, because the ctor() function will be called automatically when the scene object is created.

Make sure that you add all of the resources in resources.js before using it, as you did in Listing 24-5A. The main menu will display on your screen.

Creating the Game Layer, Toolbar Layer, and Game Map Layer

Now it is time to create the game play scene. The first thing to do when creating a game play scene is to build a game layer. It contains all of the other layers, such as the Game Map layer, Tower layer, Monster layer, Bullet layer, and Toolbar layer.

You should create a GameLayer.js file and add it to appFiles array. The code to do this is provided in Listing 24-8.

Listing 24-8. Defining the Game Layer and Add Sub-layer to it (GameLayer.js)

```
// Extern GameLayer from standard cc.Layer.
var GameLayer = cc.Layer.extend({
    _maps:null,
    _winSize:null,
    init : function(){
        this._super();
        this._winSize = cc.Director.getInstance().getWinSize();
        // init game maps
        this.initMaps();    //Add and init your game map.
```

```
            // add tool bar
            this.initToolsBar();    //Add tool bar.
    },
    initMaps : function(){
            this._maps = GameMaps.create();
            this._maps.setPosition( cc.p( 0, 30));
            this.addChild(this._maps);  // Add game map to game layer.
    },
    initToolsBar : function(){
            var toolLayer = cc.Layer.create(); // We will add monsters menu items to this tool
layer later.
            var sToolsBar = cc.Sprite.create(s_ToolsBar);
            sToolsBar.setPosition( cc.p( this._winSize.width / 2 ,
sToolsBar.getContentSize().height / 2));
            toolLayer.addChild(sToolsBar);
            this.addChild(toolLayer, 2);  // Add toolbar layer into game layer.
    }
});
```

You have created a toolbar layer and add it to game layer. You also defined a initMaps() for Game Map layer, now let's implement it and add it to the Game layer.

As to Game Map layer, you use the Tile map editor *Tiled* to create the map (See Figure 24-15). You can download this powerful tool from www.mapeditor.org/download.html.

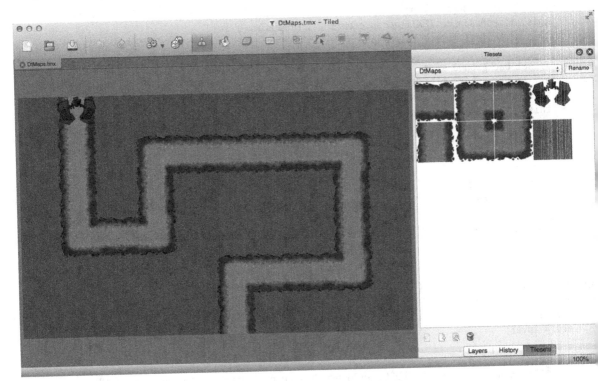

Figure 24-15. *Tower Defence game map*

The map has three layers:

- tlBackgroud

- tlWayPoint

- tlStartPoint

tlWayPoint defines the path that the monsters will take, and tlStartPoint is the place where the monsters are born.

Tiled will export two files: DtMaps.tmx and DtMaps.png. Add these files to the /TowerDefence/res/ folder. Cocos2d-html5 natively supports .tmx files, so it is easy for you to add the map to the scene.

Now let's create the Game Map layer, step by step. First, you need to create a GameMaps.js file and add it to appFiles array. Then define the Game Map layer and add it to the Game layer. The sample code in Listing 24-9 shows you how to define a Game Map layer. Refer to GameMap.js for details of the setting.

Listing 24-9. Defining GameMaps Class in GameMaps.js

```
var GameMaps = cc.Layer.extend ( {
    _tiledMap : null ,
    _mapSize : null ,
    _mapContentSize : null ,

    init : function ( ) {
        this._super ( ) ;
        cc.log( "game maps init.");
        // init background tilemap
        this._tiledMap = cc.TMXTiledMap.create ( s_DtMapsTmx ) ;
        this.addChild ( this ._tiledMap ) ;

        // set background size
        var layer = this._tiledMap.getLayer ( "tlBackground" ) ;
        this._mapSize = layer.getLayerSize ( ) ;
        this._mapContentSize =layer.getContentSize ( ) ;

        // init start point
        this.initStartPoint ( ) ;

        // init way points
        this.initWayPoints ( ) ;

        cc.log("map size:" + this._mapSize.width + " " + this._mapSize.height ) ;
    }
) ;

GameMaps.create = function ( ) {
    var layer = new GameMaps ( ) ;
    layer.init();
    return layer;
;
```

cc.log() is an important debug API of Cocos2d, which you can use to print debug messages on Chrome debugger consoles. You can also debug game code step by step on the Chrome debugger or set a breakpoint on it.

As Listing 24-8 shows, you have added the toolbar layer and the Game Map layer to Game layer. Now that the Game layer is ready, you can connect it to the game scene, as shown in Listing 24-10.

Listing 24-10. Connecting the Game Layer to Game Scene in GameLayer.js

```
var GameScene = cc.Scene.extend({
    onEnter:function(){
        this._super();
        var layer = new GameLayer(); // Create the GameLayer.
        layer.init();
        this.addChild(layer);
    }
});
```

Now the game scene is ready to run, and it should look like Figure 24-16.

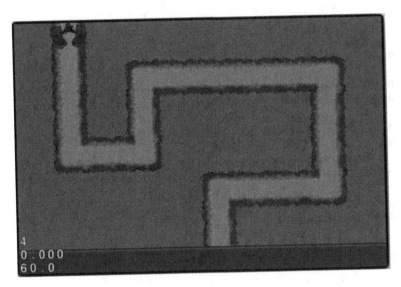

Figure 24-16. *Tower Defence Game Map layer and Tool Bar layer*

There are three numbers at the bottom-left corner. These numbers represent the following statistics:

- Draw calls
- Second per frame (SPF)
- Frame per second (FPS)

You should try to keep draw calls as few as possible and keep the updating time (SPF) as low as possible to get a high CPU idle time. For example, the cocos2d engine will cache the tile map automatically to improve performance, because the tile map is created by lots of tiles, and their position is always the same. This is why the draw calls only reads 4 with lots of tiles displayed on the screen. SPF will be indicated as 0 when it is less than 1ms.

Adding the Enemy Menu and the Show Range of the Game

In this part, you allow users to control monster creation manually. Thus you will add a menu item to the toolbar layer to control this.

All of the menu items will be added to the tool layer that you already defined. The code to do this is shown in Listing 24-11 through Listing 24-13.

Listing 24-11. Creating theGreen MonsterMenu Item in GameLayer.js

```
// add monster menu item of Green
var green = cc.Sprite.create ( s_Monster [ 0 ] ) ;
var greenSelected = cc.Sprite.create ( s_Monster [ 0 ] ) ;
greenSelected. setColor(cc.c4b( 125 , 125 , 125 , 125 ) ) ;
var menuMonsterGreen = cc. MenuItemSprite.create (
    green ,
    greenSelected ,
    function ( ) {
        this.addMonster ( Monster.createGreen ( ) ) ;
    } , this ) ;
menuMonsterGreen. setPosition ( cc.p( 118 , -245*0.6 ) ) ;
```

The code in Listing 24-11 through Listing 24-13 should be added in initToolsBar() of GameLayer.js. Listing 24-11 shows that you created a green monster sprite with an image for normal status. You then made its selected status grey. It then used the normal sprite and the grey sprite to create a menu item in the cc.MenuItemSprite.create() API. The menu item will be added to the menu later. The callback function of the menu item is addMonster. It will create a monster and add it to the game when clicked.

Similarly, you add the purple and orange monsters and set their position. Refer to GameLayer.js for the implementation. You also need an item to show the attackable range of the tower. It is created by cc.MenuItemFont (see Listing 24-12).

Listing 24-12. Creating a "Show Range" Menu Item in GameLayer.js

```
var menuShowRange = cc.MenuItemFont.create ( "Show Range" , function ( ) {
        // callback function, for showing the attackablt range.
    } , this ) ;
menuShowRange.setFontSize ( 14 ) ;    // set font size.
menuShowRange.setPosition ( cc.pAdd ( menuMonsterGreen. getPosition ( ) , cc. p( -120 , 5 ) ) ) ;
```

After creating all of the menu items, you will use the cc.Menu.create() function to build the menu and add it to the ToolBar layer. The code to do this is shown in Listing 24-13, and the result is shown in Figure 24-17.

Listing 24-13. Creating a Menu with All Items in GameLayer.js

```
var menu = cc. Menu.create (
    menuMonsterGreen ,
    menuMonsterPurple ,
    menuMonsterOrange ,
    menuShowRange
    ;
oolLayer. addChild ( menu ) ;
```

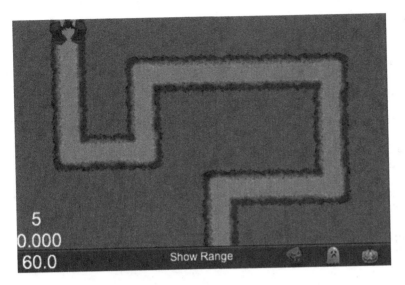

Figure 24-17. HalloweenDefence menu items

Creating Towers and Bullets

There are two different towers and two different types of bullets. The low-level tower attacks monsters with low-level bullets, while the high-level tower attacks monsters with high-level bullets.

The towers are created by four properties: tower building, weapon type, attackable range, and bullet speed. You will create a Monster layer to contain all of the monsters and add it to Game layer. The towers support positional movement with touch input and automatically generated bullets with monsters robotically attacking when they enter the attack range.

The towers need to register an input delegate when you want to use touch to control tower positions. You use TargetedTouchDelegate and enable the target type API cc.registerTargetedDelegate() to swallow the input event. Listing 24-14 provides the code to register touch for tower.

Listing 24-14. Register Touch for Towrers in Tower.js

```
var Tower = cc. Layer.extend ( {
    onEnter : function ( ) {
        this ._super ( ) ;
        cc.registerTargetedDelegate ( 0 , true , this ) ; //Register input delegate
    } ,
    onExit : function ( ) {
        this ._super ( ) ;
        cc.unregisterTouchDelegate ( this ) ;                // Unregister input delegate
    } ,
    onTouchBegan : function ( touch , event ) {
        // check rect
        if ( ! this.containsTouchLocation ( touch ) )
            return false ;
        this ._curPosition.x = this.getPositionX ( ) ;
        this ._curPosition.y = this.getPositionY ( ) ;
        this ._beganTouch = touch. getLocation ( ) ;
        return true ;
    } ,
```

```
      onTouchMoved : function ( touch , event ) {
          var touchPoint = touch. getLocation ( ) ;
          var moveTouch = cc.pSub ( touchPoint , this ._beganTouch ) ;
          this.setPosition ( cc.pAdd ( this ._curPosition , moveTouch ) ) ;
      } ,
      onTouchEnded : function ( touch , event ) {
          // check position
          var location = this ._gameLayer. checkTowerLocation ( this.getPosition ( ) ) ;
          if ( ! location ) {
              // If it is a invalid location, set to previous position.
              this.setPosition ( this ._curPosition ) ;
          } else {
              // Set the tower to new position.
              this.setPosition ( location ) ;
          }
          this ._curPosition.x = 0;
          this ._curPosition.y = 0;
      }
} ) ;
```

After registration of touch, you will have an input event in OnTouchBegan, OnTouchMoved, and OnTouchEnded. The code shows that the tower will move to the new position when the position is in a valid location. Please refer to Tower.js for implementation.

There are two types of bullets. The difference between them is that the low-level bullet will disappear after it hits a monster, and it can only hurt one monster at a time. Conversely, high-level bullets can go through and hurt all of the monsters.

High-level bullets extend from cc.Node, coming from a high-level tower and are removed when a lifetime is over. It has lifetime property and attack function. (Refer to Tower.js for the implementation.) The high-level bullets will be added to the bullet layer.

Low-level bullets are created when monsters come within the attack range of low-level towers. Low-level bullets are simply a sprite with a MoveTo action, and every bullet will hit one monster and then disappear. Thus you don't need to check the collision of low-level bullets, you just add them to game layer instead of the bullet layer (refer to the Tower.js file). The code of low-level bullets is shown in Listing 24-15.

Listing 24-15. Low-level Bullets in Tower.js

```
var bullet = cc.Sprite.create ( s_Bullet ) ;
bullet. setPosition (
    cc. pAdd ( this.getPosition ( ), this ._sBall. getPosition ( ) ) ) ;
this ._gameLayer. addChild ( bullet ) ;

var move = cc. MoveTo.create ( 0.1 , monster. getSprite ( ).getPosition ( ) ) ;
bullet. runAction ( cc. Sequence.create (
    move ,
    cc. CallFunc.create ( function ( ) {
        bullet. removeFromParent ( ) ;        // auto removing call back.
    } , bullet )
) ;
monster. lostBlood ( 20 ) ;                    // it will shoot at monsters always.
```

The low-level bullets use cc.Sequence to create a series of actions, which will be executed in order. The cc.CallFunc function enables bullets to remove themselves when the action sequence is completed.

Creating Enemies and Actions

It is time to set up the enemies and make them move in the direction defined in the tile map tlWayPoint layer. There are three types of monsters, and all of them can display themselves and update the hit points. (Refer to Monster.js for the implementation.)

Monsters can be created both automatically and manually. The ToolBar allows you to create monsters manually, and you will use a schedule to add monsters to the game automatically. Listing 24-16 provides the code to accomplish this.

Listing 24-16. Adding the First Monster, and Starting a Schedule for Automatically Adding Monsters in GameLayer.js

```
var GameLayer = cc. Layer.extend ( {
    init : function ( ) {
        this.addMonster ( Monster.createOrange ( ) ) ;
        this.schedule ( this.autoAddMonster , 2 ) ;  // Add a monster every 2 seconds.
    } ,
} ) ;
```

The code will add a monster randomly every two seconds. Monsters will move on the path defined with cc.CardinalSplineTo, as shown in Listing 24-17.

Listing 24-17. The addMonster Function in GameLayer.js

```
addMonster : function ( monster ) {
    if ( ! this._monsterLayer ) {
        this._monsterLayer = cc.Layer.create ( ) ;
        this.addChild ( this ._monsterLayer ) ;
    }
    this ._monsterLayer.addChild ( monster , 1 ) ;

    var array = this._maps.getWayPositions ( ) ; // Get the way point frome tlWayPoint layer.
    var action1 = cc.CardinalSplineTo.create ( 20 , array , 0 ) ;   // create the action.
    var remove = cc.CallFunc.create ( function ( ) {

        // You will lose when monster passed the gate. We will create the GameOverScene later.
        cc.Director.getInstance().replaceScene(new GameOverScene(false));
        this.removeFromParent ( ) ;
        // cc.log("remove monster");
    } , monster ) ;
    monster.showRange ( HD .SHOW_RANGE ) ;
    monster.getSprite ( ).runAction ( cc.Sequence.create ( action1 , remove ) ) ;
```

It will create a monster layer and then add the monsters to it. After adding monster layer to the game layer, your screen should look like the one shown in Figure 24-18.

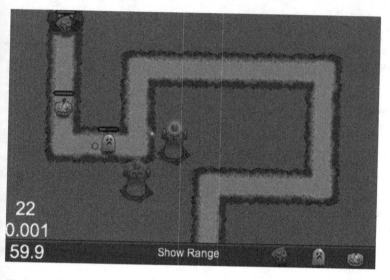

Figure 24-18. *Tower Defence game's enemies and actions*

Monsters will be removed when they die or after completing the cc.CardinalSplineTo action. If the monster completes the journey, you will lose the game, and see the GameOverScene. When the monster dies, you will receive a score equal to monster's hit points. If the score is higher than 2,000, you will win and also see the GameOverScene. I will discuss creating the GameOverScene later in this chapter.

Simple Collision Detection

Monsters and high-level bullets will move all over the screen. Sometimes the unlucky monster will get hit, and so you need to add collision detection to the game.

The prototype for collision detection in this game is known as QuadTree. Visit http://en.wikipedia.org/wiki/Quadtree to learn more about it, and refer to QuadTree.js for the implementation. QuadTree recursively splits the screen into four regions, and it checks the collision in each region. If objects in one region are larger than the maximum defined number, the region will be split again. The code to invoke QuadTree initially is as follows:

```
this ._quad = new Quadtree ( 0 , cc. rect ( 0 , 0 , this ._winSize. width , this ._winSize. height ) ) ;
```

With the Update function of GameLayer, you use QuadTree to check whether or not the monster is attackable. The code to do this is shown in Listing 24-18.

Listing 24-18. Checking Monster Attackability in GameLayer.js

```
this ._quad.clear ( ) ;
for ( var i = 0 ; i < monsters.length ; i ++ ) {
    this ._quad.insert ( monsters [ i ] ) ;
}
for ( var i = 0 , iLen = towers.length ; i < iLen ; i ++ ) {
    var tower = towers [ i ] ;
    var list = [ ] ;
```

```
    this ._quad.retrieve ( list , tower ) ;     // Get the check list
    // cc.log("length:" + list.length);
    for ( var j = 0 , jLen = list.length ; j < jLen ; j ++ ) {
        towers [ i ].checkAttack ( list [ j ] ) ;   // Check attackable
    }
}
```

In this game, the collision range of monsters and bullets is a circle shape, so you use circle-to-circle collision detection. It only needs to get the distance between monster and bullet, and check whether it is smaller than the sum of the bullet radius and the monster radius.

Adding Music and Sound Effects

For music and sound effects, you need to preload them and play them when desired. Note that you need at least two audio formats to support all browsers (mp3 and ogg, for instance). If you choose to play an mp3 or ogg file, the engine will choose the file that is supported by the installed browser. The code defining sound effects is shown in Listing 24-19.

Listing 24-19. Defining Sound Effects in resource.js

```
var s_AttackEffect_mp3 = "res/Music/AttackEffect.mp3" ;
var s_AttackEffect_ogg = "res/Music/AttackEffect.ogg" ;
var g_resources = [
    ... ...
    //effect
    { src : s_AttackEffect_mp3 } ,
    { src : s_AttackEffect_ogg }
] ;
```

After defining a sound effect in resource.js, you can play it when desired. The cc.AudioEngine is a singleton object in Cocos2d, and you can call it to play sound effects directly. The code for playing sound effects is as follows:

```
cc.AudioEngine.getInstance().playEffect(s_AttackEffect_mp3)
// play mp3 or ogg--you don't need both.
```

You also should add a "Sound" menu item on ToolBar to control the on/off function for audio.

Creating the Game Over Scene

This is the final part of the game. The method for creating the game over scene is almost the same as that for creating the main menu, as learned previously. It shows you whether you win or lose, your score, and a start button. The win and lose game over screens are shown in Figure 24-19.

Figure 24-19. *Tower Defence Game over scenes*

Now create a GameOver.js file and add it to appFiles array. The game over scene contains only one GameOverLayer. The GameOverLayer can be created as shown in Listing 24-20.

Listing 24-20. Defining the GameOverLayer in GameOver.js

```
var GameOverLayer = cc. Layer.extend ( {
    init : function ( win ) {
        this._super ( ) ;
        var backgroudImage = null ;
        var titleImage = null ;
        var winSize = cc.Director.getInstance ( ).getWinSize ( ) ;

        if ( win ) {
            // Congratulations, you win
            backgroudImage = s_StartBG ;
            titleImage = s_Win ;
        } else {
            // Oh, no, you lose
            backgroudImage = s_LoseBG ;
            titleImage = s_Lose ;
        }
        // init background
        var background = cc.Sprite.create ( backgroudImage ) ;
        background.setPosition ( winSize. width / 2, winSize.height / 2 ) ;
        this.addChild ( background , 0 ) ;

        // init title
        var title = cc. Sprite.create ( titleImage ) ;
        title.setPosition ( winSize. width / 2, winSize.height * 3 / 4 ) ;
        cc.log ( winSize.width / 2 ) ;
        cc.log ( winSize.height / 2 ) ;
        this.addChild ( title , 1 ) ;

        // add the score on the screen
        score = cc.LabelTTF . create ( "Score:" + HD. SCORE , "Arial" , 28 ) ;
        score.setAnchorPoint ( cc. p( 0.5 , 0.5 ) ) ;
        score.setHorizontalAlignment ( cc. TEXT_ALIGNMENT_CENTER ) ;
```

```
        this.addChild ( score , 100 ) ;
        score.setPosition ( winSize. width / 2, winSize.height / 2 + 30 ) ;
        ... ...
        // add start button here
    } ) ;
```

You will notice that setPosition accepts two types of parameters: x and y or cc.p().
After creating GameOverLayer, connect it to GameOverScene, as shown in Listing 24-21.

Listing 24-21. Connecting the GameOverLayer to GameOverScene in GameOver.js

```
var GameOverScene = cc.Scene.extend ( {
    ctor : function ( win ) {
        //cc.log(win)
        this._super ( ) ;
        var layer = new GameOverLayer ( ) ;
        layer.init ( win ) ;
        this.addChild ( layer ) ;
    }
} ) ;
```

As the code in Listing 24-21 shows, the GameOverScene will be created with a different background and a different title according to the win parameter.

Deploying the Game

After finishing the game coding, you can package all of the JavaScript files into a single obfuscated file for security. Before packaging, you should add all of your JavaScript files to build.xml, which is found in the /root/Cocos2d-html5-v2.2.2/HalloweenDefence folder.

Open Terminal app. Use the cd command to switch to the directory where build.xml is stored, and execute ant, as shown in Listing 24-22. The resulting screen appears in Figure 24-20.

Listing 24-22. Packaging JavaScript Files

```
cd ~/work/HalloweenDefence/Cocos2d-html5-v2.2.2/HalloweenDefence
ant
```

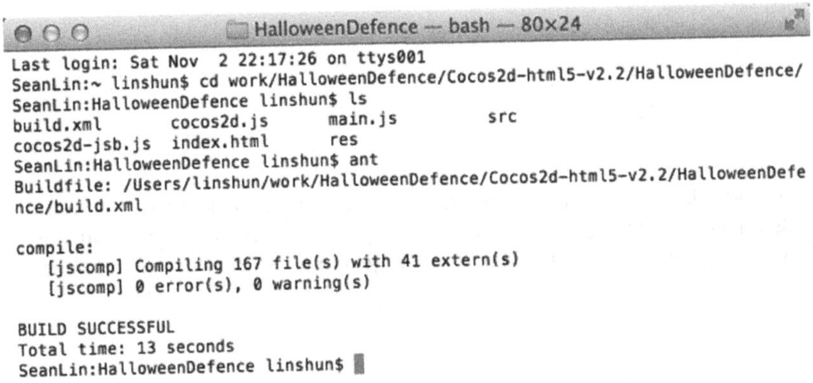

```
Last login: Sat Nov  2 22:17:26 on ttys001
SeanLin:~ linshun$ cd work/HalloweenDefence/Cocos2d-html5-v2.2/HalloweenDefence/
SeanLin:HalloweenDefence linshun$ ls
build.xml        cocos2d.js        main.js        src
cocos2d-jsb.js  index.html        res
SeanLin:HalloweenDefence linshun$ ant
Buildfile: /Users/linshun/work/HalloweenDefence/Cocos2d-html5-v2.2/HalloweenDefe
nce/build.xml

compile:
    [jscomp] Compiling 167 file(s) with 41 extern(s)
    [jscomp] 0 error(s), 0 warning(s)

BUILD SUCCESSFUL
Total time: 13 seconds
SeanLin:HalloweenDefence linshun$ ▊
```

Figure 24-20. *Packaging game files*

42

The ant tool will be executed with build.xml, and it will call the Google closure compiler to release the file HalloweenDefence.js in the same folder. Then you can configure the project to load this single file.

There are two loading modes in Cocos2d.js. What you need to do is to delete the "delete section" and uncomment the commented section. Read the comments in Listings 24-23 and 24-24 carefully.

Listing 24-23. Multi-File Loading Mode in cocos2d.js

```
window. addEventListener ( 'DOMContentLoaded' , function ( ) {
    //first load engine file if specified
    var s = d.createElement ( 'script' ) ;
    /*********Delete this section if you have packed all files into one*******/
    if ( c.SingleEngineFile && ! c.engineDir ) {
        s.src = c.SingleEngineFile ;
    }
    else if ( c.engineDir && ! c.SingleEngineFile ) {
        s.src = c.engineDir + 'platform/jsloader.js' ;
    }
    else {
        alert ( 'You must specify either the single engine file OR the engine directory in "Cocos2d.
js"' ) ;
    }
    /*********Delete this section if you have packed all files into one*******/
    //s.src = 'HalloweenDefence.js'; //IMPORTANT: Un-comment this line if you have packed all
files into one
    d.body.appendChild ( s ) ;
    document.ccConfig = c ;
    s.id = 'Cocos2d-html5' ;
    //else if single file specified, load singlefile
} ) ;
```

Listing 24-24. Single-File Loading Mode in cocos2d.js

```
window. addEventListener ( 'DOMContentLoaded' , function ( ) {
    //first load engine file if specified
    var s = d.createElement ( 'script' ) ;
    s.src = 'HalloweenDefence.js' ; //IMPORTANT: Un-comment this line if you have packed all
files into one
    d.body.appendChild ( s ) ;
    document. ccConfig = c ;
    s.id = 'Cocos2d-html5' ;
    //else if single file specified, load singlefile
 ) ;
```

After changing the loading file to HalloweenDefence.js, the game will load this obfuscated file. You also can use Texture Packer to package all of the game images into sprite sheets, which are supported by Cocos2d-html5 natively. The last thing you need to do is to deploy the HalloweenDefence folder or full project folder to the web server folder and visit it via the browsers. Enjoy!

Releasing a Cocos2d-html5 App to a Native App

Cocs2d-html5 and Cocos2d JSB have the same set of completely compatible JavaScript APIs. Thus a Cocos2d-html5 project can easily be run on HTML5-ready browsers. It also supports running game code as a native application via the Cocos2d JSB without code modification.

The Power of Distributing an HTML5 Game as a Native Package

Cocos2d JSB for C/C++ is the wrapper code that sits between the native code and JavaScript code. JSB enables the calling of the native code from the JavaScript code and vice versa, as illustrated in Figure 24-21.

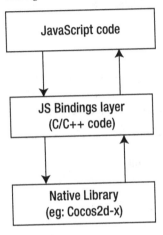

Figure 24-21. *Cocos2d JSB*

SpiderMonkey interprets JavaScript code, Mozilla's JavaScript virtual machine (VM). The JavaScript VM is extended by JSB to support Cocos2d-x types, structures, and objects. SpiderMonkey is Mozilla's open source JavaScript engine written in C/C++, and it can be linked into any C++ program, not just web browsers.

C++ code accesses SpiderMonkey via the JSAPI. The *JSAPI* provides functions for setting up the JavaScript runtime, compiling and executing scripts, creating and examining JavaScript data structures, handling errors, enabling security checks, and debugging scripts. You can find the Cocos2d-x JSB wrapper code under the directory [Cocos2d-x root]/scripting/javascript/. This technology is used for rapid game development and game prototyping.

Setting Up the Cocos2d JSB Environment

Cocos2d-x is a multi-platform 2D game engine. As an example, the porting steps that follow focus on Android and iOS. Most of the steps for porting to these two platforms are the same, and I will point out the few differences.

CREATING A PROJECT FOR IOS

For iOS, follow these steps.

1. Install Xcode from the App Store.

2. Open your web browser, and navigate to the Cocos2d-x download page.

3. Get the latest stable version of Cocos2d-x, and extract it to a location of your choice. This sample game used the latest version Cocos2d-x at the time of writing, which was v2.2.2.

4. Open Terminal app. Use the `cd` command to switch to the directory where you extracted the Cocos2d-x archive, like so:

```
cd ~/work/HalloweenDefence/Cocos2d-x-2.2.2/tools/project-creator
```

5. Create the project using `create_project.py`, as follows:

```
./create_project.py -project HalloweenDefence -package org.Cocos2dx.HalloweenDefence
-language javascript
```

If you see the information shown in Listing 24-25, the project has been created successfully.

Listing 24-25. Successful Project Creation Log

```
proj.ios       : Done!
proj.android   : Done!
proj.win32     : Done!
New project has been created in this path:
/Users/linshun/work/HalloweenDefence/Cocos2d-x-2.2.2/projects/HalloweenDefence
Have Fun!
```

As described above, `create_project.py` automatically creates iOS, Android, and win32 projects.

Adding Resources to the Project

Copy all files under the /HalloweenDefence/Cocos2d-html5-v2.2.2/HalloweenDefence of Cocos2d-Html5 project to directory ~/work/HalloweenDefence/Cocos2d-x-2.2.2/projects/HalloweenDefence/Resources of the Cocos2d-x SB project. Your HalloweenDefence Resources group should now look like the image shown in Figure 24-22.

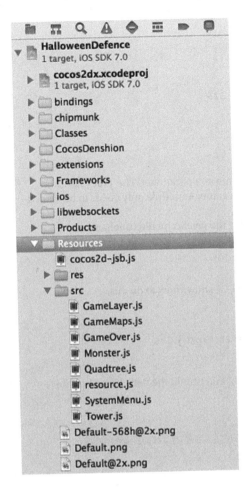

Figure 24-22. Project resources settings

Configuring the Project

The main entry between Cocos2d-x JSB and Cocos2d-html5 is different. The default entry file of the JSB project is cocos2d-jsb.js. Open cocos2d-jsb.j, shown in Listing 24-26, to review its contents.

Listing 24-26. Contents of cocos2d-jsb.js

```
require ( "jsb.js" ) ;
require ( "GameMaps.js" ) ;
require ( "Monster.js" ) ;
require ( "resource.js" ) ;
require ( "Tower.js" ) ;
require ( "GameLayer.js" ) ;
require ( "Quadtree.js") ;
require ( "SystemMenu.js" ) ;
require ( "GameOver.js") ;
```

```
        // main entry
        try {
            director = cc.Director.getInstance ( ) ;
            director.runWithScene ( new GameScene( ) ) ;
            // Show the game in full screen mode.
            cc.EGLView.getInstance( ).setDesignResolutionSize( 480, 318,
                cc.RESOLUTION_POLICY.SHOW_ALL ) ;
        } catch ( e ) {
    log ( e ) ;
    }
```

The require() function will load a JavaScript module and use a filename as a parameter. The jsb.js is the module that needs to be loaded if you are using Cocos2d-x JSB to develop a game. A module only needs to be loaded once in the runtime before it can be used anywhere else.

Load all JavaScript modules in the file cocos2d-jsb.js, and leave all of the JavaScript files unchanged.

Building for iOS

Switch to the project directory, and open the project. The code in Listing 24-27 shows how to do this.

Listing 24-27. Opening an iOS Project

```
cd ~/work/HalloweenDefence/Cocos2d-x-2.2.2/projects/HalloweenDefence/proj.ios
open TD.xcodeproj
```

Select the targets of this project in Xcode, switch to label "Build Phases," and unfold the item "Copy bundle Resources" (see Figure 24-23).

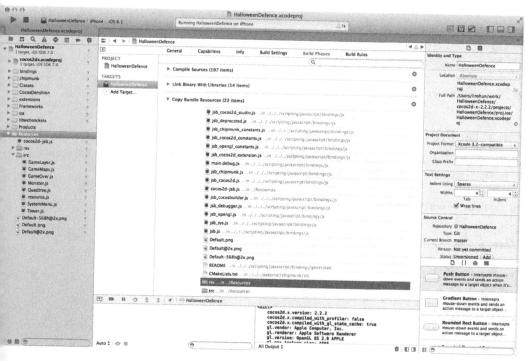

Figure 24-23. Copying bundle resources

As Figure 24-23 shows, the src and res directories are embedded as defaults.

The final step of porting a project is to run and test it. Thanks to the API's compatibility, this step is not very difficult.

Build and run the project, and check to see if there are any errors in the log panel. Test the game, and verify that every function is working the same way in the browser.

Figure 24-24 shows the Hybrid Project screen for iOS.

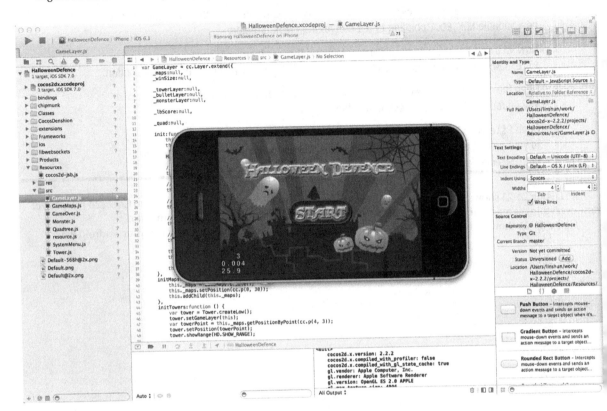

Figure 24-24. *Hybrid Project screen for iOS*

The game will be run on the iOS devices or simulators without code modification.

BUILDING FOR ANDROID

For Android, you can download the Eclipse ADT bundle from the Google ADT homepage at http://developer. android.com/sdk/index.html. Or you can install Eclipse with Java, ADT, and the CDT plug-ins. You also need to install and set up Android NDK. Refer to http://developer.android.com/sdk/index.html for further details.

There is a user's guide for Android development setup. It is automatically generated when you create a new project. The path is

~/work/HalloweenDefence/Cocos2d-x-2.2.2/projects/HalloweenDefence/proj.android/README.md

There are five steps that need to be taken to set up the Eclipse environment for Cocos2d-x. Let's set up the COCOS2DX and NDK_ROOT variables before adding the existing project to Eclipse in this section. (Skip the first two steps if you've done this before.)

1. Open Eclipse>Preference>General>Workspace>Linked Resources, and click the New button to add the Path Variable COCOS2DX pointing to the root Cocos2d-x.

2. Open Eclipse>Preferences>C/C++>Build>Environment, and click the Add button to add a new variable NDK_ROOT pointing to the root Android NDK directory.

3. Now let's add the libCocos2dx library project and the game project. Open File>New>Project>Android Project From Existing Code, and click the Browse button.

4. Open the ~/work/HalloweenDefence/Cocos2d-x-2.2.2/Cocos2dx/platform/android/java directory, and click Finish to add the project.

5. Open File>New>Project>Android Project From Existing Code, click Browse to go to your project directory, ~/work/HalloweenDefence/Cocos2d-x-2.2.2/projects/HalloweenDefence/proj.android, and add the project.

As Listing 24-25 shows, you created the Android projects, and added the game resources to Cocos2d JSB project. Now everything is ready, and you can build and run the game on Android devices or an emulator. Figure 24-25 shows the Hybrid Project screen for Android. You can get the same game in your Android device.

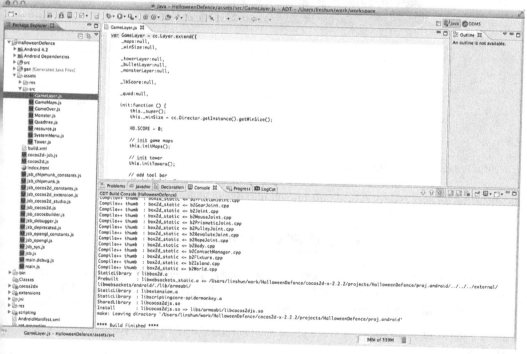

Figure 24-25. *Hybrid Project screen for Android*

Learning More

It's extremely easy to communicate with Cocos2d community. If you have a question, use public mail list: `cocos2d-js-devel@googlegroups.com`. If you find a bug or just a suggestion, please submit an issue on the issue tracker channel of `http://www.cocos2d-x.org` or post it in the forum.

If you want to learn more about Cocos2d, here are some very useful web sites:

- Official Cocos2d documentation: `www.Cocos2d-x.org/wiki`

- Official Cocos2d Forum: `www.Cocos2d-x.org/forums/19`

- The Cocos2d Community: `www.Cocos2d-x.org/wiki/Cocos2d-html5`

If you google Cocos2d tutorials, you will find tons of them out there. Besides the cocos2d-x web site, I highly recommend these two web sites:

- `www.raywenderlich.com`. This website provides many iOS related tutorials, including many awesome Cocos2d tutorials.

- `http://paralaxer.com/Cocos2d-x-book/`. Though all of the tutorials on this site are written in Objective-C or C++, the key ideas on how to construct a game with Cocos2d are the same as with Cocos2d-html5. When you read these tutorials, you can simply pick the main ideas while you start to write one with Cocos2d-html5.

How Active Is the Community?

Figure 24-26 provides a view of the entire Cocos2d family. It also illustrates the relationships between different versions of Cocos2d.

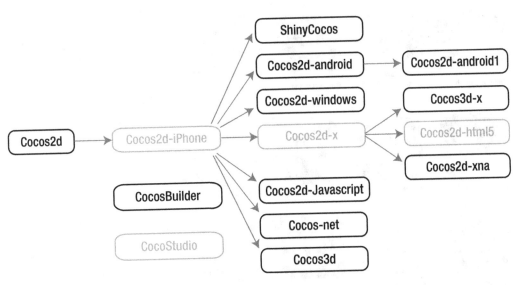

Figure 24-26. *Cocos2d family*

Cocos2d started in 2008 in Argentina. A group of Python developers attended weekly gatherings in a place called Los Cocos, a small town near Buenos Aires. These Python programmers created the basic framework, and name of the place where they met (Los Cocos) is where the framework name "cocos" came from. Later, in 2008, Ricardo Quesada ported it from Python to Objective-C, running on iOS devices. With the rise of Android two years later, the Cocos2d-x team expanded Cocos2d-x from Cocos2d-iphone, not only to focus on the Android platform but also to target cross-platform capability. In 2011, Google sponsored the Cocos2d-x team to port Cocos2d-x to Cocos2d-html5, which focuses on HTML5-ready browsers, web apps, and hybrid apps.

There are several other branches of Cocos2d, including Cocos2d-Android and Cocos2d-Android-1 (Java implementations for Android), ShinyCocos (a Ruby implementation), Cocos2d Javascript (another HTML5 web browser implementation), Cocos2d Windows (a C++ implementation for Windows), and CocosNet (a C# implementation for .NET). All of these implementations serve as examples of the widespread popularity of Cocos2d.

Currently, the most active branches of the Cocos2d family are Cocos2d-iPhone, Cocos2d-x, and Cocos2d-html5. All three branches have proven themselves in a wide range of games, with many tech giants joining the Cocos2d fold to make it more powerful, faster, and more stable.

Many Top Games Are Created with Cocos2d

You can refer to Cocos2d-x's official web site for further information about the top-selling games created with Cocos2d. Figure 24-27 shows the various types of the leading games created with Cocos2d.

Figure 24-27. Cocos2d games

What If I Have a Question?

You will find many experienced peers on the Cocos2d Forum, so use it freely to ask questions when encountering problems. Be sure to read the forum rules first before posting. The No.1 rule is to search before posting.

Also try to find answers from Stackoverflow, Google, and Google+ first. If you have no luck there, you can post your question on the forum.

Conclusion

Cocos2d-html5 is a 2D game framework for developing multi-platform games that span rapid prototyping to finished high-performance games with a complete toolchain. It helps to try out ideas as you think of them and test them as soon as possible.

This chapter provides a quick introduction to Cocos2d-html5 and what it is all about. I hope that with this introduction, along with the examples found in this chapter, you have learned enough about the structure of a basic Cocos2d-html5 game and how to use the framework to implement your ideas quickly.

This is the final chapter of the book, and you have learned much about both JavaScript and programming. Now it is time to use what you have learned to optimize your Cocos2d-html5 game, making it awesome and running your code on the Web without a plug-in, on both iOS and Android devices via Cocos2d JSB.

Index

Get the eBook for only $10!

Now you can take the weightless companion with you anywhere, anytime. Your purchase of this book entitles you to 3 electronic versions for only $10.

This Apress title will prove so indispensible that you'll want to carry it with you everywhere, which is why we are offering the eBook in 3 formats for only $10 if you have already purchased the print book.

Convenient and fully searchable, the PDF version enables you to easily find and copy code—or perform examples by quickly toggling between instructions and applications. The MOBI format is ideal for your Kindle, while the ePUB can be utilized on a variety of mobile devices.

Go to www.apress.com/promo/tendollars to purchase your companion eBook.

Apress®
THE EXPERT'S VOICE™